ELECTRONIC & MICROPROCESSOR CONTROLLED SECURITY PROJECTS

VAUGHN MARTIN & DEAN DAVIS

TAB BOOKS Inc.
Blue Ridge Summit, PA 17214

Burglar Baffler, Perimiguard, and Sentinel are trademarks of
Specialty Electronic Services, Inc.
Sonalert is a trademark of Mallory Corp.
Wild Rover is a trademark of Refac Electronics Corp.
Zippertubing is a trademark of Zippertubing, Inc.

FIRST EDITION

FIRST PRINTING

Copyright © 1985 by TAB BOOKS Inc.

Printed in the United States of America

Reproduction or publication of the content in any manner, without express permission of the publisher, is prohibited. No liability is assumed with respect to the use of the information herein.

Library of Congress Cataloging in Publication Data

Martin, Vaughn, 1946–
Electronic and microprocessor — controlled security projects.

Includes index.
1. Electronic security systems—Amateurs' manuals.
2. Microprocessors—Amateurs' manuals. I. Davis, Dean, 1944– . II. Title.
TH9737.M375   1985   643′.16   85-4626
ISBN 0-8306-0957-1
ISBN 0-8306-1957-7 (pbk.)

Cover illustration by Darron Fredricksen.

Contents

	Acknowledgments	v
	Introduction	vi
1	**Home Security**	1
	Types of Systems—System Components	
2	**Light Controllers**	13
	Burglar Baffler—Programmable Light Dimmer—Programmable Timer	
3	**Entry Detection System**	59
	Circuit Description—Battery Charger—Front Panel Controls—Integrated Circuits—Construction	
4	**Microcomputer/Controller**	71
	Power Requirements—Board Components—Board Troubleshooting—Board Construction—System Checkout	
5	**Microprocessor-Based Systems**	83
	Perimiguard with Delayed Entry—Perimiguard without Delayed Entry—Software Light Dimmer	
6	**The Sentinel**	117
	Circuit Description—Simple Sentinel—Precision Sentinel—Quad Precision Timer	
7	**Automatic Telephone Dialer**	137
	Telephone Basics—MK5375 Repertory Dialer—Telephone Dialer Project	

Appendix A	**EMI Supression**	**169**
Appendix B	**Program Listing**	**187**
Appendix C	**Suppliers**	**211**
Bibliography		**219**
Index		**227**

Acknowledgments

We are indebted to C. A. Roper for the information contained in *The Complete Security Handbook—for home, office, car, boat, anything* (TAB Book No. 1320). This excellent volume addresses nearly every aspect of security imaginable and reviews the great variety of commercial products available, including switches and intrusion alarms, two areas of specific concern in our book. Rather than duplicate Roper's admirable efforts, we would instead recommend *The Complete Security Handbook* to readers who wish to broaden their knowledge of security systems and how they work.

Thanks are also due to Carol Ebert and Kirby Beard of Gates Energy for their generous contribution of both batteries and technical data; Richard Schultz of Mountain West Security for making the equipment necessary to prototype these systems available to us at cost; and Bob West of EECO, Inc., for artwork and samples of the miniature switches used in these projects.

We extend our special appreciation to John Cater, our former boss, who conceived the idea of the one-board microcomputer, later modified as described in this book.

From Dean Davis, thanks also to Stephanie and Stacy Davis and Sherill; from Vaughn Martin, thanks to my research assistant, Dorothy M. Rosa, whose enthusiasm provokes and provides me with inspiration.

Introduction

This book is for the experienced kit builder, experimenter, student, or professional who wants to build and truly understand the design of a home, office, or business security system. The systems we present can be built for a fraction of the cost of a commercially installed system. Six completely original designs are presented along with several variations for a total of ten security projects. All have been built, bench-tested, and proven in actual use. They can be constructed and installed separately. All can be built directly from this book with parts available from standard suppliers. The printed circuit foil patterns can be used directly from the book. They are 1:1 reproductions. Chapter 2 discusses several methods for non-photographically lifting these patterns from the page. Components, printed circuit boards, and partial kits for the microprocessor-controlled projects are also available from Specialty Electronic Services, Inc.

Three of the designs—The Burglar Baffler, the Sentinel, and the Programmable Light Dimmer—are innovative, state-of-the-art lighting control devices offering both enhanced conventional features and functions so novel that they are not yet commercially available. Three others are technologically advanced perimeter-protection systems: the Electronic Entry Detection System and the computer-controlled Perimiguard Systems. The last project is an automatic telephone dialer that is part of a silent alarm system.

The first part of this book deals with the projects that are built without microprocessor control. The projects in the second part are built with microprocessor control using the 4 1/2 IC single-printed circuit board computer/controller. This extremely compact PC board includes an 8-pin 555 minidip timer IC, a 6502 microprocessor, (the same one used in the Apple, Ohio Scientific, Commodore PET, and ATARI home computers), a 6532 RIOT (RAM-I/O Timer) chip, and a 2716 EPROM (ultraviolet light-erasable PROM) with a 2-kilobyte capacity.

Each project description includes a schematic drawing, and a parts list. Some feature a component placement drawing, complete timing diagrams, and charts to aid in troubleshooting before and after installation is complete. Printed circuit board patterns (1:1 scale positives) are provided for each of the computer-controlled projects as well as four of the other five projects. The assembly language program listing in Appendix B is clearly annotated in plain English to allow you to follow each step and detail of the program with ease.

In an effort to minimize the cost of completing the microprocessor projects, several distinctive features have been introduced. For example, a single-sided printed circuit board instead of a double-sided board is used for the power supply/battery backup boards. And while each of the three computer-controlled projects operates on a completely different program, all three programs are contained within a single 2716 EPROM on the microcomputer/controller board, thereby eliminating the need for a specially programmed EPROM for each project. This EPROM is also available from Specialty Electronics Services, Inc. for $10. Readers may wish to select cost-cutting options of their own: the LM350 voltage regulator specified for the power supply/battery backup board, for example, may be either a metal-cased TO-3 IC or a plastic tab three-pin in-line TO-220 package. While the board provided will accommodate either one, the plastic tab IC costs approximately two thirds less than the metal-cased TO-3, yet delivers the same load current of 3 amps.

The book concludes with several appendices. Appendix A covers the suppression of EMI. Appendix B contains the program for the microprocessor projects. Appendix C contains suppliers of electronics components and security-related items. The Bibliography has entries of magazine articles and manufacturer's literature that specifically addresses security systems and closely allied areas. We assume that you may want to build one or more of these security projects but may also want to modify them. This carefully selected bibliograpy of practical tips on security will be particularly helpful in this regard.

1
Home Security

FEW WORDS EVOKE STRONGER EMOTIONS. Home is where the heart is. We keep the things we care about, the treasured possessions of a lifetime of hard work, in our homes.

Unfortunately, home isn't as safe as we'd like to think it is. Every year, more than 2,000,000 homes are robbed of cash, jewelry, stereos and video equipment, silver, appliances, antiques, furs, stamp and coin collections, and other valuables. Some of these crimes involve physical harm, or the threat of harm, to those at home when the burglar chooses to strike. Surprisingly, two thirds of these *crimes of opportunity,* as the United States Department of Justice describes them, do not involve break-ins. The burglar merely walks through an unlocked door, or climbs through an unlocked, even open, window, takes what he wants, and leaves. Only rarely is his presence ever detected, or the stolen goods ever recovered.

Over $400,000,000 is lost to burglars every year. In the United States alone, one residential burglary occurs every nine seconds. And while the nationwide crime rate seems to be declining slightly (refer to Fig. 1-1) certain urban areas are experiencing dramatic increases; recently the crime rate in Los Angeles jumped almost 5%, while it rose a staggering 20% in Houston.

The overwhelming majority of burglars—almost 94%—are male, and of these, 79% are under the age of 24. Ninety percent are under 35, and 80% are amateurs, rather than professionals. As a rule, amateurs are younger than professionals; they're generally looking for cash and items that are easily pawned or sold on the street for drug money. They choose their targets more or less at random! Often less sophisticated than professional thieves, young burglars may be more easily discouraged or

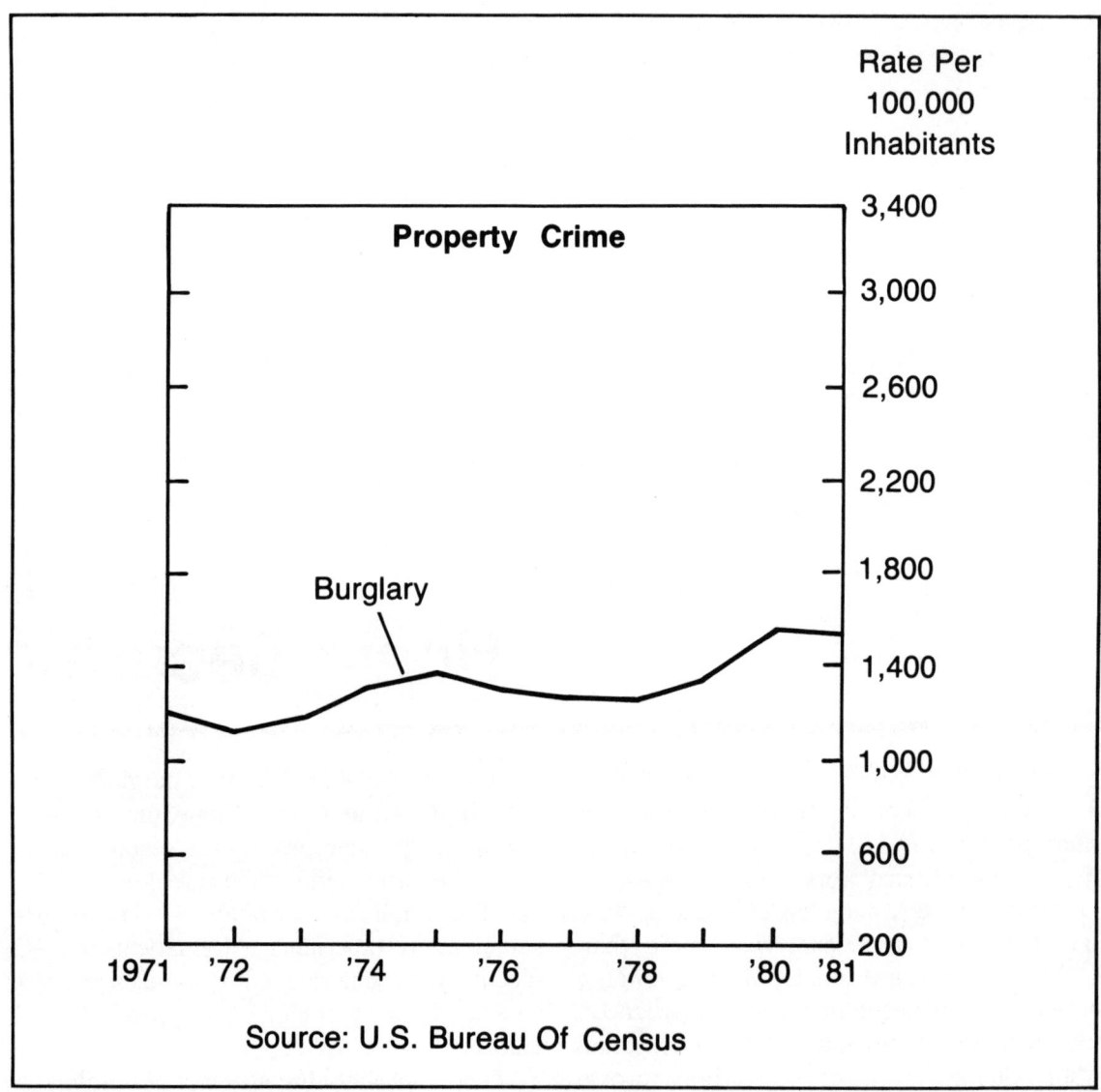

Fig. 1-1. The trend in crimes against property

frightened away by electronic detection and subsequent alarms. Often more skittish than professionals, they may also be more dangerous.

Professionals, on the other hand, plan and execute their crimes with greater thought and care. The driver of a strange van that pulls up to the front door of an unoccupied summer home, and proceeds to empty it of cash, jewelry, and priceless antiques is likely to be a seasoned professional rather than a drug-crazed adolescent. As a professional, he's more likely to know how to spot the unprotected home and diminish the chances of apprehension. Once motivated, he can be difficult to discourage and harder to catch.

Young or old, amateur or professional, burglars have one thing in common: they're lazy. (If they weren't, they'd be out making an honest living like the rest of us.) They'd rather tackle an easy job than a tough one. Given the choice of two homes of comparable appeal, they'll select the easiest entry and the easiest escape.

In 1983, Americans spent more than $5,000,000,000 on security devices and systems to guard against burglary. These devices ranged from the simple and inexpensive ($5 for a simple window lock, for example) to the costly and complex installation of a comprehensive security system in a typical home,—an apartment, or condominium—which can begin at $2500 and soar to $20,000 and beyond, as the level of protection increases.

Whether installed separately or as part of a more elaborate system, every device in this book can help you protect your home against loss. But other measures can and should be taken as well:

1. Use the security devices you already have, regardless of however inadequate they may appear; any locked door or window presents a greater challenge to the would-be intruder than an unlocked door or window. Upgrade existing protective devices; replace spring locks with deadbolts; keep little cash on hand and stow valuables away in a safety deposit box.

2. Turn on existing lighting and install additional lamps to illuminate entries and walkways.

3. Cut back foliage that might conceal a would-be burglar. Use small, compact plants for landscaping close to the house.

4. Keep an eye on the neighborhood and report any suspicious activity. Studies show that when communities organize and publicize "block watch" programs, the crime rate goes down—often dramatically. (To form a neighborhood watch program, contact your local police department. The National Neighborhood Watch Program, coordinated by the National Sheriff's Association, offers an informational packet for $2. Contact that organization at 1250 Connecticut Avenue, N.W., Washington, D.C. 20036.)

5. Post decals indicating that an alarm system is on guard, even if it isn't. Good spots for decals are on doors and first-floor windows and where telephone lines enter the house. (The point here is to make the burglar believe that an alarm will sound if the lines are cut.)

6. Don't broadcast your absence from home. Leave an ambiguous message on your telephone-answering machine; never say "I'm not at home right now." Tell the neighbors when you leave and when you expect to return so that they can keep after mail and other deliveries. If you announce a family occasion in the newspaper—a wedding or funeral, for example—be sure to engage a house-sitter or arrange for other protection during your absence. Don't brag about coming vacations in public places. You may be overheard, and your planned absence noted with interest. If you have air conditioning, leave it turned on low; a warm house on a sizzling day announces its unoccupied status.

Most importantly, if you come home and find any sign of forced entry—a window broken, curtains awry, a door ajar, or any sign whatsoever—leave at once and call for help. Don't risk confronting a startled thief; in such circumstances, your cool head can keep burglary—basically a crime against property—from becoming a crime on interpersonal violence.

TYPES OF SYSTEMS

Throughout this book you will encounter the terms *outer* and *inner* loop. Let us establish a definition for each term and a previously agreed upon convention as to their use.

The *outer loop* corresponds to a closed-circuit system and the *inner loop* corresponds to an open-circuit system. More specifically, in a closed-loop system, current flows through the entire loop. There is a complete circuit from the power source through the sensors or switch contacts and back to the control box. In the control box, a sensitive relay is typically held energized in older systems. In the case of our more modern systems, a logic state is detected. In an open-circuit or inner-loop system, no current flows through the circuit until one of the sensors is activated. But more will be said about this later. Let's concentrate on the closed-circuit system now.

Closed-Circuit Systems

The closed-circuit system that uses a relay has the relay drop out when a sensor (typical-

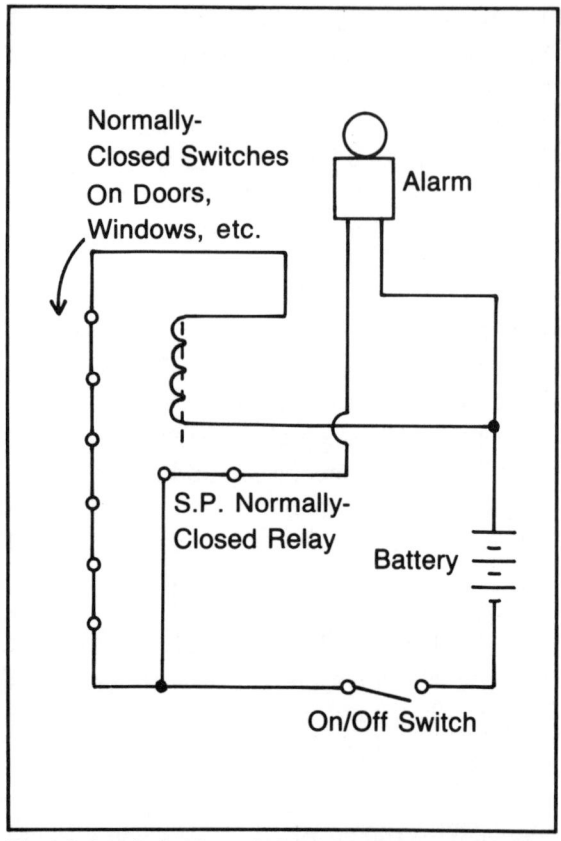

Fig. 1-2. A typical wiring scheme in a closed-circuit system.

Table 1-1. Wire Run Length Versus Wire Gauge Size.

LENGTH OF RUN	20 FT.	50 FT.	200 FT.
AWG – TYPE OF MULTIPLE STRAND WIRE	26 AWG	24 AWG	22 AWG

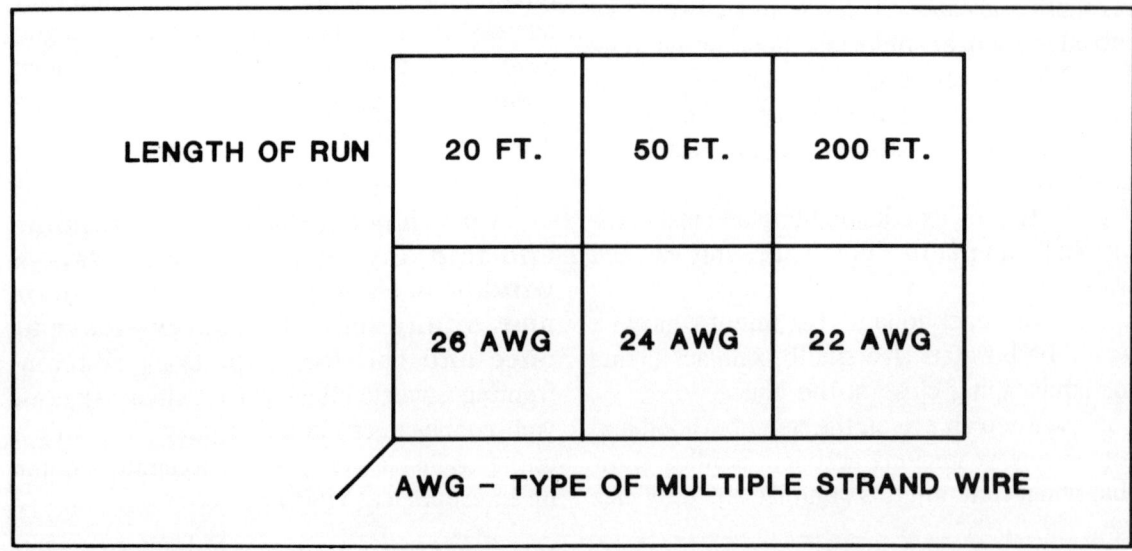

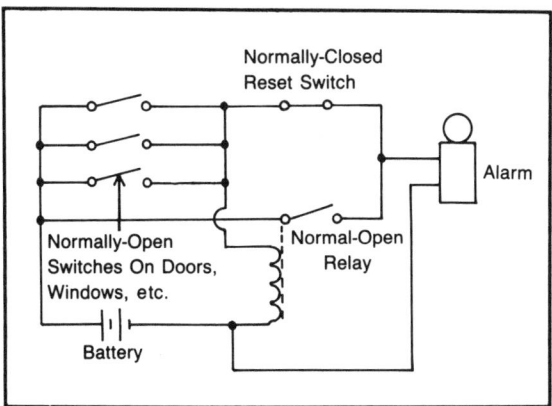

Fig. 1-3. A typical wiring scheme in an open-circuit security system.

ly a switch on a door or window) is opened. This action energizes the alarm, as shown in Fig. 1-2. This type of security system has the advantage that if the intruder cuts the wires, the alarm is automatically set off. There are disadvantages though. Probably the foremost problem is the low-current requirements on the switch, which makes long electrical lines impractical because of the inherent voltage drop unless heavy gauge wire is used. Table 1-1 provides a suggested wire size for a given wire run length.

Open-Circuit Systems

As previously stated, an open-circuit system has no current flowing through it until one of the sensors (switch contacts) is activated. Open-circuit systems are typically used where less than an absolute maximum degree of protection is required. Typical examples of open-circuit systems are ones using a smoke/fire detector, a doormat that experiences switch closure when stepped upon, door and window switches, or an ultrasonic or microwave motion detector. Figure 1-3 shows an open circuit system.

The advantages to this type of system are the elimination of a power drain on the dc power source. There is also a diminished likelihood of false alarms.

What many security books recommend and likewise what we have not only designed here but have very successfully installed in our own homes is a combination of both types of systems. You will note later on how both systems working in conjuction with one another can have inner-loop security devices selectively disabled while the outer loop remains intact. This approach allows entry detection while still enabling normal human behavior or activity to transpire within the house without setting off the alarm.

SYSTEM COMPONENTS

The following discussion lists several typical electronic security system components. Most are really rather simple in their theory of operation. The microwave motion detector, however, is a bit more sophisticated than the rest of these security components. It is, therefore, discussed first and in greater detail. The Sentinel System in Chapter 6 works in conjuction with this device. The microwave motion detector specified in these projects is a typical one. Therefore, it is covered in this section as a representative sample of all such detectors.

Microwave Motion Detectors

These useful devices are gaining increasing popularity due to recent manufacturing advances that are enhancing performance while dramatically reducing prices. A microwave motion detector senses or detects motion by use of the doppler radar principle, often just called the doppler effect. This principle is most easily understood by use of a practical tangible example. No doubt you have observed an oncoming car sounding its horn or an aircraft or train approaching you while sounding its whistle. The *tone*, or actually the *frequency of the sound*, tends to change as the oncoming sound approaches and also as it goes away from you.

This phenomenon is due to the speed of sound (a constant) being altered by an amount equal to the speed of the vehicle emitting this sound relative to the listener. The speed of the sound is speeded up by this amount as it approaches and causes an apparent increase in frequency. Conversely, upon leaving or departure from the listener, a decreased apparent frequency is observed. This changing of speed of the sound relative to the speed of the sound emitting source, and furthermore relative to its direction with respect to the listener, is called the doppler effect.

This same principle, even though ever so slight, is detected by a microwave motion detector that sends out a high frequency signal (typically 10.5 GHz) and detects a returned frequency that can be a different value. This change in frequency indicates a disturbance or alteration in the field or pattern over or upon which this signal was initially cast. Keeping this doppler effect principle in mind, you can understand why each device comes with a warning not to mount it to a vibrating surface.

The microwave motion detector used for the projects in this book is the NJH6007M manufactured by New Japan Radio Company. It can be rotated 90 degrees and mounted so that the beam can be directed at a horizontal angle from the wall. The detector should not be aimed at a nearby window nor at a fluorescent light fixture that is less than five feet away. However, this unit does have a very sharp low pass filter designed to eliminate fluorescent light noise and crosstalk. Appendix A discusses the various sources of EMI (electromagnetic interference). The fact that this extremely high frequency signal is totally unaffected by sounds, air currents, or changes in temperatures contributes to its usefulness and popularity.

Here are some of the features of the NJH6007M:

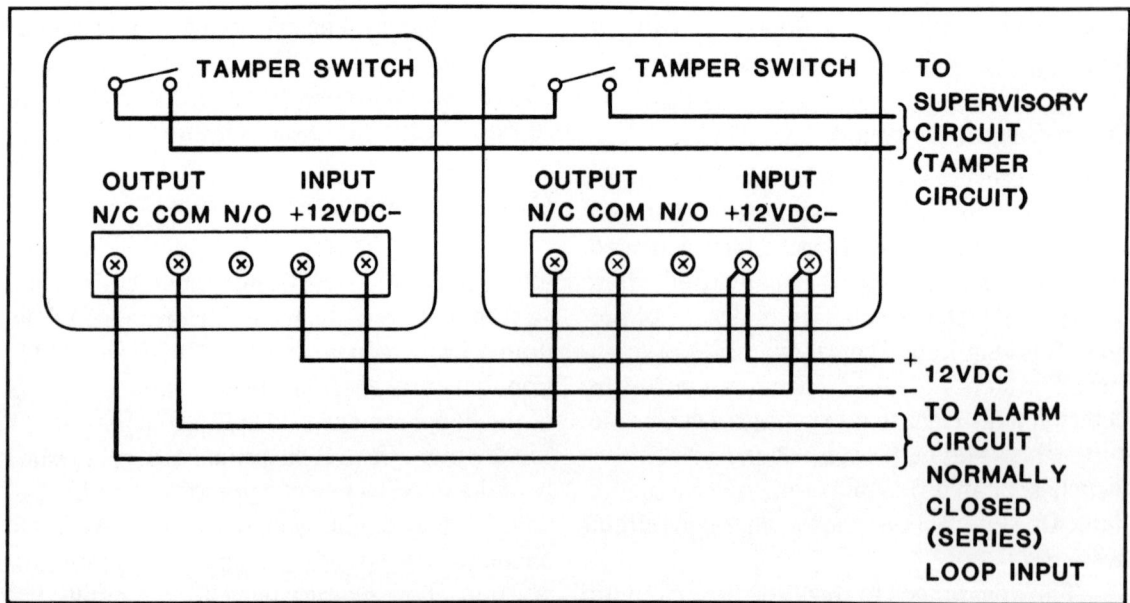

Fig. 1-4. A typical closed-loop wiring scheme for a separate monitoring or tamper circuit.

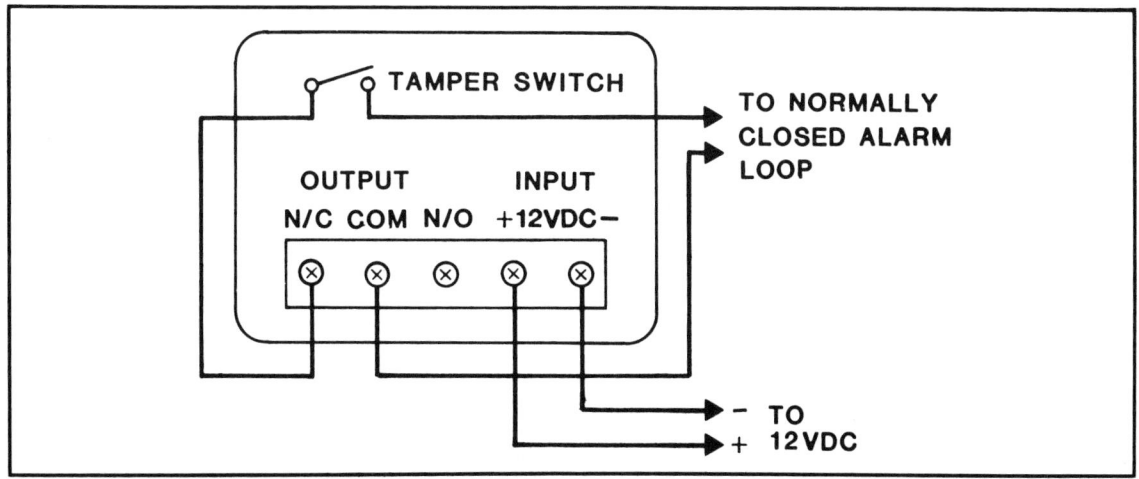

Fig. 1-5. A typical closed-loop wiring scheme for a system without separate monitoring or a supervisory circuit.

Sensitivity Adjustment. Set the sensitivity to the required level by turning the adjustment clockwise to increase or counterclockwise to decrease effective range. Do not set sensitivity higher than that actually required by the application.

System Testing. Walk test the system by observing that the LED lamp lights when motion is detected. Readjust sensitivity or reposition sensors as required. Snap front cover back into position. Thoroughly test the system for false or nuisance alarms before connecting it to an alarm sounding device or central station.

Mounting. Open the sensor housing by squeezing slightly inward on the sides of the front cover (opposite the rear mounting holes). Attach the adhesive backed foam strip supplied to the back of the unit housing aligning the holes in the strip with the mounting holes in the sensor. (Remove paper backing from foam strip before applying). Use the screws and washers provided to mount sensor to wood surface or through wall-board into stud. Use appropriate expanding fastener for mounting to hollow wall. Secure screws firmly but do not overtighten. The 3 1/4" mounting holes fit into standard electric flush mounting boxes.

Wiring. The gauge of wire to be used in the installation is determined by the number of sensors in the run and the length of the run (see Table 1-1). The wiring is brought into the sensor through the hole in the rear of the unit housing, or through the "knockout" hole on the bottom side below the terminal strip. Connect sensors to alarm circuit as shown in Figs. 1-4 and 1-5.

Power Supply. The NJH6007M operates normally with 11 Vdc (absolute minimum) to 18 V (absolute maximum). The unit has a built in voltage regulator, thus it does not require regulated dc; however, the voltage ripple should be less than 100 mV.

Multiple Sensor Applications. In the case of multiple sensor applications in which sensors are in close proximity to each other, there are four different frequency groups available to avoid cross talk.

Frequency	Letter	Color Code
10.540 GHz	H	Red
10.530 GHz	M	Yellow
10.520 GHz	O	White
10.510 GHz	L	Orange

The four frequency groups, H, M, O and L are marked on the module with the letters and the color code. Frequency can be specified in the range of 9 GHz through 11 GHz in order to meet individual country requirements.

Smoke/Fire Detectors

As a result of in excess of 10,000 people dying in fires within their own homes each year, some 20 million smoke detectors have been installed in American homes. These range in size, cost, and complexity from the $20 unit to the very elaborate units in excess of $150. Typical of units on the lower price end are the *Statitrol SmokeGard* with its dual alarm comparator for detection of low smoke concentrations.

A more sophisticated model is the *Fire-Lite heat detector* with its fusible link fixed temperature detector. This unit is capable of covering over 900 square feet when set at a 135° F trip temperature.

Another type of sophisticated smoke detector works off the ionization principle. This type of detector has an internal shielded radioactive material inside a shielded chamber. When smoke enters the chamber, conductivity of the electrodes is lessened. This diminished electric current is detected, thereby indicating the presence of smoke. Incidentally, the United States Nuclear Regulatory Commission has tested these devices and found them to be absolutely safe.

Switches

Switch sensors are crucial to any security system, probably even more so to the closed-circuit or outer-loop type of security system, for reasons so obvious they need not be mentioned. The first type of switch is the surface-mounted, self-adhesive type with screw terminals and usually concealed contacts. These switches are ideal for placement around doors and windows and have minimum and maximum acceptable gaps or mounting distances (refer to Fig. 1-6). There are even spacers made to go between the switch contacts to ensure a proper gap or separation distance. The Magnetic Sensor Switch in Fig. 1-7 has concealed M3 Reed contacts. It comes in slim, modern gray plastic housings (1/2" × 1/2' × 3 7/8"), molded from high temperature, impact-resistant polystyrene. Rhodium contact material eliminates contact "freezing" in this hermetically sealed switch. Alnico 5 magnets assure very long life under continuous operation. Two-inch magnets work with spacings or applications near steel. If extremely powerful magnets are used, it is possible to install M3-001 and M3-003 magnets too close to the switch. Usually a 1/2" minimum gap is satisfactory. Test magnet and switch with an ohmmeter if in doubt. The switch is rated at 15 W or 400 Vdc, 1 A.

There are also a number of other types of magnetic switches with unique features. The *Select-a-Gap* made by Sentrol has set screws at the end of the switch to set the gap. These type switches are polarity sensitive and, therefore, must be aligned properly as shown in Fig. 1-6. A very complete discussion of all types of magnetic switches may be found in Chapter 7 of *The Complete Security Handbook* by C. A. Roper (TAB Book No. 1320).

Specific switch part numbers by actual manufacturer are given and discussed in Chapter 5 of this book when the actual installation of the systems is described. However, the following three magnetic switches are unique in one aspect or another and should serve as representative examples. First, the switch in Fig. 1-8 is typical of a magnetic contact switch that is rated for 10 million cycles or activations,

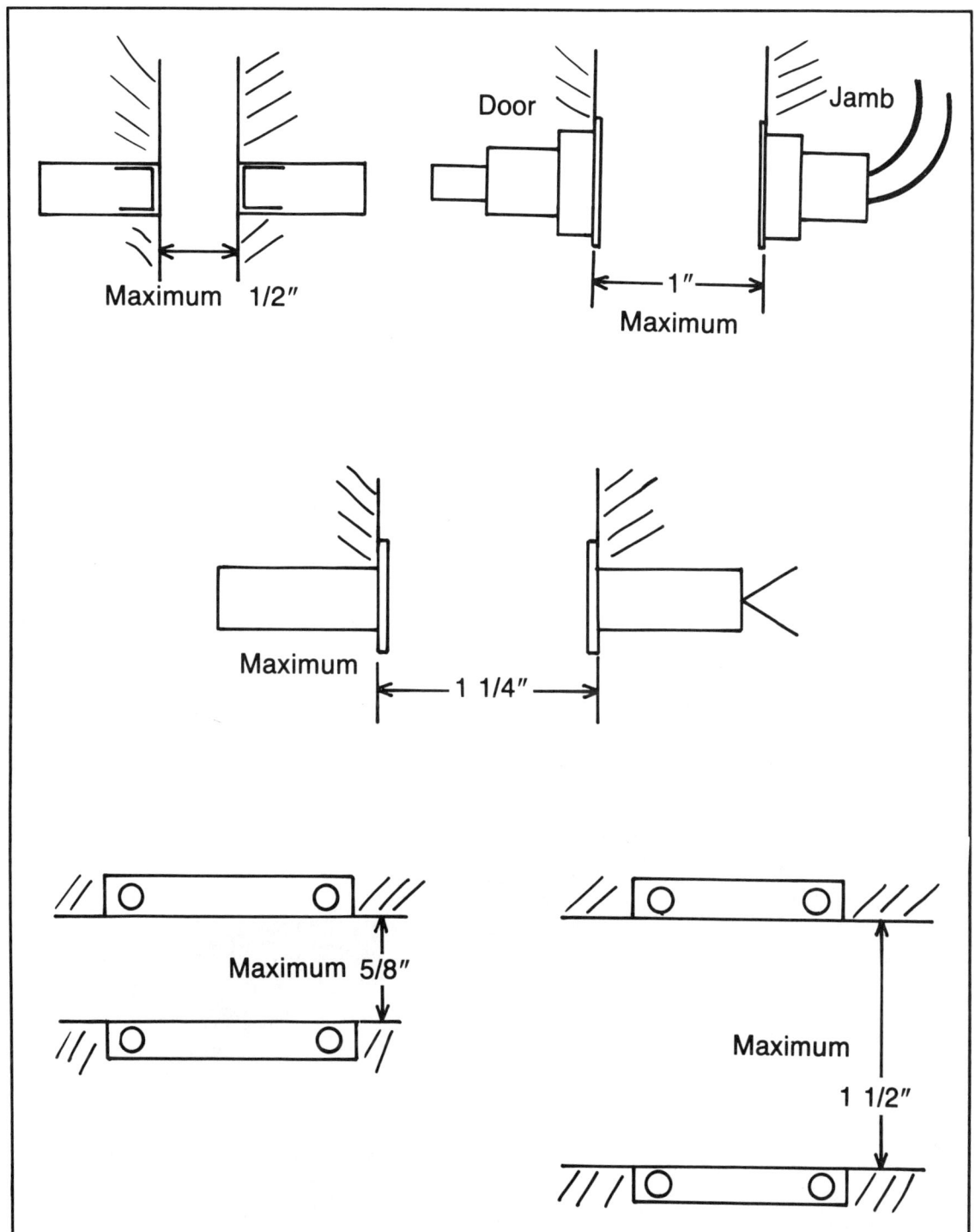

Fig. 1-6. Maximum mounting distances for magnetic switches.

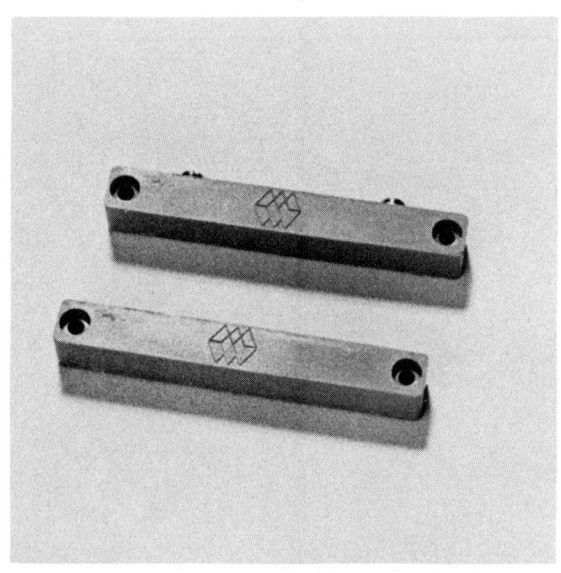

Fig. 1-7. Model M3-002 magnetic sensor switch from Mountain West.

an indication of how rugged and reliably it has been made. It is a Sentrol model S5-021 Closed Contact 1/2" Gap Magnetic Switch. These quality magnetic contacts use rhodium plating. Choice of white or mahogany brown allows system to match most decors. Wider working gaps reduce false alarms due to wind, loose doors, and door shakers, making alignment less critical. It is rated as follows: Closed loop 100 Vdc, .5 A, 10 W; SPDT 30 Vdc, 25 A, 3 W.

The magnetic switch in Fig. 1-9 works on the principle of hermetically sealed reed relays making and breaking contact upon closure in a manner that is so reliable that Mountain West will give its user $40 worth of merchandise for every failed switch returned to them to undergo inspection. This rugged design operates with a 1/2" or less gap and has a hermetically sealed

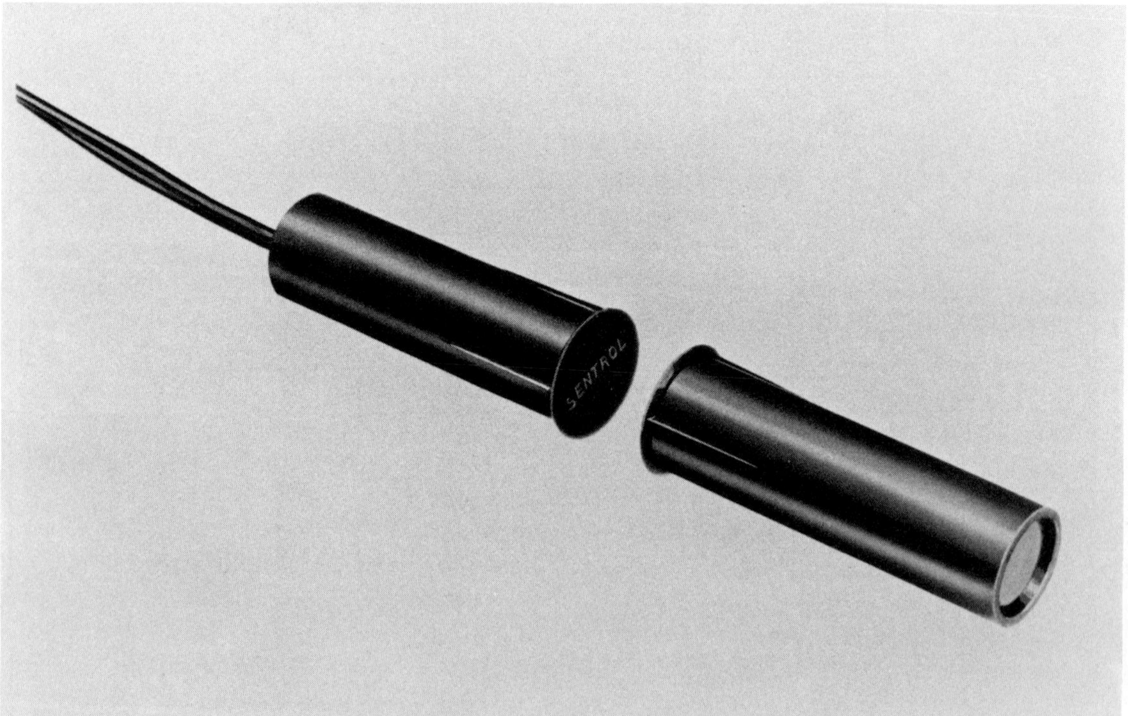

Fig. 1-8. Sentrol model 55-021 closed-contact magnetic switch.

Fig. 1-9. Mountain West M18-005 closed-contact magnetic switch.

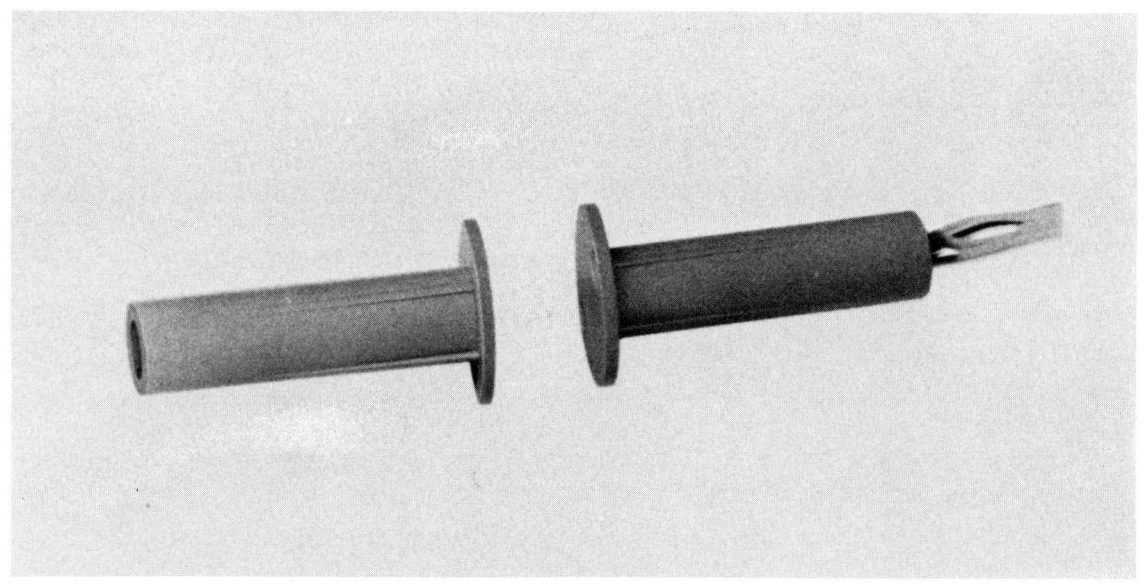

Fig. 1-10. Model 55-032 high-security magnetically biased switch from Sentrol.

reed switch inside that is guaranteed for the life of the installation and experiences less than 1 miss per one million closures.

The switch in Fig. 1-10 is a magnetically *biased* switch. It will trip when in the presence of a magnetic field. Some clever burglars may try to use magnets to bridge gaps in normal switches, but not in this one. This switch will detect this type of trick and surprise this sophisticated attempt at entry/burglary.

2
Light Controllers

THIS CHAPTER PRESENTS THREE BURGLAR deterrent projects. They are all concerned with controlling lights within your home, apartment, or place of business. In all three projects, the lights are controlled in a manner that suggests or simulates the presence of someone within the unoccupied dwelling.

The first project, appropriately entitled "The Burglar Baffler," is a pseudorandom light controller. It turns the lights on and off within the operator selected hour, but it does so in a seemingly unpredictable manner. The predictability of lights coming on and going off in a repetitive fashion is the most serious drawback of traditional light timers. Additional Burglar Baffler features include a zero-crossing detector circuit to ensure that a lamp's cold filament never receives a sudden surge of current and total solid state ac activation by LASCR's (light activated SCR's) working in conjunction with a triac to ensure added reliability by eliminating potentially unreliable relays.

The second and third projects are closely related to one another. They even share a common PC board. The second project is a lamp dimmer that dims the lamp in equaluminous steps, but it does this so smoothly that it makes it appear as if it is being done by a human rather than electronically. The smoothness in dimming is so effective that it resembles expensive theatrical lighting.

The third project uses this same dimmer circuit and PC board, but instead of being set and controlled by an 8-position manual DIP rocker switch, it uses a PNG (pseudorandom number generator) to apply varying pulses to a group of logic circuits. This in turn varies the point at which a triac activates the light. By varying this parameter in a random fashion, the triac, and in turn the light, turns on in a fashion simulating a flickering effect, and a very realistic set of "shadows" results. The net effect is one of a person or persons walking between the light and the drawn drapes. So if you were to view this from outside, say standing on the sidewalk, you would definitely get the impression that someone was walking between the light source and the draperies.

These three light-controller projects all simulate normal human activity in one manner or another while you're away and your residence is left unattended. In all three instances these projects result in extremely realistic burglar deterrents. These three projects are deterrents, not detectors or alarms; these more sophisticated devices will be covered in subsequent chapters.

In addition to the light controller circuits in this chapter there is another security application project called the *Sentinel* that turns on a light but really isn't a "smart" light controller. It appears in Chapter 6 and performs an interesting task. As a person approaches the porch or an entry point of a dwelling where a microwave motion detector is installed, a light is automatically turned on and remains on for a programmable (operator selectable) amount of time. This serves as a deterrent to someone who isn't supposed to be lurking around the premises while simultaneously serving as a convenience aid to a person who is a welcomed visitor approaching the porch in the dark.

BURGLAR BAFFLER

The conventional light timer in itself is the most economical practical burglar deterrent in existence; however, this device, in its current state, has three severe limitations. The Burglar Baffler overcomes these problems and is easy to build and test. It is highly effective, yet surprisingly inexpensive!

The first and the most objectionable limitation of a light timer is the predictability of the lights being turned on and off at the same time over and over again along with the inability to turn on lights more than once or twice within an hour or within a 24-hour period. This established pattern quickly becomes discernible to a lurking or cruising burglar and is almost an invitation to literally drop in! Secondly, the limited life and cost of frequently replacing the conventional light timer due to its mechanical nature must be considered a negative aspect. For example, the current carrying contacts soon become pitted, undependable and, therefore, largely ineffective. Lastly, there is another subtle often overlooked limitation of not protecting the incandescent light bulb filament against current surges which reduce the life of the light bulb and more importantly might cause the light bulb to fail while the homeowner or apartment dweller is away, thus rendering it totally useless!

Solving the Limitations

The Burglar Baffler expands upon the basically sound idea and principle of the light timer and overcomes the problems by making it programmable over several days, adds pseudorandom actuations, and allows 28-day cycling results. You can build and test this project in two evenings for approximately $30. Additionally, the foil pattern for the printed circuit board is included. The circuit is designed so that the project can be tested with a simple multimeter rather than an expensive oscilloscope. When completed, the Burglar Baffler will give years of satisfactory troublefree service and provide your family with an extra measure of added security.

Limited Timer Life. The problem of the limited life of the timer is resolved by total solid state design—even in the light activation portion which uses an LASCR (light-activated

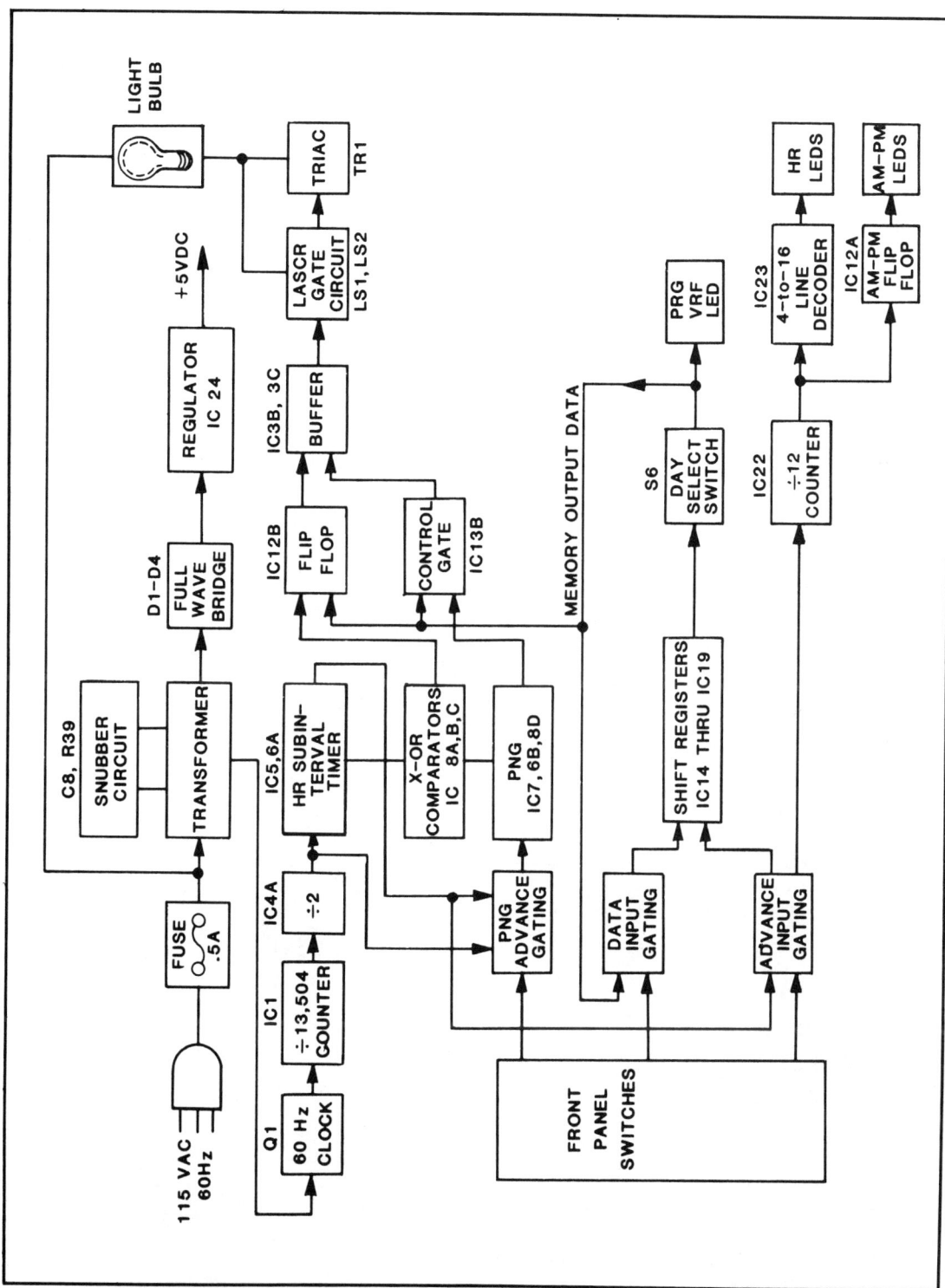

Fig. 2-1. The Burglar Baffler block diagram.

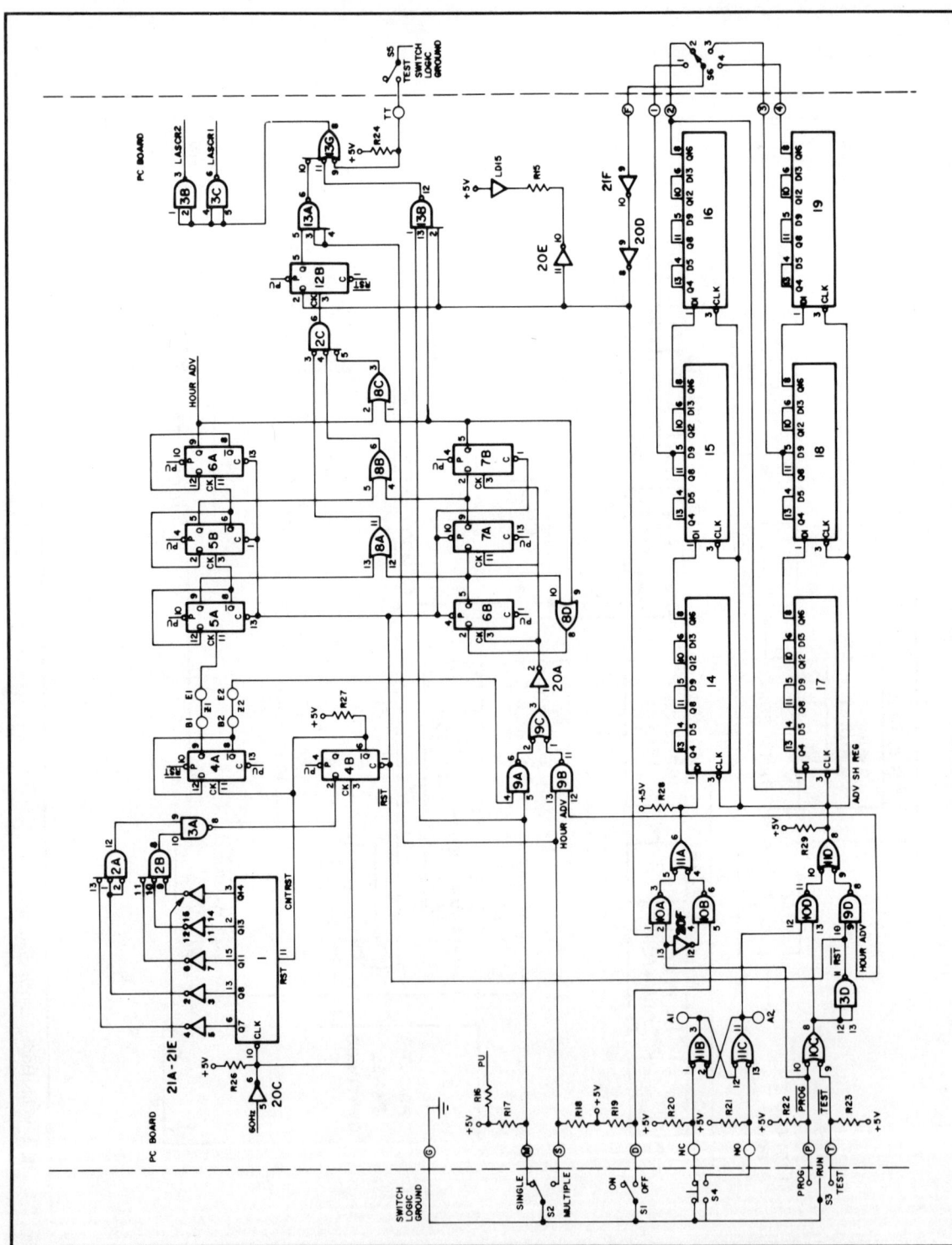

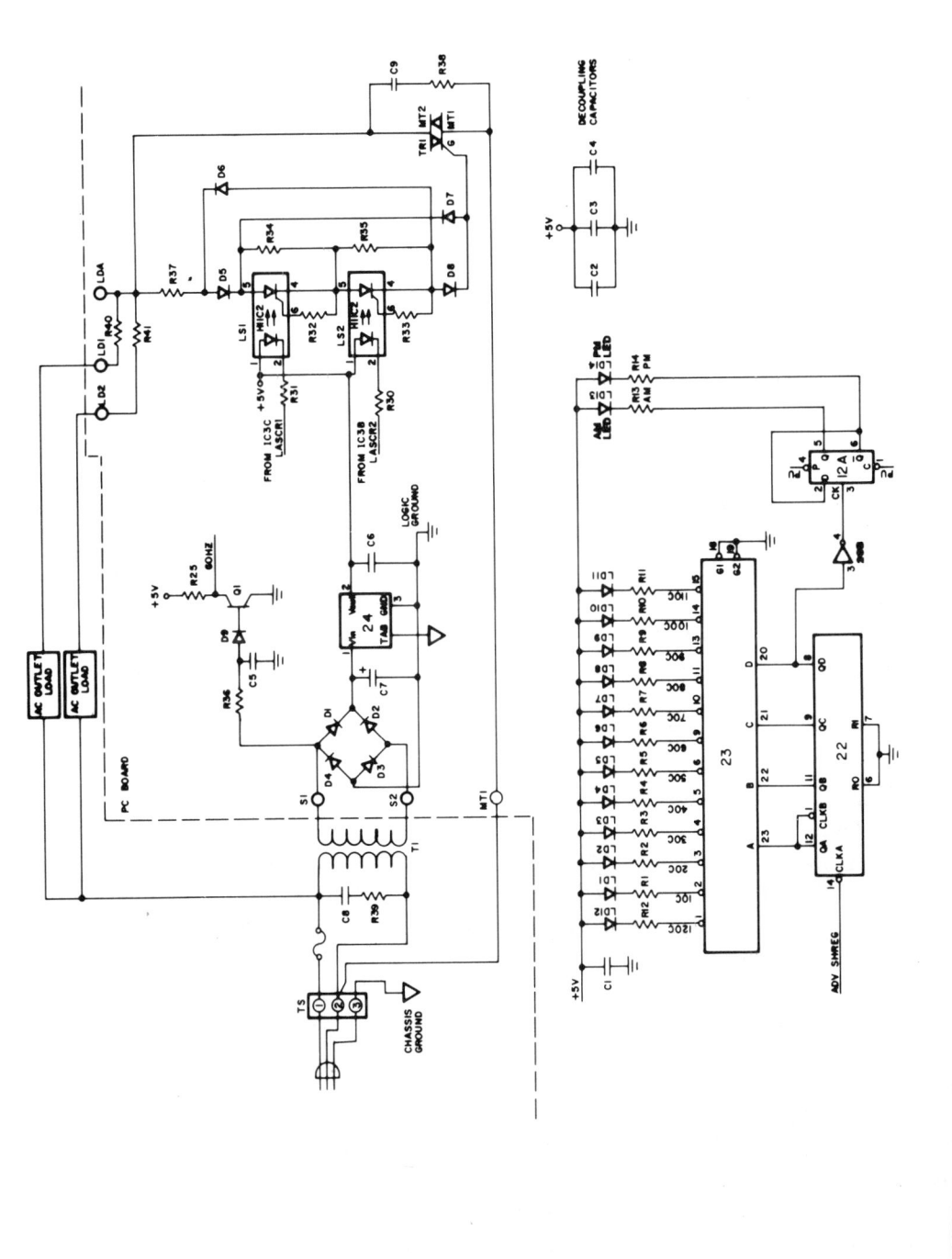

Fig. 2-2. The Burglar Baffler schematic.

SCR) and triac. This also greatly enhances dependability and reliability of operation. Refer to the schematic of the Burglar Baffler, and its block diagram in Figs. 2-1 and 2-2. Note the ac activation portion of the overall circuit.

Limited Bulb Life. The problem of limited light bulb life is solved by a circuit called a *zero-crossing detector*. This circuit ensures that the filament is protected by self heating. The importance of this "electronic shock absorber" is that it avoids applying full voltage to a cold filament. This is dramatically illustrated by the following example. First, an RCA triac applications note states that a cold filament has 1/12 to 1/18 the resistance of a warm filament. Secondly, if at turn on, the ac is at either a negative or positive peak, approximately 170 volts will appear across the filament. This is the $\sqrt{2} \times 120$ Vac. Applying this to a resistance of only 1/18 the normal "on" filament resistance results in 25 times the normally drawn current. This is a possible surge of nearly 25 amperes for a 100 watt bulb. This is why the zero-crossing detector is definitely needed! Also, the voltage applied at turn on is now, as a result of the protective action of this circuit, guaranteed to be at or near zero volts.

Predictable Light Patterns. The problem of predictable patterns of lights being turned on (or of lights being turned on at exactly the same time after each hour) is solved by use of the following two circuits. A pseudorandom number generator controls activation times. Also, shift registers, acting as very simple memories, store a program of up to four days of operator *programmable* light activations. Each day can then have a unique pattern. Likewise the operator can program as many activations as desired. The pseudorandom number generator, (PNG), or linear sequence generator, as it is also known, is not as formidable as it sounds. The PNG is composed of serially connected flip-flops forming a shift register. The trick is to tap the right points off of the shift register, apply these to an exclusive-OR gate, and then feed this signal back around to the D input of the first flip-flop. When the right taps are made and the state of all binary zeros is suppressed, a sequence results that appears totally random.

When enough flip-flops are used, you get a truly weird sequence. This project uses just three flip-flops, the minimum number possible, resulting in seven distinct states which correspond to light activation at 1/8 to 7/8 of an hour after the selected or programmed "on" hour. A longer PNG sequence can be realized by using more flip-flops. Figure 2-3 illustrates this idea. It also shows you where within this flip-flop "chain" the taps should be made. Once the timer has gone through its unpredictable pattern it returns for recycling 28 days later. This simulates normal human behavioral patterns which in themselves are very unpredictable. That is, possibly staying up late at night and moving from room to room turning on lights, music, and television, etc.

Single or multiple activations of lights within the programmed "on" hour are also possible through a SPDT (Single-Pole Double-Throw) front panel toggle switch. This adds more unpredictability to the project since the number of activations, when in the Multiple mode, is also controlled by a 3-bit PNG, and is therefore also unpredictable.

Operation

The front panel is arranged in a manner for convenient use by either right-handed or left-handed people. This also provides an orderly and logical format which is easily understood. This attention to detail with respect to human factors engineering should be followed in order to make this project easy

N	2^N	2^N-1	NO. BITS	FEEDBACK CONNECTION
1	2	1	2	11
2	4	3	3	011
3	8	7	4	0011
4	16	15	4	1001
5	32	31	5	00101
6	64	63	5	01001
7	128	127	6	000011
8	256	255	6	100001
9	512	511	7	0000011
10	1,024	1,023	7	1000001
11	2,048	2,047	8	00011101
12	4,096	4,095	8	01110001
13	8,192	8,191	9	000010001
14	16,384	16,383	9	000100001
15	32,768	32,767	10	0000001001
16	65,536	65,535	10	0010000001
17	131,072	131,071	11	00000000101
18	262,144	262,143	11	01000000001
19	524,288	524,287	12	000001010011
20	1,048,576	1,048,575	12	100101000001
			13	1000000000111
			14	01000000000111
			15	000000000000011
			16	0000000000101101
			17	00000000000001001
			18	000000000010000001
			19	0000000000000100111
			20	00000000000000001001

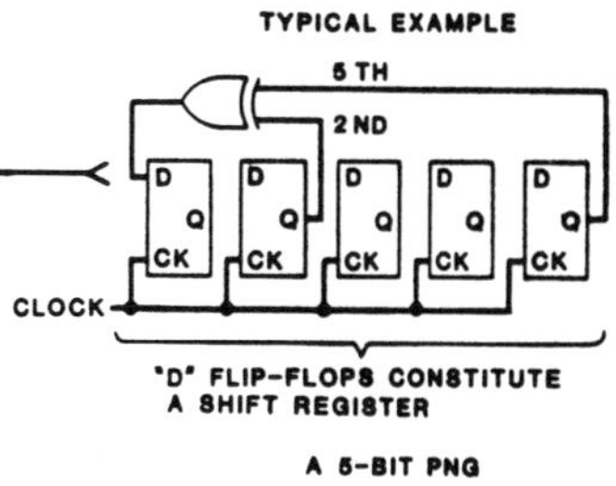

Note: Where 1s occur within the "feedback connection" column, feed these bits back around through an Exclusive OR gate to the input of the shift register. Note the example for a 5-bit PNG and where the taps were taken.

TYPICAL EXAMPLE

A 5-BIT PNG

"D" FLIP-FLOPS CONSTITUTE A SHIFT REGISTER

Fig. 2-3. Psuedorandom number generator bit patterns. The taps are shown for various word lengths.

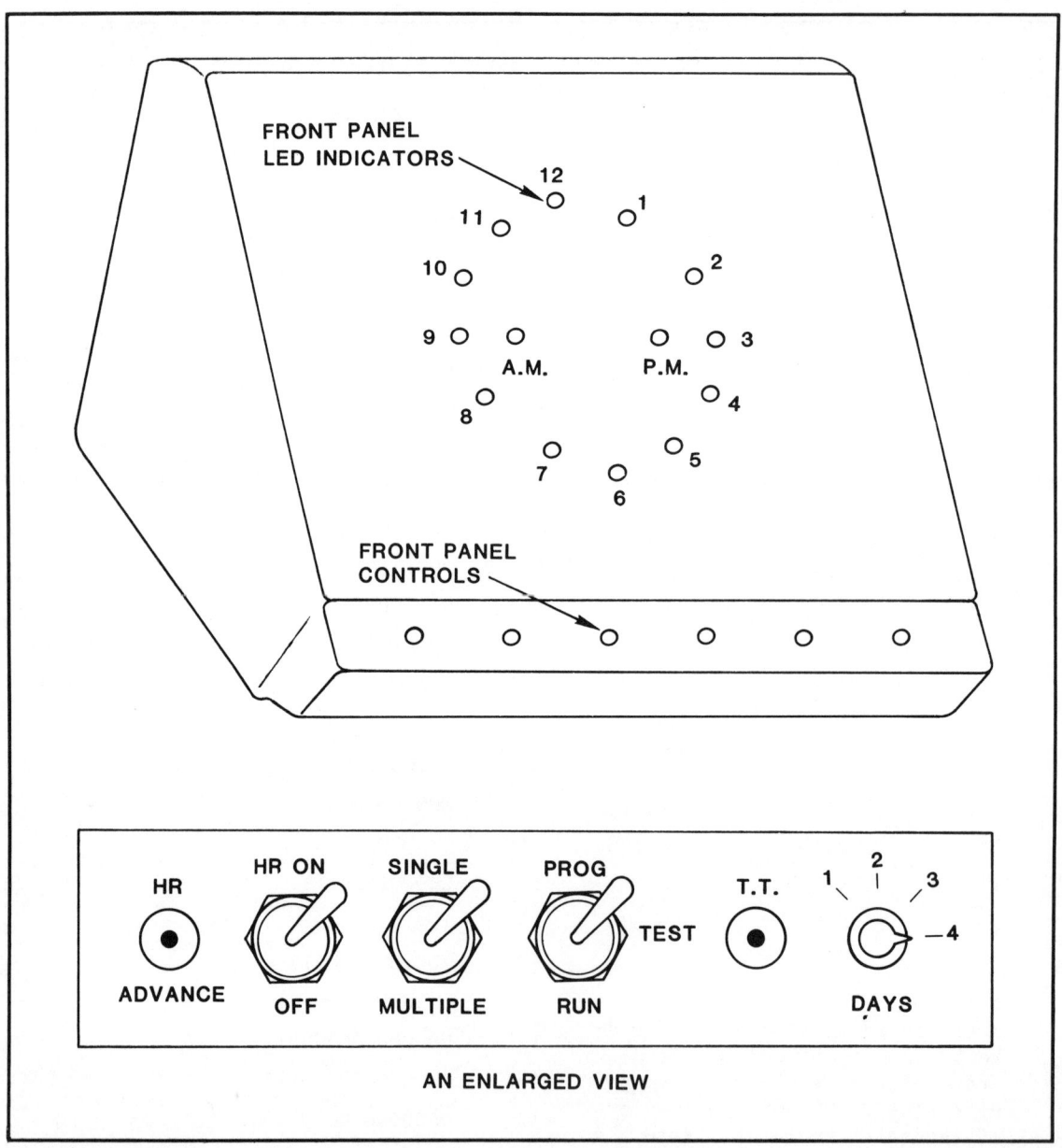

Fig. 2-4. The front panel of the Burglar Baffler.

to use by the whole family.

There are six front panel switches, as shown in Fig. 2-4. There are three toggle switches, two pushbutton switches, and a four-position switch. Two of the three toggle switches are SPDT (switches without a center off position). These are labeled SINGLE/MULTIPLE and HR ON/OFF. As their names imply, they are for either selecting single or multiple light activations within a programmed "on" hour. The HRS ON/OFF switch is used in conjunction with the HR ADVANCE pushbutton for loading the light activation program into memory.

As the hours are advanced by depressing the HR ADVANCE momentary contact switch, that particular hour will be on if the HRS ON/OFF switch is in the on position. Conversely, if the off position is selected, the hour advanced to will have no light activation within that hour.

The T.T. pushbutton switch stands for Triac Test and is used to test the triac and the associated ac activation circuitry. If an electrical device is plugged into the Burglar Baffler, it will come on when this button is pressed. Do not worry about damaging the light bulb in this mode because the timer is still protected by the zero-crossing detector.

The four-position switch called DAYS 1,2,3,4, selects how much memory is to be used. That is, if one day is selected, 24 bits will be enabled, for two days 48 bits are enabled, etc. up to four days or 96 bits. This corresponds to one bit per hour.

The last toggle switch with a center off position is labeled RUN/PROG/TEST. When set to the PROG position, the timer may be programmed to control light activations of each and every hour of the day even if a multiple number of days is selected.

Programming

Programming is very simple. Merely repeatedly depress the HR ADVANCE pushbutton switch while setting the HR ON/OFF switch to the position you desire with respect to the light activations within that hour. As an example, if you are at 11 AM and you have the HR ON/OFF switch in the on position, during the 11 AM hour the light will come on. Also, when in the PROG mode you need not worry about what program was previously entered in the shift register memory. This is because you are literally pushing out the old data as you open up the loop and this old data is then replaced with new data. This is a familiar operation to those of you who use more sophisticated calculators with the so called push-down stack operation of entering data into memory registers. Another analogy in real life might be a single file of soldiers marching out a door one-by-one until the old regiment is gone (old program) and is replaced by a new regiment of men coming in a different door (the new program). The opening of the recirculating loop is synonymous with the PROG mode and the purging operation just described. This is not to be confused with the TEST mode to be described later which looks at the new program but does not open up the loop. This might be analogous to a regiment passing in review only to do an about face and then to repeat their processional.

There are 12 LEDs placed in a circular configuration on a clock's face. There are two more LEDs to indicate whether the hour is AM or PM, and they are labeled as such. The last of the 15 LEDs is labeled PRG VRF for program verification.

You will note that after you pass the 12 o'clock position the AM and PM LEDs swap states; that is, the LED that was formerly on is now off and vice versa. This use of an AM and a PM LED allows the use of 12 LEDs and a PM and AM LED to represent all 24 hours of the day, rather than the unwieldly number of 24 LEDs.

Program Verification

Once programmed, the operator may wish to have a look at what lies within memory. After all, his or her hand could have slipped during programming or the person could have been momentarily interrupted by a member of the family. This is accomplished by switching the three position toggle switch to the TEST position. If the four day option has been selected, you must have used all 96 hours. If you program less than 96 hours, you will cause a start at an incorrect time. Once in the TEST position, step through the program by pressing the HR ADVANCE pushbutton 96 times. The PRG VRF (program verification) LED will come on if that particular hour is supposed to experience a light activation. Naturally if the PRG VRF LED remains off then lights within that hour will likewise remain off.

Once the program is entered and checked, if so desired, the switch may be placed in the RUN mode. This position starts the timer going and keeps track of actually how much time is passing.

For ease of explanation, we will enter a very simple program. This example will nonetheless show how the timer is programmed, and you can then enter in as complicated a program as you wish once you master the basic procedure. Assume for our example that it is now 10 minutes before 5 PM. Therefore, we push the HR ADVANCE pushbutton twice until it is at 7 PM, now we switch the HRS OFF/HRS ON switch to the HRS ON position. This means that a 7 PM or sometime during that hour the lights will come on. Press the HR ADVANCE pushbutton switch twice until it is at 9 PM. That will cause the lights to remain on at 8 PM. If the HRS OFF/HRS ON switch is switched to the HRS OFF position, the lights will turn off sometime during the 9 PM hour. Pushing the HR ADVANCE pushbutton switch twice again with the HRS OFF/HRS ON switch off will cause the 9 PM and 10 PM hours to be off. Now we are at 11 PM, and we want the lights to be on during the next two hours. We first make certain that the HRS OFF/HRS ON switch is in the on position, and then press the HR ADVANCE pushbutton two times. The last hours of 1 AM to 7 PM we wish the lights to remain off, therefore we make certain that the HRS OFF/HRS ON switch is in the HRS OFF position and then just push the ADVANCE pushbutton 18 times so that the next 18 hours will remain off. This same pattern can be entered in the second day.

You are probably saying why make it such an obvious pattern by repeating it the second day since you said that the predictability of lights coming on at a set time was one of the drawbacks of the conventional light timers? A good question! The answer lies in the fact that this timer has a pseudorandom number generator which controls the times during the selected hour the lights go on and off as well as the number of times they come on within that hour.

However, before worrying about the pattern's predictability which is no problem at all, as will become apparent when the circuit's actual electronic operation is described, let us concern ourselves with verifying the program. All that is needed is to set the PROG/RUN/TEST switch into the TEST position and then hit the HR ADVANCE pushbutton while watching the little LED's zing around the Burglar Baffler's clocklike face. When these numbers, in conjunction with the PM or AM LEDs light and coincide with a PRG VRF LED on, it is indicating hours in which the lights will come on.

Block Diagram

Starting with the power supply requirements (refer to Fig. 2-1 and Fig. 2-2), the timer has both TTL and CMOS logic and requires a +5 Vdc at 500 mA dc regulated source. Also required is a 12 Vac source which is easily derived from the transformer's secondary.

Transformers rated at 9 to 18 Vac at 1 A will do nicely. Actually, the regulator input can withstand from 7 to 34 Vdc. Diodes D1 through D4 form the full wave bridge rectifier and should have a 50 V PRV minimum. The timer also requires a 1/2 A fuse. The transformer primary has an RC network across it (C8, R39) which is commonly called a *snubber circuit*. This circuit prevents ac line transients from being inductively coupled through the secondary to other parts of the system. Capacitor C7 is the input smoothing or filter capacitor.

IC24 is the +5 Vdc voltage regulator. The voltage regulator is a TO-220 plastic or ceramic tab device. Its function is to provide a very stable +5 Vdc output voltage regardless of sudden radical changes in the amount of current drawn during operation. Capacitor C6 bypasses to ground any ripple that might appear at the +5 Vdc output.

The 60 Hz clock circuit provides timing critical to the system and is conveniently derived from the utility company's ultrastable 60 Hz, 115 Vac wall outlet frequency. This circuit is composed of transistor Q1, R36, C5, D9, and R25. The 17 volt peak voltage from the 12 Vrms transformer secondary is applied to another RC network (R36 and C5) to form a low-pass filter that rolls off at 60 Hz. This circuit also reduces transients. Diode D9 is inserted for noise immunity. Essentially, this circuit is a clipper by which the base of transistor Q1 is purposely overdriving to cut off the top of the sinewave. This forms a squarewave with slow rise and fall times. The rise and fall times are improved by applying transistor Q1-s collector output to inverter 20C. This has a Schmitt trigger effect that sharpens the shape of the squarewave. The counter is mainly composed of IC1 which is a 14-stage CMOS binary counter.

A few precautionary notes concerning handling and interfacing CMOS with TTL are in order. First, do not remove the CMOS IC from the black conductive foam upon which it is shipped until you are ready to use it. Secondly, use a grounded soldering iron. Lastly, make certain that you are not at a different voltage potential while handling the CMOS IC. That is, if possible, before handling the device avoid scuffling around on hylon wall-to-wall carpet which generates static charges. Concerning interfacing, TTL will easily drive CMOS; however, CMOS will not as easily drive TTL. Driving TTL logic with CMOS requires CMOS buffers or special inverters such as a 4009, 4010, 4049, or 4050. The timer's CMOS counter uses 4009 buffered inverters 21A, B, C, D, and E to drive the 7427 3-input gates (2A and 2B).

The CMOS inverter (IC1) is composed of 14 serially connected negative edge triggered "D" flip-flops with a common reset. This common reset provides a convenient means of recycling by having the counter's selected outputs go high and then be gated back to the reset pin to set all outputs back to zero for counting through another predetermined number of pulses. This number is 13,504 which, in terms of a 60 Hz wall frequency, converts to 3 minutes and 45 seconds or 1/16 hour.

After 13,504 pulses have been experienced, the counter, (IC1), will have outputs Q7, 8, 11, 13 and 14 all high. These are buffered and inverted by inverters 21A, B, C, D, and E. These low outputs from the inverters are again inverted by NOR gates 2A and 2B. NAND gate 3A provides another inversion. This signal is now applied to flip-flop 5B and then to flip-flops 5A, 5B and 6A which form a divide-by-eight ripple through counter. This is called the *hour subinterval counter*. This circuit recycles every hour, advances by one count every 1/8 hour, and applies the three flip-flop's Q outputs to exclusive-OR's 8A, 8B, and 8C.

Reviewing the truth table of an exclusive-

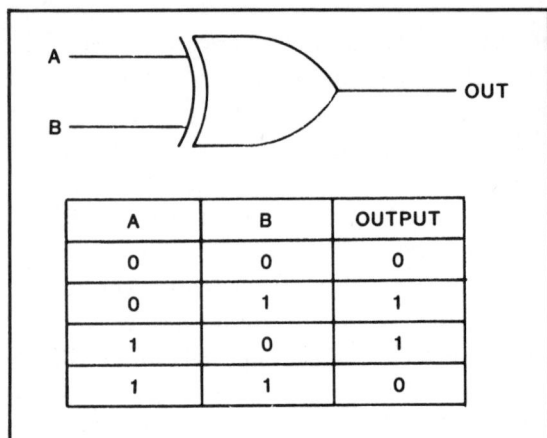

Fig. 2-5. An exclusive-OR truth table.

OR gate (see Fig. 2-5) reveals that it is a digital comparator. That is, when both inputs are either simultaneously high or low, a logic low output results. This is convenient because during the hour each time an eighth hour transpires, a different binary number from 000 to 111 is represented by flip-flop 5A, 5B, and 6A's outputs. This three bit number is compared with the three bit number, representing the output of the PNG (6A, 7A, and 7B). The three exclusive-OR gates have all logic low outputs when the two 3-bit numbers match. This is the only combination that will force the three input NOR gate (2C) high. When 2C goes high or on the positive going or rising edge, this signal clocks flip-flop 12B which transfers what appears at its data or "D" input to the flip-flop's Q output. This all holds true during operation in the SINGLE mode. During operation in the MULTIPLE mode, this inhibits the hour subinterval counter's output but it still advances each 1/8 hour; however, no comparison is made between that 3-bit word and the PNG's 3-bit word.

In the MULTIPLE mode the hour subinterval counter's 3-bit word is not compared and the PNG is advanced every 7 1/2 minutes (1/8 hour) from the $\overline{Q}$ output of flip-flop 4A. While in this mode the R17 pull-up resistor causes a logic high to be applied to one of the three inputs of NAND gate 13B. The other two inputs are the MSB (Most Significant BIT) of the PNG and the output of the shift registers (ICs 14 to 19) represent a capability of storing a four day or 96 hour period. Refer to Table 2-1

Table 2-1. Number of Shift Registers Required Versus the Number of Days Programmability.

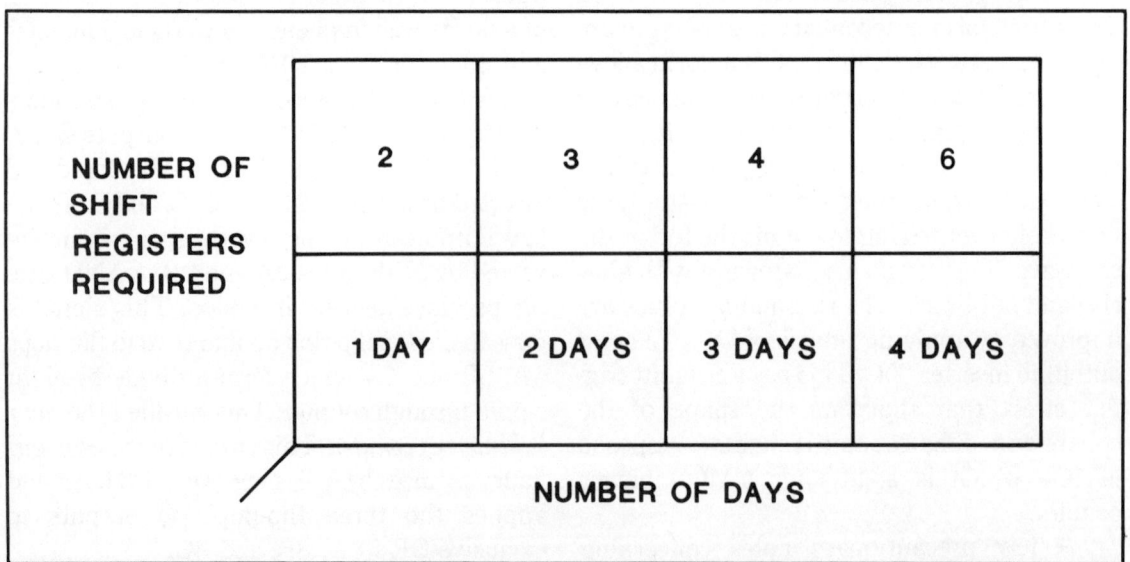

for a chart to select the number of shift registers required for the number of days that are desired. Each shift register represents 16 hours through its 16 bits. The equating of an exact hour per bit is derived by clocking these serial shift registers exactly once per hour by the hour subinterval counter. Note that the HOUR ADV line from flip-flop 6A is applied to NAND gate 9D which in turn gates this squarewave to the clocks of all the shift registers. Taps are provided at multiples of 24 bits each representing the exact duration of one day multiples.

Switch S6 provides a flexible means of altering the number of days that can be programmed. Or, if you prefer to have an exact nonvariable fixed duration, you may hardwire between points 1 through 4 and F on the PC board. Refer to Fig. 2-6 for the PC board foil patterns. Hardwiring a number of days less than 4 could save the number of shift registers required (again refer to Table 2-1). This design feature of the Burglar Baffler is like buying a computer today with spare card slots designed to accommodate future memory expansion as the situation warrants.

Input Gating

This shift register memory is loaded with highs and lows representing hours on and off respectively by means of input gating. Input gating is accomplished when the PROG or TEST position NAND gate 10C inhibits NAND gate 10D which causes the shift registers not to advance. While in the PROG position, programming occurs. Advancing the hour to the upcoming hour is accomplished by depressing the HR ADVANCE momentary contact pushbutton switch. If an hour is desired to be an hour during which the lights will come on, the HRS ON/OFF toggle switch is put into the on position, or conversely into the off position if the opposite is desired. This advancing causes cross-coupled NAND gates 11C and 11B to have a pulse applied to NAND gate 10D, which in turn, causes NAND gate 11D to toggle the shift register's clocks. This is accompanied by the HRS ON/OFF switch applying a logic high through gates 10B and 11A to the "D" or data input of the shift registers while in the on position. While in the off position, a logic low is applied to the shift register's "D" input.

The SINGLE/MULTIPLE mode switch causes the AND-OR-INVERT combination of gates 9A, 9B, 9C, and 20A to either make the digital comparison with exclusive-OR gates 8A, 8B, and 8C in the single mode or makes no comparison in the MULTIPLE mode. In the MULTIPLE mode, the MSB of the PNG activates the light if the shift register's output through inverter 20D is a logic high corresponding to a programmed in "on" hour. If a logic low has been entered, corresponding to an OFF hour, then no activation will occur because one of the three inputs to gate 13B will be low.

This randomness of the hour's starting time as well as the randomness of the number of multiple activations makes the lurking burglar unable to determine any set patterns of the timer. If this were not enough, there is a purposely induced error of approximately 2 1/2 minutes per week because of the inexact division of the CMOS counter. That is, the counter recycles after 13,504 counts rather than the 13,500 counts which would be exactly one-sixteenth of an hour.

The randomness of the PNG can be more appreciated by observing the decimal equivalent of the PNG's binary output. It is 7-3-1-4-2-5-6-7-3 etc. depending upon where you enter this sequence. Without the aid of Table 2-2, it is impossible to tell where in the sequence you are, or for that matter, what the se-

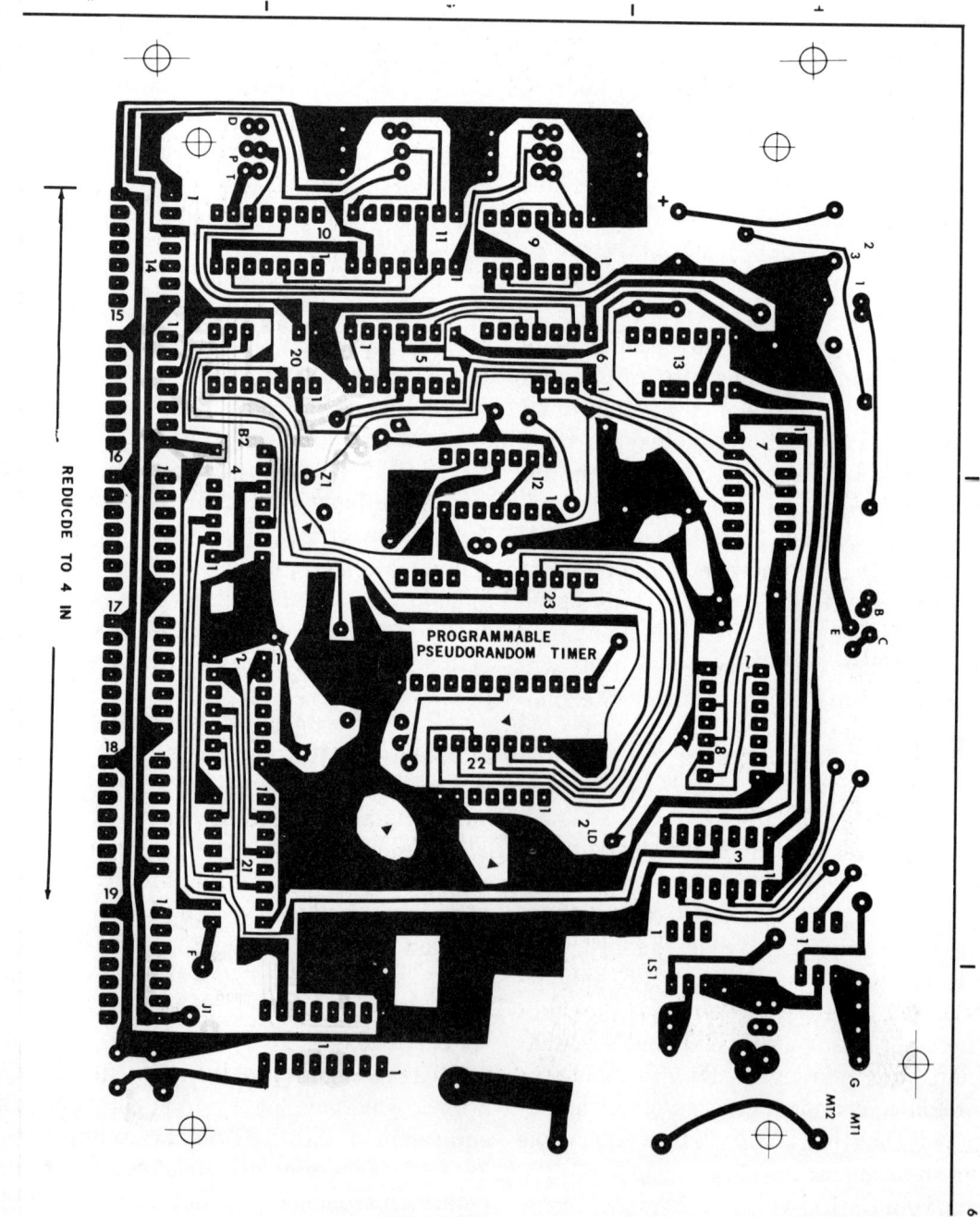

Fig. 2-6. PC board foil pattern for the Burglar Baffler.

27

Table 2-2. Psuedorandom Number Generator Truth Table and Hour Activation Schedule.

PNG BINARY STATES	PNG COUNTER STATES - Q OUTPUTS			TIME OF LIGHT ACTUATION AFTER HOUR BEGINNING - IN SINGLE MODE MIN:SEC	LIGHT ON-OFF IN MULTIPLE MODE (7½ MINUTES FOR EACH INCREMENT)
	6B	7A	7B		
8	1	1	0	22:30	OFF
7	1	1	1	52:30	ON
6	0	1	1	45:00	ON
5	1	0	1	37:30	ON
2	0	1	0	15:00	OFF
4	0	0	1	30:00	ON
1	1	0	0	7:30	OFF

* PNG LOGIC RESET STATE

quence is. This is perfect because it is an ideal way to cope with the conventional light timer's nasty habit of coming on with precision like exactness.

Incidentally, for a PNG to work properly, if an exclusive-OR feedback technique is used, a state of all binary zeros must be suppressed. Conversely, if exclusive-NOR gates are used, a state of all binary ones must be suppressed.

AC Activation

The actual turning on of an electrical device is accomplished by a LASCR, triac, and associated circuitry. When any of the three inputs to the three-input NAND gate 13C are low the output is high. This high output is inverted by NAND gates 2B and 2C which are buffered gates or *power gates*. They can sink twice as much current as a normal two-input TTL NAND gate. That is, they can sink 32 mA instead of the normal 16 mA an ordinary TTL gate can sink. The current that they are sinking, or in other words that flows into them, is from two LEDs. These LEDs are contained within a six-pin mini-DIP along with an SCR. As gates 2B and 2C go low they cause a near five volt potential to develop across the LEDs of the LASCRs. These LEDs naturally give off light as they conduct and this infared light triggers the infrared light sensitive SCRs. Remember not to look for separate SCRs and LEDs because they are probably not recognizable since they are on a six-pin DIP. These two 200 volt LASCRs are connected in series to handle loads up to 400 volts. They are barely stressed when turning on lights, which will improve system reliability. Refer to the schematic of the Burglar Baffler and note resistors R34 and R35 which are equal 270 K, 1/4 W resistors. These equivalent series resistors ensure an exact ac voltage division between the two LASCRs so one is not stressed more than the other, again in an attempt to enhance reliability. The outputs of the series LASCRs, when activated, are applied to the gate of the triac enabling it to permit the ac to flow and in turn turning on the electrical device plugged into the Burglar Baffler.

Power Capacity

A total power capacity of 500 watts can be drawn from the Burglar Baffler in the form of a resistive load. Small transistorized radios and tape recorders can still have their inductive (transformer) inputs effectively powered by the Burglar Baffler. Plugging a refrigerator into the Burglar Baffler would not only be ridiculous but also harmful to the Burglar Baffler since it is designed for lower-power resistive loads.

Precautions

Certain precautions should be followed when a large amount of power is being controlled. Heatsinks for the latching devices (the LASCR and the triac) must be used with great care. Three rules should be followed. Use minimum lead lengths when mounting SCR's. Do not connect heat dissipating devices to the SCR leads. Shield heat radiating devices such as lamps, power transformers, and resistors from radiating their heat directly onto the SCR case. Using the PC board foil pattern of the board itself will help avoid the majority of these pitfalls. Further precautions are discussed in the construction section.

One last item, when consulting the parts list, the IC's that begin with 74 are TTL ICs, and the others that begin with CD40XX are CMOS ICs and should be handled with extreme care regarding potential static electricity hazards, as has already been mentioned. If you scrounge from military surplus ICs, you should be aware that a 54 prefix is the same as a 74 prefix, the only difference is that the 54 prefix is a military temperature range ceramic packaged TTL IC.

Construction

Mount the transformer, assuring proper clearance, followed by the power supply circuit. Use a temporary heatsink in the form of a piece of metal, preferably aluminum or copper, attached to the hole on the +5 volt "tab" regulator. Measure the regulator's output voltage. Assemble the remainder of the board's components taking cognizance of the proper mounting side (see Fig. 2-7). The parts list is shown in Table 2-3. Do not assemble the triac or LASCR circuitry on the PC board yet. Add wires by matching B1, E1 points and then matching B2, E2 points on the board. Allow adequate service loop on the switch wiring so that the wires do not have to be changed when the board is mounted inside the cabinet. Perform a check on the logic. Assemble the triac ac activation circuitry. Use a separate heatsink for the triac while checking the board. Use only a 25 or 60 watt bulb until the triac is mounted to the cabinet. Next, mount the board to the cabinet. Mount the regulator to the chasis using a mica insulating washer, and silicone grease. (For a more detailed explanation in this area refer to "IC Voltage Regulator Sourcebook with Experiments" by Vaughn Martin, TAB Book No. 1557, pages 190 and 196.) Carefully observe the triac pin configuration before mounting. Before mounting the triac and regulator to the cabinet, thoroughly clean the surface with steel wool to ensure absolute flush mounting surfaces between the triac, regulator, and cabinet's surface. The triac requires an insulator between it and the cabinet's surface. Use an audio oscillator and apply the output to the 60 Hz clipper input at R36. If you do not have an audio oscillator, a one-shot multivibrator oscillator can be easily constructed (see Fig. 2-8) and then applied to the input of inverter 21A.

Do It Yourself

Should you choose to breadboard or lay out

Table 2-3. Parts List for the Burglar Baffler.

Item	Reference Designation	Qty	Description
1	IC9, 10, 11	4	Integrated Circuit, 7400
2	IC20	1	Integrated Circuit, 7404
3	IC13	1	Integrated Circuit, 7410
4	IC2	1	Integrated Circuit, 7427
5	IC3	1	Integrated Circuit, 7437
6	IC4, 5, 6, 7, 12	5	Integrated Circuit, 7474
7	IC8	1	Integrated Circuit, 7486
8	IC22	1	Integrated Circuit, 7492
9	IC23	1	Integrated Circuit, 74154
10	IC14-19	6	Integrated Circuit, CD4006
11	IC21	1	Integrated Circuit, CD4009 or CD4049
12	IC1	1	Integrated Circuit, CD4020
13	VR1	1	Voltage Regulator, LM340T-5.0
14	Q1	1	Transistor, 2N2222A
15	LD1-15	15	Light Emitting Diode MV5054-3 or equiv.
16	D1-D4	4	Diode, Rectifier Typically 1N4001 or equiv. Iave = 1.0 A Isurge = 3.0 A for 5 ms PRV = 50 V
17	D9	1	Diode, Rectifier - 1N4001 Iave = 100 mA Isurge = 1.0 A PRV = 50 V
18	D5-D8	4	Diode, Rectifier - 1N4004 Iave = 0.5 A Isurge = 5.0 A for 15 ms PRV = 400 V
19	R1-R15	15	Resistor 220 Ω $\pm$5% 1/4 W
20	R16-R25, R41	11	Resistor 1 KΩ $\pm$10% 1/4 W
21	R26-R29	4	Resistor 4.7 K $\pm$10% 1/4 W
22	R30, R31	2	Resistor 270 Ω $\pm$5% 1/4 W
23	R32, R33	2	Resistor 56 K $\pm$10% 1/4 W
24	R34, R35	2	Resistor 270 K $\pm$10% 1/4 W
25	R36	1	Resistor 27 K $\pm$10% 1/4 W
26	R37	1	Resistor 100 Ω $\pm$10% 1/2 W
27	R38, R39	2	Resistor 47 Ω $\pm$20% 1/2 W
28	R40	1	Resistor 1 Ω 5 W Wirewound
29	C2-C4*	3	Capacitor 0.1 μF 15 V Ceramic or Mylar
30	C5	1	Capacitor 0.1 μF 25 V Ceramic or Mylar
31	C6	1	Capacitor 1.0 μF 15 V Ceramic or Tantalum
32	C7	1	Capacitor 220 μ $\pm$10% 35 V Electric Radial Leads
33	C8, C9	2	Capacitor 0.1 μF 400 V a. Sprague Type 160P #4TM-P10 b. Cornell Dubilier #PKM4P1
34	S1, S2	2	Switch, SPDT
35	S3	1	Switch, SPDT - Center Off
36	S4	1	Switch, SPDT Pushbutton
37	S5	1	Switch, 4 Position Rotary - Short between switch common and one contact at a time. + Knob
38	T1	1	Transformer Primary: 117 V 60 Hz Secondary: 12.0 $\pm$1.0 Vac 1.0 $\pm$0.2 A RMS

Item	Reference Designation	Qty	Description
39	TR1	1	Isolation: 1000-1500 Vac Triac Iave = 8 A RMS Isurge = 100 A RMS for 15 ms Peak Voltage = 400 V
40	LS1 (LS2)	1 or 2	Light Activated SCR a. H11C1, H11C2, or H11C3 General Electric b. MCS2 Monsanto
41	F1	1	Fuseholder Buss #HKP or equivalent
42	F1	1	Fuse Buss ABC5 or equivalent
43		1	Line Cord 115 Vac 10 A 3 Wire 6 Foot
44	TB1	1	Barrier Terminal Block Cinch #2-140 or equivalent
45	TS1	1	Terminal Strip Cinch #55 or equivalent
46		4	Spade Lugs (Fits Item 44)
47		1	ac Outlet Amphenol 160-2N (3 Prong)
48		1	Rubber Grommet H.H. Smith #91121 or equiv.
49		4	Insulated Spacer H.H. Smith #4018 or equiv. Length-0.50 inches O.D.-.25 inches I.D.-For #4 Screw
50		4"	Shrink Sleeving 1/8" Diameter
51		20"	Hookup Wire 16 AWG Appropriate for 115 Vac 60 Hz
52		70"	Hookup Wire 24-26 AWG
53		—	#6-32 Pan Head Screws
		6	3/8 inch long
		4	1/2 inch long
54		—	#6-32 Hardware
		10	Nuts
		10	Lockwashers
		6	Flatwashers
55		—	#4-40 Pan Head Screws
		4	7/8 inch long
		2	1/2 inch long
56		—	#4-40 Hardware
		6	Nuts
		6	Lockwashers
		6	Flatwashers
57		1	T0220 Mica Insulator (For Triac-Item 39)
58		2	Shoulder Washer a. Accept #4 Screw b. Fit inside T0220 tab mounting hole. c. Appropriate for 115 Vac insulation from earth ground.
59		Optional	Thermal Grease, Dow Corning Compound
60		15	Clip Lite LED Lens Holder
61		1	Cabinet LMB Box, Part #E-007-746 Available from Bill Godbout Electronics, Oakland Airport, CA 94614

*Note: C1 reference designator skipped in sequence.

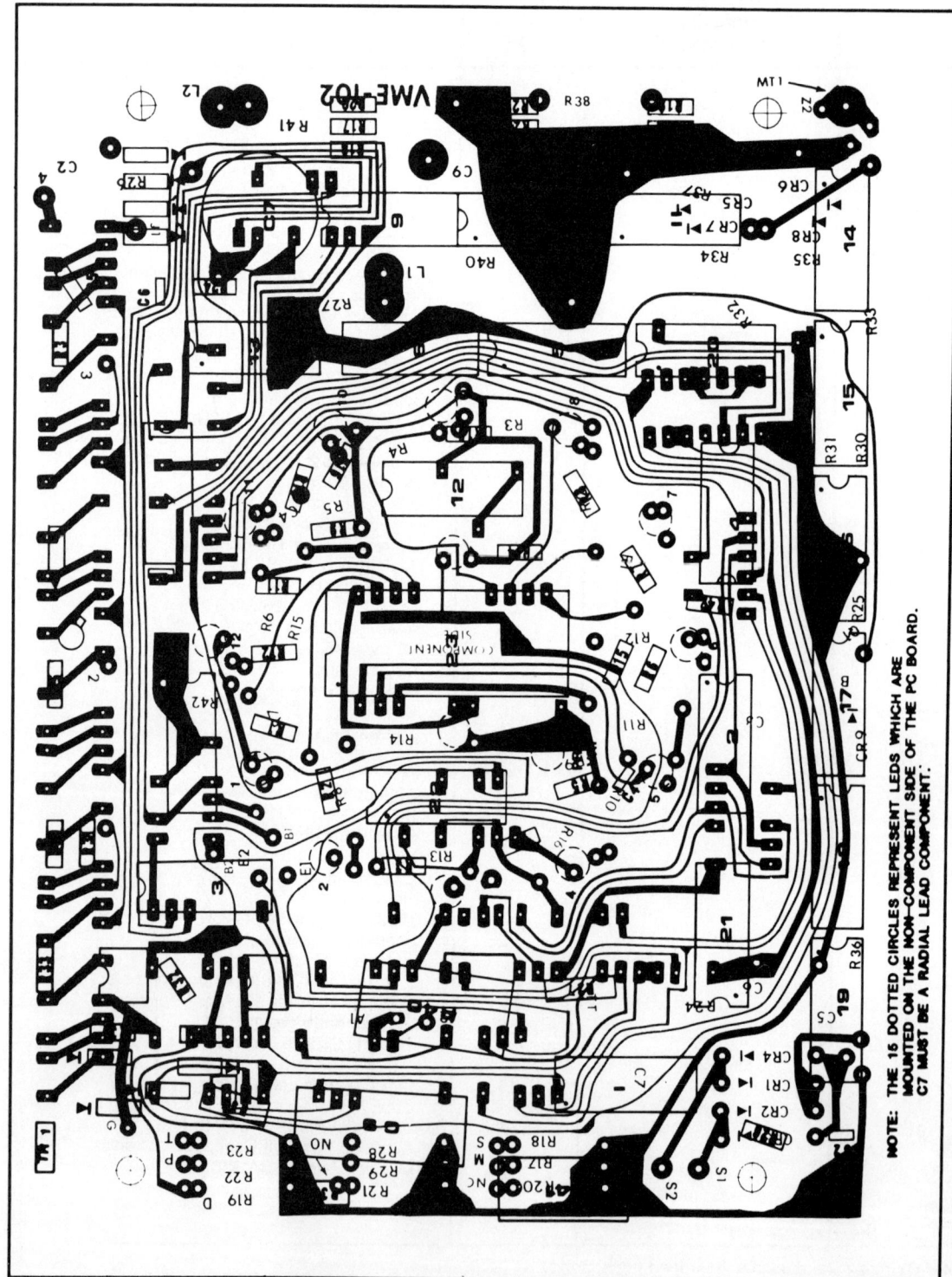

Fig. 2-7. Component placement drawing for the Burglar Baffler.

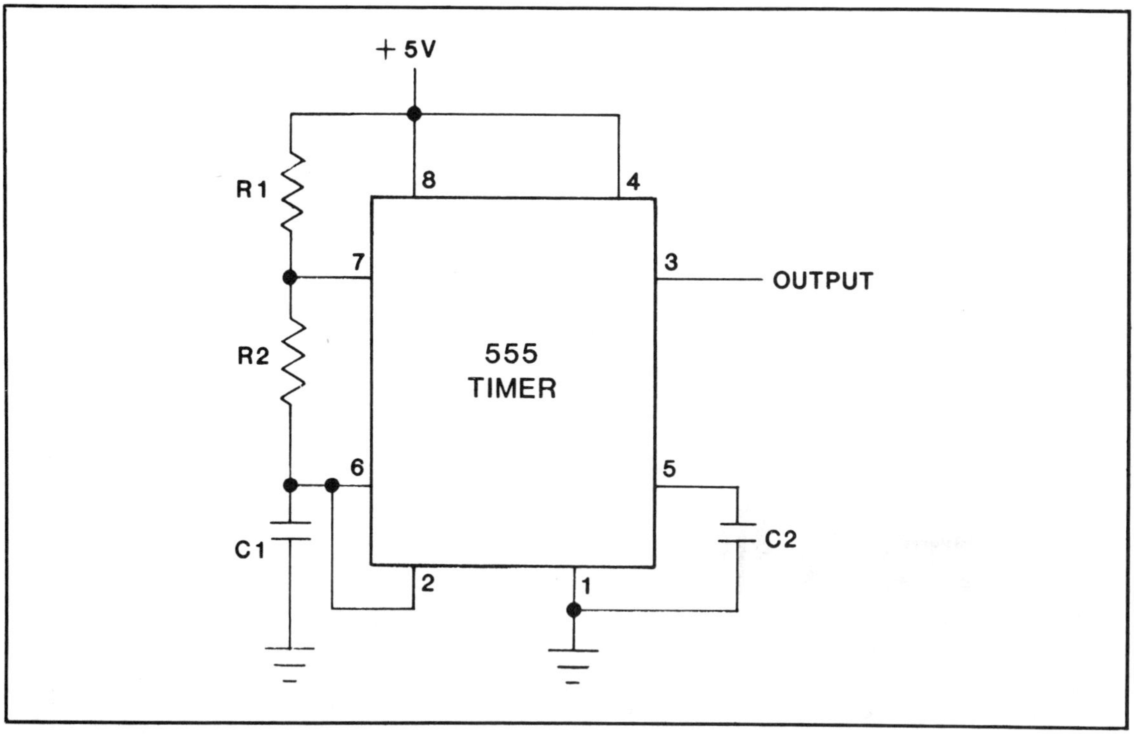

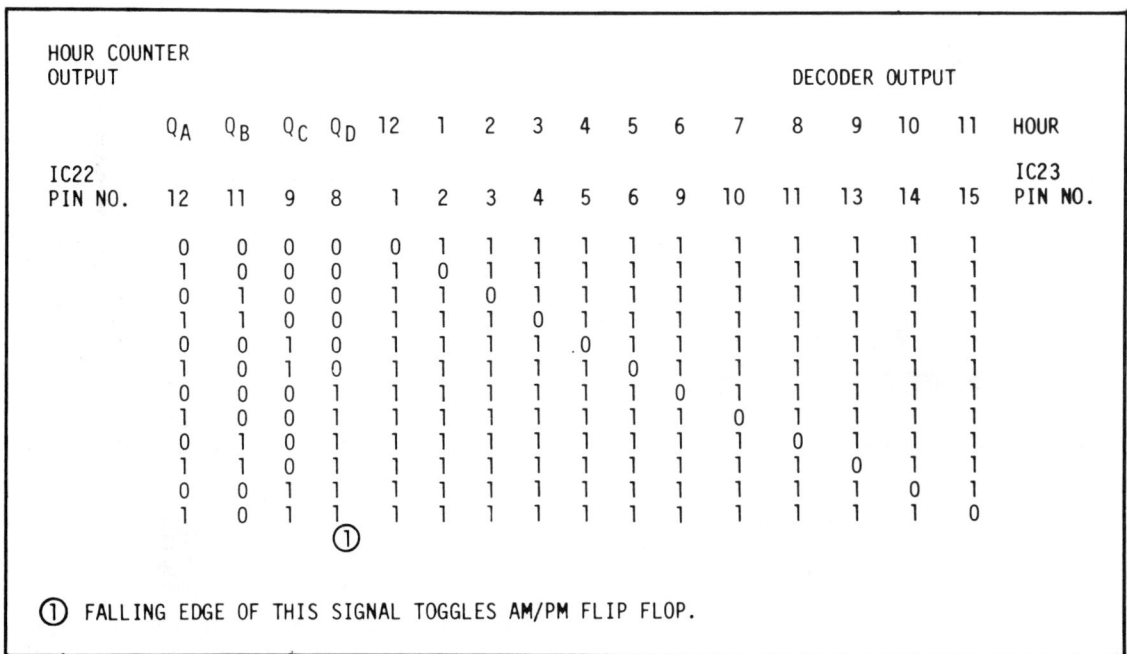

Fig. 2-8. A 555 timer circuit used as an oscillator.

Table 2-4. Truth Table for the Hour Counter and Decoder.

HOUR COUNTER OUTPUT									DECODER OUTPUT							
	Q_A	Q_B	Q_C	Q_D	12	1	2	3	4	5	6	7	8	9	10	11	HOUR
IC22 PIN NO.	12	11	9	8	1	2	3	4	5	6	9	10	11	13	14	15	IC23 PIN NO.
	0	0	0	0	0	1	1	1	1	1	1	1	1	1	1	1	
	1	0	0	0	1	0	1	1	1	1	1	1	1	1	1	1	
	0	1	0	0	1	1	0	1	1	1	1	1	1	1	1	1	
	1	1	0	0	1	1	1	0	1	1	1	1	1	1	1	1	
	0	0	1	0	1	1	1	1	0	1	1	1	1	1	1	1	
	1	0	1	0	1	1	1	1	1	0	1	1	1	1	1	1	
	0	0	0	1	1	1	1	1	1	1	0	1	1	1	1	1	
	1	0	0	1	1	1	1	1	1	1	1	0	1	1	1	1	
	0	1	0	1	1	1	1	1	1	1	1	1	0	1	1	1	
	1	1	0	1	1	1	1	1	1	1	1	1	1	0	1	1	
	0	0	1	1	1	1	1	1	1	1	1	1	1	1	0	1	
	1	0	1	1①| 1	1	1	1	1	1	1	1	1	1	1	0	

① FALLING EDGE OF THIS SIGNAL TOGGLES AM/PM FLIP FLOP.

your own PC board, extreme care should be exercised with respect to three critical items. First, the ac activation portion of the timer with associated triac circuitry has to have the proximity of adjacent high current carrying runs and their widths carefully observed and a 1/4 inch spacing must be maintained. Secondly, the divide-by-twelve IC (7492) has an unusual power-ground pin assignment. The power is applied to pin 5 and ground is pin 10. Third, the output of the 74154 16 line to 4 line decoder/demultiplexer integrated circuit has a peculiar output code.

Several pins representing outputs are skipped to give a continuous count from the 74154 demultiplexer. Therefore, be careful when connecting the LED's to the correct pin, or else a weird noncontinuous and skipping sequence will result in the LED hour activation pattern. Table 2-4 will aid in checkout with respect to this. Using the board as illustrated in the foil pattern in Fig. 2-6 will avoid these problems.

Figure 2-9 shows three kits that are commercially available from Datak and GC Electronics. These kits will nonphotographically lift PC artwork patterns from a book or magazine page. With this film positive, a board can be made by etching. Next, you will have to drill the holes for the component leads after this etching process is complete.

Care should be taken when putting the components on the PC board. Figure 2-7 is an illustration of how the components are to be mounted. Note that the 15 LEDs, represented as circular dotted-in figures, are **not** mounted on the component side of the PC board. They have to be mounted on the foil or noncomponent side because they must mount flush with or slightly stick through the front panel. They also have a number within this "dotted-in circle" which appears to be in error because of the counterclockwise rotation with respect to the numbers ascending in order, but remember—it is the mirror image you are viewing since they actually stick out from the other side of the board. The circular pads with a point sticking out from them are for the anode. The LEDs used have the anode as the longer of the two LED leads and this seems to be a standard convention used by all LED manufacturers. Check polarity though to make certain before you assume the longer lead on the LED is the anode. Also, ICs 13 and 15 are not mounted in the same orientation as other ICs in that column and the adjacent column. Take note of the dot in the corner of the ICs as well as the notch in the center at the end of the IC. This denotes pin 1.

The schematic in Fig. 2-2 also has a dotted line which defines the board's edge. Circles with either letters or numbers within them at the board's edge denote where wires either enter or exit the board.

There are seven signal connections and one ground connection which are in the lower right hand portion of the PC board's component side. Additionally, there is some on board wiring. On the noncomponent side there is a pad with the reference designator Z1 beside it. This is for a Z-wire, or a straight solid strand wire to be pushed through, soldered on both sides, and then snipped off flush with the board's surfaces. It connects between the two sides of the board.

Other on board wiring is designed to aid in troubleshooting this circuit in an orderly manner. Specifically, note the following pairs of pads on the board and their reference designators: B1 and E1, B2 and E2, and A1 and A2. If the counter and 60 Hz circuit is working, there will be an output at points B1 and B2. In fact, these points will toggle every 7 1/2 minutes. Obviously, this is too long for even the most patient kit builder to wait, so you may wire from points A1 and A2 to points E1 and E2 respectively and by pressing the monentary

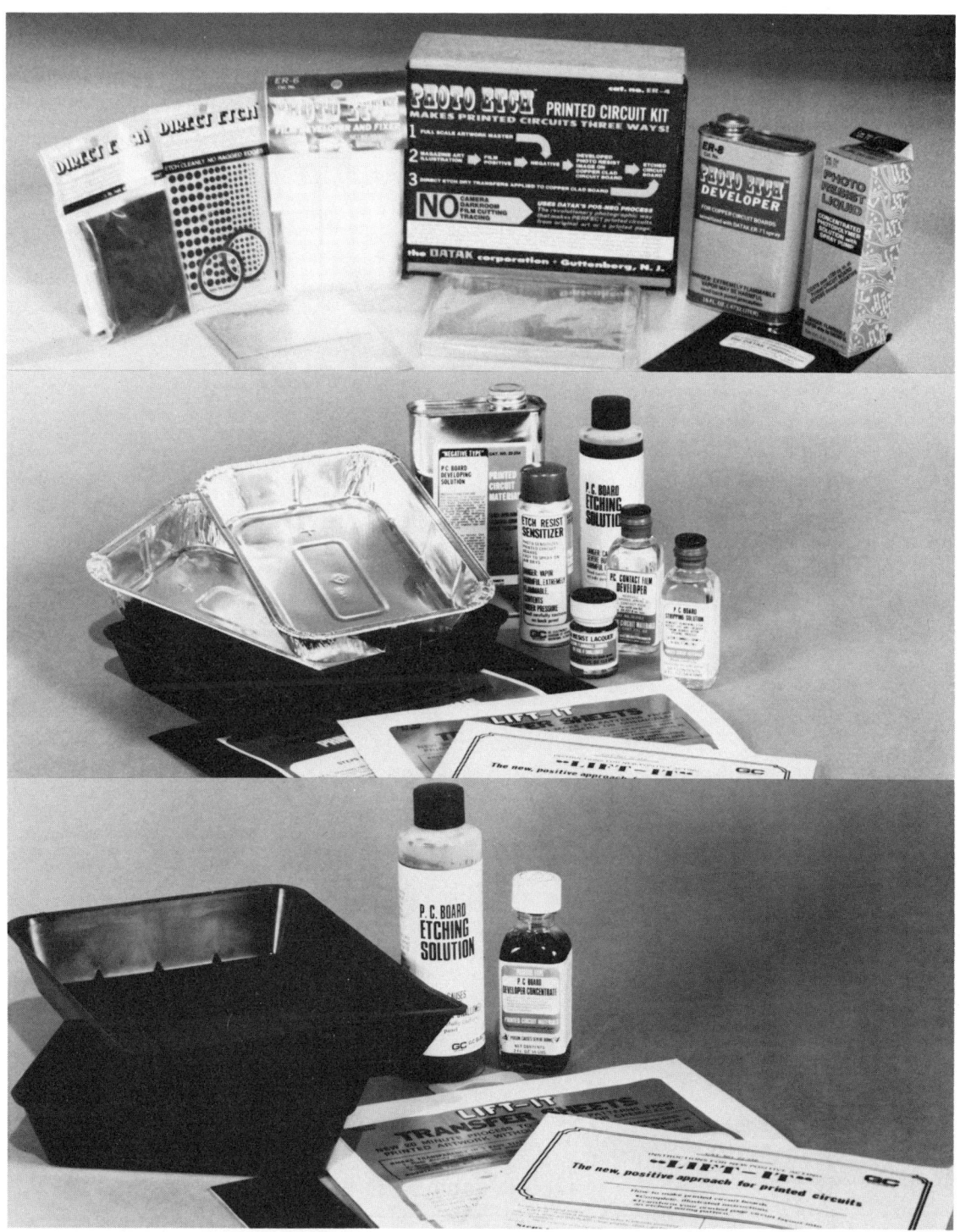

Fig. 2-9. Three kits for photographically lifting PC board patterns from a book's pages.

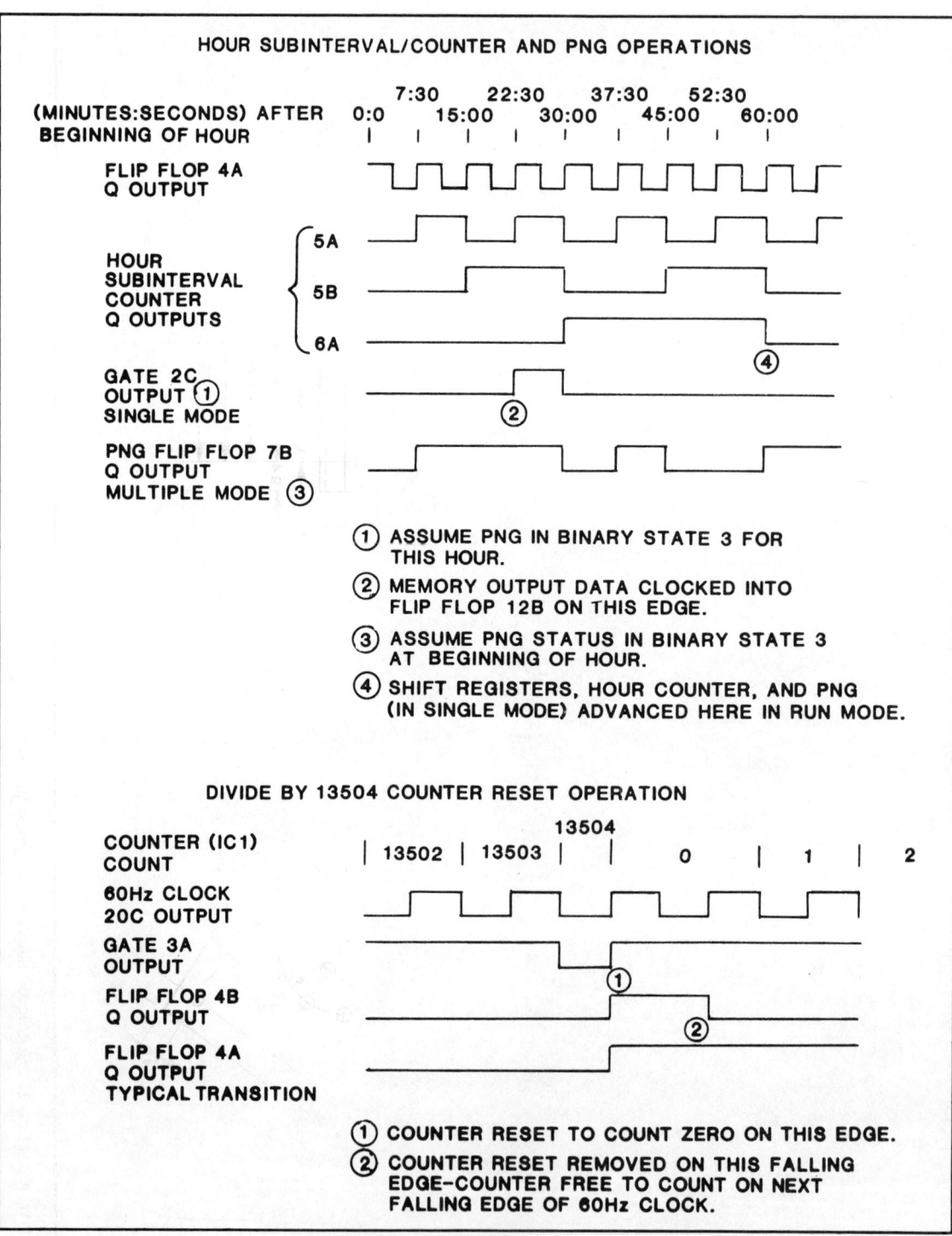

Fig. 2-10. A timing diagram/troubleshooting chart for the Burglar Baffler.

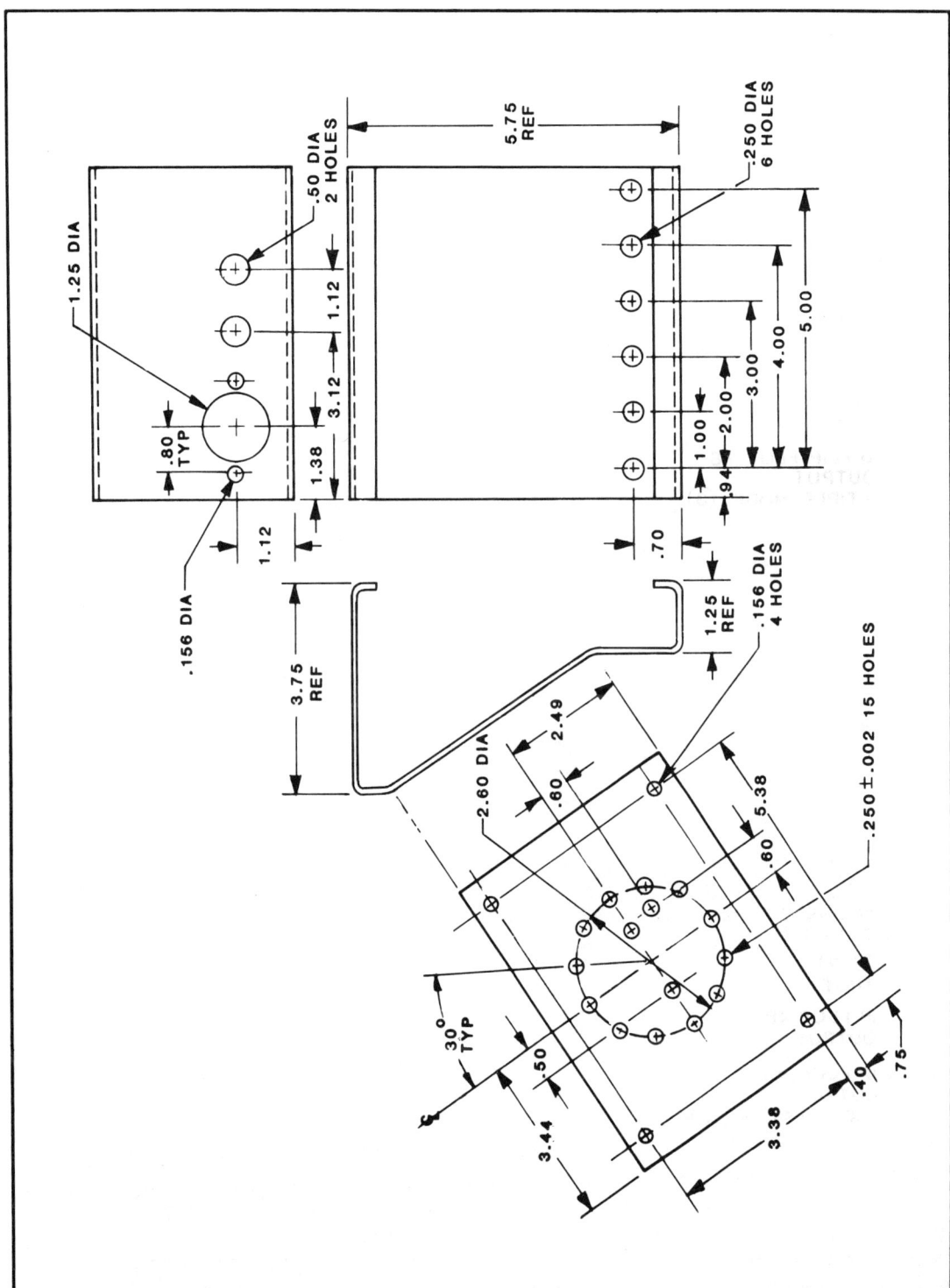

Fig. 2-11. A front panel construction diagram for the Burglar Baffler.

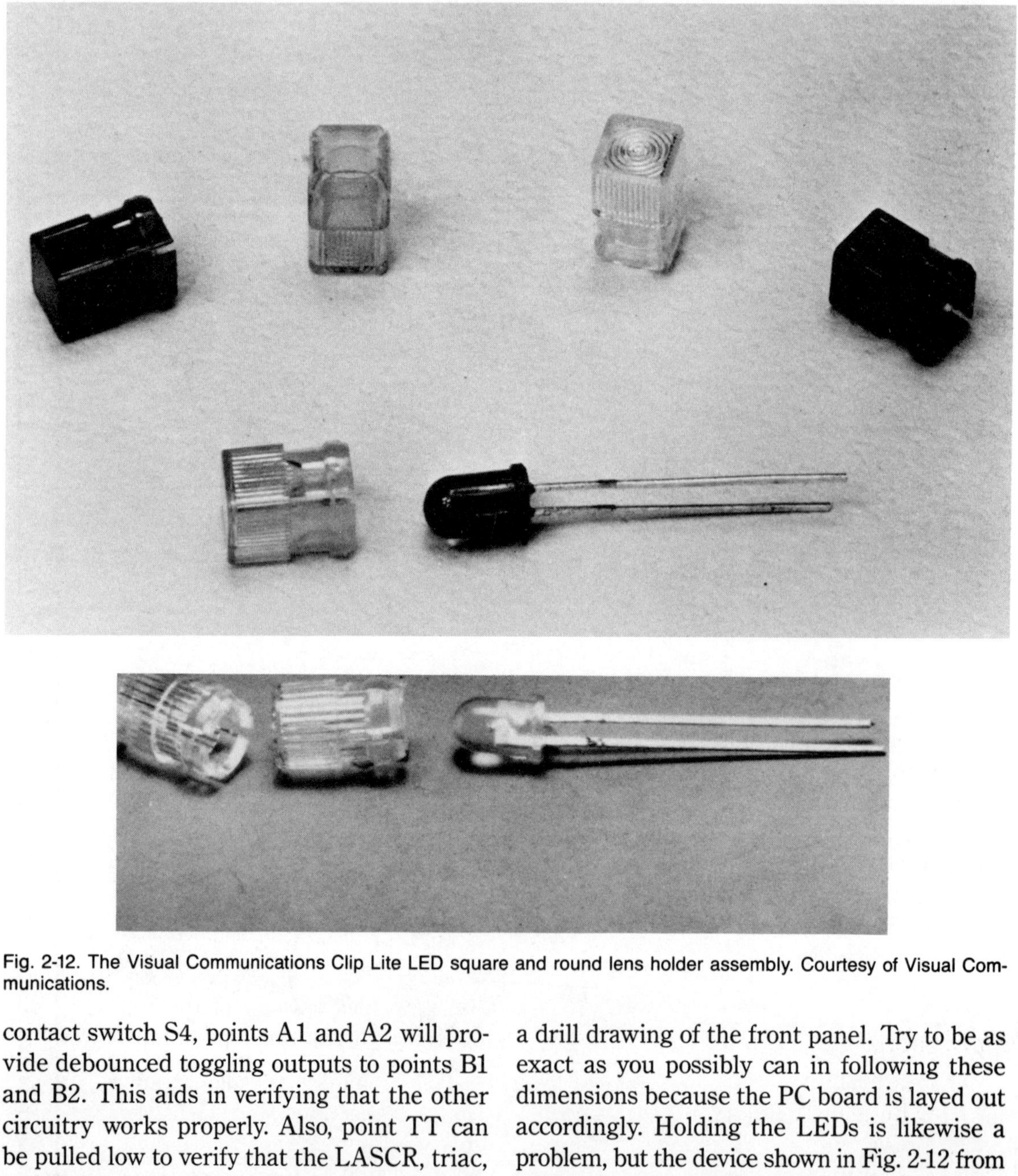

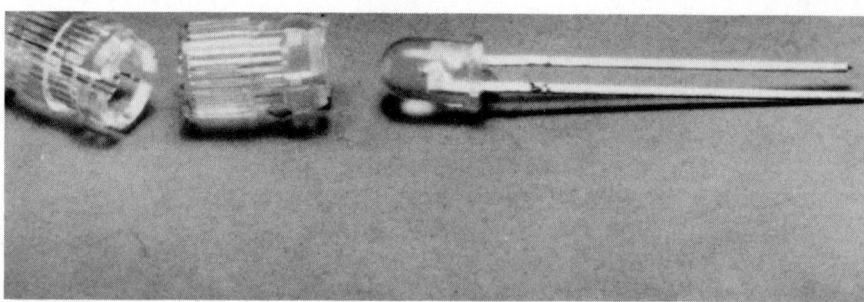

Fig. 2-12. The Visual Communications Clip Lite LED square and round lens holder assembly. Courtesy of Visual Communications.

contact switch S4, points A1 and A2 will provide debounced toggling outputs to points B1 and B2. This aids in verifying that the other circuitry works properly. Also, point TT can be pulled low to verify that the LASCR, triac, and their associated circuitry functions properly. The timing diagram shown in Fig. 2-10 will also help in troubleshooting the logic circuitry.

The most difficult problem in construction is aligning the 15 LEDs. Observe Fig. 2-11 for a drill drawing of the front panel. Try to be as exact as you possibly can in following these dimensions because the PC board is layed out accordingly. Holding the LEDs is likewise a problem, but the device shown in Fig. 2-12 from Visual Communications can greatly help. This device is called the Clip Lite. It is both an LED lens and an LED holder! The beauty of this device becomes apparent when a poor alignment has resulted and the bent leads of the

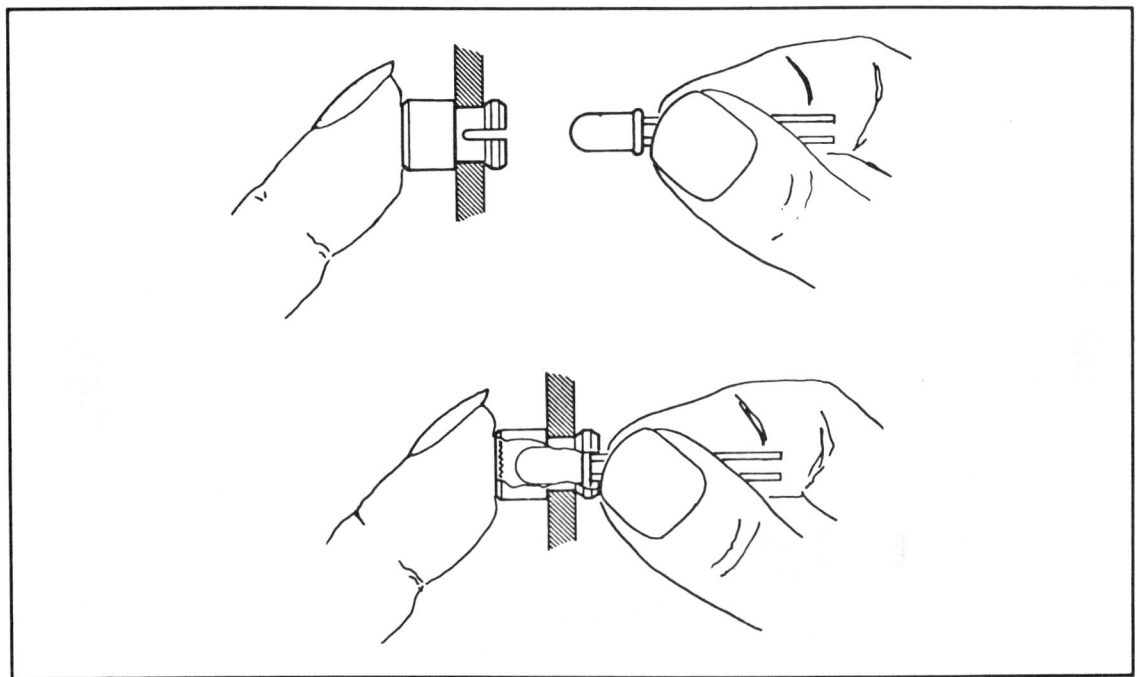

Fig. 2-13. A mounting/insertion procedure for the Clip Lite. Courtesy of Visual Communications.

LEDs experience a stress on them making them at times intermittent. This is what we experienced in our first prototype model of this project before we got the alignment problem solved. Figure 2-13 shows the proper insertion method for these devices. Additionally, there are four mounting holes at the corners of the PC board. Drill these slightly oversized on purpose so that the board can be maneuvered a bit in any direction.

Applications

There are numerous ingenious schemes in which the Burglar Baffler can be used to serve as an effective burglar deterrent. One application involves using two Burglar Bafflers. One Burglar Baffler may be programmed to come on during even hours while the other may be programmed to come on during odd hours. Also one of these Burglar Bafflers may be set for multiple activations while the other is used in the single activation mode. Working together, we can assure you that they will effectively gap and overlap one another in a scheme totally emulating normal human behavior!

The first two Burglar Bafflers, as just mentioned, might well be used with a third Burglar Baffler. This third Burglar Baffler could turn an eight-track tape recorder on and off. We suggest an eight-track instead of a cassette or reel-to-reel recorder because of the repeating or recycling ability of this type of tape recorder.

There is almost an endless number of ways in which such a timer could be used in conjunction with other conventional light timers. As an example, if three Burglar Bafflers were used with three 60 watt lightbulbs over an entire weekend and assuming that electricity costs 6 cents per kilowatt hour, then a total of 9 cents worth of electricity would be dissipated.

This is a very cheap form a homeowners or apartment-dweller's insurance!

The Burglar Baffler can also be used in applications of a nature totally divorced from security. As an example, upon mentioning this project to a friend of mine, he proposed using it with a heater patch with an adhesive on the back. This patch would be driven by the ac from the Burglar Baffler's output and placed directly under the thermostat "tricking it" into not turning on the heat or turning it on less often during the night. Most people prefer a cooler house at night in the winter while they sleep and it has been stated that setting your thermostat at one spot and not tampering with it will give greater fuel savings. Actually, the timer could also be programmed to go off several hours before you planned to awaken, and as such, could provide you with a warm house to get up to and still provide you with considerable savings while doing so.

Modifications

One obvious drawback to the Burglar Baffler is a power failure? Unfortunately, the system goes down until the power comes back on, and when the power returns, the program that we entered in the shift registers is lost. The rudimentary memory made up of these shift registers is unfortunately a *volatile* memory. What then resides in memory is a random pattern of 1s and 0s. A battery backup system would solve this problem and at least keep the digital circuitry alive until the ac went back on. Such a backup system is discussed in Chapter 5.

Another possible modification would be to alter the period determining circuitry in a manner yielding a longer period at one time and a shorter period at another time. You will recall that at present we have 13,504 pulses per period instead of 13,500 pulses, which would be an exact 1/16 of an hour. But varying this even more by manually switching the outputs of IC1 into and out of the inverters made up of IC21A through 21E would compensate for the days getting shorter as the winter nears and the days lengthening as the early summer's long days approached. Considering how smart the Burglar Baffler is, maybe this is more trouble then it might be worth. We only mentioned it as food for thought! You determine for yourself what is best.

PROGRAMMABLE LIGHT DIMMER

The second light controller project in this chapter is the Programmable Light Dimmer. This project draws on the versatility of the CD4046 CMOS PLL (phase-locked loop), primarily manufactured by RCA and Motorola. This linear IC is so integral and fundamental to the operation of this project that it deserves explanation in the form of an encapsulated overview of basic PLL theory.

After reading this overview of PLLs, you may opt to alter this or similar "favorite" circuits of your own. You will be able to do so much more effectively by being armed with an understanding of this versatile and powerful IC. If the operation of this IC is of little or no interest to you, then you may skip the next section. You will not significantly suffer in understanding the explanation of the Programmable Light Dimmer.

PLL Theory

A PLL is quite simply an electronic feedback system. The block diagram in Fig. 2-14 shows the three main elements of a PLL. Each of these elements will be covered in some detail.

Phase Detectors. The phase detector or phase comparator produces an average or dc voltage proportional to the phase difference between two input signals. In the case of the PLL,

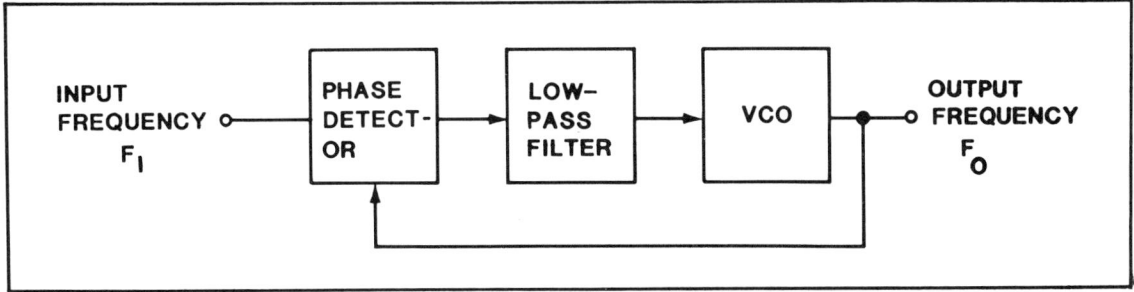

Fig. 2-14. A block diagram of a phase-locked loop.

these two signals are the phase/frequency reference and the signal fed back from the output or the PLL's VCO. There are two basic types of phase detectors. One type is used for analog PLLs, and the other is used for digital PLLs. The analog PLL uses double-balanced mixers while the digital PLL uses either an exclusive-OR (XOR) or some variation of edge-

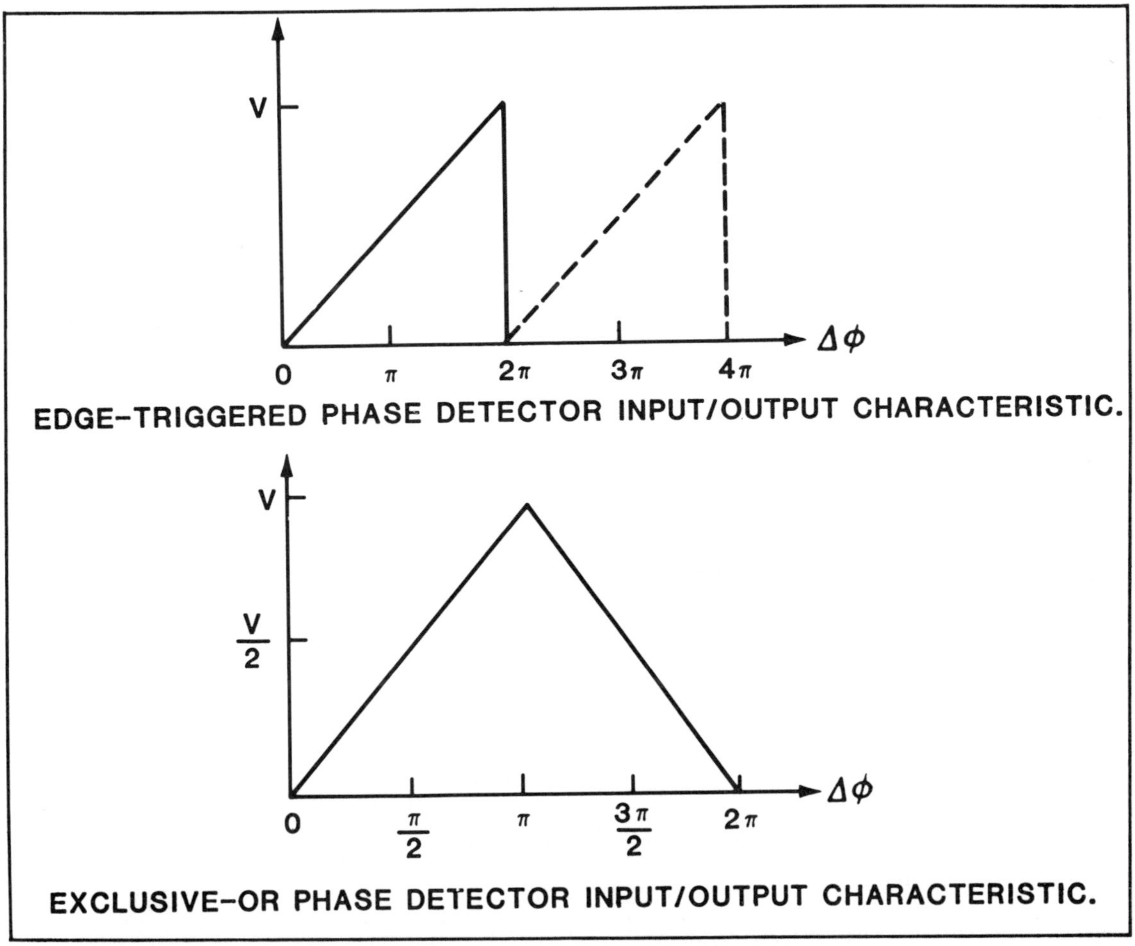

Fig. 2-15. A plot of output voltage vs. phase difference for two types of phase detectors.

triggered circuitry. The CD4046, the PLL used in this project, is a digital phase-locked loop so we will concern ourselves only with XOR and edge-triggered phase detectors.

A properly functioning XOR phase comparator requires a symmetrical or 50% duty cycle VCO squarewave. The other type of phase detector, the edge-triggered variety, does not require a 50% duty cycle squarewave. This then enables pulses of short duration to trigger edge-triggered detectors which are usually flip-flops. A plot of the average output voltage as a function of phase difference between these two types of phase detectors, is shown in Fig. 2-15. This plot demonstrates that the edge-triggered type has twice the linear range of the XOR detector.

This phase detector theory translates into practical usable characteristics with respect to the CD4046 CMOS PLL by its having two phase detectors, one of each type. The block diagram of the CD4046 is given in Fig. 2-16. The XOR type requires exactly a 50% duty cycle squarewave for the system to remain in lock despite being more impervious to high ambient electrical noise; however, this type detector has more of a tendency to lock onto input frequencies close to harmonics of the VCO center-frequency. You will note in the articles referenced under PPL theory in the Bibliography that there are several articles on how to divide by an odd number and still have a resultant 50% duty cycle symmetrical squarewave. The interest in this 50% duty cycle is obviously for the XOR type phase detector.

The edge-triggered type of phase detector used in the CD4046 is really a digital memory unit or a simple set of four flip-flops and three-state logic output circuitry made up of PMOS and NMOS type drivers. If the signal is not symmetrical this does not bother the CD4046 PLL edge-triggered phase detector since it is only looking for the occurrence of a positive edge. In actual operation, if the input signal frequency is higher than the comparator input fre-

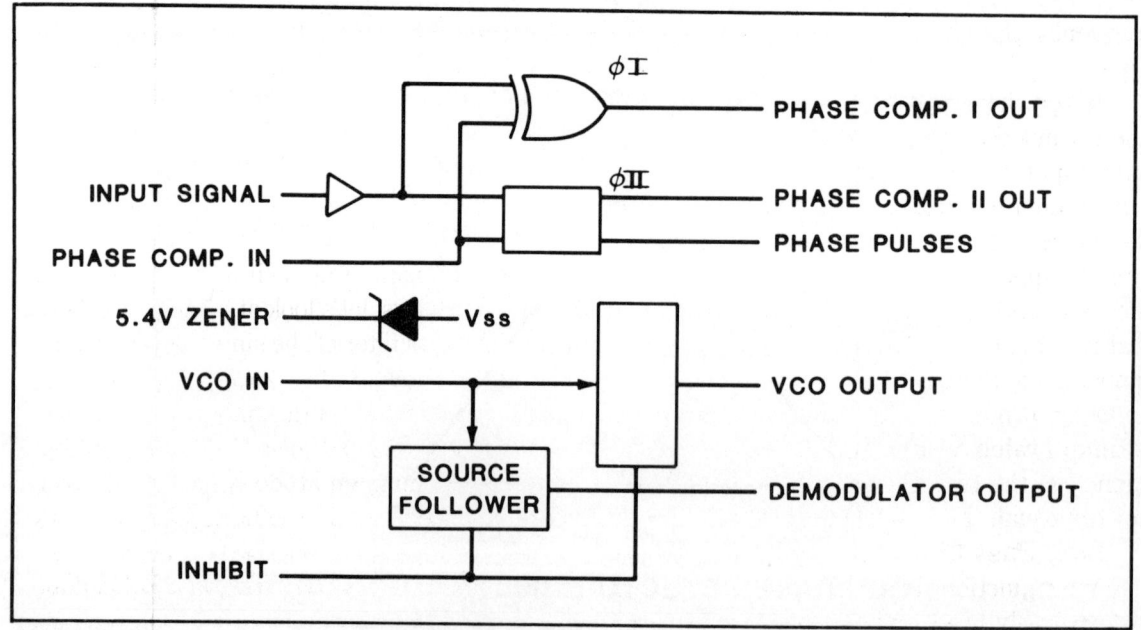

Fig. 2-16. A block diagram of the CD4046 phase-locked loop.

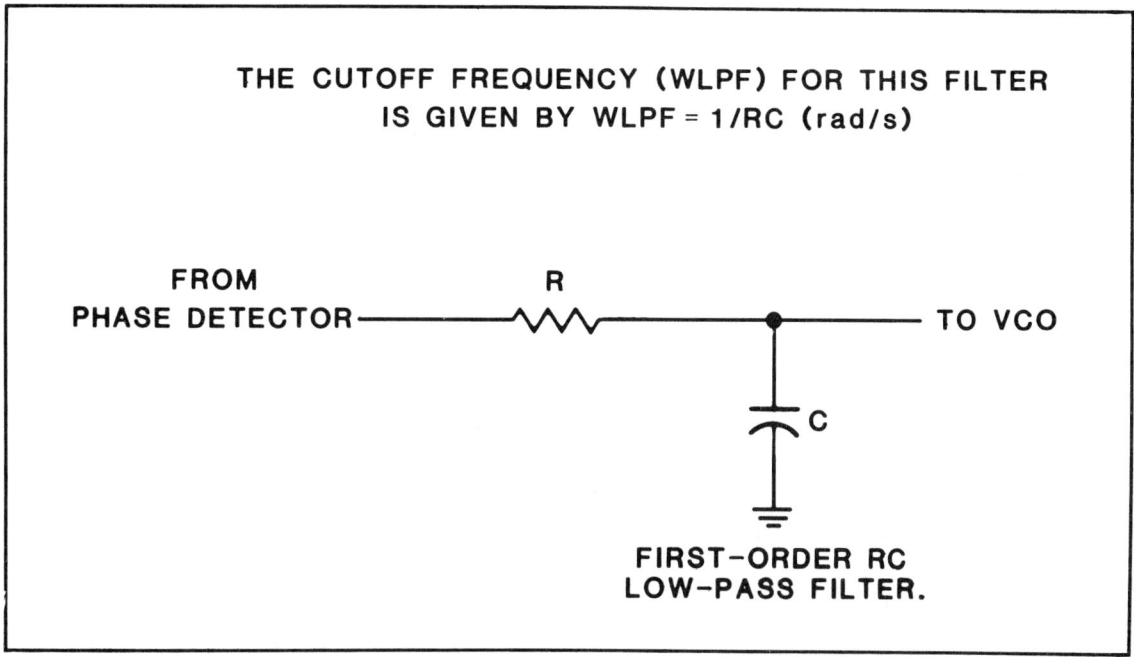

Fig. 2-17. The simplest type of low-pass filter.

quency, the p-type output driver is predominately on and conversely if the input frequency is lower than the comparator input frequency, the n-type driver is on most of the time.

When these two inputs are the same frequency but the comparator input lags the applied input signal in phase, the p-type output driver remains on for a time corresponding to the phase difference. What may be becoming already apparent to some of you, even before the VCO and low-pass filter are discussed, is that the capacitor voltage of the low-pass filter connected to this phase comparator is adjusted up and down or iterates, narrowing in on the optimum value, where both the phase and frequency of the two signals to the phase detector are equal. This is the goal of a PLL!

Low-Pass Filter. The low-pass filter has two main functions in a PLL system. The first and probably most obvious one is to remove, by filtering, any noise/spikes or high frequency/harmonic components from the PLL's output (the VCO). Secondly, and probably less obvious in function are the tasks of determining loop performance, which is primarily characterized or described by these three parameters:

- ☐ Capture and lock ranges.
- ☐ Bandwidth.
- ☐ Transient response.

Before examining each of these low-pass filter parameters, let's look at some actual first-order low-pass filters. The simplest type would be the one shown in Fig. 2-17. the formula for the cutoff frequency of this filter or the frequency at which the amplitude is 3 dB less than that of the maximum amplitude frequency is given within the illustration. Another passive network providing a lead/lag function is shown in Fig. 2-18. This basic lead/lag function can also be accomplished with the op amp circuit shown in Fig. 2-19.

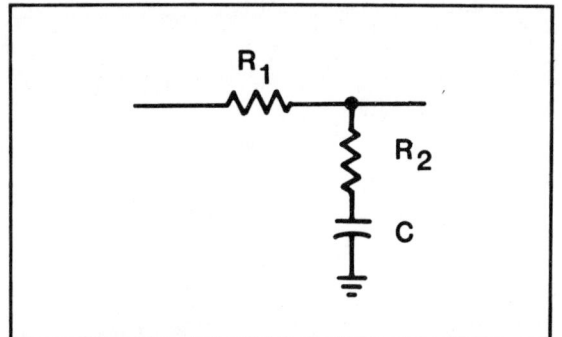

Fig. 2-18. A lead/lag filter that accomplishes the same effect as a low-pass filter.

The *lock range* of the PLL is the frequency over which the system will faithfully follow changes in the input. The *capture range* is the frequency band in which the PLL can acquire phase lock or how close an input frequency must be to the VCO free-running frequency before the loop acquires phase-lock. The *bandwidth* of a PLL is the difference in frequency between the frequency of maximum amplitude and the frequency where the amplitude is 3 dB lower than this maximum point.

The *transient response* of a PLL is the phenomenon describing when an input frequency is changed and the output of the VCO tries to follow but oscillates around this new frequency for a while before eventually settling in on it. The speed with which the output "settles down" is described by the loop damping factor and is controlled by the loop low-pass filter.

Voltage Controlled Oscillator

A VCO is merely a network of electronic components connected or configured in a manner that yields an output frequency that is directly proportional to an input control voltage. Therefore, a VCO is nothing more than a voltage-to-frequency converter. During phase lock (the normal operating condition of a PLL), this output frequency will be identical to the input frequency except if a digital frequency divider is inserted in the feedback loop as we do here in this application. In that case, the output frequency is "N" times greater than the input frequency with "N" being the number by which the digital divider is programmed to divide. Such a configuration of a PLL circuit is commonly called a frequency synthesizer since you can create or "synthesize" frequency by controlling the digital divider.

The PLL we are using is the RCA CD4046A and it has a VCO built right on the chip itself. The high impedance inherent in the input to this VCO, typically 10^{12} ohms, enables the low-pass filter which accompanies this VCO to have a wide range of permissible resistor-to-capacitor ratios. Also, in order for this VCO not to load down the low-pass filter, an FET source follower output is provided at pin 10 (the DEMODULATED OUTPUT).

As previously stated, the VCO can be connected either directly or indirectly through a digital divider back around to the comparator input of the phase comparators. There are applications where the power consumption of a circuit is a major concern. This ICs VCO has an INHIBIT pin for this function. More specifically, if a logic "0" is applied to this INHIBIT pin this enables the VCO and its source follower. Conversely, a logic "1" on this same pin causes a powered down state where both circuits lie in a "stand by" state and thereby save power.

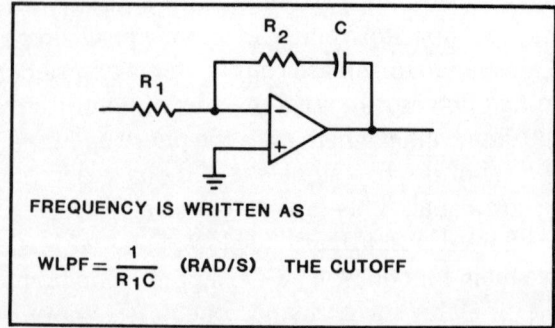

FREQUENCY IS WRITTEN AS

$$W_{LPF} = \frac{1}{R_1 C} \quad (RAD/S) \quad \text{THE CUTOFF}$$

Fig. 2-19. An active, op amp lead/lag filter.

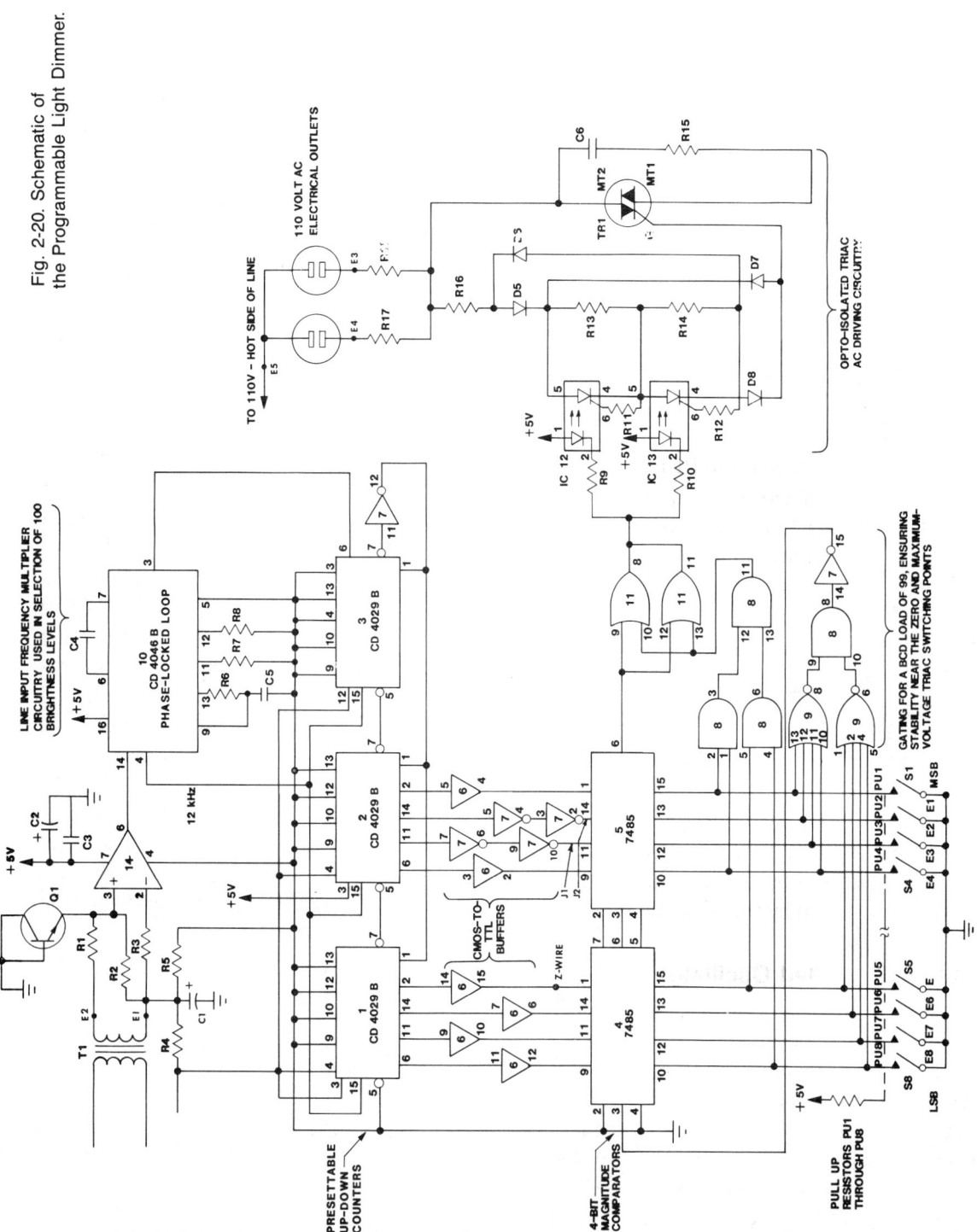

Fig. 2-20. Schematic of the Programmable Light Dimmer.

Operation

For our specific application of the CD4046 CMOS PLL, refer to the schematic in Fig. 2-20. Note that there are five discrete components associated with this circuit. These are resistors R5, R6, and R7 and capacitors C4 and C5. With respect to the VCO, it is possible to use one capacitor and either a single resistor on pin 11 or a pair of resistors on pins 11 and 12 to go to ground. This RC pair from pin 11 and the capacitor across pins 6 and 7 determine the frequency range of the PLL, while the resistor from pin 12 to ground establishes a frequency offset. Refer to Fig. 2-21 for an illustration of the effect of frequency offset.

The VCO (pin 4) can be either directly or indirectly connected to the comparator inputs of the phase comparator. Note how there are basically three digital ICs between the comparator input (pin 3) and the VCO output (pin 4). These three ICs, numbered 1 through 3 in Fig. 2-20 are DC4029 CMOS presettable up/down counters, and they are programmed by having their JAM inputs (pins 3, 4, 12 and 13) either tied high or low. In this configuration, they are set for a divide by 200.

Recalling the basic purpose of a PLL, you will note now that a divide by 200 is inserted between the VCO output and comparator input (pin 3). The other comparator input (pin 4) is experiencing a 60 Hz wall outlet ac frequency. The op amp comparator is overdriven into clipping or saturation, and in so doing, the overdriven 60 Hz sine wave changes or "shapes up" into a squarewave of the frequency. But, remember that the other comparator input wants to see this same frequency so that VCO must run at 200 times this frequency of 12 kHz

CHARACTERISTICS	PHASE COMPARATOR USED	DESIGN INFORMATION	
		VCO WITHOUT OFFSET $R_2 = \infty$	VCO WITH OFFSET
VCO FREQUENCY	1	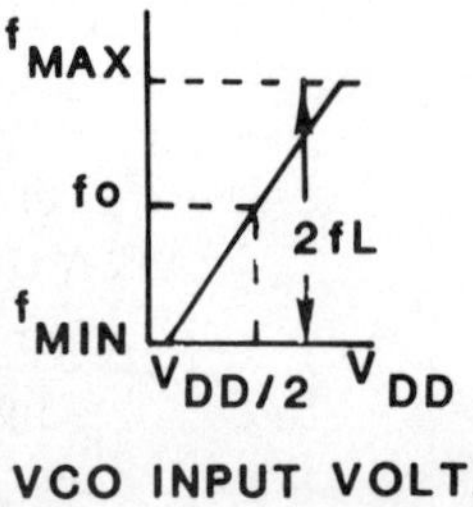 f_{MAX}, f_o, f_{MIN} vs VCO INPUT VOLTAGE ($V_{DD}/2$, V_{DD}), $2f_L$	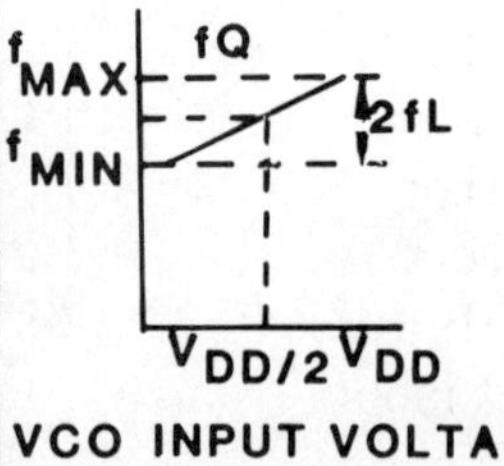 f_{MAX}, f_Q, f_{MIN}, $2f_L$ vs VCO INPUT VOLTAGE ($V_{DD}/2$, V_{DD})
	2	SAME AS FOR NO. 1	
FOR NO SIGNAL INPUT	1	VCO WILL ADJUST TO CENTER FREQUENCY f_o	
	2	VCO WILL ADJUST TO LOWEST OPERATING FREQUENCY f_{MIN}	

Fig. 2-21. The effect of frequency offset.

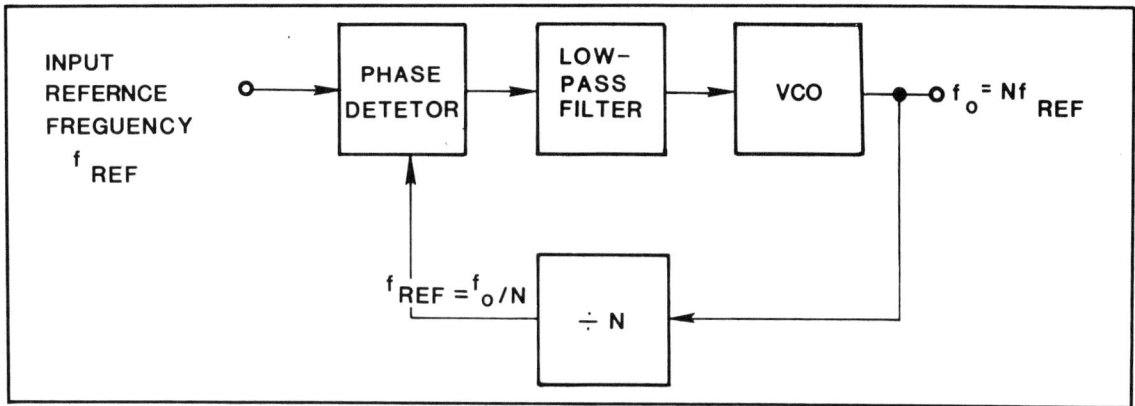

Fig. 2-22. A divider in the feedback loop to increase the VCO output frequency.

because this 12 kHz, once divided down by 200 by ICs 1 through 3, yields 60 Hz, or just what the other input of the phase comparator needs to remain balanced. Refer to Fig. 2-22 for an illustration of this divider in the feedback loop principle.

The outputs of the first ICs in this three IC divider chain are buffered and applied to ICs 4 and 5. These two ICs are TTL semiconductor logic requiring the extra buffering or drive capability offered by ICs 6 and 7. You will note that this project uses both CMOS and TTL logic as the Burglar Baffler did, and these buffer ICs are again required when CMOS has to drive TTL.

The two driven ICs, ICs 4 and 5, are TTL 74LS85 4-bit magnitude comparators. Their function is to take a 4-bit word on its A inputs and another 4-bit word on its B inputs and determine if A is greater than, less than, or equal to B. Refer to Fig. 2-23. Note also the cascaded inputs from IC4 to IC5. This is to allow the outputs to be serialed into these inputs and form words greater than 4-bits in length. We are doing comparisons on 8-bit words here because of the three lines linking ICs 4 and 5 together.

To summarize, when the first two of the three programmable up/down counters count down and reach a number equal to the 8-bit number set in by switches S1 through S8, the A = B output on IC5 (pin 6) becomes active and goes low. This action of going low causes the two LEDs in the series connected LASCRs to go low, allowing the IR (infrared) LEDs within these devices to conduct and the gate of the triac is enabled or turned on. A more detailed explanation of this ac activation portion of the circuit may be found in the Burglar Baffler discussion earlier in this chapter. The end result is that the 8-position switches constituting a number between 0 and 255 control the point at which the triac fires and likewise how much of the ac cycle will be allowed to conduct which in turn dictates light intensity.

Modifications

One of the 8-bit ports from the 6532 RIOT (RAM-I/O Timer) on the microcomputer/controller board from Chapter 4 could also control this light by providing what might be called a "random ramp" to these eight inputs. The "random ramp" is nothing more than counting up in sequence and then down at a different rate. This approach will be covered later in Chapters 5 and 6.

Another method of adding true randomness to the manner in which this light dim-

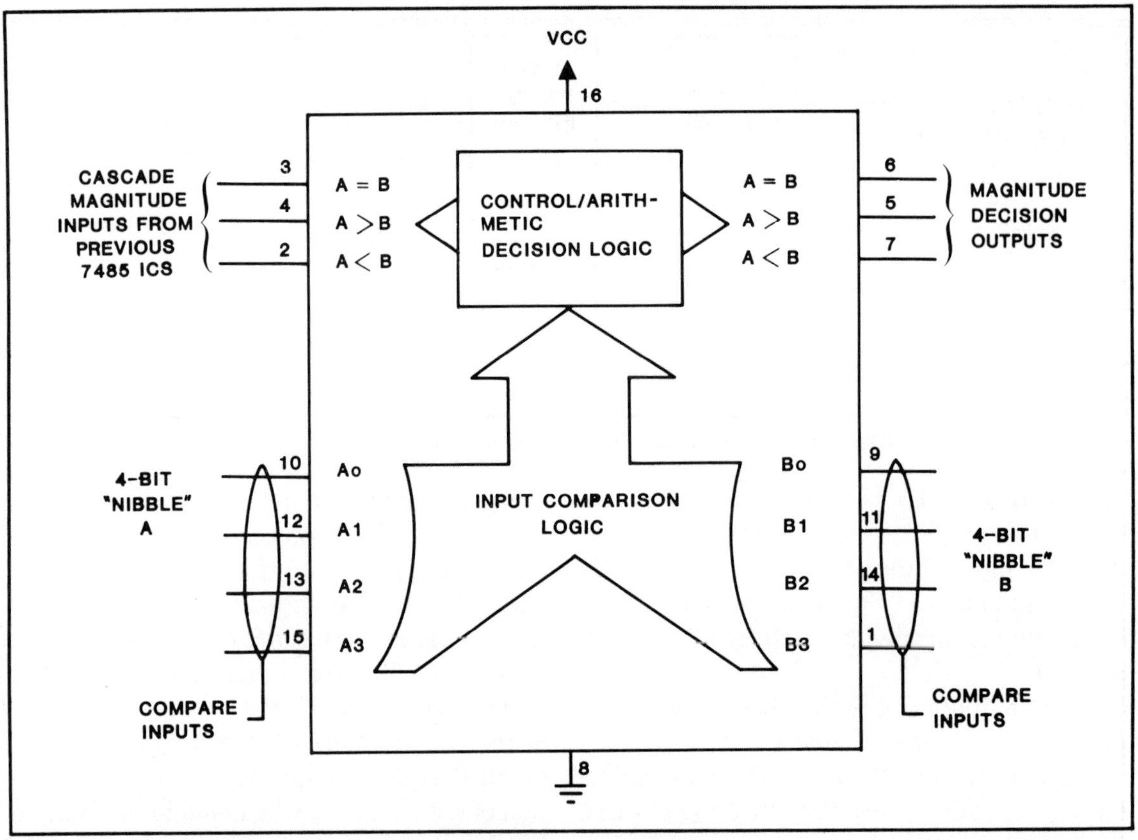

Fig. 2-23. The block diagram of the 7485 4-bit magnitude comparator.

mer is controlled is with a PNG or pseudorandom number generator, as described in the Burglar Baffler section; however, there is one small drawback to this. Refer to Fig. 2-24 and note that any digital PNG using the traditional shift register technique with selective

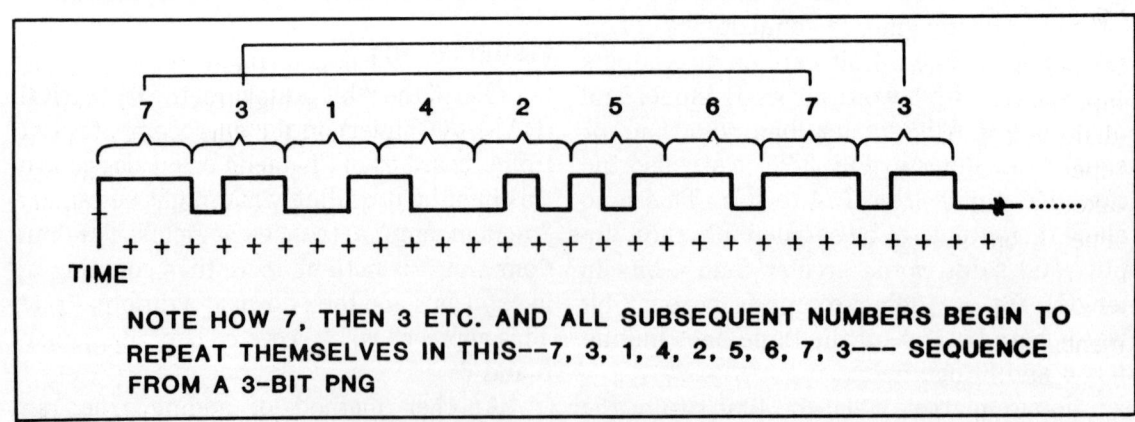

NOTE HOW 7, THEN 3 ETC. AND ALL SUBSEQUENT NUMBERS BEGIN TO REPEAT THEMSELVES IN THIS--7, 3, 1, 4, 2, 5, 6, 7, 3--- SEQUENCE FROM A 3-BIT PNG

Fig. 2-24. The repetitive waveform of a psuedorandom number generator.

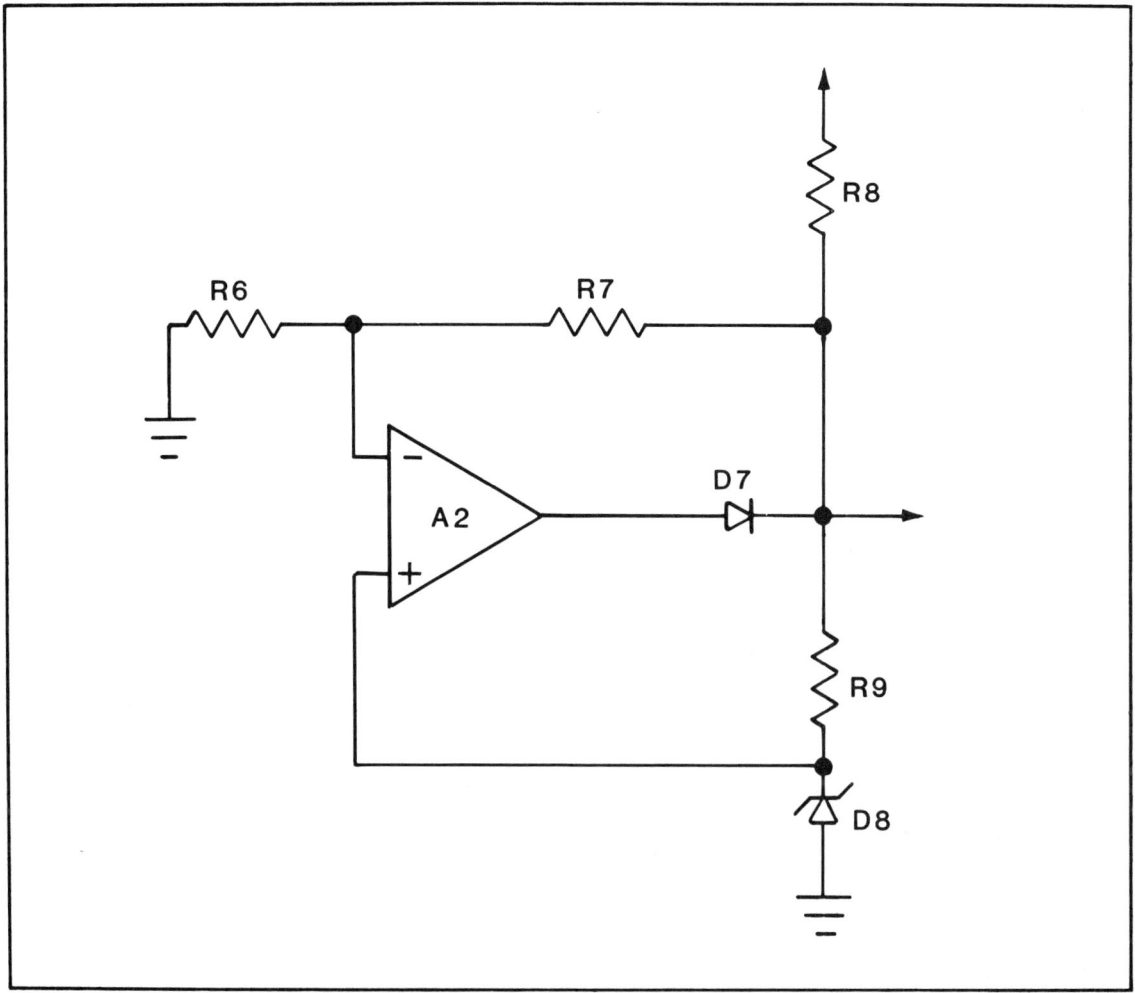

Fig. 2-25. A PNG derived from the analog thermal noise phenomenon.

taps made and XORed back around to the D-input of the first flip-flop in the shift register chain results in a circuit with a periodic or repetitive pattern. Granted, a 16-bit PNG will take $2^{16} - 1$ different combinations before it repeats, but it will still repeat!

Actually, for all practical purposes this long of a period would do fine, but for the sake of mental exercise consider the circuit in Fig. 2-25. This circuit uses the thermal noise inherent in a zener diode's pn junction which is truly random. This low level noise is applied to a FET op amp. A FET op amp (field-effect transistor) is used because of its high (typically 100 Ω) input impedance. The FET's drain (output) in the op amp comparator, as in the 60 Hz squarewave shaper to the PLL in this light dimmer circuit, also ramps up because of its tremendously high gain and purposely overdrives a sine wave until it is clipped or shaped like a squarewave. However, quite unlike the 60 Hz constant nonvarying frequency from the ultrastable utility company, this input frequency, as previously stated, is totally random because of the thermal noise inherent in any semiconductor.

The result is truly random squarewaves of vastly varying frequencies and pulse widths that produces a flickering effect emblematic of a person walking between a light source to anyone standing outside on the sidewalk observing. This effect assumes, of course, that the drapes are drawn as in customarily done when a home is left temporarily unattended.

Line Frequency Accuracy

The utility company's ultrastable 60 Hz source previously referenced in this chapter must be qualified. Granted, over an entire year (a very large sampling period), this frequency will not be off by any more than a 3 Hz total; however, the daily variations are typically somewhat greater. During the day, as factories and places of business are being lit, cooled, or heated, and electrical consumption is at a maximum, the line frequency will be ever so slightly slower. Conversely, at night it is slightly greater than 60 Hz. The end result, though, is a frequency that is extremely close to this idealized frequency over a short or long sampling period.

PROGRAMMABLE TIMER

The third and last light controller circuit uses the same PC board as the dimmer circuit just discussed. The difference though is that the 8-position DIP switch (S1 through S8) is replaced by one of two PNGs (pseudorandom number generators) driving the spots where the switches were, namely points E1 through E8 on the PC board. The PNGs take the form of one of two circuits found right on the dimmer circuit board itself. You merely select which PNG you wish, the digital or analog one. The digital PNG theory has been covered earlier in this chapter, but suffice it to say that in this specific application, it consists of IC15 and IC16 which make up an 8-bit PNG. The first integrated circuit, IC15, is an 8-bit shift register, and the XOR gate that taps this shift register in selective paces and returns this back around to the "D" input is IC16. You merely need to take these eight shift register outputs and connect them to the 8 switch inputs E1 through E8. You can connect any of the shift register's outputs to any of these switch inputs as long as only one input is tied to one output. Due to the randomness of the PNG, it really doesn't matter.

Construction

This project uses the same PC board as the Programmable Light Dimmer. Refer to Fig. 2-26. A component placement drawing is shown in Fig. 2-27. The part's list is given in Table 2-5. A few notes on the construction is warranted. First, note in the component placement drawing (Fig. 2-27) the small 8-position DIP switch. It does not go on the component side of the PC board. The board was designed to place it on the wiring side. It was designed this way so that when mounted in a small metal box, it would be accessible to the outside world. In this way, it can be manually operated just like an ordinary light dimmer. Naturally, if it is used with a hardware PNG then it is this PNG output that is 8-bits in length, and the PNG shift register outputs are fed to the eight spots on the board where this 16 pin DIP pattern resides.

An outboard PNG can be built on a perf board or on a board designed to accommodate Molex pins as shown in Fig. 2-28. Also, a multiple tap transformer will be required as shown in Fig. 2-29. This will not only provide the necessary 60 Hz wall frequency signal from which all timing is derived, but it will also (on the other secondary winding) provide a +5 Vdc

Table 2-5. Parts List for the Programmable Light Dimmer and Programmable Timer.

IC1, 2, 3	CD4029B	(CMOS)
IC4, 5	7485	(TTL)
IC6	CD4050	(CMOS)
IC7	CD4049	(CMOS)
IC8	74LS08	(TTL)
IC9	7425	(TTL)
IC10	CD4046B	(CMOS)
IC11	74LS32	(TTL)
IC12, 13	LASCR H11C1, H11C2, H11C3, (G.E.) or MCS2 Monsanto	
IC14	LM101 type op amp	
R1, R6	36 K	1/4 W 5%
R2	4.7 K	1/4 W 5%
R3	4.3 K	1/4 W 5%
R4, R5	10 K	1/4 W 5%
R7	8.1 K	1/4 W 5%
R8	3 K	1/4 W 5%
R9, R10	270	1/4 W 5%
R11, R12	56 K	1/4 W 5%
R13, R14	270 K	1/4 W 5%
R15	47	1/2 W 10%
R16	100	1/2 W 10%
R17, R18	1	5 W wirewound
PU1	9 resistor pull-up pack (1 K)	

Voltage Regulator
LM 340T-5 5 V 1 A voltage regulator
Transistor Q1 2N2222

Transformer

Two Secondaries - one rated at 12.6 V @ 25 mA
                      - one rated at 6.3 to 12.6 V @ 100 mA

Triac   - 200 V, 6 A SK 66127 or equiv. *

*These triacs are available from Speciality Electronic Services, Inc. for $2.00 postpaid. Check the list of suppliers at the end of the book. Texas residents add 5% sales tax.

C1	47 µF	25 Vdc	polarized
C2	20 µF	25 Vdc	polarized
C3	0.1 µF		
C4	0.03 µF		
C5	0.1 µF		
C6	0.1 µF	400 Vdc	
C7	1 µF	25 Vdc	polarized
C8	100 µF	25 Vdc	polarized
D1 to D4	1N4001 or equiv.		
S1	8 position	SPST	DIP cluster switch

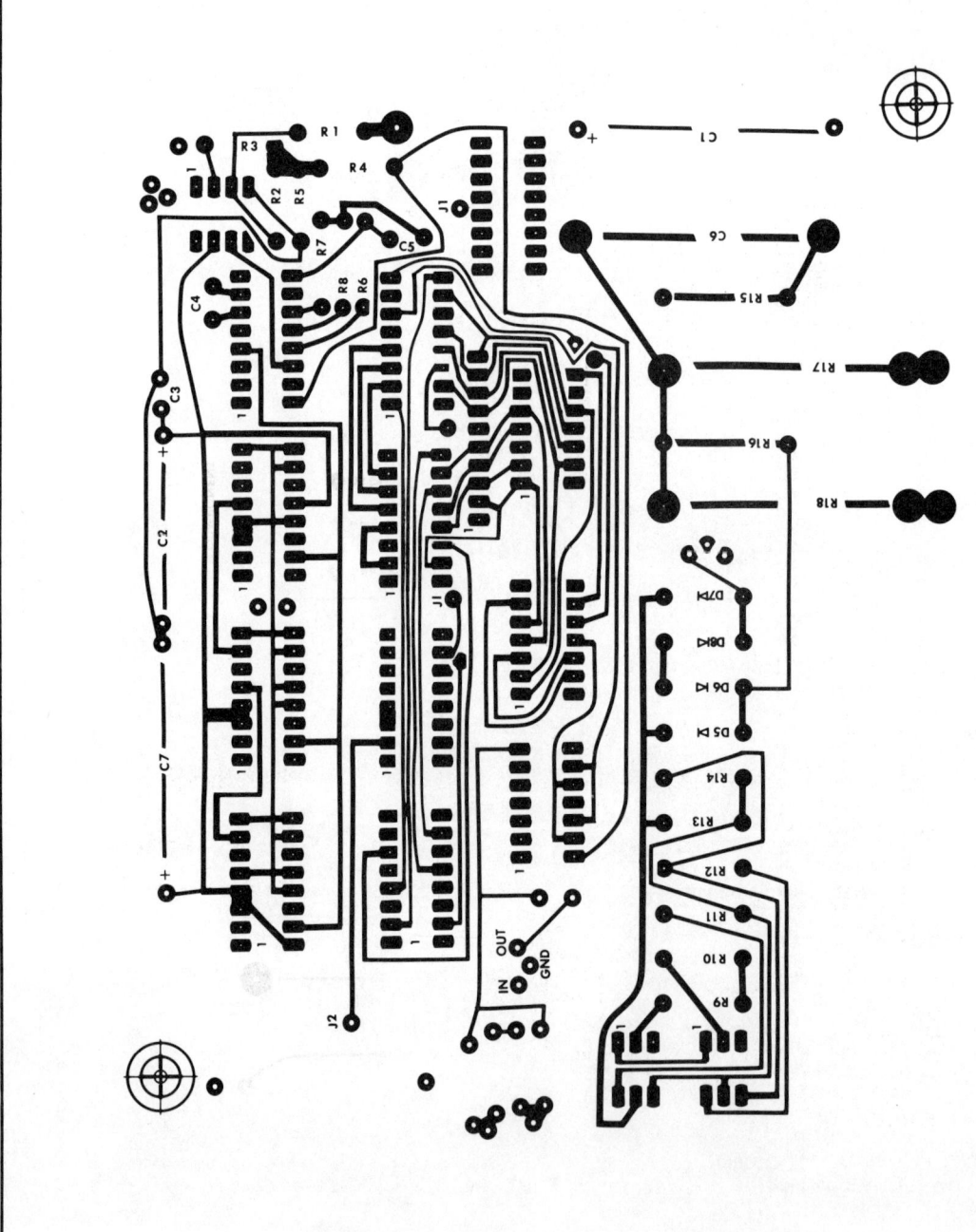

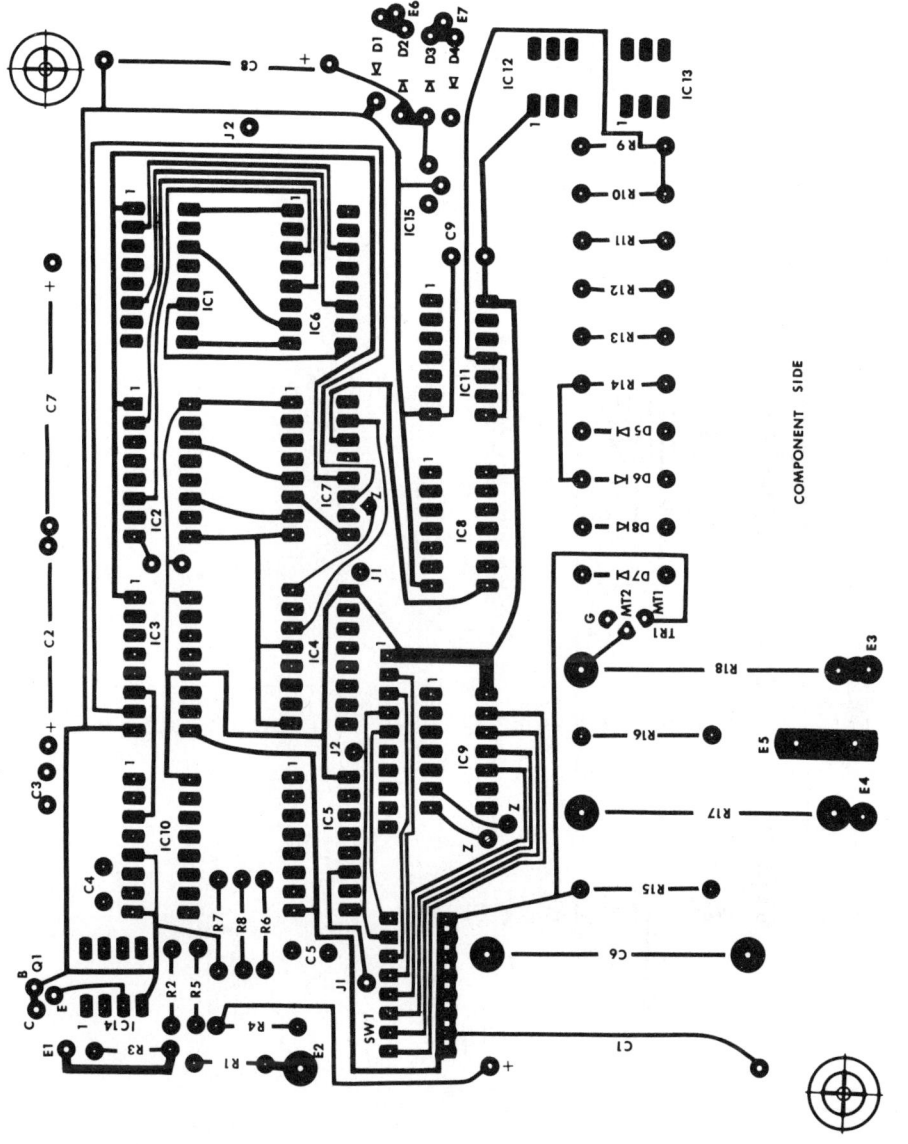

Fig. 2-26. PC foil pattern for the Programmable Light Dimmer and Programmable Timer.

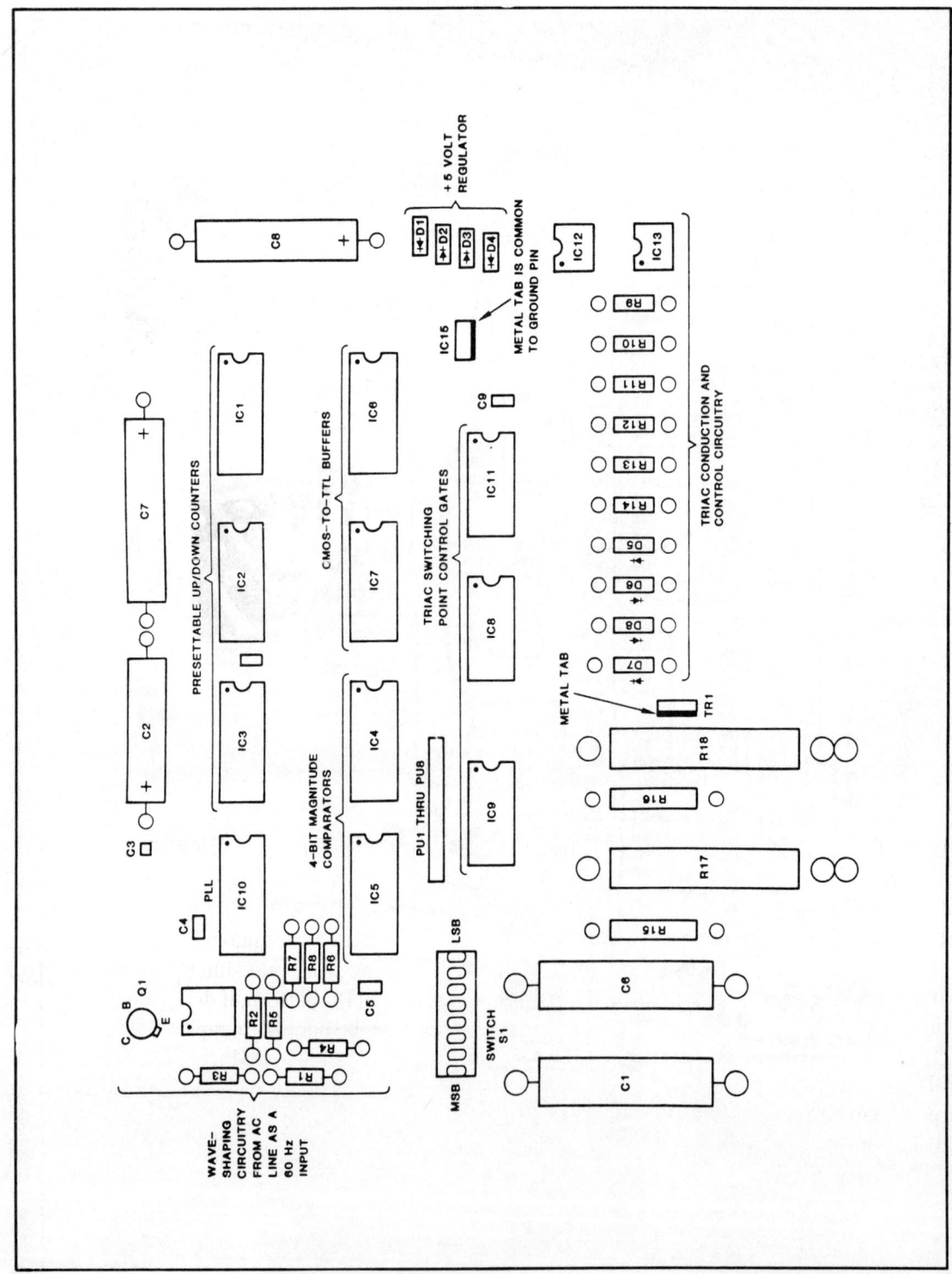

Fig. 2-27. Component placement drawing for the Programmable Light Dimmer and Programmable Timer.

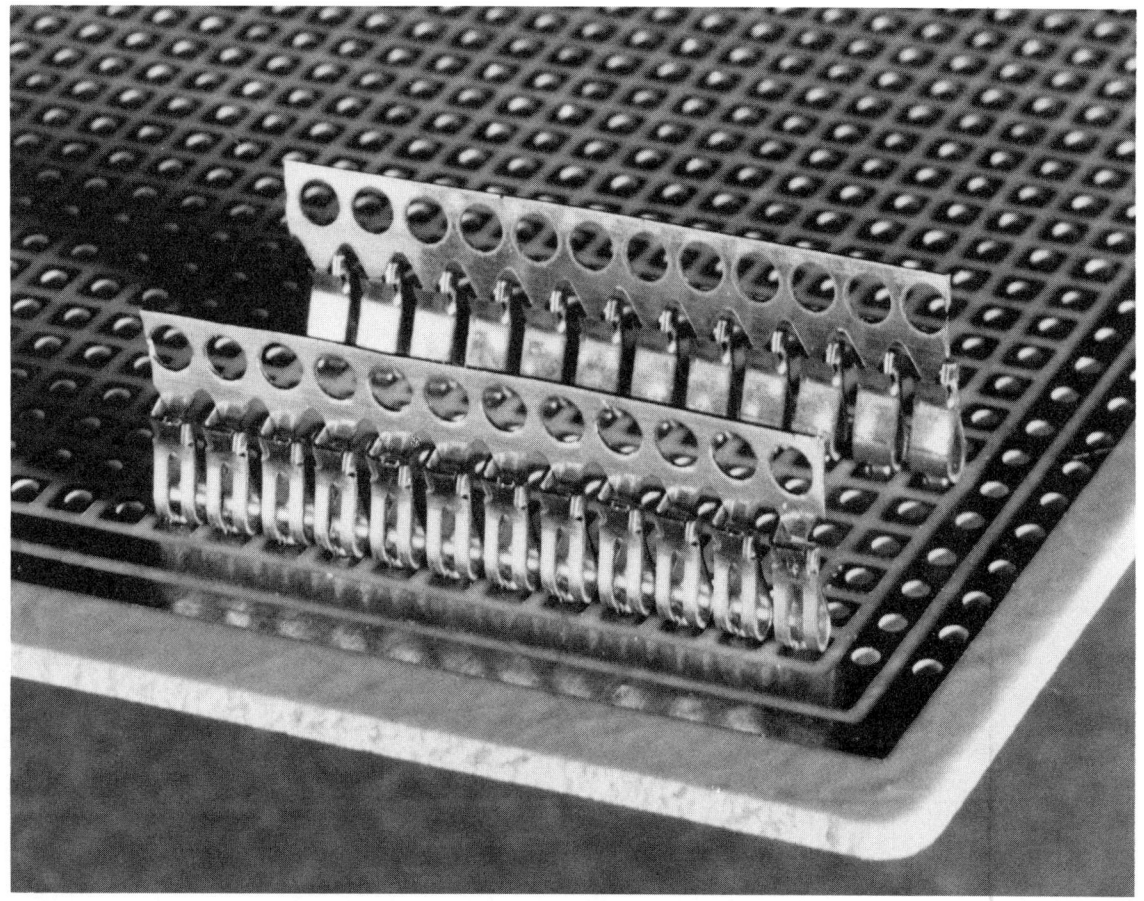

Fig. 2-28. A board with Molex pins to accommodate phototyping a quick PNG circuit.

output. The +12 V you see in Fig. 2-24 can be derived from the positive (+) side of the input filter capacitor to the +5 Vdc voltage regulator, shown in Fig. 2-29. If it is not exactly +12 Vdc, or if it is not too well regulated, or has up to 500 mV of ripple on it, that is still satisfactory.

Returning to the actual construction of the PC board, there are two jumpers and one "Z" wire. As can be seen from the schematic in Fig. 2-20, the lines from the inverting CMOS buffer, IC7, namely pins 2 and 10 need jumpers over to IC5, pins 14 and 11 respectively. Also, note on the schematic the "Z" wire in line with IC6 pin 15 to IC4 pin 1. A "Z" wire is merely a solid strand wire or a clipped off component lead from a 1/4 watt resistor that is inserted in one side of a PC board and soldered on both sides to afford a continuous path of current flow by bridging from one side of the board to the other. This PC pattern, if duplicated from these pages, can be nonphotographically lifted by one of the kits shown in Fig. 2-9. Therefore no plated through holes will exist to make continuity from one side of the board to the other.

There are also "E" numbers on the schematic of the programmable dimmer in Fig. 2-20. These are where a wire either enters or leaves the PC board. As an example, note E1 and E2 in the upper left hand corner of Fig.

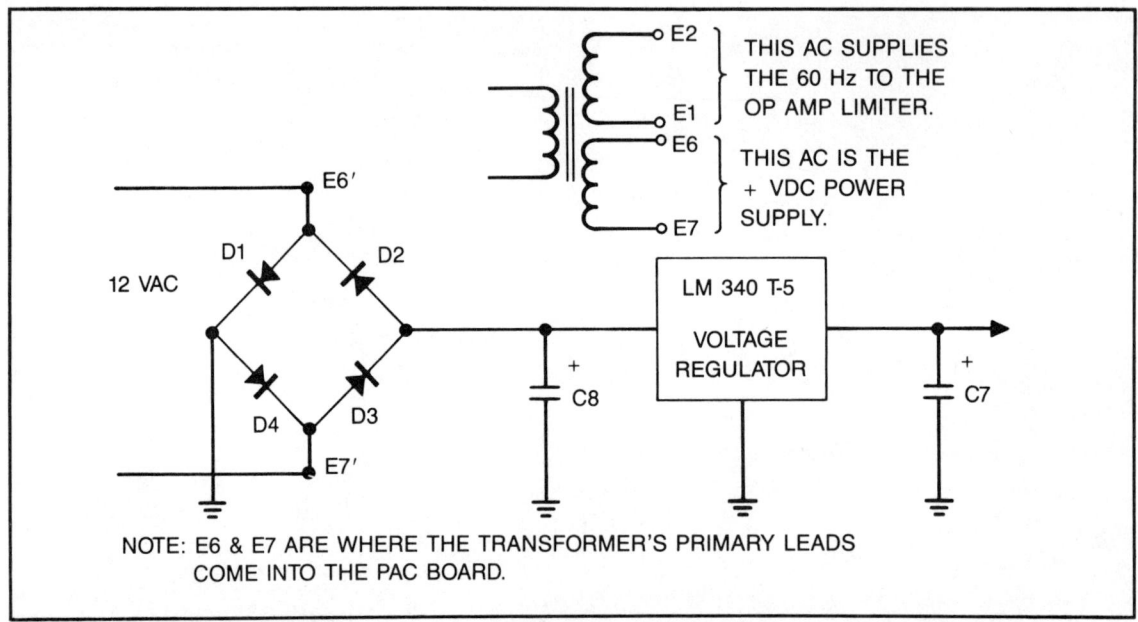

Fig. 2-29. A multiple winding transformer with one winding providing timing and the other winding providing 5 Vdc.

Table 2-6. Power and Ground Pin Assignment for the Programmable Light Controller Board.

+5 V Power (pin numbers)	Ground (pin numbers)
IC1 - 16,3,4	IC1 - 8,5,9,10,12,13
IC2 - 16,3,4	IC2 - 8,9,10,12,13
IC3 - 16,12	IC3 - 8,3,4,9,10,13
IC4 - 16	IC4 - 8,2,4
IC5 - 16	IC5 - 8
IC6 - 1	IC6 - 8
IC7 - 1	IC7 - 8
IC8 - 14	IC8 - 7
IC9 - 14	IC9 - 7
IC10 - 16	IC10 - 8,5
IC11 - 14	IC11 - 7
IC12 - 1	IC12 - NO GND PIN
IC13 - 1	IC13 - NO GND PIN
IC14 - 7	IC14 - 4
C2	Q1 - B and C
C3	C1
C7	C2
C9	C3
C10	C5
Pullup Resistor Pack	C7
R4	C8
	C9
	C10
	S1 through S8 switches
	R15
	R5
	D1
	D4

2-20. These are where one of the secondaries of the transformer with a typical 12.6 Vac rms output is applied to the board.

Lastly, the triac specified should be good for a minimum of 4 A to yield a safe 250 watt capacity. Also, the power supply for this project as shown in Fig. 2-29 has been provided for on the PC board.

Precautions

The TTL 4-bit magnitude comparator ICs come in both the standard 7400 series and the low power 74L00 series as well as the 74LS00 series. The problem is that this is the only TTL IC we have encountered to have different pin-out configurations in the 7400 versus 74L00 series. Therefore, if you use the PC pattern shown, use the 7485 ICs and not the 74L85 or 74LS85 TTL ICs.

Troubleshooting

Should you encounter any problems, the first thing to do is to check to see if all of the voltages and grounds are what they should be, refer to Table 2-6. Next, give the board a quick visual inspection. If trouble still persists, then check to see if the two jumpers have been installed and that the "Z" wire has been inserted into the PC board and soldered from both sides. If this is done and no satisfactory results occur, then switch the DIP switches and trace their actions throughout the circuit starting with the magnitude comparison phase, and then check the programmable counters followed by the VCO on the PLL, and last check the ac activation circuitry by looking for a changing logic level on the gate or input to the two LASCRs (light activated silicon controlled rectifiers).

3
Entry Detection System

THIS CHAPTER EXAMINES A MORE TRADITIONAL, less sophisticated, yet very effective security system composed of all small scale integration (SSI) ICs from the transistor-transistor logic (TTL) semiconductor family. Chapter 5 later examines, in greater detail, two other systems accomplishing these same tasks; however, these are done under microcomputer control.

Many of the features found in the sophisticated microcomputer alarm systems in Chapter 5 are inherent in this design. As an example, there is a delayed entry feature, an arming light indicator, and a status loop indicator light. This circuit, though, uses somewhat dated (five to ten year old) technology so no PC (printed circuit) board was laid out for this design. It was built and bench tested, and it worked really well.

Refer to the schematic in Fig. 3-1, and note the presence of five very simple SSI TTL ICs used rather cleverly along with a fair amount of transistors and discrete components. Please note the two squares denoted as A1 and A2, these are separate input detection circuits in themselves and exist on separate perf boards such as shown in Fig. 3-2. They can be easily cut with a saw to any shape or size you might desire.

Beginning with the block A1, refer to Fig. 3-3, its schematic, and note that it consists of two transistors in a complementary npn-pnp arrangement with direct coupling through a *steering diode* (a device ensuring current flow in one and only one direction) to the base of the second transistor. What this input detection device does is allow its output, denoted as OUTPUT and physically consisting of the collector of the second transistor, Q2, to go high when the loop is closed and to go low when the loop

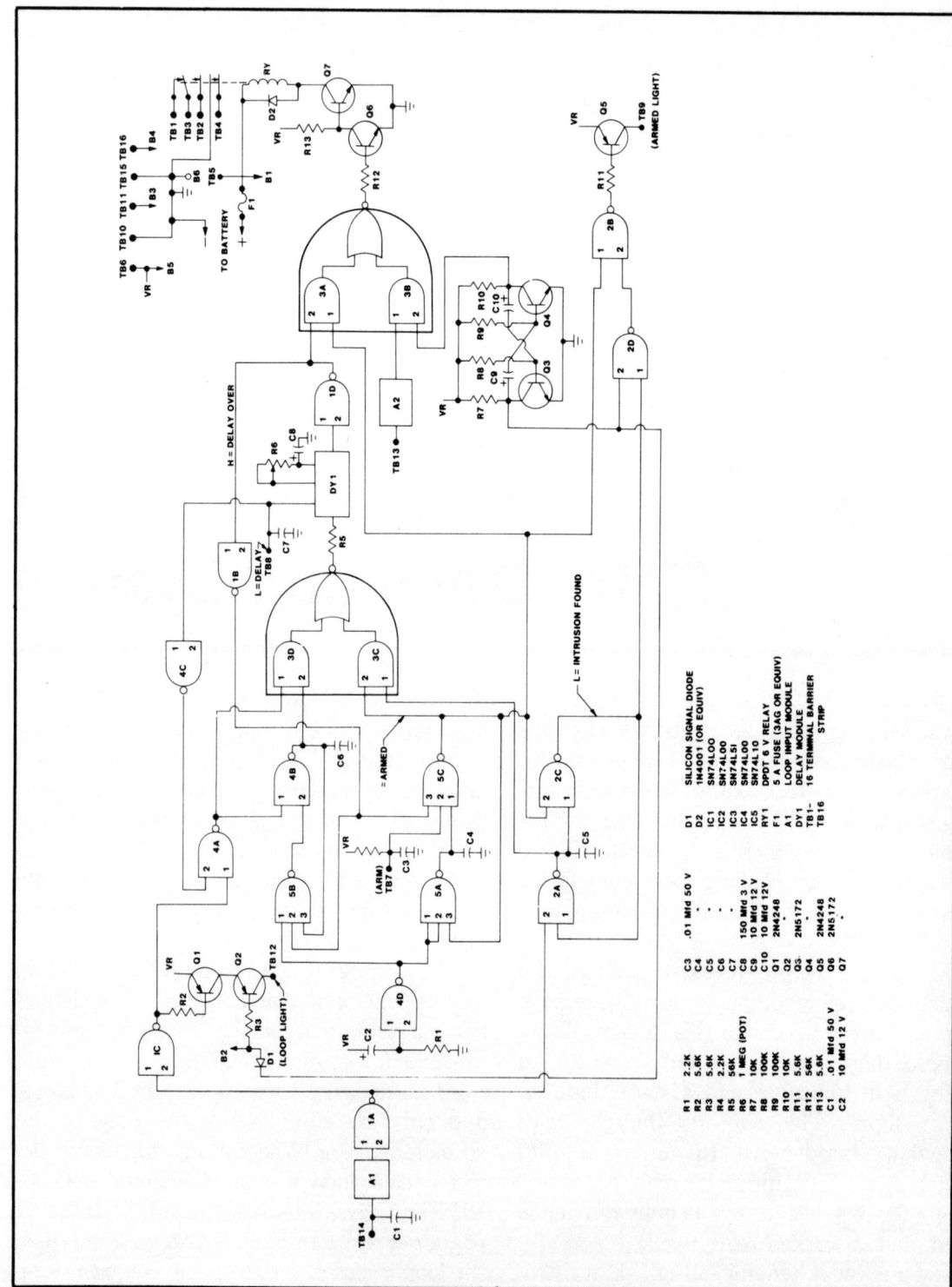

Fig. 3-1. Schematic for the Electronic Entry Detection system.

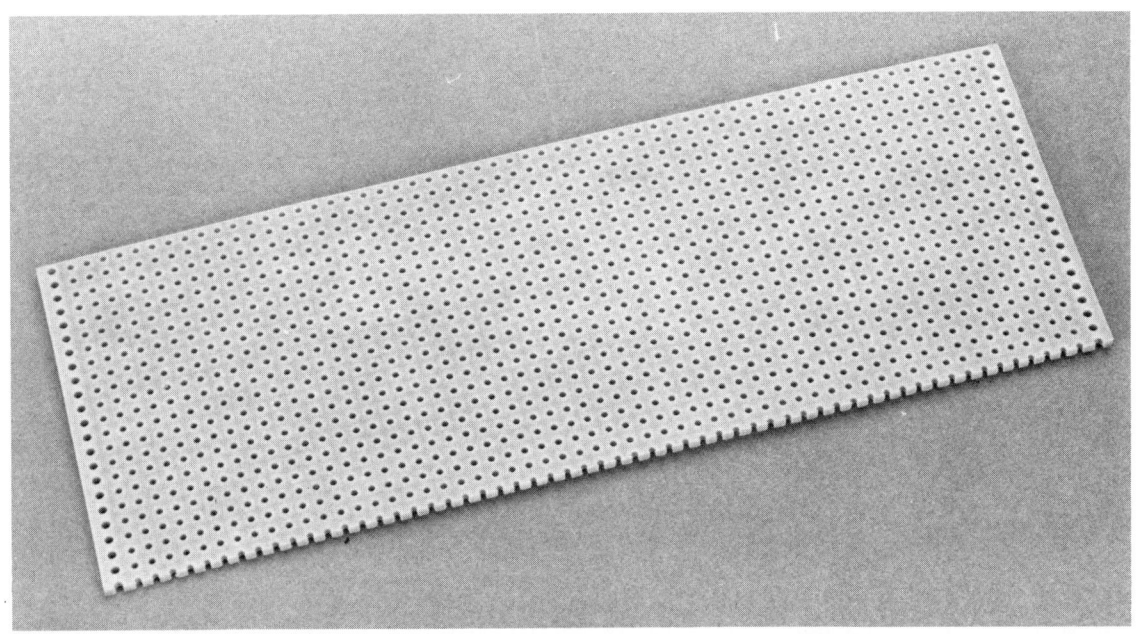

Fig. 3-2. Circuits can be built on perf boards like these.

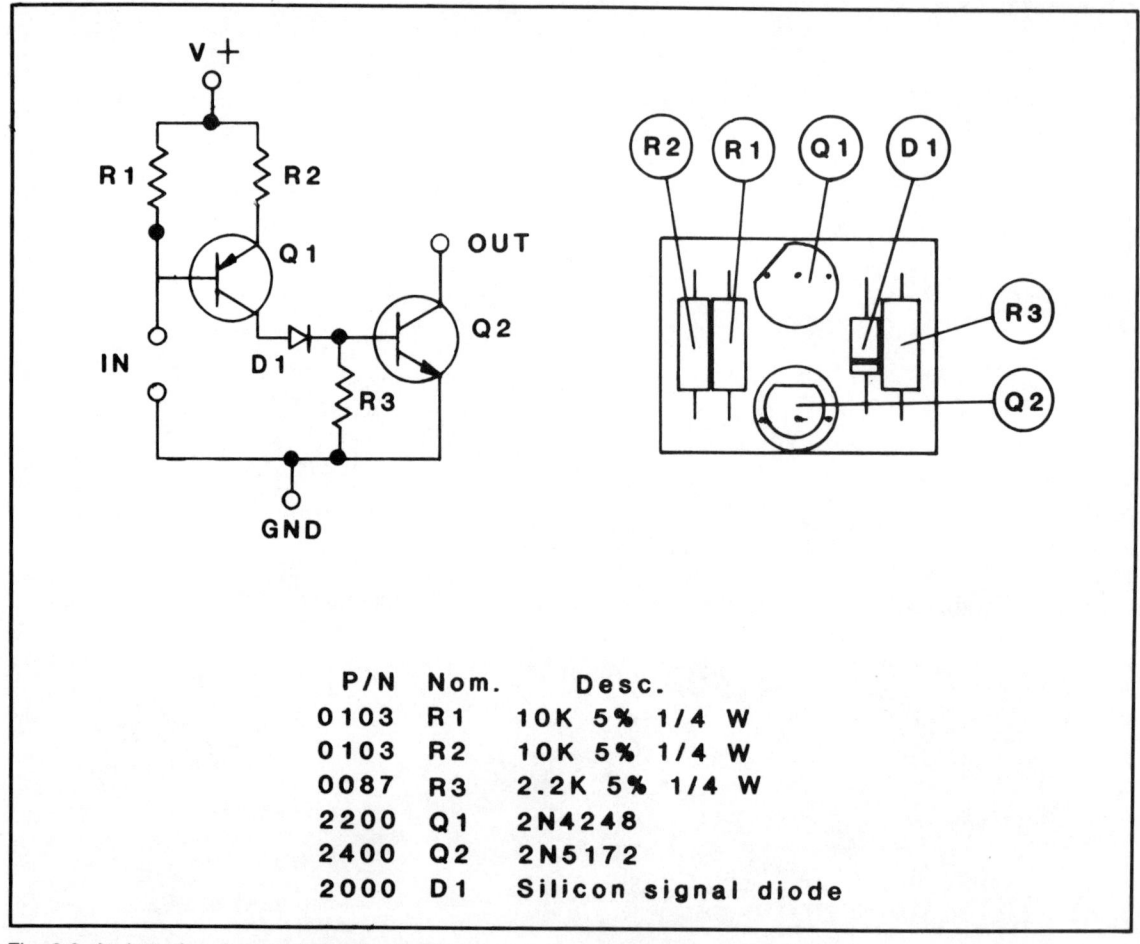

Fig. 3-3. An intrusion detector input circuit.

is opened. By the term *loop* let us precisely define what this entails in more exact language. This definition applies throughout this book as a convention for common usage. A loop is a series of connected switches that are normally closed (N.C.) and provide a path for a complete circuit to be made. If this loop is broken, the circuit is no longer made and this two transistor detection circuit so indicates this.

Consider how the loop would be broken. Obviously, if a breakin were to occur, then the two contacts of the magnetic switch would be pulled apart and it would be an open-circuit condition or an indication of a burglary. If one of the switch contacts were placed on a stationary spot and the other switch contact were placed on a door or window's frame subject to being moved, then as the door or window were opened, the contacts would be broken and the circuit, in its truest sense, would be opened.

CIRCUIT DESCRIPTION

Let's assume that all of the switches are in their proper states and that the output of Q2, the output transistor in the input module, is high. This will cause IC1A to be low and IC1C to be high which causes the loop light to be on, indicating that the loop is in the correct state and that the switches are all closed. The system can next be armed by use of an ON/OFF nonmomentary contact. A two-position keyswitch that is set in its proper position by turning a key that is later removed works well. The arm signal is connected to terminal barrier strip terminal no. 7, denoted TB7, on the schematic.

The signal on the schematic called ARMED, which is the output of the 3-input NAND gate 5C, indicates this state and does so when all of its three inputs are high. The two cross-coupled transistors, Q3 and Q4, formed a simple bistable multivibrator or flip-flop with the RC pairs (R10, C10 and R7, C9) determining the period. This rather long period of approximately 1/4 second, corresponds to a 4 Hz flashing rate for the ARMED LIGHT to flash and indicate that the system is armed. The delay module is symbolically represented in the schematic in Fig. 3-1 as a block with DY1 within it. The actual schematic of DY1, for delay circuit, is shown in Fig. 3-4. Note the open terminals for C_T and R_T. These stand for timing resistor and timing capacitor and are there to insert the RC pair of your choice for however long of a time constant or delay you wish. Resistors above 5 M should be avoided because of the inaccuracy that might be associated with the capacitor. The leakage currents will be within 1 or 2 orders of magnitude of the minute charging current with this size resistor.

The purpose of the delayed-entry feature is to allow you some time to exit the premises before the security system is armed. This time

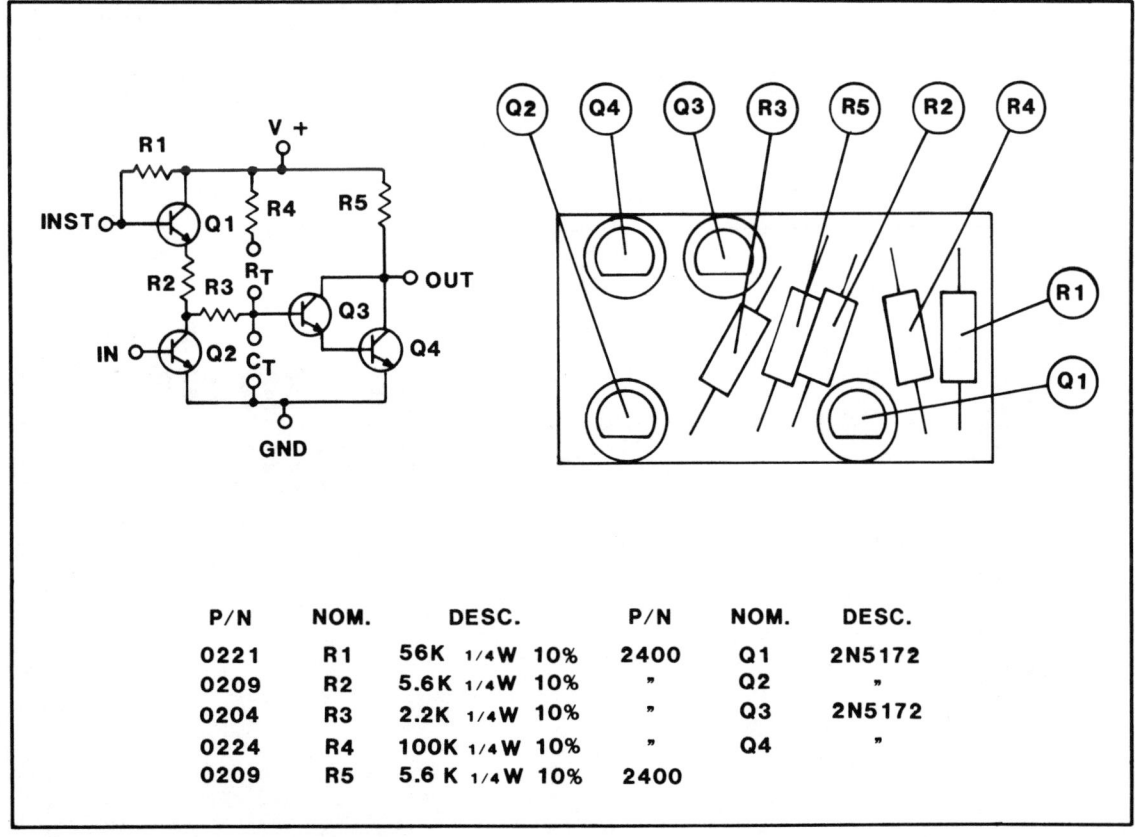

P/N	NOM.	DESC.	P/N	NOM.	DESC.
0221	R1	56K 1/4W 10%	2400	Q1	2N5172
0209	R2	5.6K 1/4W 10%	"	Q2	"
0204	R3	2.2K 1/4W 10%	"	Q3	2N5172
0224	R4	100K 1/4W 10%	"	Q4	"
0209	R5	5.6 K 1/4W 10%	2400		

Fig. 3-4. The delayed entry time-out circuit.

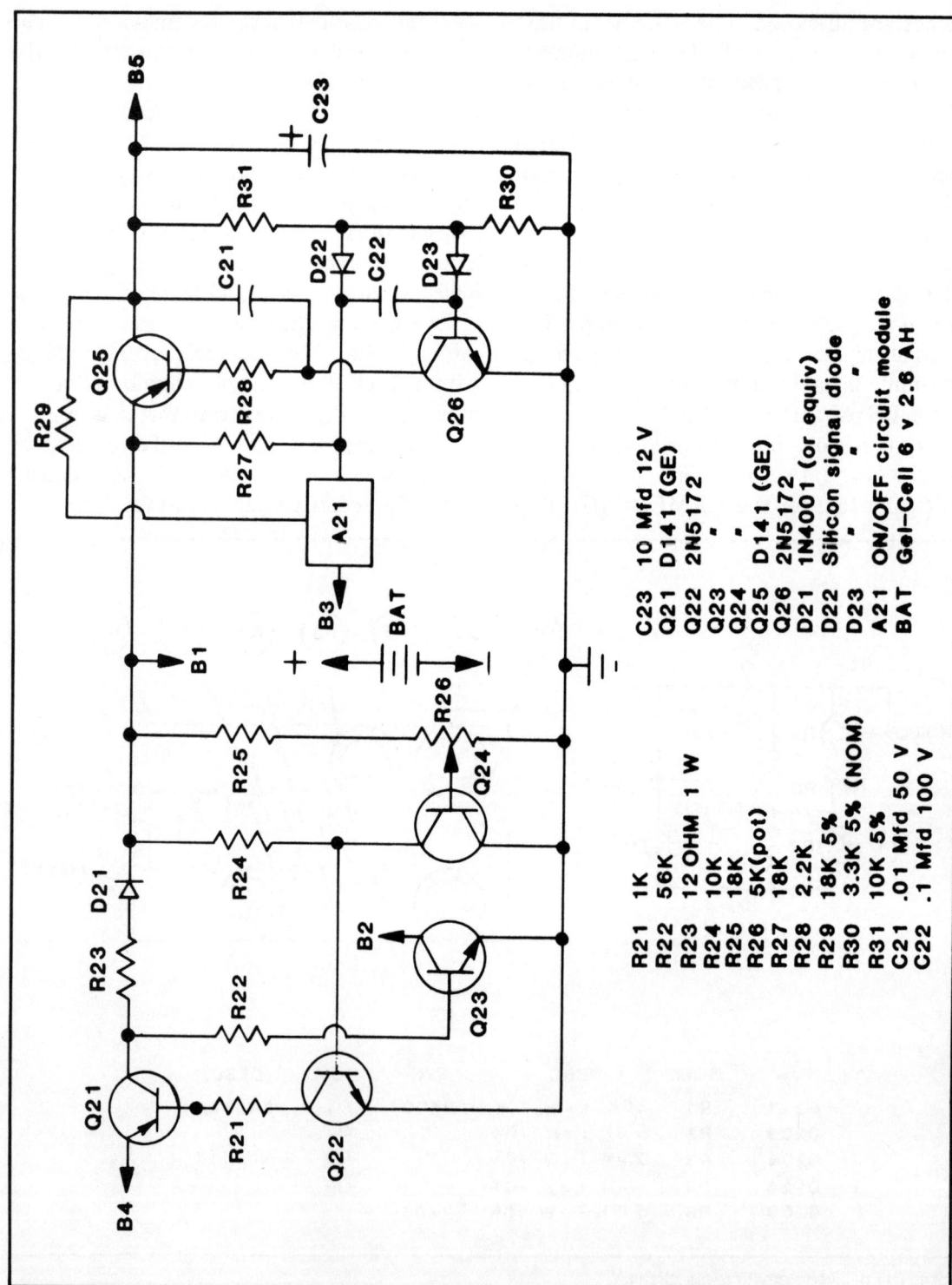

Fig. 3-5. The battery charger/voltage regulator circuit.

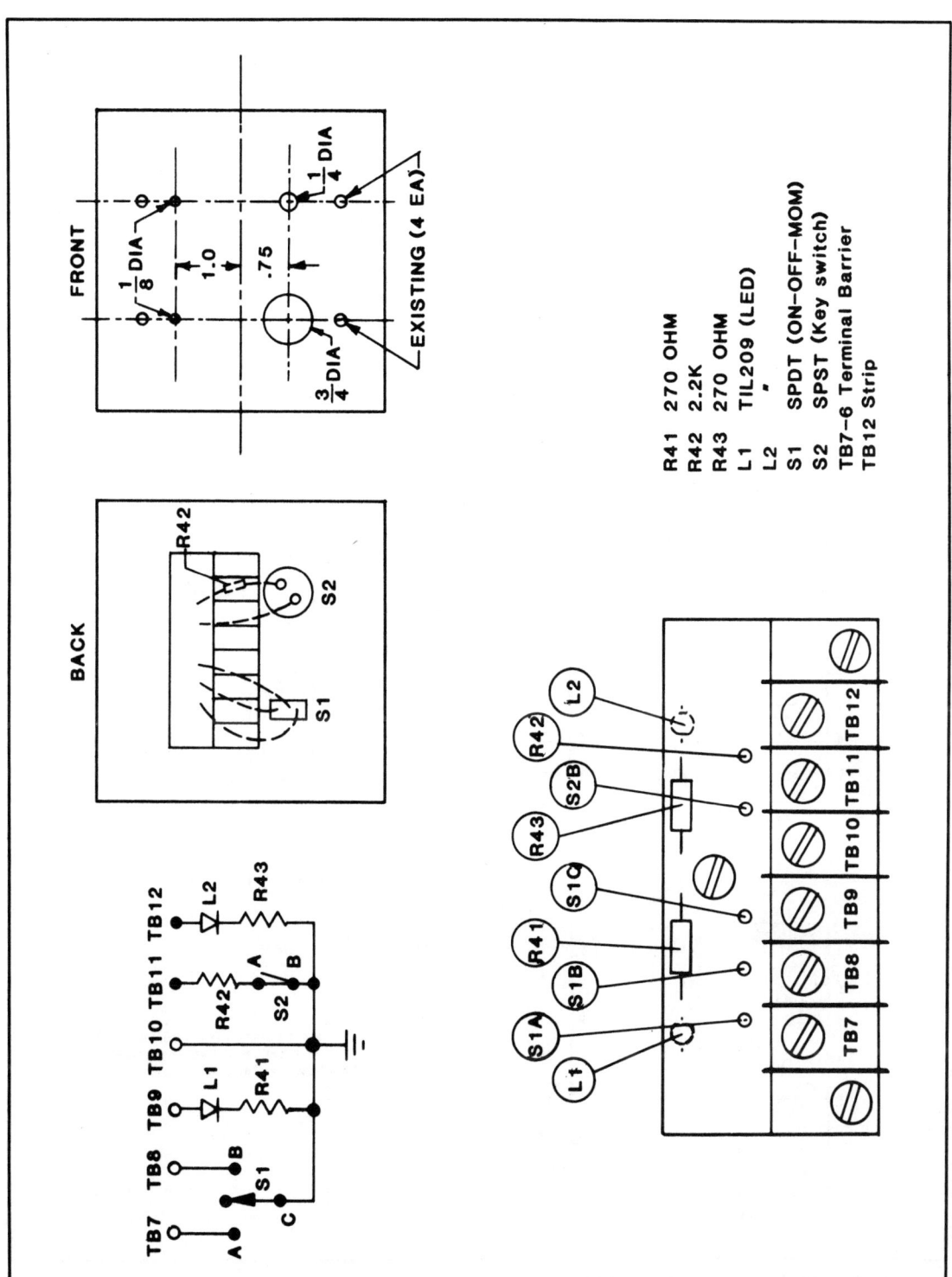

Fig. 3-6. The LED driver/series limiting circuit.

is a function of the values of the RC pair you select for R_T and C_T.

BATTERY CHARGER

This security system has a battery backup feature and uses a gel cell or rechargeable battery. The voltage regulator and rechargeable battery charging circuit are shown in Fig. 3-5. The battery charger/voltage regulator circuit uses a very efficient discrete design to accomplish the +5 V output for the TTL circuits. Essentially, the four transistor configuration of Q21 through Q24 establish a voltage reference that is very stable and is adjustable by virtue of pot R26. This reference voltage is applied to a series pass transistor, Q25, and its output is filtered by C23 before being applied through the rest of the system as +5 Vdc. Incidentally, the TTL logic ICs used here require a +5 Vdc ±1/4 Vdc so there is a need for a good stable well regulated circuit as we have here. Additionally, when constructing this project, be certain to build the voltage regulator circuit first and measure its output with a DVM (digital

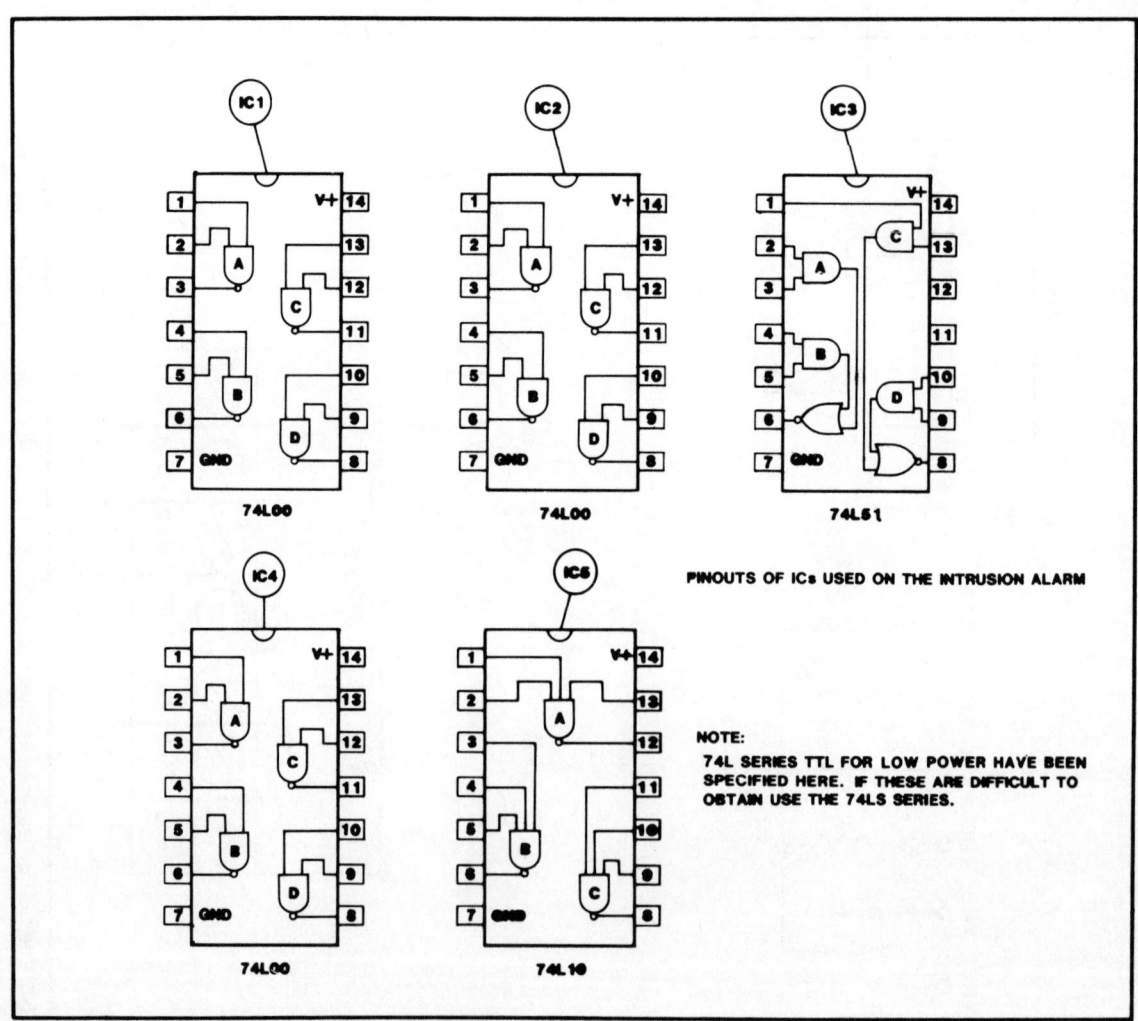

Fig. 3-7. Pinouts of the ICs used on the intrusion alarm.

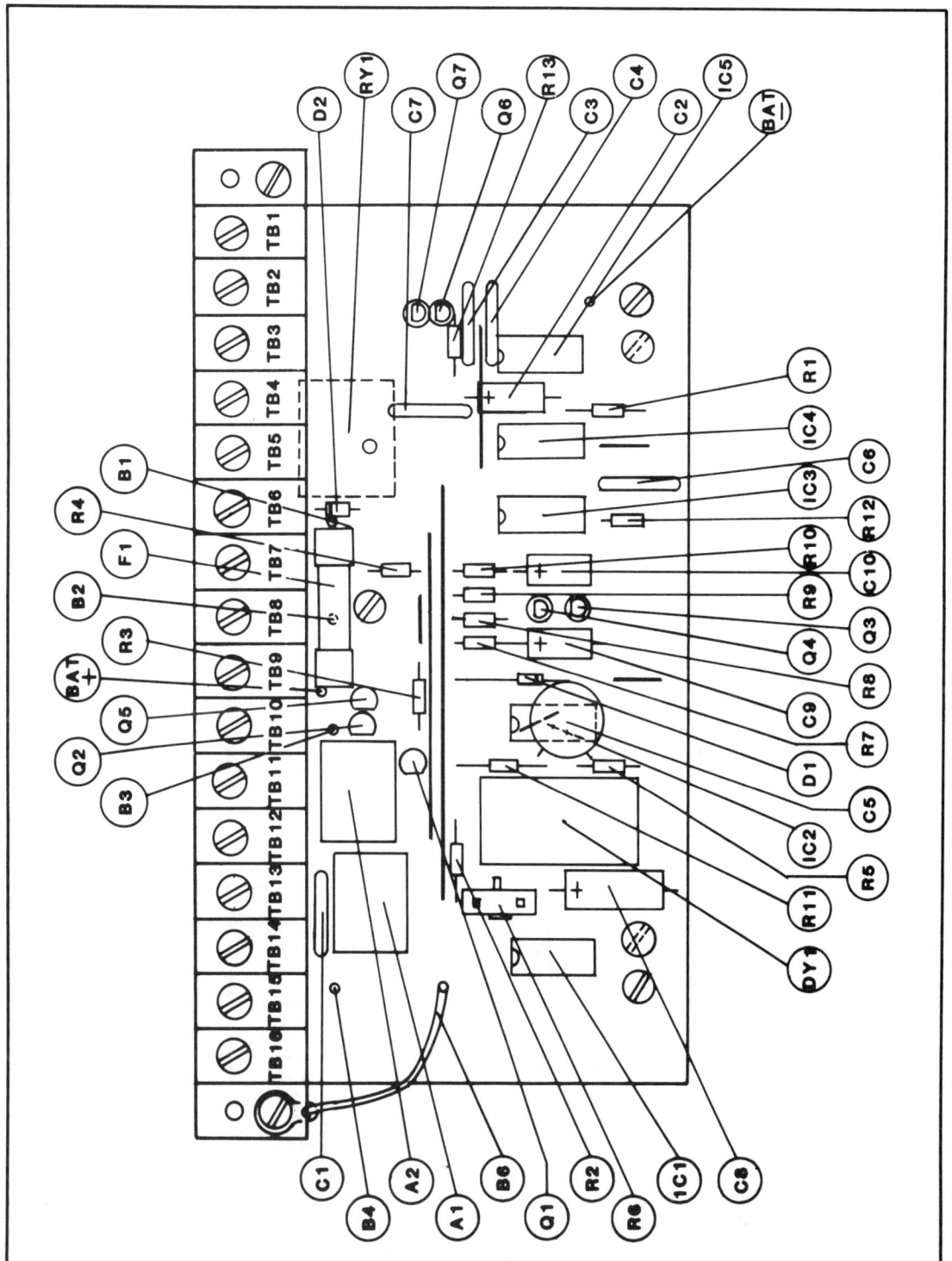

Fig. 3-8. The physical layout of the detection circuitry.

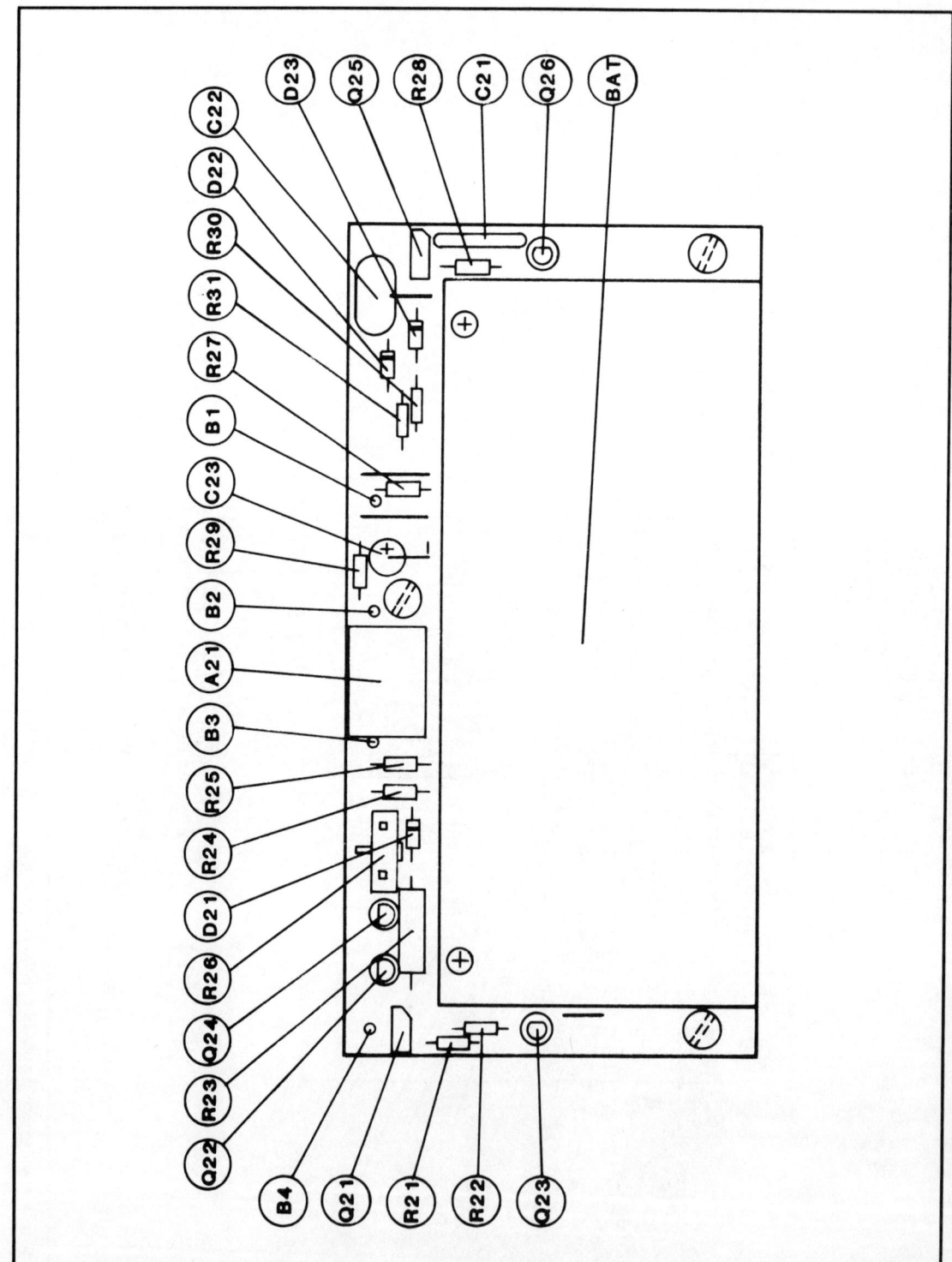

Fig. 3-9. The physical layout of the battery charger/voltage regulator circuitry.

```
1.  RELAY (N.C.)
2.  RELAY (N.O.)
3.  RELAY (COM)
4.  BELL (NEG)
5.  BELL (POS)
6.  ARM
7.  DELAY
8.  ACCESSORIES
9.  LOOP LIGHT
10. COMMON PANEL
11. KEY
12. ARM LIGHT
13. LOOP (FIRE)
14. LOOP (ENTRY)
15. LOOP (COM)
16. POWER
```

Note: The order in which these functions appear corresponds to the drawings associated with this project. However, you can, if you wish, vary this order.

Fig. 3-10. Signal names and pin assignments for the barrier terminal strip.

voltmeter) first to determine and adjust the output to exactly +5 Vdc.

The A21 ON/OFF module is merely the keyswitch which provides either a closure allowing the circuit to complete itself or to remain off and in effect OFF.

FRONT PANEL CONTROLS

The two LEDs (L1 and L2) in Fig. 3-6 indicate the ARMED and DELAYED ENTRY status. They are physically mounted on another separate board. Note the two switches S1 and S2 which correspond to these functions with S1 being the delayed entry and S2 being the system arming switch. The resistors associated with these LEDs are merely for series current limiting. Most LEDs withstand an absolute maximum forward current of approximately 18 to 20 mA.

INTEGRATED CIRCUITS

As previously stated, this security system uses TTL or transistor-transistor logic and although the 74 "L" series, or the low power series, is specified, the 74 "LS" low power Schottky series may also be used, as the note in Fig. 3-7 indicates. Both the L and LS as well as the regular 7400 series TTL parts all have identical pinout configurations and so all are interchangeable. The TTL 7400 series is somewhat discouraged because its power consumption is higher than the other two series. The reason for the selection of these low powered series of TTL parts is to minimize power consumption so that when there is a power failure the system will still remain operational as an intrusion detector and alarm for as long as possible. The particular gel-cell rechargeable battery used here has a 2.6 AH (ampere-hour) capacity. It will run horns or alarms that require 1/2 A of current for about 5 hours. It will run the system without an alarm being activated for approximately 2 1/2 days.

CONSTRUCTION

The actual system was built on the two perf boards shown in Fig. 3-8 and Fig. 3-9. Figure 3-9 shows how the logic board (Fig. 3-8) can be placed on top of the battery with the battery charger board below it. This approach sandwiches the battery between the two boards. The barrier terminal strip pin assignments used is shown in Fig. 3-10. This system was housed in a metal cast box manufactured by Bud Boxes. The relay, RY1, is one of your choice, it need only by a 6 Vdc relay capable of driving the alarm you select.

4

Single Board Microcomputer/Controller

BEFORE DELVING INTO THE ACTUAL MICROprocessor-based security projects, an explanation of the single board microcomputer/controller is warranted. Construction details on this 4 1/2 chip computer are also given here. A partial kit is available for this project from Specialty Electronics Services, Inc.

POWER REQUIREMENTS

This single board microcomputer runs off of a +5 Vdc ±1/4 volt regulated power source. The power enters this board from an 18-pin edge connector. Refer to Fig. 4-1 for an illustration of this type connector which can be cascaded to reach the proper number of contacts. Figure 4.2 shows the signals assigned to each of these 18 terminals. You will note that pin 1 is ground and pin 18 is +5 Vdc. The convention of putting power and ground on opposite ends of a connector is to lessen the likelihood of a direct short between power and ground. Pay particularly close attention not to reverse these two pins, (pins 1 and 18) or else irreparable damage to the board will result.

BOARD COMPONENTS

This board consists of one 6502 microprocessor, a 40 pin LSI IC manufactured by Rockwell, Commodore, and Synertek. Additionally, the I/O IC enabling communications to and from the outside world, is a 6532 40 pin LSI IC manufactured by these same sources. This IC has internal to it 128 bytes of addressable RAM, 16 bits of I/O in the form of two 8-bit ports denoted port A and port B. These two 8-bit ports are identical for all intents and purposes with the exception that port B can source approximately 50 percent more current than port A. Each of these 16 I/O pins on the chip can be configured as either inputs or outputs or any combinations thereof. The 6532 also has a presettable timer that can be run off of the

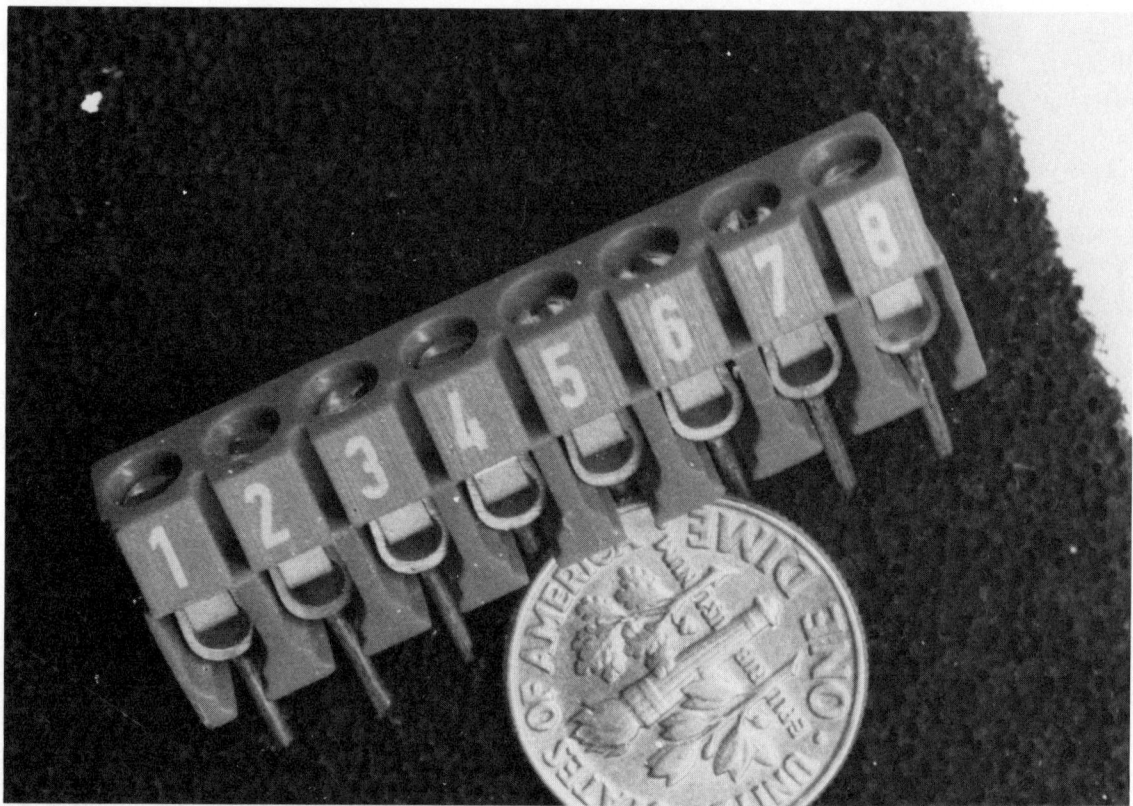

Fig. 4-1. A typical edge-mounted connector with 0.2 inch spacing for mounting on the microcomputer/controller.

phase 2 ($\phi 2$) clock from the 6502 microprocessor.

The permanent or nonvolatile memory is a 2716 EPROM which has a 2K by 8-bit wide capacity. This is a memory that will retain its data after the power is removed. Its contents are eraseable only when exposed to ultraviolet light in the 3,500 Angstrom wavelength range for approximately 20 minutes. The actual physical PC board proper was laid out to accommodate this memory. In other words, when the PC design was first formulated, all runs ran out from this 24 pin IC rather than beginning elsewhere and wiring over to this IC. This is important because it allowed for all 24 connections to be made from the wiring or noncomponent side of the board. This approach allows the use of an IC socket, and it does not require solder connections underneath the plastic socket. When such connections must be made, it results in burnt, melted away portions of the socket.

An 8-pin mini-DIP NE555 timer manufactured by Signetics, National Semiconductor, and numerous other semiconductor manufacturers also exists on the board with the primary function of power-on reset. A 74LS04 TTL hex inverter IC is the fifth and last chip on board. It inverts certain signal lines for the correct signal polarity and also two inverters are used in conjunction with a 1 MHz crystal to establish a very accurate time source from which all timing loops and delays are eventually derived. This 1 MHz squarewave is applied to phase 0 ($\phi 0$).

Upon powering up, the 555 timer pulls the

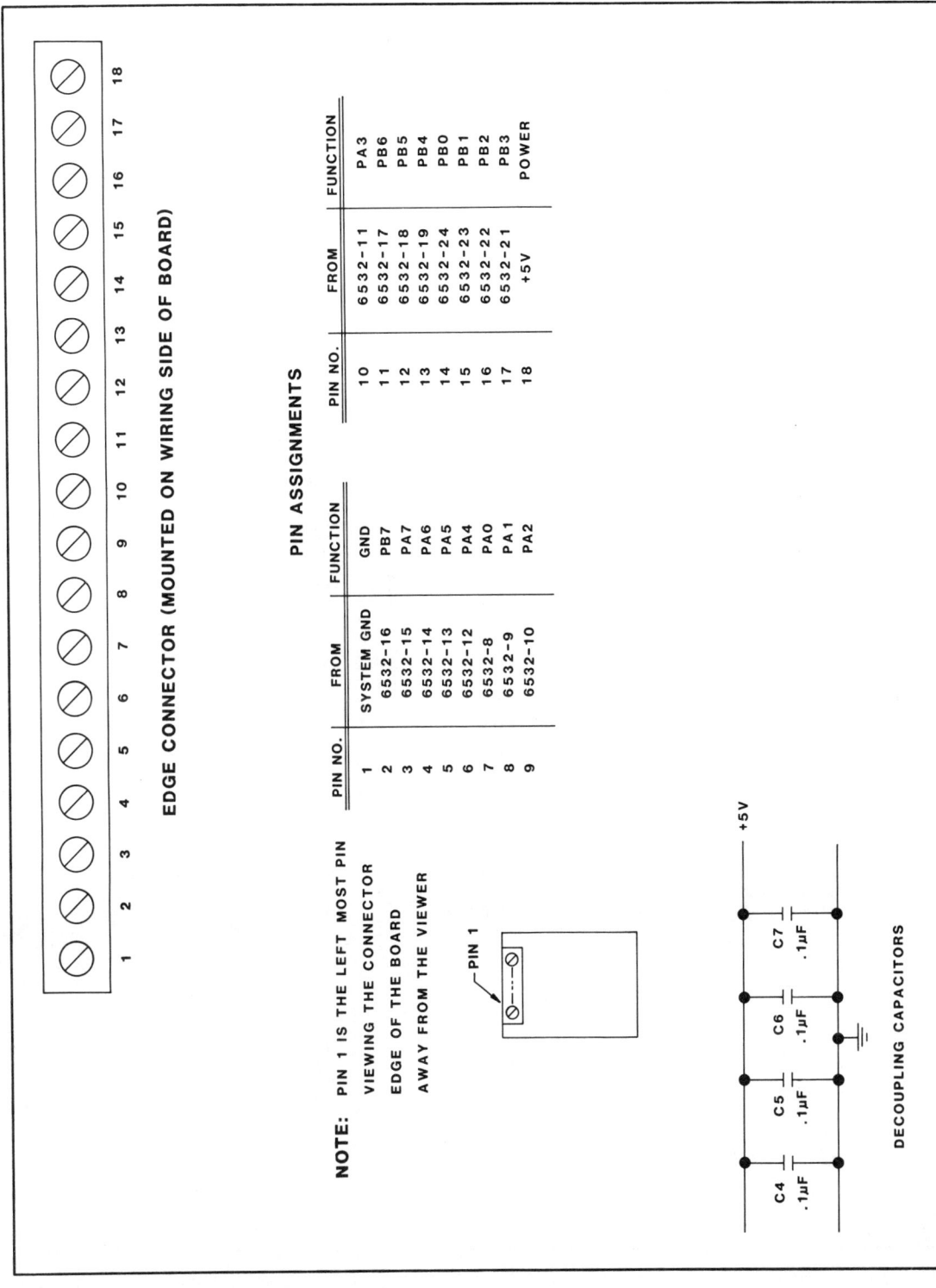

Fig. 4-2. Pin assignments by signal names for the edge connector.

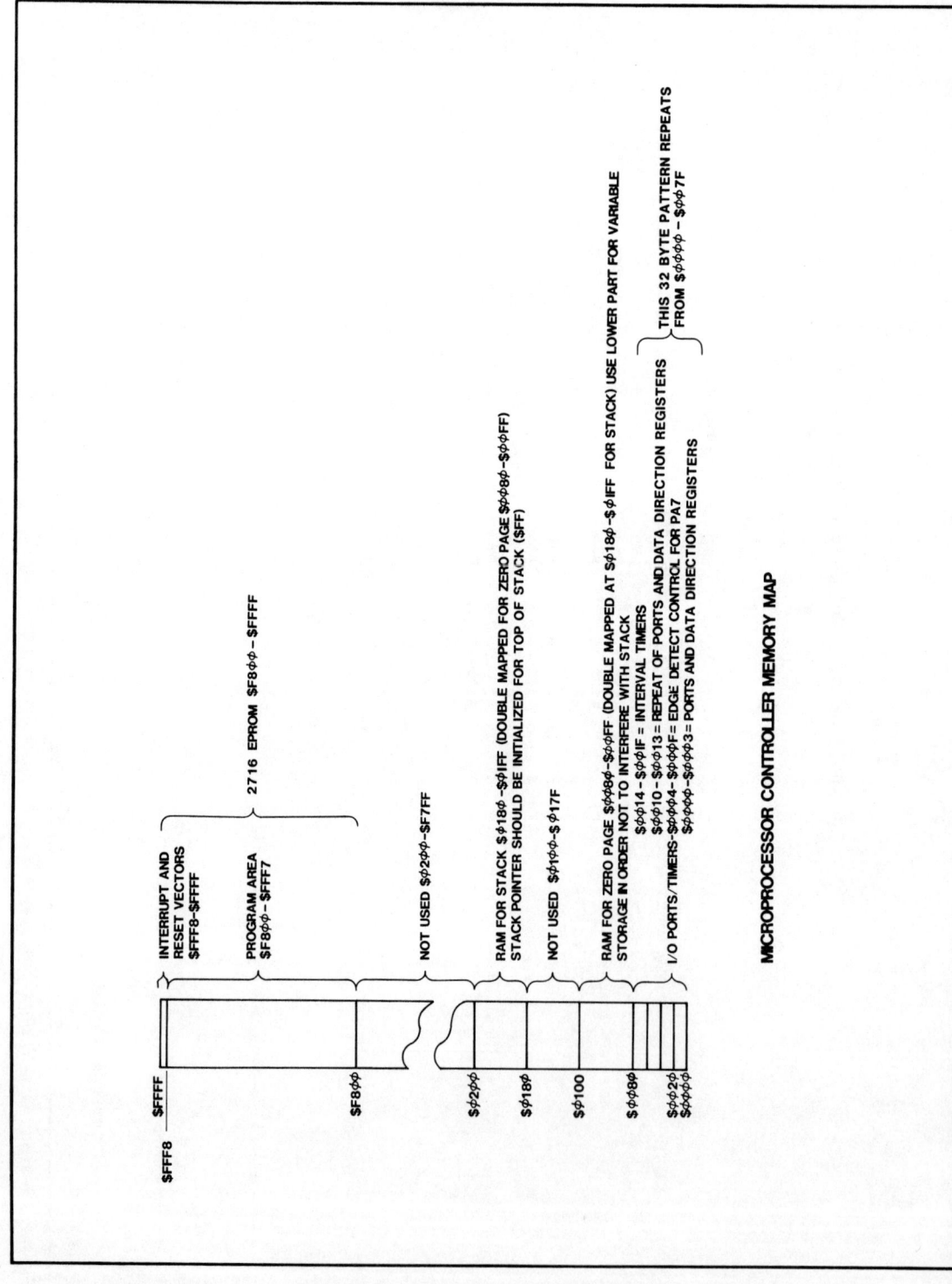

Fig. 4-3. The microcomputer memory map.

RESET line low (pin 40 on the 6502 and pin 34 on the 6532 RIOT). When the timer times out this RESET signal goes high, enabling the 6502 microprocessor to begin executing instructions contained in the 2716 EPROM. The microprocessor has no internal RAM of its own. It depends on the 128 bytes in the 6532 RIOT (RAM - I/O Timer) for this.

The system is configured according to the memory map in Fig. 4-3. The A and B 8-bit ports on the 6532 are addressed with port A corresponding to 00 in hex and port B corresponding to 01 in hex. The data direction register of port A is addressed at 02 in hex and the same register for port B is addressed at 03 in hex. The data direction registers determine which one of the 8 bits are to be inputs and which ones are to be outputs. The next 12 bytes up to 0F in hex are for determining the period or the amount of time the 6532 RIOT takes to time out. Registers exist within this chip to determine timing constants; for example, if the phase 2 ($\phi 2$) clock is divided by 64, 1024, etc., and how many of these divided down clock cycles or timing constants it will take before the 6532 RIOT times out. Therefore, a total of 32 bytes are taken up with this data and this pattern is repeated for a total of 4 times or 32 bytes times 4 identical occurrences for a total of 128 bytes (the capacity of the 6532's RAM). What occurs at address 07 in hex would then occur again at 27, 47, and 67 in hex.

This repetition of a program four times in the 6532 transpires because of the lack of full decoding to this chip select line ($\overline{CS2}$) which is tied to A15, the MSB of the address bus and because the $\overline{RS}$ RAM Select line (pin 36) is inverted from A7 while A0 through A6 write to the RIOT's RAM. This repeating process within RAM is due to simplified decoding hardware. It could have been fully decoded for the projects in this book, but it would just be an overkill. The beauty of the simplified decoding is that it allows for a 4 1/2 IC board to be a full fledged legitimate computer.

BOARD TROUBLESHOOTING

If trouble appears, or as a preliminary precautionary checkout, you should visually inspect the board for any opens or gaps on the board, especially where two conductors meet at a right angle. This should be followed by a visual check for shorts, especially adjacent runs that are closely spaced to one another. If a short appears or a suspiciously close spacing between adjacent conductors is in evidence, use an ohmmeter to make a continuity check. If your suspicions are confirmed and the gap has been bridged by soldering iron or solder wick to open this bridge. If the bridge is a manufacturing error in the board itself (a highly unlikely possibility) take a razor's edge to separate the shorted conductors.

BOARD CONSTRUCTION

Install all of the chips. Solder them on both the bottom and top of the board, and solder all discrete components as well from both sides of the board per the instructions in Table 4-1. Figure 4-4 illustrates how the parts go on the microcomputer/controller PC board. Pay particularly close attention to the proper orientation of the ICs. Note that pin 1 is adjacent to the notch on the ICs and that on the PC board a dot exists beside each pin one to denote this.

This PC board is extremely useful and diverse from the numerous projects that run off it in this book to a whole host of tasks that can be accomplished with a stand alone microcomputer PC board. This board's utilitarian nature is further enhanced by the space in its corner with a number of 14, 16, 24, and 40 pin DIP sockets upon which numerous expansion ICs of your choice may be placed via

Table 4-1. Board Construction Guide.

MICROPROCESSOR BOARD
ASSEMBLY INSTRUCTIONS

1. LOCATE COMPONENT SIDE OF MICROPROCESSOR BOARD. (THE COMPONENT SIDE IS THE SIDE OPPOSITE FROM THE REFERENCE DESIGNATIONS.)
2. INSERT THE 6532 RIOT CHIP IN POSITION, MAKING CERTAIN PIN 1 ON THE RIOT MATCHES PIN 1 ON THE OPPOSITE SIDE OF THE CIRCUIT BOARD.
3. USING A SMALL WATTAGE SOLDERING IRON (25 WATTS OR LESS), AND A SMALL TIP, SOLDER ALL PINS ON TOP AND BOTTOM.
4. INSERT THE 6502 MICROPROCESSOR INTO PLACE, MAKING CERTAIN PIN 1 MATCHES PIN 1 ON THE BOTTOM OF THE BOARD, AND SOLDER ALL PINS TOP AND BOTTOM.
5. INSERT THE 74LS04 MAKING SURE PIN 1 ALIGNS WITH PIN 1 ON BOTTOM OF BOARD. SOLDER ALL PINS TOP AND BOTTOM.
6. INSERT THE NE555 TIMER MAKING SURE PIN 1 ALIGNS WITH PIN 1 ON BOTTOM OF BOARD. SOLDER ON BOTTOM OF BOARD.
7. INSERT THE TERMINAL STRIP FROM OPPOSITE SIDE OF THE BOARD. SOLDER PINS ON COMPONENT SIDE OF BOARD.
8. INSERT THE CRYSTAL FROM COMPONENT SIDE OF BOARD AT LOCATION MARKED XTAL1. LEAVE CRYSTAL SPACED ABOUT 3/16" OFF BOARD IN ORDER TO SOLDER THE PAD ON COMPONENT SIDE. SOLDER BOTH PADS ON BOTTOM.
9. INSERT R1, R2, C1, C2, C3 ON COMPONENT SIDE OF P.C. BOARD, SOLDER ALL ON BOTTOM SIDE OF BOARD. SOLDER ONE END OF R2 ON COMPONENT SIDE OF BOARD. CUT OFF EXCESS WIRE FROM THESE COMPONENTS. SAVE WIRE FOR LATER USE AS JUMPERS.
10. INSERT R3, R4, R5, R6. SOLDER ON BOTTOM SIDE OF BOARD. SOLDER ONE END OF R5 ON TOP SIDE OF BOARD.
11. INSERT C4, C5, C6, C7. SOLDER ON BOTTOM SIDE OF BOARD. SOLDER C7, AND ONE END OF C4 ON TOP OF BOARD. CUT OFF EXCESS WIRE.
12. USING WIRE PREVIOUSLY CUT OFF FROM RESISTORS, INSERT WIRES IN HOLES MARKED ON BOTTOM OF BOARD WITH TAILS LIKE THE LETTER "Q". SOLDER WIRES ON BOTH SIDES OF BOARD. CUT OFF EXCESS.

NOTE

There are a number of pads on the PC board that serve as "Z" wires. That is, they are bridges for a conductor line that terminates, seemingly in free space, at one of these pads. There is likewise a corresponding pad on the opposite side perfectly aligning itself with this "Z pad". A solid piece of wire is inserted in these holes and soldered on both sides to affectuate or enable reliazation of an electrical path from one side of the board to the other, in the absence of plated through holes. These special pads look like any other pad on the board so a convention had to be adopted allowing them to be immediately recognizable. The convention employed here is the use of a tick mark beside the pad making the pad look like the capital letter "Q".

13. SOLDER THREE JUMPER WIRES ON PINS 18, 20, AND 24 OF THE 2716 ON BOTH SIDES OF THE BOARD. TRIM THE WIRES ON THE COMPONENT SIDE OF THE BOARD AS CLOSE TO THE BOARD AS POSSIBLE BECAUSE THE 2716 SOCKET MUST FIT OVER THE JUMPERS. INSTALL THE 24 PIN I.C. SOCKET FOR THE 2716 AND SOLDER ON BOTTOM OF THE BOARD ONLY. INSTALL THE 2716 IN THE SOCKET. THIS COMPLETES THE ASSEMBLY OF THE MICROPROCESSOR BOARD.

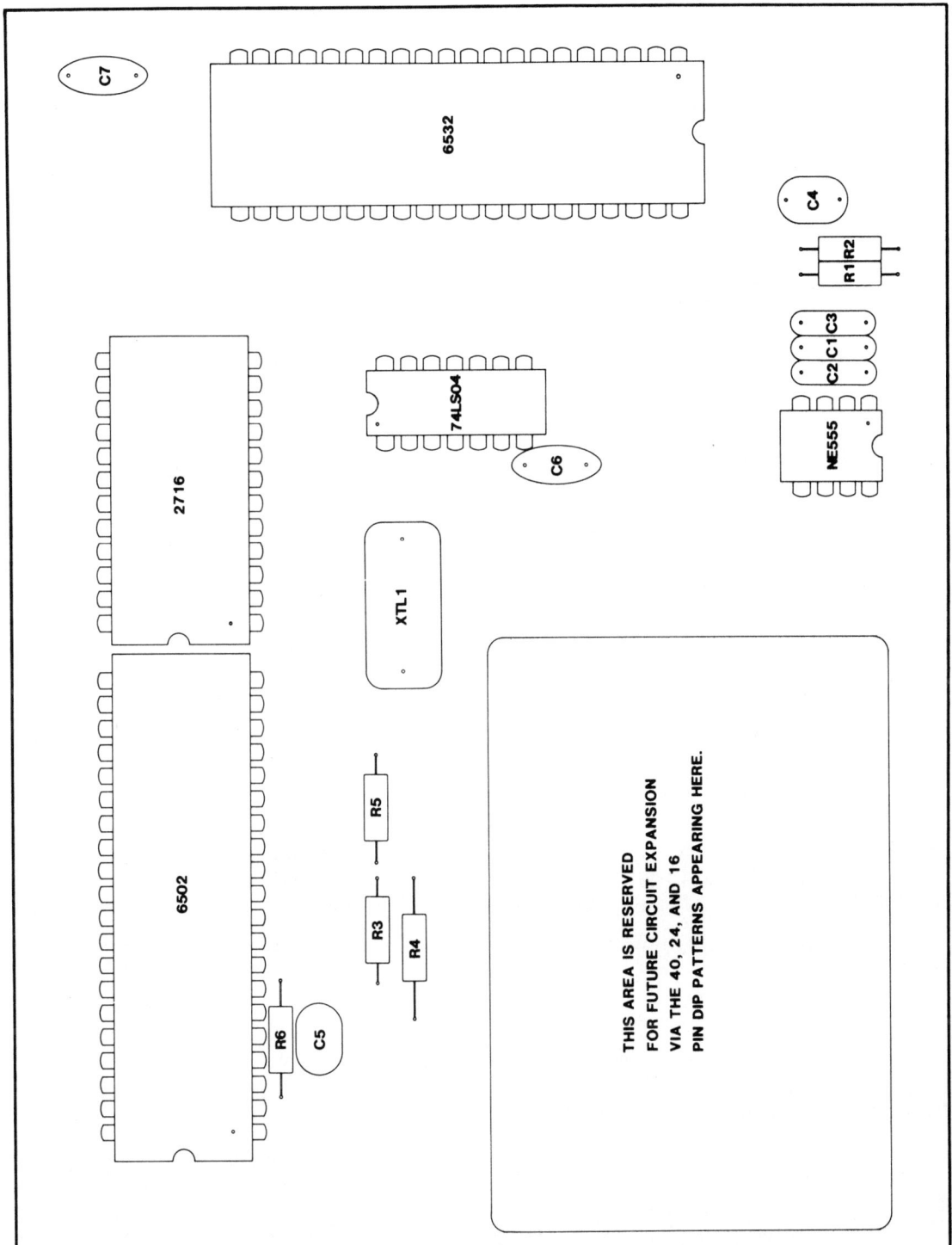

Fig. 4-4. Component placement diagram.

wire-wrap socket or a component header which allow for custom designs and modifications to this basic microcomputer board.

The board itself is available for $16 (etched and drilled) from Specialty Electronic Services, Inc. The programmed EPROM is also available from the authors for $10 through the same source. Refer to the Supplies section at the back of the book.

After another board checkout, as just described, it is now time to install a program in the 2716 EPROM and insert it in the EPROM

TEST STEP	IF PROBLEM IS FOUND, THEN CHECK
1. Measure voltage from 6502 Pins 8,2,6,4, and 21 to ground. If all read +5VDC go to step 2.	Check solder joints on both sides of P.C. board, check for proper value of R6.
2. With voltmeter connected between 6502 Pins 40 and 1, momentarily short between points marked A and B on NE555. Voltage should go from +5VDC to 0VDC and back to +5VDC. If O.K. go to step 3.	Check for bad solder joints, defective NE555 or defective 74LS04. Check for proper values of R1, R2, C1, C2, and C3.
3. With an oscilloscope, check for 1MHZ waveform at 6502 Pin 39 and 6532 Pin 39. If O.K. go to step 4.	Check for defective 74LS04 or crystal. Check for proper values of R3, R4, and R5. Check solder joints.
4. With oscilloscope connected to 2716 Pin 20, momentarily short points A and B near NE555. If pulses appear on oscilloscope, go to step 5.	Connect oscilloscope to pin 34 of 6502 and momentarily short A and B. If pulses appear, check for defective or improperly installed 74LS04.
5. Connect oscilloscope to 6532 Pin 37 and momentarily short A and B. If pulses appear, go to step 6.	Connect oscilloscope to 6532 Pin 36 and momentarily short A and B. If pulses appear go to step 6. If not, check for defective 74LS04.
6. Check voltage on 6532 Pins 20 and 38 to ground. If +5VDC go to step 7.	Check for bad solder joint or broken trace on P.C. board.
7. Check voltage on 2716 Pins 21 and 24 to ground. If +5VDC go to step 8.	Check for bad solder joint or broken trace on P.C. board
8. Check voltage on NE555 Pins 4 and 8. If +5VDC go to step 9.	Check for bad solder joint on top of R2.
9. Check voltage on 74LS04 Pin 14. If +5VDC go to step 10.	Check for bad solder joint or broken P.C. trace.
10. Last possibility is defective 2716 EPROM, 6502, or 6532	

Fig. 4-5. Checkout/Troubleshooting guide for the microcomputer board.

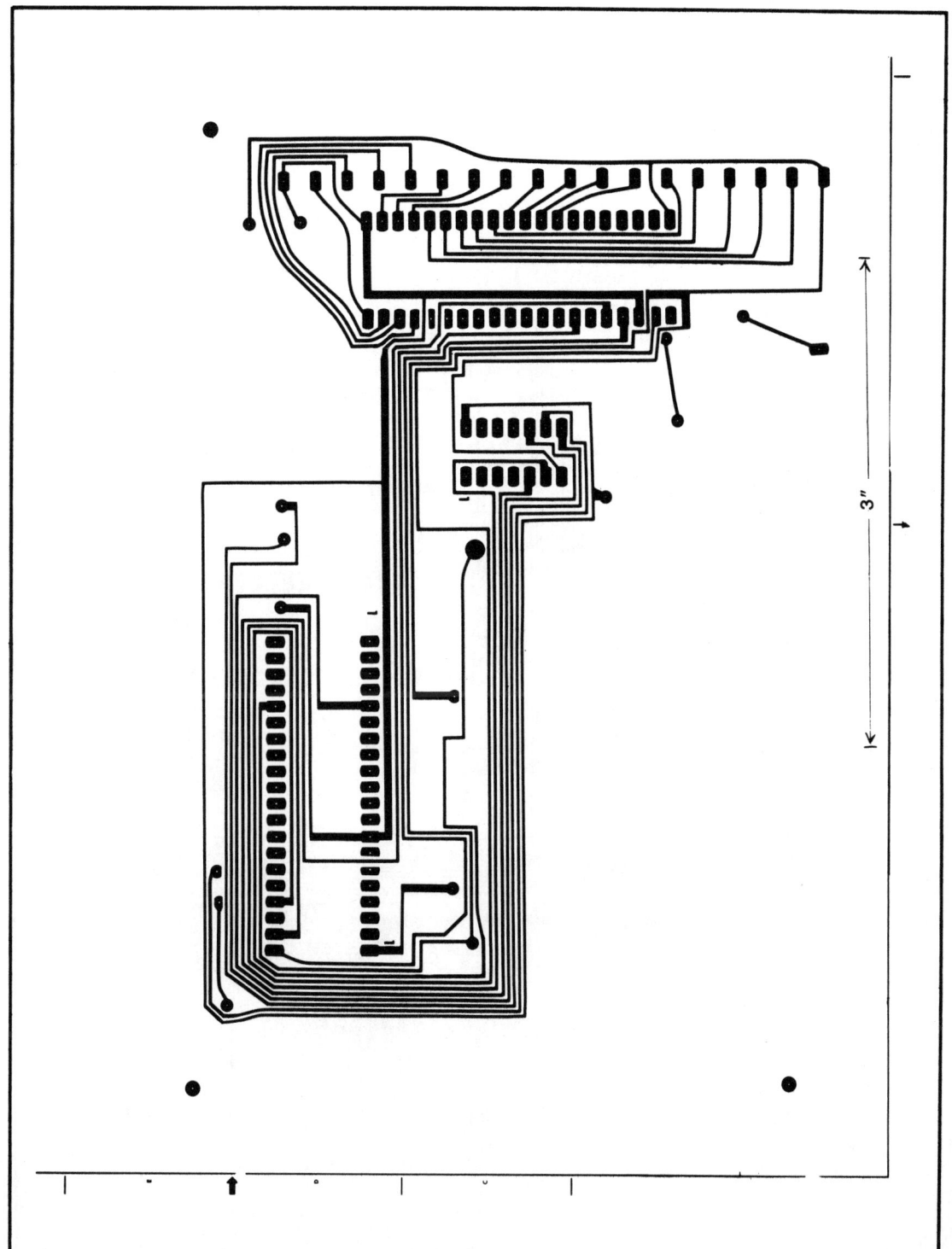

Fig. 4-6. Foil patterns for the microcomputer board (cont'd on page 80.)

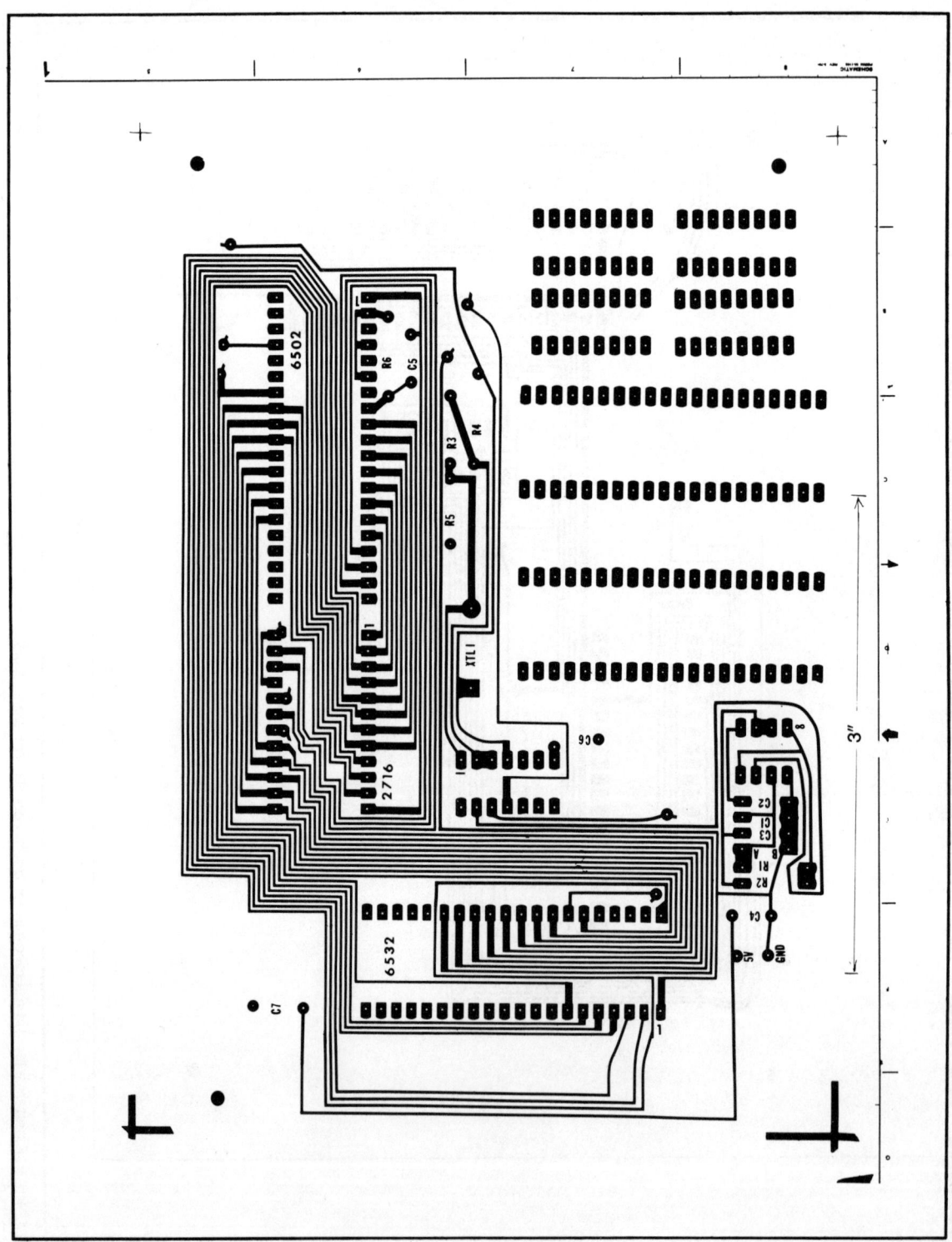

socket. You can program the EPROM from the listing in Appendix B with an EPROM programmer. A simpler alternative is to purchase an already programmed EPROM from Specialty Electronic Services, Inc.

SYSTEM CHECKOUT

If the program does not execute properly after turning on the power, first check the power and ground on each IC. If the voltages checkout properly, use an oscilloscope to monitor the 1 MHz clock on pins 37 and 39 of the 6502 microprocessor and pin 39 of the 6532 RIOT. Refer to Fig. 4-5. Also, monitor the address lines A0 through A10 and connect a short or a normally open momentary contact switch across points A and B of the 555 timer IC. Two solder pads on the PC board denoted "A" and "B" have already been provided expressly for this purpose. Refer to the foil patterns of the PC board in Fig. 4-6. When you engage the momentary contact normally open pushbutton switch, the address lines should change states or exhibit some activity on the scope.

If the microprocessor is functioning properly by having the address lines exhibiting a like activity of changing logic states, then first check the chip select ($\overline{CS}$) line on the EPROM and if it occasionally goes low, then check the ($\overline{CS}$) line and the read/write ($R/\overline{W}$) lines on the 6532 RIOT. These should be alternating states. Next, go down the address and data lines and observe that no two adjacent lines have identical data on them. They may appear similar but they should never be identical. This will be obvious if viewed on a dual trace scope. If exact duplications occur on adjacent lines, then a short exists and it should be removed by the procedure outlined in the Troubleshooting section.

If the system still does not function properly or only marginally, the next step is to examine the I/O lines on ports A and B of the 6532 RIOT. Realizing that in all our applications the A port pins are all inputs, you can short the two ports together and then intermittingly short and open port A lines and observe the respective port B lines following this action on the scope, indicating that the board is operating properly. The reason the A ports were selected to be inputs is that, as previously mentioned, the B ports sink more current, or have more current drive capacity.

5
Microprocessor-Based Systems

THIS CHAPTER DISCUSSES THREE SECURITY systems, all under the control of the 6502 microcprocessor. They all use the single board microcomputer discussed in Chapter 4.

The first system discussed is the delayed entry security system, followed by a simpler yet similar system without the delayed entry capability. The last system discussed uses the programmable light dimmer board already developed in Chapter 2.

PERIMIGUARD WITH DELAYED ENTRY

The Perimiguard System with the delayed entry feature is a comprehensive security system. It uses the 4 1/2 IC single-board computer that was described in Chapter 4. Altogether, this system has five loops. There are two normally closed loops. One can be used as the main outside perimeter loop and the other as an inside or outside perimeter loop. There is also a panic loop and a normally closed inside loop for use with smoke/fire detectors and/or motion detectors. Lastly, there is a delayed entry loop. Each of these loops will be discussed in more detail.

This system uses a pushbutton keypad to control the system. Additionally, this system can monitor switches, fire and smoke detectors, and motion detectors. Upon a signal from any of these sensors, an alarm can be registered. As you can see, it is a versatile and complete system.

Circuit Description

A 12 Vac transformer with a 4 A current capacity is required. To protect this system and the wiring internal to your residence or place of business where this is installed, it is recommended that you use a transformer with an internal fuse. The reason that an external transformer was selected in lieu of wiring it into the security system itself is that in certain states and municipalities there is a requirement that

Fig. 5-1. This plug-in transformer plugs directly into the 110 Vac wall outlet. Brackets exist for secure mechanical fastening. This 12 Vac model comes with a 4 A capacity.

voltages above 25 volts be run in conduit. The 12 Vac transformer shown in Fig. 5-1 meets this less than 25 volt requirement. Standard zip cord can be used to wire to the security system from the transformer.

Once the 12 Vac is run over to the Power Supply/Buffer Board, shown in Fig. 5-2, the ac is full wave rectified by diodes D1 through D4, which are IN4006 or equivalent type rectifier diodes. Refer to the parts list within this figure. This rectified ac is changed to dc with a significant amount of ripple on it and is filtered by filter capacitor C1.

The input voltage is approximately 18 Vdc and is applied to the voltage regulator, IC2, which is a 3 A regulator that is programmable. The output voltage is determined by transistor Q1 and the resistor network consisting of resistors R5, R6, and R7. This transistor and its resistors control the voltage on the ADJ (adjust) pin of the voltage regulator. These produce an approximate voltage of 12.6 volts at the junction of diode D5. Resistor R8 is a 2 A current limiting resistor which limits the amount of current the charging battery can accept. If the rechargeable battery is completely discharged, the regulator will current limit at 2 A and the regulator voltage will match the voltage of the battery. As the battery is charged to its normal rated voltage, the current limiting will not be in effect to its maximum extent, and the voltage regulation function of IC2 will then predominate.

The purpose of the battery is naturally to supply voltage to the circuit in case of a power failure. When doing so, it is necessary for

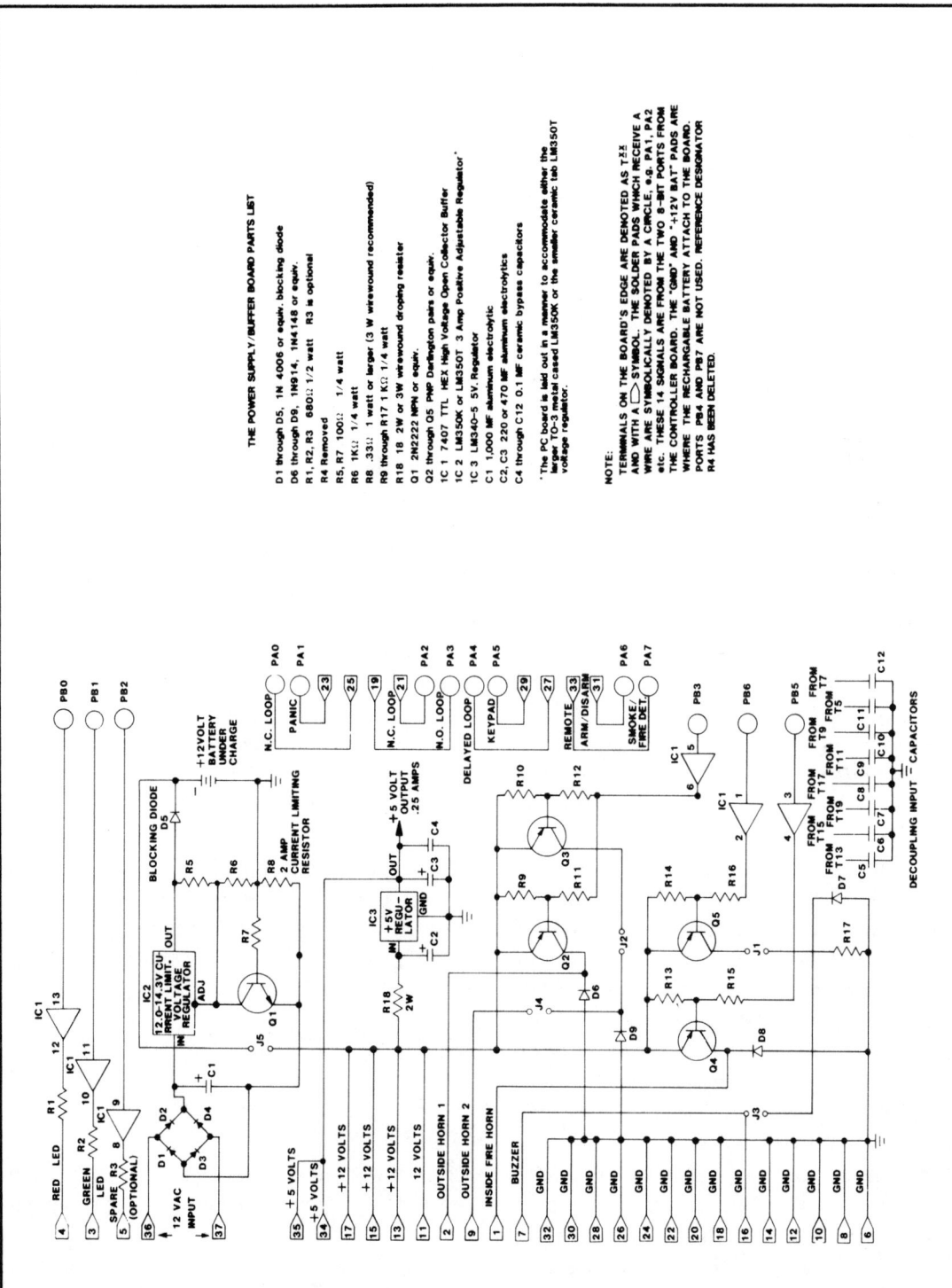

Fig. 5-2. Schematic of the power supply/buffer board for the Perimiguard with delayed entry.

voltage from the battery's output terminal not to be fed into the voltage regulator's (IC2's) output terminal. Diode D5 was inserted there for this blocking function.

The rest of the circuit essentially operates off of the battery, and it supplies power to accessories such as the touch pad switches, an external microwave motion detector, or horn/alarm etc. Also, there is a +5 Vdc voltage regulator, IC1 in this circuit that supplies a +5 Vdc voltage to the logic circuitry and the external microprocessor board. Note resistor R18. This resistor is merely a series limiting resistor that drops approximately 4 volts so that IC1 has only a +8 volt input and, therefore, less power to dissipate because of this reduced input voltage.

There are four pnp Darlington pairs (directly-coupled very high gain transistor pairs) that are labeled Q2 through Q5 and driven by IC1, an open collector noninverting TTL buffer. This buffer is driven by the B port of the 6532 RIOT (RAM I/O Timer) from the microcomputer board.

The A ports of the microcomputer board are all connected as inputs and the B ports are all outputs. These A and B ports are brought out to the outside world or to an edge connector on the microcomputer board. Refer to Fig. 4-2 for an illustration of this as well as a listing of signals if you've skipped that portion of Chapter 4. Note how these A ports come out to several loops on the right side edge of the schematic, Fig. 5-2. Note the N.C. (normally closed) loop which is the main outside perimeter loop that constitutes a series circuit with possible points where it can be broken (switches on windows and doors) to detect entry. There is also a N.O. (normally open) loop that could be either an outside or inside perimeter loop. A normally open device would typically be mats with switch closure construction features that are actuated when stepped upon.

The panic loop is where the burglar alarm is set off, by a PANIC pushbutton switch, regardless if the system is set or not. Its typical use would be when you heard a prowler. Regardless of the armed state of the burglar alarm, it would activate immediately.

There is another normally-closed inside loop for use with smoke/fire detectors and/or microwave motion detectors. This feature of the Perimiguard System might prove very useful when you are awake and going from room to room within your house. Your perimeter entry detection devices can continue to function while the interior loop devices such as motion detectors are disabled. Refer to Fig. 5-3 for an illustration of methods to selectively disable security devices while still maintaining the integrity of the perimeter's entry detectors.

A *delayed entry* loop is also provided and exists only on the door upon which you would want to have the keypad attached. There is also an input from the keypad itself which arms and disarms the system. Another input exists in the form of a remote disarm function which would be particularly useful when the garage door opener was activated. Naturally under these quite normal circumstances, you would not want the alarm to go off. This feature only functions as a disarm input and the system cannot naturally be armed by this input.

All inputs are normally closed with the exception of the N.O. LOOP, the PANIC, and the KEYPAD inputs. The KEYPAD input is a momentary input to arm and disarm the system.

Output Devices

As previously stated, the A ports are inputs and the B ports are outputs with these outputs typically being through IC1, an open-collector noninverting TTL buffer. Starting with PB0, it goes through a buffer and

A. Normal connections for normally closed loop devices.

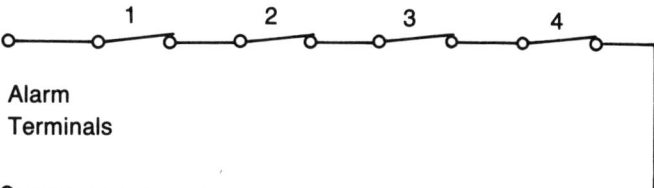

1. For selective disable of devices 3 & 4 connect as below.

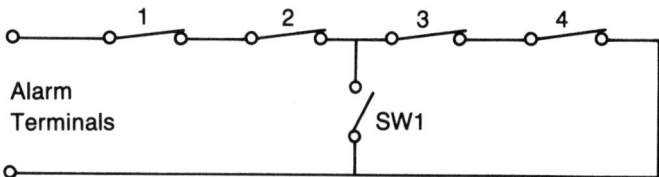

2. When SW1 is closed, devices 3 & 4 are disabled. When SW1 is open, all devices–1, 2, 3 & 4 are enabled.

B. Normal connections for normally open loop devices.

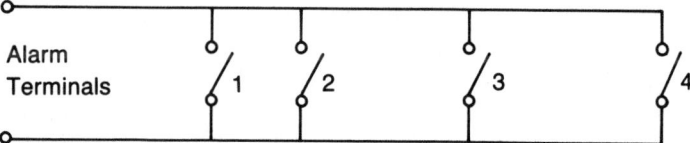

1. For selective disable of devices 3 & 4 connect as follows.

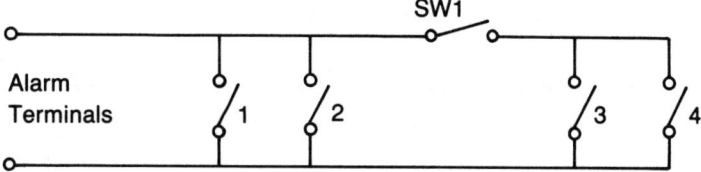

2. When SW1 IS open, devices 3 & 4 are disabled. When SW1 is closed, all devices–1, 2, 3, & 4 are enabled.

Note: The reason for selective disable of devices is so that inside detectors, such as motion detectors or switch mats, may be disabled by toggle switches so that the perimeter alarm devices can still function and the alarm system may be armed while someone is inside the house.

Fig. 5-3. A method to selectively disable inner-loop security devices.

its signal is current limited by resistor R1 which is attached to a red LED which in turn indicates that the system is armed. When the *delayed entry mode* is activated, this same red LED flashes. The next B port output, PB1, drives a green LED in a similar fashion. When the green LED is on, it indicates that the system is disarmed and all the loops are closed. When the green and red LEDs are both off, they indicate that the loops are not in the proper mode.

There is a third LED driven by PB2 which is not used with the present software package. It is reserved for expansion and may be used at a later date. The next B port output, PB3, is the main output for this security system. This B port drives Q2 and Q3, two pnp Darlington pairs, which in turn drive two outside horns (OUTSIDE HORN 1 & 2). This driving of the outside horns indicates that the security system has detected an entry or motion within the premises or a device tamper switch has been activated. You might want to place one of these warning devices outside and the other one inside. The B port outputs, PB4 and PB7, have purposely been skipped, and for a good reason, as will soon become apparent. The B Port PB5 drives Darlington pair Q4 and may be the inside fire indicator and is labeled the INSIDE FIRE HORN on the schematic. In addition to this horn being set off or activated by a detection of the presence of fire or smoke, the horn will likewise be activated in unison with the outside horns.

The buzzer driven by PB6 can be a piezoelectric type, typically drawing less than 50 mA and indicating, along with the flashing red LED that the *delayed entry* has been activated. These continue to be alternately activated at a 1 Hz rate after walking through the *delayed entry* doorway until their 30 second time-out period is over. If you have not entered the proper code on this keypad by this time, the system activates and all of the alarms go off. The only way to disarm the system after this happens is to enter in the proper keypad code.

Power Capacity

When the power is functioning properly, the battery experiences a charging and no drain on it occurs; however, when a power outage occurs, the 5 AH (ampere-hour) battery in Fig. 5-4, will easily run this 1/2 A system for at least 10 hours. If a break-in occurs during this time and the alarms sound, then it will still last four hours even if the alarms draw 1 or slightly more amps at 12 volts.

Keypad Functions

When the green LED is on, it indicates that all the loops that should be closed are indeed closed and that the other sensors are in their proper mode. This indication informs you that the system is ready to be armed, and this is done by entering a predetermined code into the keypad. As soon as the proper code is entered, the green LED goes off and the red LED begins flashing at a 1 Hz rate. This will be alternately accompanied by the warning buzzer.

This means, in practical terms, that you have 30 seconds in which to exit the building before the alarm is set off. If you exit the delayed entry door within this 30 second period then the system will be armed and the red LED will be on continuously without the buzzer being activated as an indication of this armed condition. If you do not exit before this 30 second period with red LED flashing and the buzzer buzzing, then the delayed entry would activate again and you would have another 30 seconds before activation of the siren. The armed state is again indicated by the red LED being on and no buzzer sounding.

If another entry point in this system is

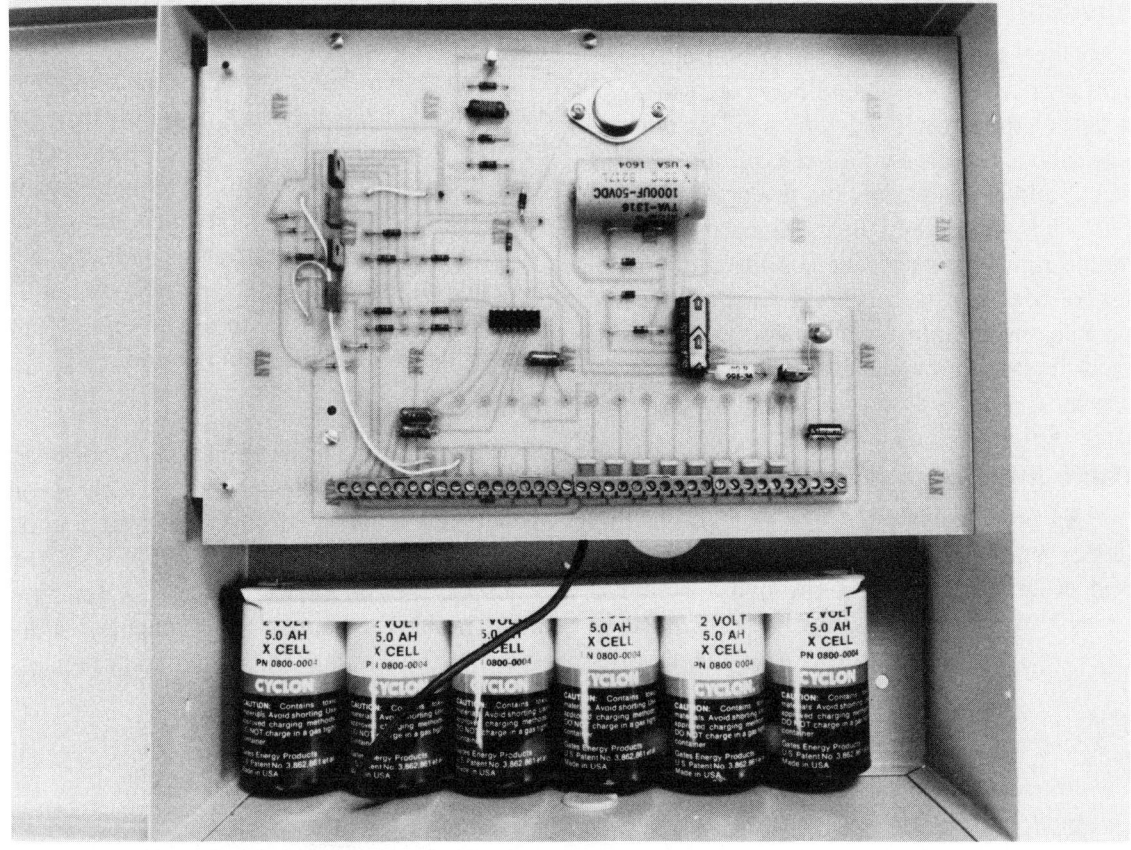

Fig. 5-4. A 5 ampere-hour rechargeable battery.

breached the alarm goes off immediately, and the only way to disarm it is to enter the proper code into the keypad. Upon entering the building or your home again, you would come through the delayed entry door, and the system will begin counting down this 30 second time period during which you can then enter the proper code. If this code is properly entered, the green LED will then be on in a steady nonflashing mode, indicating that all of the loops and sensors are in the proper state. If the proper code has not been set during this 30 seconds, the alarms in the form of horns, sirens, etc., will go off.

When the system's alarm is set off, it goes into a five minute timing loop in which you have the opportunity to put all of the elements within the loop in their correct state. Once this is done, the sirens and other alarms will cease and the system will come up in the ARMED state. If, however, you have failed to put these devices in their proper states, then at the end of this five minute timing loop, the alarms will continue to sound and you will have entered another five minute timing loop. This return to the five minute period will continue as long as at the end of that period the elements, typically switches, constituting the perimeter security system have not been placed in their proper states.

Fire/Smoke Alarm

Once activated, the fire/smoke detectors will only set off the inside horn regardless of whether the security system is set or not set. The alarm remains on for five minutes and if at the end of this period, the fire or smoke condition has ended, then the inside horn will cease sounding. If, however, the condition of smoke and/or fire persists, the inside horn will remain on and the sampling period will repeat itself again just as it was described for the security alarm.

Panic Switch

As previously stated, the purpose of this device is to set off the alarms, both inside horn and outside alarm when the panic switch is pressed to ward off a prowler that you may believe is lurking outside. This switch works in any situation whether or not the system is ARMED.

This system feature, just like the previously mentioned alarms, has the five minute time out feature. It will check the status of the switches to determine if an entry has occurred within this period. The proper keypad code must be entered within the time out period, and the switches on the doors and windows, etc., must also be in the proper state at the end of this period for the alarm to stop sounding.

Remote Disarm

The Remote Disarm function is optional, and is a normally closed loop, which when opened, automatically disarms the system if the system has been previously ARMED. If the system is not ARMED, then this function causes nothing to happen. You cannot ARM the system if the Remote Disarm loop is open. As

Fig. 5-5. Fire Burglary Instruments Model 546 Digital Remote Keypad.

an example, if this loop were hooked up to a garage door opener, then as long as the garage door remained opened, the system then could not be armed.

Keypad Installation

The keypad that we recommended for this system is the Fire Burglary Instruments Model 546. It is available from Mountain West, part number F9-063. Check the list of suppliers at the end of the book for their address and phone number. The keypad is shown in Fig. 5-5. This versatile unit features two LEDs for loop and system status, over 5,000 possible codes, an audible signal as digits are selected, a 24 hour panic switch, and a tamper switch. It is useable in a momentary contact or shunt mode of operation. Variable exit/entry delays can be used. A buzzer announces entry/exit, day loop violation or fire trouble.

Other keypad systems will work; however, they must be able to run off of +5 or +12 Vdc. They also have to be the type of keyboard with momentary normally open (N.O.) closure on the key codes. A red and green LED should be an integral part of the keypad with a buzzer also integrally attached. However, the buzzer feature is optional in that an externally attached buzzer would also work.

The instructions contained within the Fire Burglary Instruments Model 546 keypad are specific and complete. They include such vital information as how to set the four digit code. Everything you need to know is contained in the instructions with the following exceptions which are unique to our security system design.

Refer to Table 5-1, the Fire Burglary Model 546 Keypad Connections, and note the following jumper connections which are imperative for our system to function properly. First, note the brown and green wires, these apply to the operation of the buzzer. Jumper J1 must be placed in the "B" position and the green wire goes to terminal 7 on our 37 pin connector. This makes the buzzer sound when voltage is applied.

There are also normally open (N.O.) and normally closed (N.C.) contacts on the keypad. We use the normally open contacts. This affords the ability for continuously closed contacts on one activation and open on the second activation, or it can be set up for a timed momentary operation. Our system specifically required this second function which is selected by jumper J2 being placed in the "A" position. This allows the relay contacts to pull in for a period of time which is selectable by the trimmer PC pot denoted as R7 on the keypad. Adjust the trimmer PC pot R7 for at least a two second delay time. It can be longer.

Wiring this keypad to the Perimiguard System is easy. You should wire ground (the WHITE/ORANGE keypad wire) to one of the numerous ground terminals on the power supply/buffer board's 37 pin terminal, preferably terminal 16. The +12 Vdc input power (WHITE/YELLOW) on the keypad, should be connected to terminal 17, as should the WHITE/RED red LED (+) wire from the keypad. The GREEN buzzer wire goes to terminal 7. The ORANGE relay common contact wire should go to terminal 30, the keypad ground terminal. The RED keypad wire for the N.O. contacts gets connected to the KEYPAD loop terminal 29. The BROWN buzzer and the YELLOW N.C. contacts wires from the keypad are not used. The red LED (−) WHITE wire goes to terminal 4, and the WHITE/BROWN wire goes to terminal 3. The WHITE/GREEN and WHITE/BLUE wires for the panic and tamper loops go to terminals 22 and 23 respectively.

Door and Window Switches

Door and window switches can be any

Table 5-1. Fire Burglary Model 546 Keypad Connections.

WIRE COLOR	FUNCTION	CONTROLLER CONNECTION
BROWN	BUZZER INPUT GROUND=BUZZ	NOT USED
GREEN	BUZZER INPUT +12V BUZZ	BUZZER OUT TERMINAL 7
RED	N.O. CONTACTS	KEY PAD TERMINAL 29
ORANGE	COMMON CONTACTS	KEYPAD GROUND TERMINAL 30
YELLOW	N.C. CONTACTS	NOT USED
WHITE	RED LED (−)	RED LED TERMINAL 4
BLACK	RED LED (+)	+12V TERMINAL 17
WHITE/BROWN	GREEN LED (−)	GREEN LED TERMINAL 3
WHITE/RED	RED LED (+)	+12V TERMINAL 17
WHITE/ORANGE	GROUND	GROUND TERMINAL 16
WHITE/YELLOW	INPUT VOLTAGE	+12V TERMINAL 17
WHITE/GREEN	N.O. CONTACTS FOR TAMPER & PANIC	PANIC TERMINAL 23
WHITE/BLUE	N.O. CONTACTS FOR TAMPER & PANIC	PANIC GROUND TERMINAL 22

JUMPERS INSIDE KEYPAD	JUMPERS POSITION
BUZZER J1	B
RELAY MOMENTARY J2	A

Fig. 5-6. AMSECO model H5-011 Electronic Siren.

switch with magnetically operated normally closed (N.C.) contacts. There are several switches that will work. Radio Shack sells mini-magnetic switches that come in a package with a switch and a magnet (part number 49-497). They can be bolted on or fastened with a self-sticking adhensive applied to their backs. The cost of this switch is approximately $4.

Another useful type of switch available from Mountain West Security is the M18-005 closed circuit type switch for $4.25. This bolt on type of switch and magnet has screw terminals appropriate for holding wires. Another switch from Mountain West is part no. M3-002, a closed contact magnet switch for $5.50. The switch that we used on the crucial delayed entry door was the S5-032 miniature 3/8 inch flush flange mountable switch that will withstand up to a one-half inch gap and still properly function. These are more expensive, approximately $16.50, and are available from Mountain West.

A caution, though, is in order with respect to magnetic switches. Some of the newer doors are steel doors, and in order for them to be better insulated and more thermally efficient, they sometimes have magnetic perimeter seals such as are found around refrigerator doors. Therefore, mount any magnetic switches well to the inside of the door away from the magnetic seal. Otherwise they may not activate properly.

Alarm Devices

Many alarm devices are useful in these applications. We recommend a device that will

Fig. 5-7. AMSECO model A11-031 Inside Firehorn.

This is an adequate volume. The horn is pictured in Fig. 5-6. This high-intensity warning sounds in either warbling (common for burglar alarms), or European-type high/low. The siren is a completely self-contained weatherproof unit made from tough ABS plastic. This unit comes with an outdoor, tamper-proof steel box, as an option.

The internal fire alarm horn should be a device such as a buzzer that is distinctly different in sound from the outside burglar alarm horn which warbles or has pulsating sound blasts. The buzzer recommended is the AMSECO buzzer available again from Mountain West, part # A11-031. This +12 Vdc device draws 500 mA when in operation. It is shown in Fig. 5-7. This unit may be used on ac or 6 or 12 Vdc with the unit drawing 600 mA at 12 V. There are dual horns within the unit for added reliability.

Smoke and Fire Detectors

The requirements here are for a +12 Vdc unit with normally closed (N.C.) contacts. One of the best, most reliable units is the photoelectric heat and smoke detector available from Mountain West for $109 (part number F1-005).

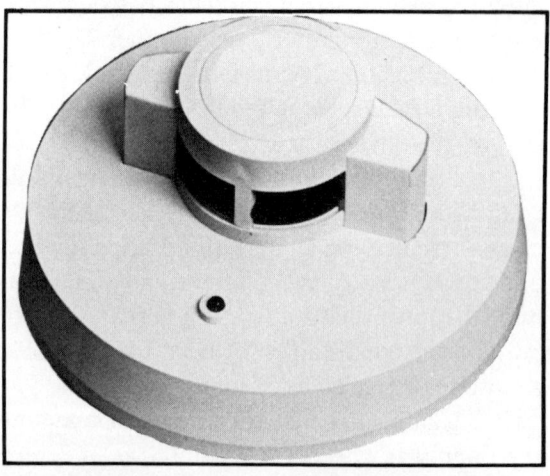

Fig. 5-8. A Sentinel model F1-005 Smoke and Fire Detector.

operate from a +12 Vdc source and draw less than one ampere of current. This current requirement is out of a regard for battery operation when the main power to the house is interrupted.

Of the variety of devices typically available, there are sirens, bells, and horns. The horn is what we used in the form of a *"warbler"* which is a tone that is modulated by another frequency to give an effect of almost multiple sound sources within one source. The unit we chose is available from Mountain West for $25 and has a part number of H5-001. It operates from 6 to 12 Vdc and draws 750 mA at 12 Vdc while producing a 110 dBm sound level at 10 feet.

It is shown in Fig. 5-8. Smoke particles entering the detector reflect light from a constant light source into a photoelectric detector. The alarm signal activates when 1.5% per foot obscuration occurs. Rate-compensation features detect fast-burning fires from flammable liquids or plastics that generate black smoke. A smoke increase within the detection chamber exceeding rates of 0.5 to 1% per foot increases detector sensitivity by 5 to 1, thus permitting early alarm. Each detector has one set of SPDT contacts for annunciation, door release, etc. All are rated 2 A @ 125 Vac. Model No. F1-030 is an end of line relay assembly that will alarm in event of detector power failure.

Preset temperature switches would also work, as long as they are the normally closed type that open when their threshold temperature is reached or exceeded. If the fire and smoke detection function is not desired, you may jumper a wire across these contacts and use it as a straight burglar alarm.

Software

First, the 2716 EPROM used with this and the other microprocessor controlled projects contains all of the programs, eliminating the need for separate EPROM's for each project. Therefore, if you buy one EPROM from Specialty Electronic Services, Inc., you can use it on all three projects. You can, of course, program your own EPROM from the program listing with an EPROM programmer.

This multiple use innovation is possible due to two unused or uncommitted output ports of the eight B ports, these are PB4 and PB7 as you will note in the program listing soon to follow. This allows the hardware to have either logic highs, lows, or combinations thereof constituting four possibilities. When an 8-bit word is formed by two of these bits, it allows four different words or places in memory for the program to vector or jump to upon system initialization. Each address corresponds to one of four different programs, all contained within the same EPROM, a money saving approach, plus a convenient one!

Refer to the EPROM listing in Appendix B to enhance your understanding of this program as it is discussed. The software documentation begins with a definition of each of the 14 used ports of the 16 possible ports (8 for port B and 8 for port A). Starting with PA0, this is the normally closed (N.C.) loop, PA1 is the perimeter loop associated with the panic switch, PA2 is the interior loop which would correspond to the microwave motion detector in hardware devices, and this bit would be the one to be disabled when you were moving about the house while at home. Port PA3 is the normally open (N.O.) loop bit, and PA4 is the delayed entry bit. Ports PA5, PA6, and PA7 are for the keypad switch contacts, the remote disable bit and the fire and smoke detectors respectively.

Directly below PA7 in the listing are ports PB4 and PB7. These are the two software switching bits just mentioned.

Note on the B ports, (they are all outputs by definition), that PB0 is the red LED used to signify that the system is armed. Port PB1 is the green LED signifying everything is OK when lit. Port PB2 is an optional LED whose present function is reserved for software expansion on future projects. Port PB3 is the ALARM SIREN bit and, as previously stated, PB4 and PB7 are software switching bits. Port PB5 is the fire alarm bit and port BP6 is the keypad warning buzzer.

This is followed in the listing by definitions of the places in memory corresponding to the 6532 RIOT's (*RAM-I/O T*imer) timer functions. Next, temporary memory storage positions are defined, beginning at 0080 in hex. Incidentally, as is customary with the 6502 and 6800 assembly instructions, a dollar sign ($) denotes a hexadecimal number.

The program begins at 0800 (F800-8800 offset=0800) in hex. The first thing it does is to disable the interrupts, followed by a clear decimal mode instruction that puts the instructions in the binary mode. The next software function to occur is an intentionally inserted delay so that all of the devices can be reset since not all devices reset at equal time intervals. Typically, the 6502 microprocessor resets first, followed by the ports within the I/O chip.

The stack pointer is initialized to FF in hex which is the top of the stack in RAM used by the 6532. The next occurrence is the setting of all the A ports as inputs, and the B ports are configured as outputs with the exception of PB4 and PB7, the software switching bits. Next, these two software switching bits (PB4 and PB7) are read, and depending upon their state, the program branches accordingly.

Since the majority of the software is for the delayed entry alarm application and the other projects are merely subsets of this main program, the following discussion is therefore predominately concerned with this program. The delayed entry alarm is symbolically represented by DLYALR in the listing, and the program begins at F8B4. The first functions performed are the setting up of the ports, the flags, and then checks are made on the status of the keypad contacts. Upon powering up, sometimes these contacts are closed so another loop is purposely inserted here providing the keypad with sufficient time for the contacts to open.

Once the keypad contacts are open, the program sets initial values, sets the alarm flag to the no alarm status, initializes the software flip-flop, and then goes into a loop mode where it constantly checks the status of the loops, First the program checks the normally closed (N.C.) perimeter loop. Then it checks the normally open (N.O.) interior loop, followed by the panic loop. Next it checks the N.C. inside loop, the delayed entry loop, and then the keypad contacts. Next it checks for the remote disarming function, and then the fire/smoke alarm. If it finds a *remote disable* it immediately branches and disarms the alarm that is set. If it finds the fire/smoke alarm set, then it activates the fire/smoke alarm. Flags are set with respect to each of these previously mentioned loops, and if none are set off, it then checks the software flip-flop corresponding to the activation of the alarm. If everything is normal and no alarm is to be set off, flag status is then checked again, and here, if everything is again in a proper state, the green LED will be lit. As previously stated, this green LED is a status OK visual indicator.

The routine called SETLED determines which LEDs are turned on or off. If the alarm is activated and all the loops are configured properly or are in their correct states the red LED will be on in a steady nonflashing manner. If all of the loops are in the proper state and the alarm is not activated the green LED is on. If there is a problem with one or more of the loops and the alarm is not activated then both LEDs will be off.

If everything is OK with respect to the loops after this check, the program then jumps to the beginning of the loop called CHECK. If the alarm has been activated for the check mode it then checks the flags again, sets the LED and then goes to the routine called GOOD FL. A 30 second delay is entered in which the red LED is blinking at a 1 Hz rate. The warning buzzer is also buzzing; however, this occurs as two distinctively alternate states so the LED is never flashing when the buzzer is buzzing, and vice-versa. At the end of this 30 second period, the burglar alarm is armed. You must therefore exit before this 30 second period or the burglar alarm will go off. If you have exited within this time the red LED will come on and will jump back to the loop and continue checking the loops.

If smoke or a fire has been detected, the program branches to a routine called SMOKEA and this activates the fire horn for five minutes. After this period, another check of the fire/smoke sensor status is made. If at the end of this five minutes the loop is OK, the system then rearms and proceeds with the further execution of the program. If, however, at the end of this five minute period, the fire/smoke detector is still active the five minute period of the fire horn being on will recycle itself and remain on until one of the two following conditions are met. These are: 1) the proper code is entered into the keypad or 2) the fire/smoke detectors have been reset and this state occurs at the end of the five minute period when a check is made again for the occurrence of the correct keypad code entry.

The subroutine labeled REDIS is a remote disarm subroutine. It checks the remote loop and if this loop requests a disarm then the system is disarmed and it goes into a normal idle state with the green LED on. If it is not a remote, it then checks to see if it is a delayed entry activation. If it is a delayed entry, it branches to a subroutine called DELENT, and this goes into the 30 second loop again with the alternate 1 Hz flashing of the red LED and the warning buzzer. If at the end of this 30 second period you have not entered the proper code into the keypad, the system's alarm is activated in the form of the outside alarm horn sounding. If the correct code has not been entered this horn remains activated for five minutes by jumping to a routine called SETALR. This SETALR subroutine checks for a five minute timeout or the correct code entered at the keypad.

The check flag subroutine, CHKFLG, checks each of the flags. There is a storage place called FLAGS and this reflects the status of each flag in the form of a set or reset bit and this set of status bits is circulated on a bit-by-bit basis by being rotated to the right through the accumulator. The normal status is to have all bits cleared (logic zeros), if a bit is set (a logic one) then that represents an abnormal condition and must be attended to immediately. If at the end of the CHKFLG subroutine there is one flag that is not correct, there will be a *carry set*. This is followed by separate subroutines to check each loop. Examples of each follow and are explained in detail.

The CHKNCL is the subroutine that checks the normally closed loop, this is the perimeter loop. This subroutine loads into the 6502 microprocessor's accumulator the status of the A port bits, and then it masks off all bits except the one for the normally closed (N.C.) loop and checks to see if there is a logic one or zero in that place. If the loop is OK, then a zero is placed in that spot. Conversely, if the loop is opened at some place, a logic one is then set in that position. So essentially what you are doing when you check a loop is to set bits in the flag position. The same procedure is gone through with the normally open (N.O.) loop. The PANIC LOOP is the same, and if a bit is set corresponding to the PANIC LOOP, the alarm is then activated whether or not it was previously armed. The alarm is set by clearing the stack pointer and immediately jumping to the subroutine called SETALR. The inside N.C. loop and the delayed entry loop have the same sequence of events with their respective flags being set.

The keypad contacts are checked in a similar manner, and if the microprocessor discovers that a keypad contact is closed, it goes into a short delay and checks it again until they open. Then it resets the software flip-flop called ALARFF, for alarm flip-flop. It is this flip-flop that is checked by other subroutines within the system.

The SETLED routine loads the temporary storage register for the flags and checks each loop to see if it is in the correct state. If they are all in the correct state, it checks the alarm flip-flop. If the alarm flip-flop is not set, the program branches to turn on the green LED. If there is a problem with one of the loops mentioned earlier, both the green and red LEDs are off. If the alarm flip-flop is set and all of the loops are in their proper states, then the red LED is on. The CHKSMO routine checks the fire/smoke detector. The CHKREM checks the remote disarming stations and manipulates the corresponding flag bit accordingly.

The subroutine called SIREON is the portion of the program responsible for turning on the outside siren or horn. Conversely, the subroutine entitled SIROFF turns the siren or horn off. The subroutine called SMOKON turns on the inside fire/smoke alarm horn. And like its counterpart subroutines, the subroutine appropriately entitled SMOKOF, turns off the inside fire/smoke horn. The routine to check the five minute time out on alarm is a nest of delay subroutines based on the one millisecond delay loop. This is called DYLIMS for one millisecond delay loop. This establishes a number to be loaded into a divider that goes through eight clock cycles. The other delay subroutine DLY1SC is for a one second delay. This counter subroutine actually counts the one millisecond delay 250 times for a total period of 250 milliseconds or 1/4 second. This is done for a total of four times which equals one second. The five minute delay is derived in a similar manner by the DLY30S subroutine which counts 30 one second intervals. Likewise, these 30 second periods are counted five times for a 150 second total. This 150 second total is futhermore counted twice for 300 seconds which equates to exactly five minutes, the basis of our five minute timeout interval.

The procedure of nesting subroutines is analogous to parentheses in mathematics in that the operation in the innermost set of parentheses is performed first and the operations performed in sequence from there progressively move to the outside from this innermost initial operation. Likewise, in programming, the innermost nested routine is done first and subsequent functions proceed outward but are all based on or derived from this innermost operation of a 1 millisecond loop in our application here.

At the end of these software timers it goes back to checking the loop again. The next subroutine is the CHANGE function which changes the state of the alarm software flip-flops from the outside alarm driving state back off and vice-versa as any flip-flop does as it toggles from one of its two states back to the opposite state.

The software listing concludes with an alphabetized symbol table of four columns with 37 listings of symbols per column.

Installation/Checkout

The following discussion examines the installation/checkout procedure of the power supply/buffer/battery backup board which is responsible for supplying uninterrupted power to the system and for directly driving the alarms, horns, and keypad.

Note. On the initial checkout of this PC board, the microcomputer/controller and the battery both should not be connected.

First, install all of the parts as shown on the component placement drawing, in Fig. 5-9. Carefully observe polarities of diodes and

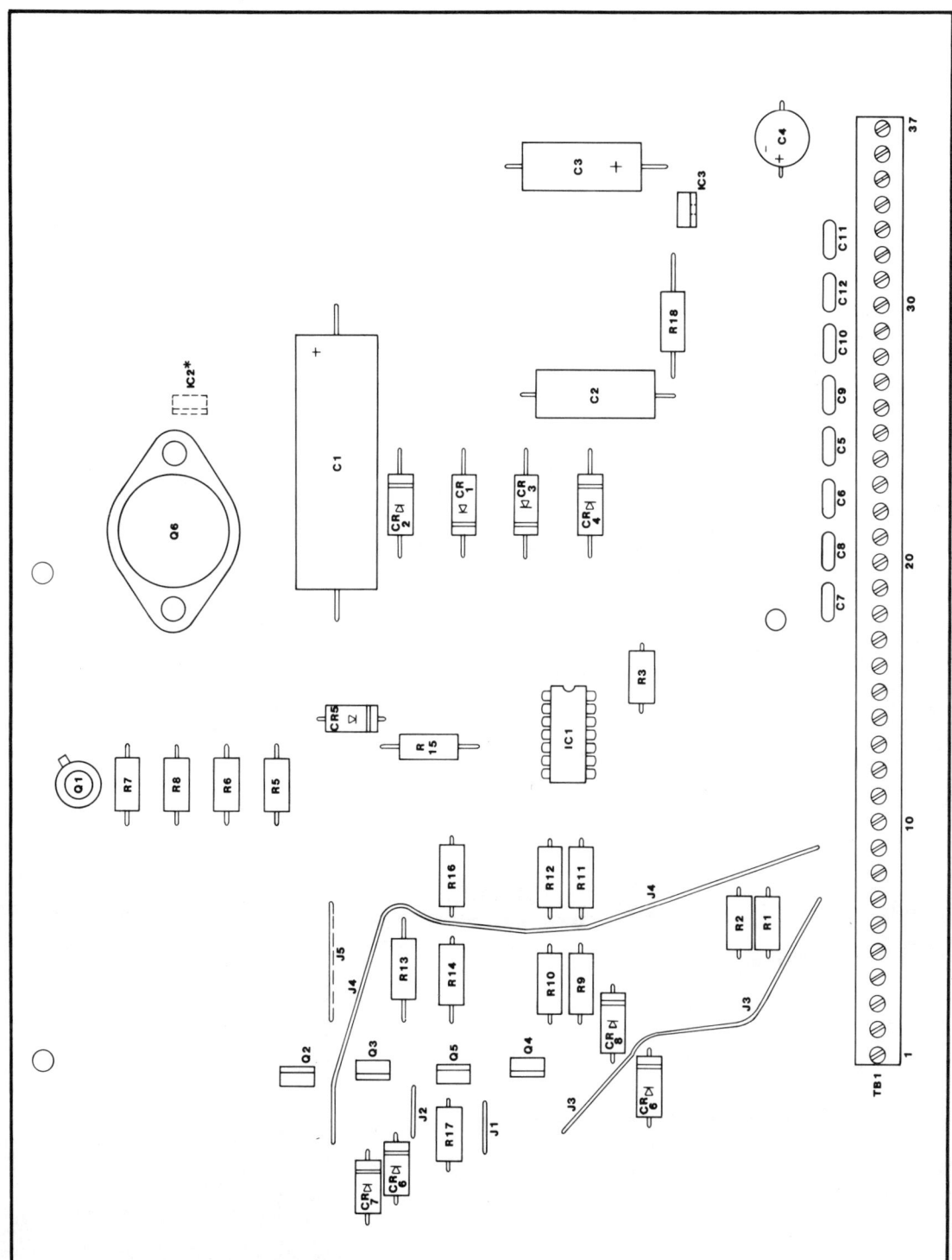

Fig. 5-9. A component placement drawing for the power supply/buffer board with delayed entry.

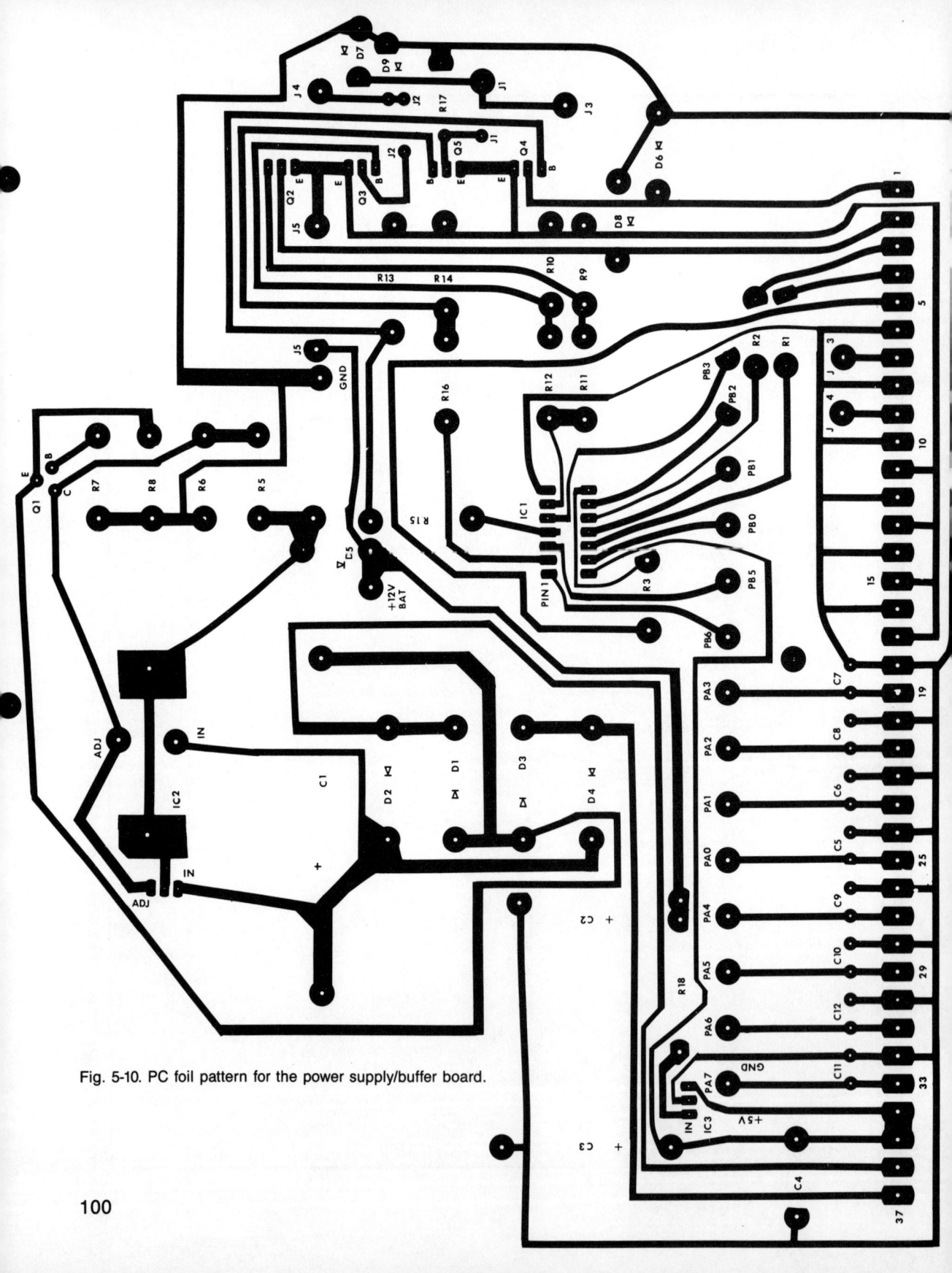

Fig. 5-10. PC foil pattern for the power supply/buffer board.

Table 5-2. List of Jumper Pins to Bridge in System Checkout of Perimiguard with Delayed Entry.

Function	Pin No.	Condition Checked
N.C. Loop	25	Jumpered
Panic	23	Open
N.C. Loop	21	Jumpered
N.O. Loop	19	Open
Delayed Loop	27	Jumpered
Keypad	29	Jumpered Momentarily
Remote Arm/Disarm	31	Jumpered
Smoke/Fire Detector	33	Jumpered

capacitors and the proper orientation of ICs, voltage regulators, and the four Darlington pair transistors in the TO-220 plastic tab case. Figure 5-10 is a 1:1 foil positive for the PC board.

Next, apply the 12 Vac to terminals 36 and 37 (refer to Fig. 5-2). Measure the voltage across filter capacitor C1 after applying the ac. It should be approximately 16 to 20 volts dc with an element of ripple in it. Next, check the system's +12 Vdc voltage without the battery attached. It should be in the 12 to 13 Vdc range. This verifies the operation of the 12 volt voltage regulator, IC2. If, however, you do not have this voltage at that point, check all solder joints and the values of R5, R6, and R8 to be certain these are the correct values. Further, check Q1, IC2, and D5 for polarity. These could have been installed backwards.

Assuming that the +12 Vdc does exist, the next item to check is the +5 Vdc that should appear across capacitors C3 and/or C4. The voltage here should be +5 Vdc $\pm 1/4$ Vdc. Again, assuming this second voltage regulator, IC1, is functioning properly, the next item to check is pin 14 of IC1 to ensure that +5 Vdc exist at this point and that a ground exists at pin 7.

If everything has checked out satisfactorily to this point, disconnect the 12 Vac source and connect the battery and microcomputer/controller board. Reapply the 12 Vac source and again measure the two voltages for +12 and +5 Vdc respectively. The +12 Vdc should appear at the battery's positive (+) terminal unless it has been drastically discharged, in which case, upon being fully recharged it will again attain a +12 Vdc, or even slightly higher, reading.

The next step is to check the microcomputer/controller board in conjunction with this power supply/buffer/battery backup board. The microcomputer/controller board itself was checked out in Chapter 4. The checkout of the microcomputer/controlled board is accomplished with jumpers installed in place of the actual loops which are naturally made up of the door and window switches, etc., that detect open circuit conditions of opened switch contacts at these possible points of entry within your home or secured dwelling.

The green and red LED's (light emitting diodes) can be hooked up by connecting +12 Vdc to pins 34 and 35. These serve as valuable visible indicators during the following checkout procedures. Additionally, once again short with jumper wires between the N.C. (normally closed) loop and ground, between the N.C. (normally closed) inside loop and ground, and between the delayed entry loop and ground as well as between the REMOTE loop and FIRE/SMOKE detector loops and ground. Refer to Table 5-2 for a systematic listing of pins to bridge with jumper wires to ground. On power up, the green LED should be on in a steady nonflashing manner. To determine if the microprocessor is functioning properly, momentarily short between the keypad connections and ground. The sequence of the green LED being on and then going off followed by the red LED blinking should be observed. Next, momentarily short the keypad connection to ground and you should observe that the red formerly blinking LED is now off and that the green LED is now on in a steady nonflashing manner. This concludes the checkout of the microcomputer/controller board.

Next, hook up and/or install the various loops and sirens or warning devices. After this, check again to make certain that the green LED is on. Now key into the keypad the proper code which you've already installed into the keypad by now, and observe the red LED blinking with the accompanying green LED going off. The warning buzzer, assuming you have one, should sound, and after 30 seconds the red LED is on in a steady nonflashing display mode and this indicates that the system is armed.

To check to see if the system is indeed armed, open any switch (except the delayed entry switch) and the horn, siren, etc. (alarm) will sound. The alarm can be disabled by again keying in the proper four-digit code into the keypad. If everything functioned properly up to this point, then the entire system is working properly. If, however, the siren or alarm fails to activate then check either Q1 or Q2, or if the inside horn fails to activate check Q4. If the buzzer fails to function, check Q5 and R17.

If the green LED fails to go on check all of your jumpers to ensure that you have unbroken continuity within this loop. If after this check the siren fails to activate, check three of the B ports with a voltmeter. These are: 1) PB3, the alarm loop, which should go low 2) PB6, the buzzer driver which should go alternately high and then low in an approximately 50 percent duty cycle fashion and 3) PB5, the fire/smoke alarm buzzer, which should also go low.

This concludes the checkout of these two systems. If neither has completely checked out up to this point, then an oscilloscope will have to be used along with Tables 4-5 and 5-3. They are troubleshooting tables for the microprocessor and power supply/buffer/battery backup boards respectively.

Final Assembly

Note on the foil pattern for the battery backup/power supply/buffer board (Fig. 5-10) that the board is single sided with a few jumpers in spots where the layout could not be totally accomplished on just one side. Also note in the lower left corner the DE 1.1. This stands for "delayed entry". Version 1.1. On the board for the next project, there is a SA in the lower left corner that stands for "simple alarm". Both of these larger boards are identical in size and the smaller microcomputer/controller board fits piggyback onto either of these boards. Refer to Fig. 5-11 for an illustration of this placement. The smaller simpler microcomputer/controller board has its dimensions outlined in Fig. 5-12. Both boards fit into the metal box shown in Fig. 5-13. This box has to be modified with a hinge and a bracket. Both the modifications and the drilling dimensions of these mechanical fasteners and the metal box itself are shown in Fig. 5-14. After the project is complete, Fig. 5-15 shows how it was actually mounted in the box. The photo in Fig. 5-4 may also be helpful. Note the "piggyback" arrangement and the hinged swing out feature that lends ease to its serviceability.

Also, when mounting components onto either version of the larger power supply/buffer board, note that it has been laid out to ac-

Table 5-3. Troubleshooting Chart for the Delayed Entry System.

TEST STEP	IF PROBLEM IS FOUND, THEN CHECK
1. Measure voltage between terminal board terminals 36 and 37. If 12VAC, go to step 2.	Check for blown fuse on 12V transformer. Check 110VAC input to transformer. Check wiring from transformer to terminal board.
2. Measure voltage across capacitor C1. If between 16VDC and 20VDC, go to step 3.	Check for defective or improperly installed D1, D2, D3, D4, or C1. Check for bad solder joints at these components.
3. Measure voltage between anode of D5 and ground. If it reads between 12 VDC and 13.5VDC, go to step 4.	Check for defective or improperly installed Q6, Q1, or D5. Check for proper values of R5, R6, R7, and R8. Check for bad solder joints at these components.
4. Measure voltage between terminals 34 and 32. If 5VDC, go to step 5.	Check for defective or improperly installed IC3, C3 or C4. Check for open or wrong value R18. Check for bad solder joints at these components.
5. Measure voltage between terminals 2 and 6. If 0VDC go to step 6.	Check for shorted or improperly installed Q2. Check for defective or improperly installed IC1.
6. With voltmeter connected as in step 5, connect a jumper between PB3 and terminal 8. If 12VDC go to step 7.	Check for open or improperly installed Q2. Check for defective or improperly installed IC1. Check for proper values of R9 and R11. Check solder joints.
7. Remove jumper, connect voltmeter between terminals 9 and 6. If 0VDC go to step 8.	Check for shorted or improperly installed Q3.
8. With voltmeter connected as in step 7, connect a jumper between PB3 and terminal 8. If 12VDC go to step 9.	Check for open or improperly installed Q3. Check for proper values of R10 and R12. Check solder joints.
9. Connect voltmeter between terminals 1 and 6. If 0VDC go to step 10.	Check for shorted or improperly installed Q4.
10. With voltmeter connected as in step 9, connect a jumper from PB5 to terminal 8. If 12VDC, go to step 11.	Check for open or improperly installed Q4. Check for proper value R13 and R15. Check solder joints.
11. Connect voltmeter between terminals 7 and 6. If 0VDC go to step 12.	Check for shorted or improperly installed Q5.
12. With voltmeter connected as in step 11, connect a jumper from PB6 to terminal 8. If 12VDC go to step 13.	Check for open or improperly installed Q5. Check for proper values of R14 and R16. Check solder joints.
13. this completes checkout.	

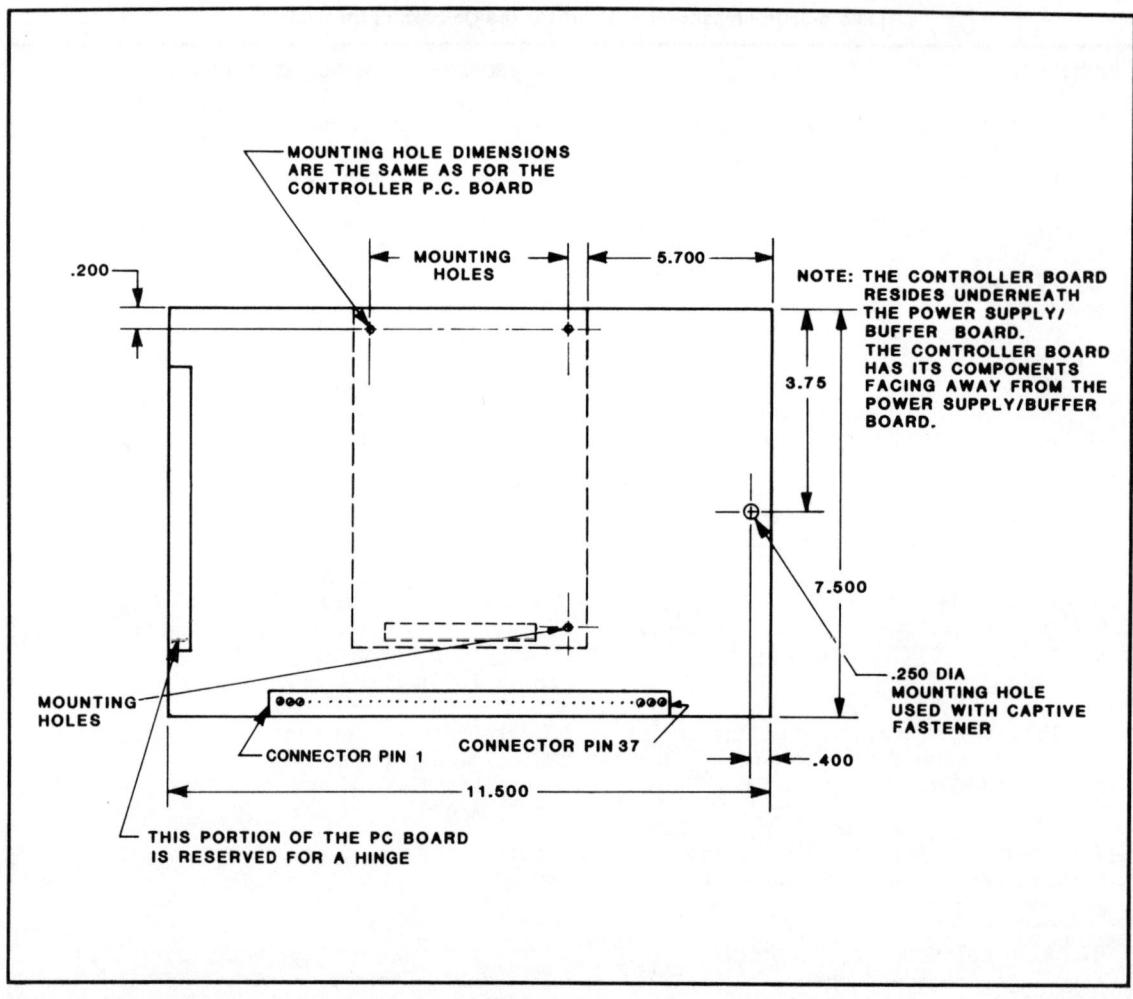

Fig. 5-11. The small microcomputer board fits underneath the larger power supply buffer board. Both are then placed into the steel cabinet that also holds the backup batteries.

commodate either a steel TO-3 type metallic case voltage regulator or a tab TO-220 type voltage regulator. Either will deliver the rated current to the load with approximately a 50 percent reserve in power capacity; however, the TO-220 packaged semiconductor will do so for about $2 versus the nearly $6 cost of the heavier cased steel voltage regulator. This was already mentioned in a small note adjacent to the schematic in the parts list for this project, but is again repeated here in case you might have missed it.

PERIMIGUARD WITHOUT DELAYED ENTRY

The Perimiguard Security System without the delayed-entry feature was purposely conceived and designed to be a less expensive, simpler, and less comprehensive security system than its more sophisticated big brother when has the delayed-entry feature. If you plan to build this simpler version, you will still want to read and understand the material for the more sophisticated model. Since most of the functions and construction details between

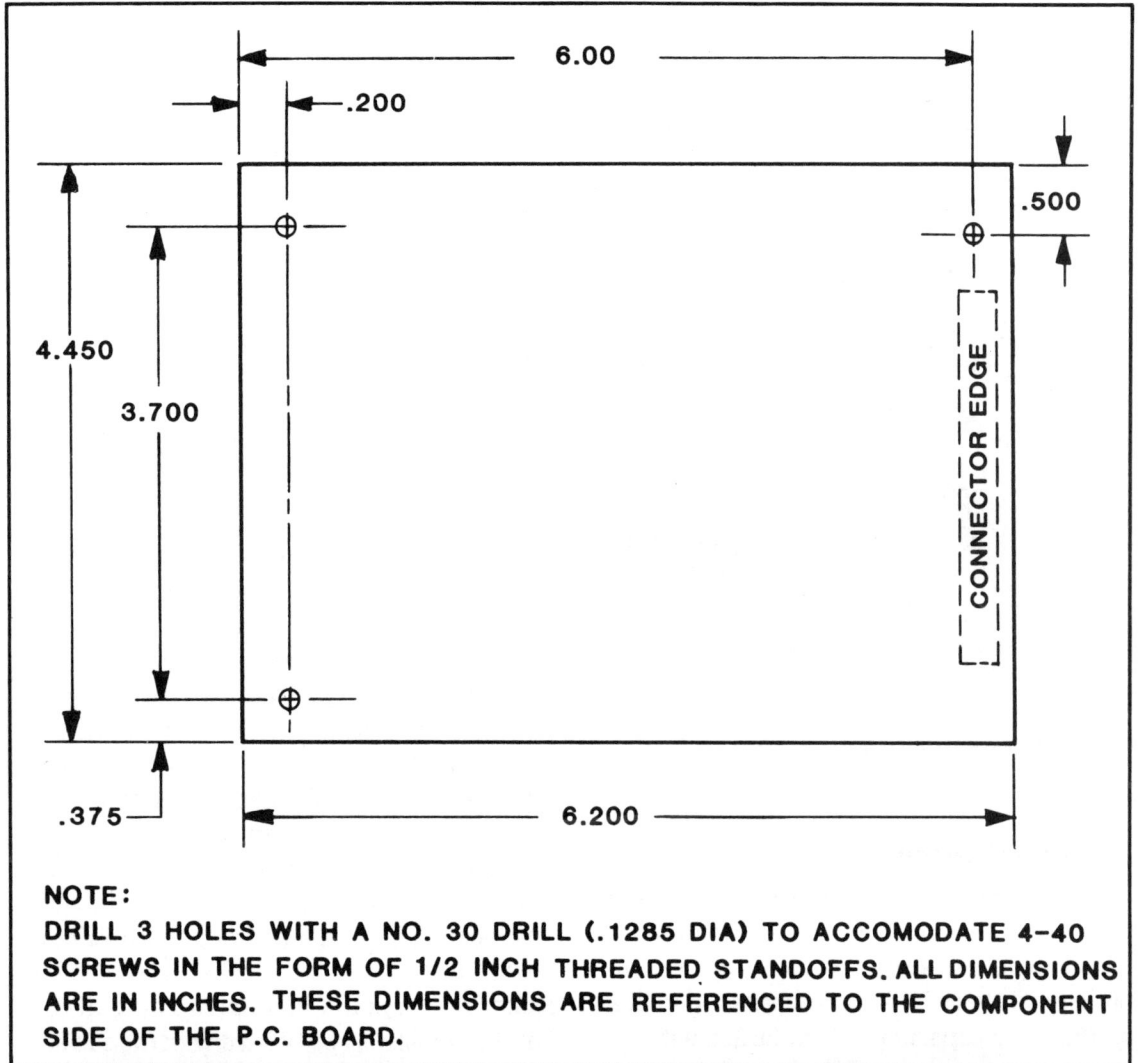

Fig. 5-12. The dimensions and placement of the mounting holes on the microcomputer/controller board.

these two units are identical, they are only explained once in the Perimiguard with delayed entry section.

Functionally, the microcomputer/controller board used with this system is the same as the one used with the delayed entry feature; however, the power supply/driver/battery backup PC board is not the same. This PC board has a little less drive circuitry. It uses fewer Darlington drivers, but other than that, it is a nearly identical board. Refer to Fig. 5-16 for a schematic of the Perimiguard system without the delayed entry feature. A component placement drawing is given in Fig. 5-17, and a PC foil pattern of this simpler security system is shown in Fig. 5-18. Note the SA 1.0 in the lower left corner. The SA stands for "simple alarm."

This system has two loops, a normally open one (N.O.) and a normally closed one (N.C.) plus

Fig. 5-13. Frankell model E2-012 Instrument Box. They come ready to mount instruments or batteries and knockouts permit easy wiring.

one siren driver for an outside horn such as was used in the delayed-entry Perimiguard system.

Circuit Differences

There are only 22 connector pins instead of 37 and only one PNP Darlington driver on this simpler security system's power supply/driver/battery backup PC board. Additionally, the filter capacitor, C1, is larger with this simpler security system in the event that the battery backup feature is not used. It is optional. The battery backup system can be thought of as an "energy reservoir" and as such provides a filtering or smoothing action to compensate for sudden demands in current by the system. If you elect not to employ this battery backup feature its effect or absence will have to be likewise compensated for by use of a larger filter capacitor. Note in the parts list within the schematic diagram (Fig. 5-16) the value of C1 and the accompanying note.

This simple Perimiguard system without delayed entry has a single ARM/DISARM key which is an off/on keyswitch and not a momentary contact type keypad switch. It affords you the opportunity to turn on the system, remove the key, and walk away knowing that the system has been armed. This feature, is identical to the Electronic Entry-Detection System described in Chapter 3. The Perimiguard is much more comprehensive than this totally hardware designed system, of course. Actually, this on-off keyswitch may have the key removed from it in either state. Both of the key switches shown in Fig. 5-19 will provide this function. They are available from Mountain West.

The Chicago Lock, Model C1-004 SPST (Single Pole Single Throw) Round Key Lock, features a pick resistant 7-pin tumbler mechanism. This type of lock comes in either SPST for (on/off) applications or SPDT switches for central station supervision. Both come with solder terminals and are specified as keyed alike (KA) or keyed differently (KD) with these designators as part of their part numbers. They are rated at 120 Vac at 2 A or 28 Vdc at 7 A.

The Medeco Model Ml5-003 is a SPDT key lock. This company produces some of the most tamper resistant locks known. These locks have keys that not only require lift pins but they must also be twisted with the exclusive angled crosscuts on the keys. The on/off model has keys removable in two positions (used for shunt locks or on/off applications). The threaded sleeve accommodates a 7/8" hole and trim washers are available. Medeco keys are exclusive and available nowhere else in the world, thus ensuring greater security.

Radio Shack, in its 1984 catalog, has a keyswitch with part number 49-511. You probably would want to purchase at the same time a keyplate (part number 49-524) with both red and green LEDs.

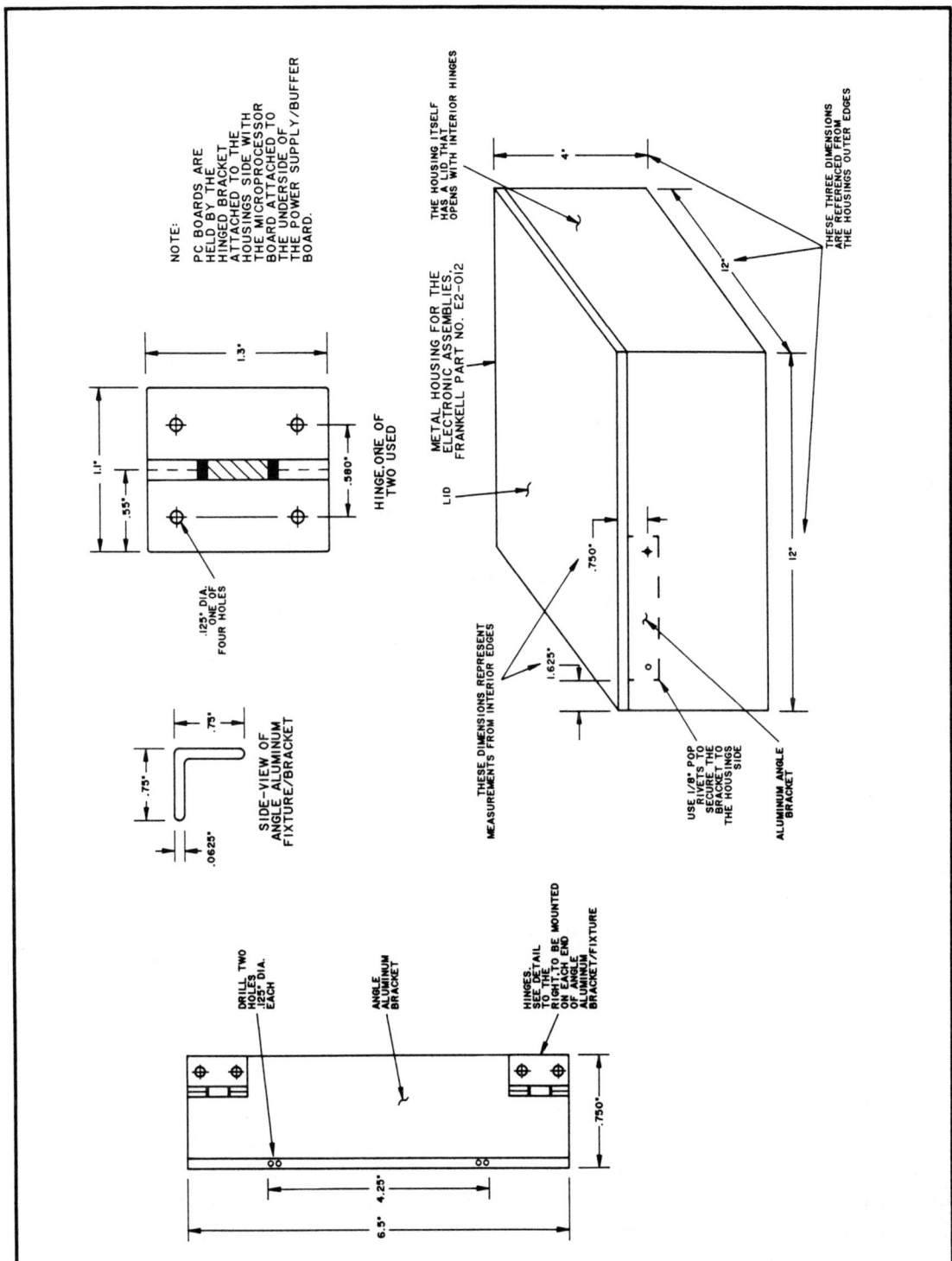

Fig. 5-14. Mechanical dimensions for the electronics housing and associated components.

Fig. 5-15. The completed project is mounted into the metal housing on hinges for ease of access in installation and maintenance.

Software

The program for the Perimiguard system without the delayed entry feature is approximately 2 1/2 pages in length. Compared to the overall program's length of 22 pages, this is admittedly rather short. This is due to two factors. The first is probably already obvious to you. This security project has less features and accordingly requires less software to accomplish these fewer functions. Secondly, and maybe less obvious to you, is that this program uses some of the previously developed software subroutines such as the ones to turn LEDs on and off as well as the detection of switch closures or their "open" status.

This security system without delayed entry feature checks the status of the two software switching bits (refer to the software description for the Perimiguard with delayed entry for an explanation of the function of these bits), PB4 and PB7. These should be high and low respectively. If they are indeed high and low then the microprocessor branches to the main program, entitled ALARM1 at address F28F. Above the ALARM 1 program is the comment "Key Switch Controlled Burglar Alarm" to let you know where the program actually begins.

The first task the program performs is to set the software flip-flop to the no alarm status. Next, the status of the N.C. (normally closed) and N.O. (normally open) loops are checked and the state of the ARM/DISARM switch is also checked. If this switch is closed, then the pro-

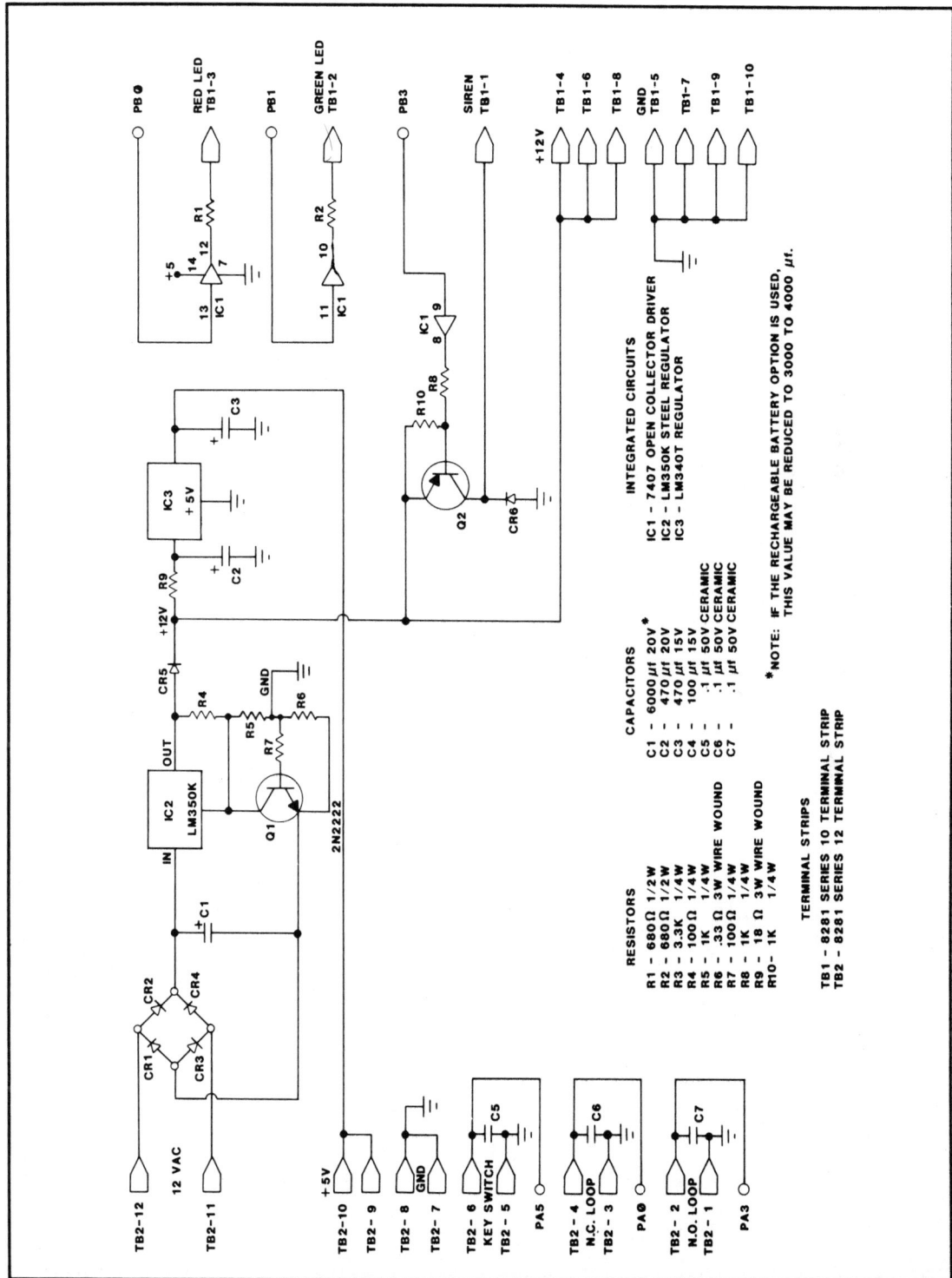

Fig. 5-16. Schematic for the power supply/buffer board for the Perimiguard without delayed entry.

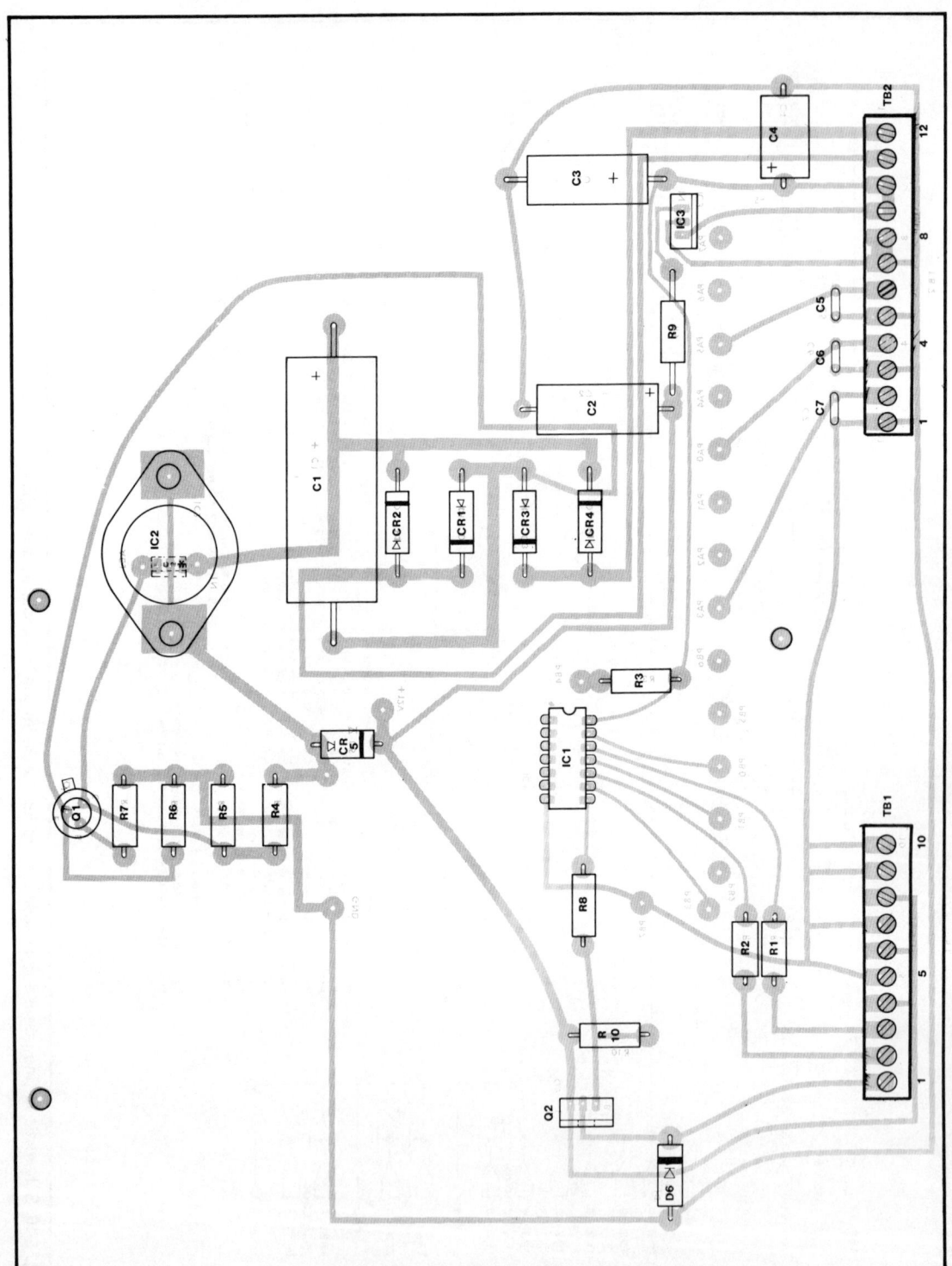

Fig. 5-17. Component placement diagram for the Perimiguard without delayed entry.

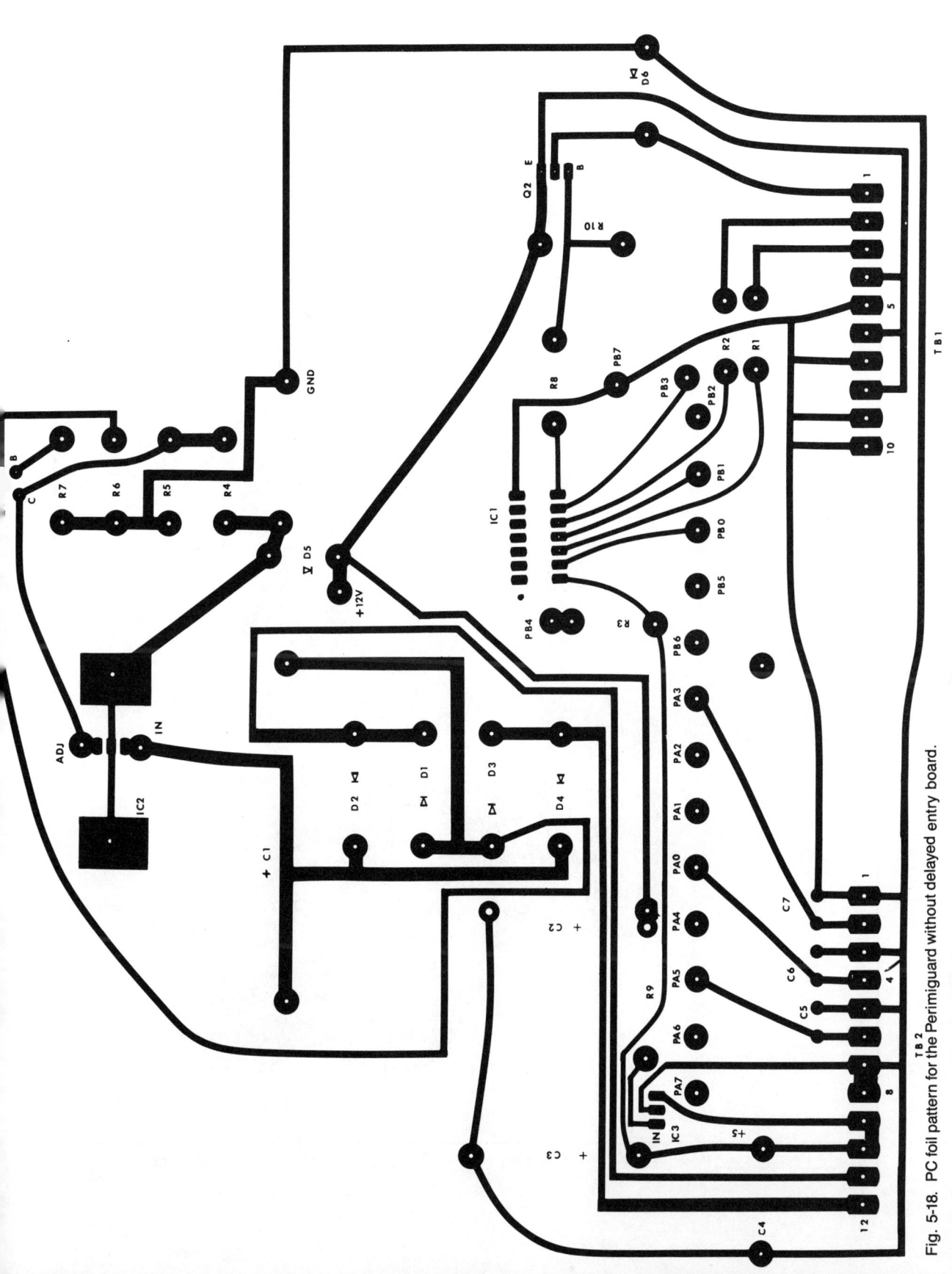

Fig. 5-18. PC foil pattern for the Perimiguard without delayed entry board.

Fig. 5-19. Chicago Lock model C1-004 SPST round key lock and Medeco model M15-003 SPDT key lock.

gram knows that the alarm should be set. If it is open, it knows that the system is to be disarmed. This is followed by a turning on of either a red or green LED, depending on the system status, and then the loop is checked over and over!

When the system is alarmed, the siren is turned on and remains activated until the system switch is turned off, if ever. There is no five minute time out period here and the system's siren or alarm will be active as long as the system is in the alarm mode.

The routine that checks the keyswitch for being either open or closed is very straightforward. It merely sets the alarm if the keyswitch is closed, and conversely if the keyswitch is open, it does not set the alarm. This portion of the program uses some of the same subroutines for turning on an LED as the delayed entry program did; however, no portion of the delayed entry program is used that involves the flashing of LEDs.

There is a NOALRM, or no alarm, routine that disarms the system when the keyswitch is again reopened. The program, as previously stated, is very straightforward and this is reflected in the system's operation. The green LED is on when the loops are all in their proper state, and then this is followed by the key being set to the on position and then removed. The red LED now comes on to indicate that the system is armed to detect any entries or disorders within the interior perimeter loop. If there is a disruption in the perimeter loop, the alarm will naturally activate. It remains on until it is turned off by the keyswitch. Again, there is no delayed feature here!

Installation/Checkout

Install all of the components according to the placement diagram in Fig. 5-17. Refer to the Installation/Checkout and Final Assembly sections for the Perimiguard with Delayed Entry project. If any troubleshooting is required use the charts in Table 4-5 and Table 5-4 as a guide. Refer to Table 5-5 for a systematic listing of pins to bridge with jumper wire to ground.

SOFTWARE LIGHT DIMMER

The Software Light dimmer combines the 4 1/2 IC computer of Chapter 4 and the Programmable Light Dimmer of Chapter 2. You may want to review the Programmable Light Dimmer project before proceeding with this project.

As mentioned in Chapter 2, the thermal noise within any semiconductor pn junction, and especially within a pn junction of a zener diode, is a totally random occurrence of varying frequencies from the audio range up to and including RF signals into the GHz region. This thermal noise is constructively used in this project. The thermal noise is bandwidth limited by the circuit in Fig. 2-23 to create random squarewaves. The frequency response of the op amp itself partially helps bandwidth limit this thermal noise. This truly random noise is amplified by a FET and then applied to an op amp comparator which amplifies and also amplitude limits by clipping the input signal. The result is a succession of squarewaves of varying frequencies, periods, and durations between occurrences. The variance in all of these parameters characterizing the resultant squarewaves is truly random. We use the term "truly random" instead of pseudorandom because the sequence never repeats itself.

The output or sequence of squarewaves that is truly random is applied to the B0 port of the 6532 RIOT and this port is read three times while masking off the other 7 bits on port B in order to generate a 3-bit random number. This resultant number is added to another random number of up to 193 to give a new random number from 1 to 200. This new number is output from all eight ports of the A-side of the 6532. These outputs are fed to the magnitude comparators on the programmable light dimmer board from the 6532 RIOT.

Software

The heart of the random light dimmer project that is controlled by software is a subroutine called RAND7 that is contained in the EPROM. This, along with TES250 and SET250, constitute a 250 millisecond or 1/4 second software timer. The unique and handy feature of this timer is that it can be tested at various intervals within the program to see if it has timed out while the rest of the program goes about performing its normal tasks.

The LIGDIM program begins at FB20. After all ports are set up, the program branches to the RAND7 subroutine which is a simple straightforward software device that generates a 3-bit random number between 0 and 7. (Note that this is done here in software while the Burglar Baffler did this in hardware with three flip-flops and an XOR gate.) In the

Table 5-4. Troubleshooting Chart for the Perimiguard System without Delayed Entry.

TEST STEP	IF PROBLEM IS FOUND, THEN CHECK
1. Measure voltage between TB2-11 and TB2-12. If it reads 12VAC, go to step 2.	Check 12VAC transformer for blown fuse. Check 110VAC input to transformer, check wiring from transformer to TB2.
2. Measure voltage across capacitor C1. If the voltage reads between 16VDC and 20VDC, go to step 3.	Check for bad rectifier D1, D2, D3, or D4. Check for bad capacitor C1. Check for bad solder joints at these components.
3. Measure voltage between anode of D5 and ground. If it reads between 12VDC and 13.5VDC go to step 4.	Check for defective regulator IC2. Check for defective Q1. Check for proper direction of D5. Check R4, R5, R6, and R7 proper value. Check for bad solder joints on any of these components.
4. Check voltage between TB2-9 and TB2-8. If it reads 5VDC, go to step 5.	Check for defective or improperly installed IC3. Check for open or wrong value R9. Check for defective or improperly installed C2 or C3. Check for bad solder joints.
5. Connect voltmeter across CR6. If the voltage is 0VDC, go to step 6.	Check for shorted or improperly installed Q2. Check for bad IC1. Check for proper value R8, R10. Check for bad solder joints.
6. With voltmeter still connected as in step 5, install a jumper between pad PB3 and TB1-5. If the voltage reads 12VDC, go to step 7.	Check for defective or improperly installed Q2 or IC1. Check for proper values of R8, R10. Check for bad solder joints.
7. This completes checkout	

Table 5-5. List of Jumper Pins to Bridge in System Checkout of Perimiguard without Delayed Entry.

Function	Pin No.	Condition Checked
N.O. Loop	TB2 - 2	Open
N.C. Loop	TB2 - 4	Jumpered
Key Switch	TB2 - 6	Jumpered when closed Open when not closed

first instance, this 3-bit random number is a value for an attack (rising) ramp. The duration of this ramp is from 1/4 to 1 3/4 seconds or from 1 to 7 times the 250 millisecond timer period. The possibility of a zero coming up randomly is taken care of by having a one automatically substituted for this zero. This means that in the normal 0 to 7 sequence, it is now a 1 to 7 sequence with 1 occurring twice to prevent a 0 from ever occurring. The one state is a "do nothing" state. Refer to Table 5-6. Therefore, a random number from 0 to 7 is generated with a resultant 1 to 7 times 250 millisecond period generated. The corresponding decay or falling ramp would be 2 seconds minus 1 1/4 seconds to 3/4 seconds long. Again, refer to Table 5-6 for a systematic listing of all of the possible combinations of random numbers with their resultant corresponding periods.

The two ramps though do not occur one

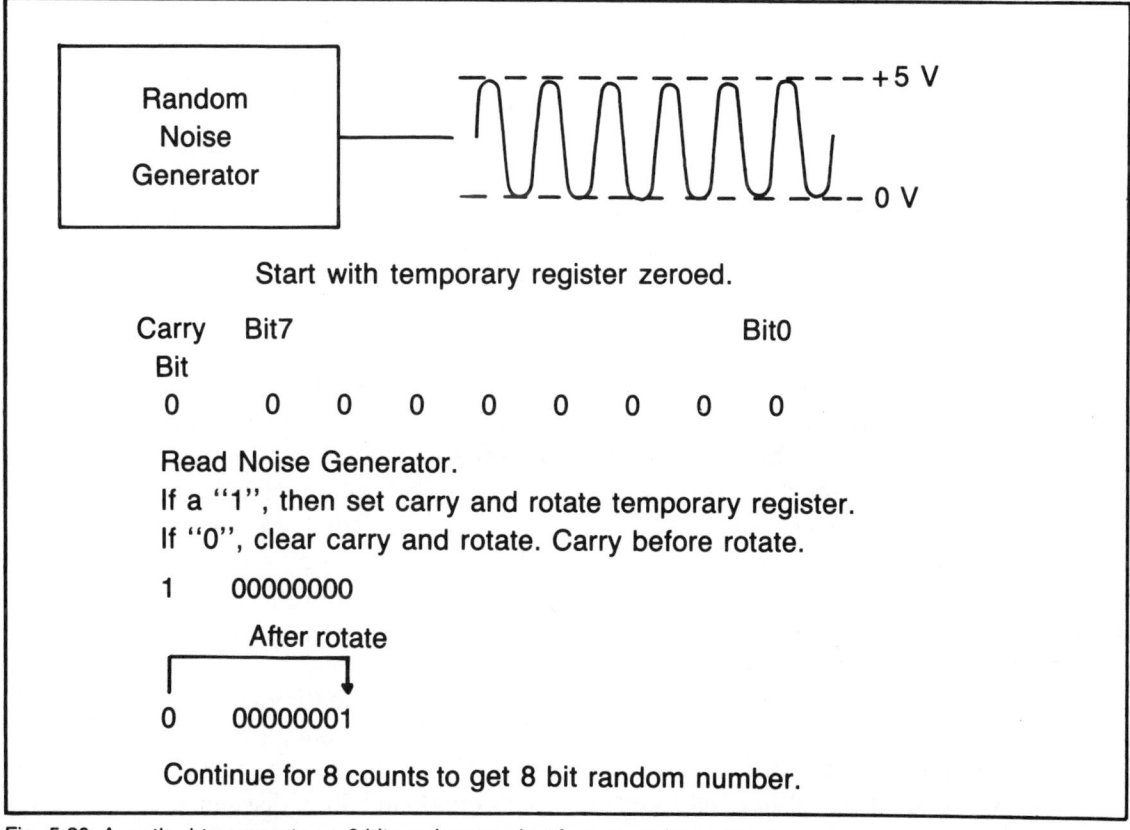

Fig. 5-20. A method to generate an 8-bit random number from a random noise generator.

Table 5-6. Resultant Period from the 3-Bit Software Random Number Generator.

Random Number	Attack (Rising) Ramp Period	Decay (Falling) Ramp Period*
0**	250 ms (1/4 s)	1 3/4 s
1	250 ms (1/4 s)	1 3/4 s
2	500 ms (1/2 s)	1 1/2 s
3	750 ms (3/4 s)	1 1/4 s
4	1 s	1 s
5	1250 ms (1 1/4 s)	3/4 s
6	1500 ms (1 1/2 s)	1/2 s
7	1750 ms (1 3/4 s)	1/4 s

*Decay Ramp Time = (2 seconds – Attack Ramp Time) or
Decay Ramp Time + Attack Ramp Time = 2 seconds

**A 0 random number automatically defaults to a state of 1
so a 250 ms instead of a meaningless 0 ms period results

right after the other. This would be an unrealistic condition for a light dimmer. What does occur next in software is the selection of a random time or period delay between the rising and falling ramps. The period of the delay between the rising and falling ramps is again controlled by the same subroutine called RAND7, only the number generated is multiplied by a 30-second time interval instead of a 250 millisecond time interval as was previously done. This results in a 30 to 210 second (1 to 7 times 30 seconds) delay between attack and decay ramps.

If the proceeding explanation was less than absolutely lucid, then the following simplified explanation may help. The explanation assumes the form of a stated problem with a proposed solution. The solution is what has been implemented in software.

Problem:

To generate a varying waveform (ramp) that has:

1. Variable time between ramps
2. Variable ramp attack and decay times
3. Variable ramp amplitude

Solution:

1. Generate a variable timer to time from 1/2 minute to 3 1/2 minutes, between ramps.

2. With total ramp attack and delay time of 2 seconds, generate a variable attack ramp between 1/4 second and 1 3/4 seconds. Subtract attack ramp time from 2 seconds to get decay ramp time.

3A. Generate variable steps for the ramp by adding some variable to previous value to maintain an 8 bit output between 0-200 counts. Stop when attack timer times out or a count of 200 is reached.

3B. Generate variable steps for decay ramp by subtracting some variable from the previous value. Stop when the decay timer times out or a count of 0 is reached.

4. Repeat cycle over from step 1.

Ramp variation (time) from 1/4 second (250 milliseconds) to 1 3/4 seconds should be able (with maximum random numbers) to reach a count of 200 in 250 milliseconds. Refer to Fig. 5-19 for a graphic illustration.

6
The Sentinel

ACCORDING TO THE DICTIONARY, THE TERM "sentinel" has a myriad of definitions, all loosely conveying the impression of vigilance, perceiving, and to stand watch or guard over something of value. Employing this same principle, you may remember the older luxury cars, such as Cadillacs, that had a small lens assembly on the dashboard called a Sentinel. This assembly perceived or detected light from an oncoming car, and as it approached, it would actuate a relay to automatically dim the car's lights if they were on high beam. This project performs a very similar task.

The Sentinel is a project that uses a microwave motion detector in conjunction with a programmable (operator selectable) elapsed-period timer to turn on the porch light as an individual approaches the front door. You may want to review the section on motion detectors in Chapter 1. The Sentinel can also be used to announce a visitor approaching your door. The indication can be visual, audible, or both. This project has three variations: the Simple Sentinel, the Precision Sentinel, and the Quad Precision Timer. The following circuit description is valid for all three variations.

CIRCUIT DESCRIPTION

The simple synchronous, or clocked, 5 IC circuit is driven by a free-running oscillator (astable multivibrator) that produces squarewaves at a theoretical rate of 16.384 kHz. This rate represents the product of two numbers, namely 4,096 and 4. Refer to the schematic in Fig. 6-1. The CD4024 CMOS counter, IC3, has taps taken off of it in a manner that decodes the number 240. This number was chosen because when it is reached, the counter conveniently produces a pulse once per minute (4 Hz times 60 seconds per minute). In actuality, this theoretical driving frequency is

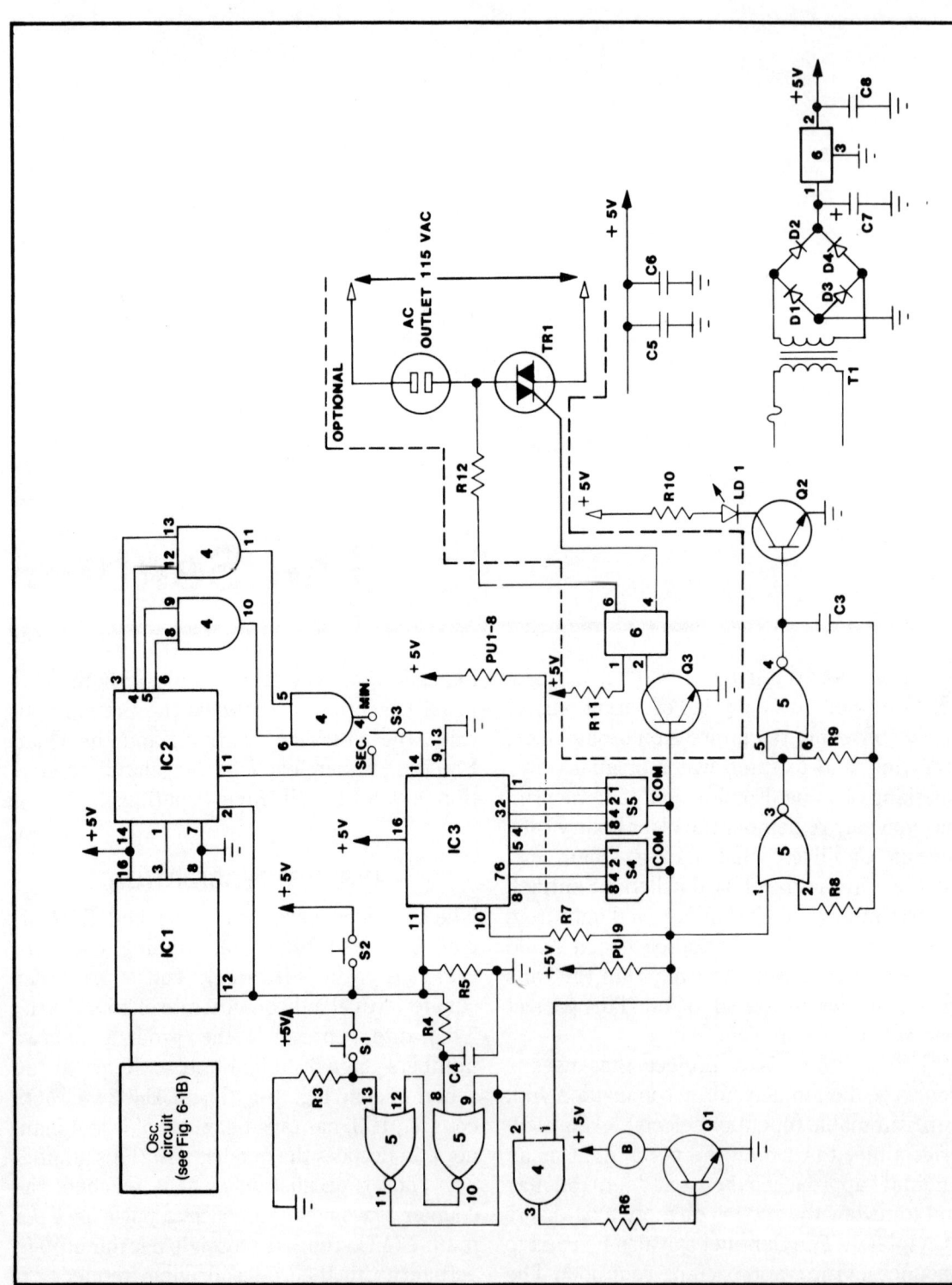

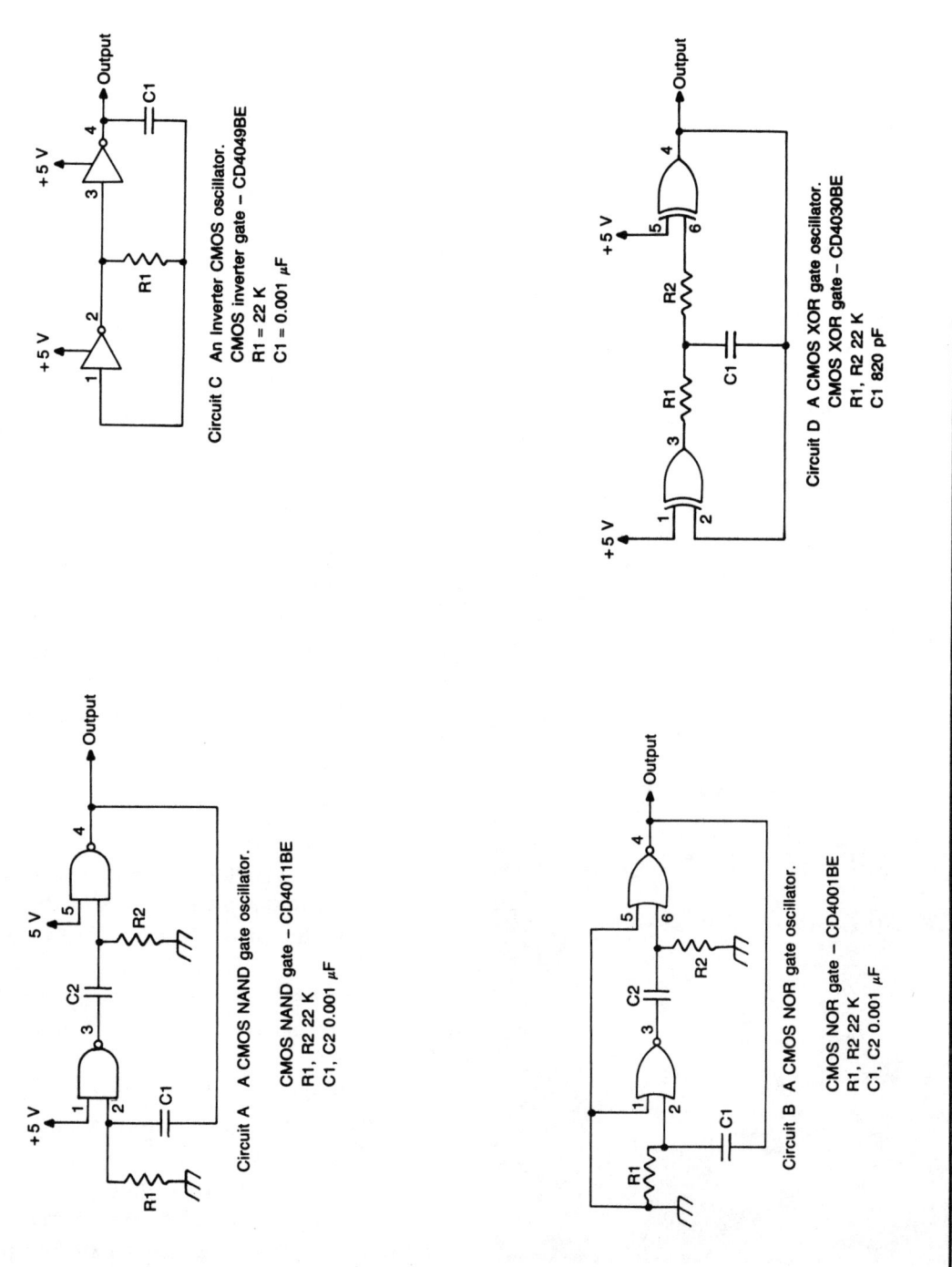

Fig. 6-1. Schematic diagram for the Simple Sentinel.

merely a design goal. It is probably only within 5 to 10% of that desired value due to the tolerances of the RC time/period determining components associated with the oscillator. In Circuit B of Fig. 6-1B, these components include R1, C1, and the two CD4049 CMOS inverters. Any of the four oscillators in Fig. 6-1B can be used. It is suggested that ceramic dielectric capacitors be used because of their excellent temperature coefficients, lack of drift, and 5% accuracy of the specified capacitance value which is integral to the determination of the frequency/period of the squarewave oscillator.

For all intents and purposes, this period of 1 minute, ±5 percent to ±10 percent, should be satisfactory for most applications since a switch selection is made by the user of from 2 to 9 minutes. It is this switch-selected time that represents the length of time that the light remains on. However, if greater accuracy and resolution is required, you may want to opt for the Precision Sentinel circuit. This circuit derives its accuracy from a quartz crystal that allows a period to be selected from 2 to 99 minutes, or from 2 to 99 seconds. The crystal itself is unusually small. As shown in Fig. 6-2, it is about the size and shape of a 1/4 watt resistor. This crystal is manufactured by a number of companies associated with commercial mass-produced digital timepieces and has become an industry standard. The frequency of 32.768 kHz is conveniently an exact power of two (2^{15}) for ease of decoding down to one second.

SIMPLE SENTINEL

Let's first discuss the less accurate RC time constant oscillator circuit in Fig. 6-1. The first divider/counter, IC2 (the CD4020 12-stage version), divides the 16,384 Hz signal by 4,096 to yield a 4 Hz signal going into the 7-stage CD4024 binary counter, IC3. IC3 puts out a pulse once per minute. The next IC, IC5, is where the real control is put into the circuit. This is a 7250 or 8250, depending on which package style and temperature range you select.

The 8250 is the more rugged version, but it is also more expensive so the less costly ICM7250 IJE was selected. This IC, made by Intersil, is one of a family of monolithic programmable timer circuits. They are intended to simplify the problem of selecting various time delays or frequency outputs available from a fixed oscillator circuit. Each device consists of an accurate, low-drift oscillator, a counter section of master-slave flip-flops and appropriate logic and control circuitry all on one monolithic chip.

The internal time base oscillator can be set with an external RC, or it can be disabled and the time base supplied from an external clock as we are doing here. The counter output taps are open collector transistors which can be programmed by a wired AND at external pins. Manual programming is easily accomplished

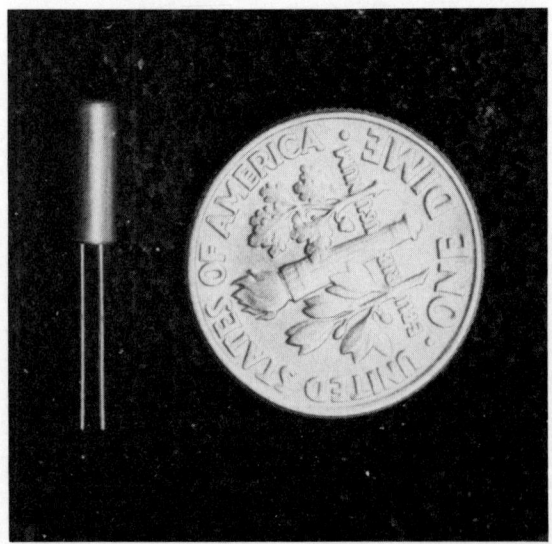

Fig. 6-2. A miniature quartz crystal.

Fig. 6-3. A ten-position switch with BCD coded outputs.

by using standard thumbwheel switches such as the EECO screwdriver slot 10-position switch. The EECO switch is shown in Fig. 6-3. Additional logic circuitry will allow timing to be programmed by computer or microprocessor. These units are also very useful for generating ultra-long delay times with relatively inexpensive RC components.

This particular time/counter is one designed to accommodate digital inputs in BCD form (2 digits) of from 02 up to and including 99. In this application, the MSD (more significant digit) or the one on the left is not used. This saves a 10-position rotary switch, since normally two are used. This limits the timed out interval, though, to between 2 and 9 minutes, but a 9 minute maximum on time for the porch lights should be more than adequate in most situations. The IC's pins 5 though 8 where the MSD switch normally should go have all been tied low or grounded. This prevents use of a second digit in the timer on period.

When a person approaches the porch, the microwave motion detector closes its normally open (N.O.) relay contacts. This pulls the START line in Fig. 6-1 high. Incidentally, this versatile motion detector has a set of both normally open and normally closed relay contacts. Once this START line goes high, it enables the TRIGGER input on the Intersil timer IC. This simultaneously resets the two CMOS counter ICs and the count begins. For illustrative purposes, let us assume that we have set the rotary 10-position switch to the "5" position for five minutes. After this interval, the reset on IC5 (pin 10) is enabled and goes high. This causes the double inverted and parallel buffered pair of four inverters to have a high output which disables the two parallel LASCRs (light-activated SCRs) and associated triac and turns off the lights after the five minute programmed interval. A more in depth discussion of the ac activation circuit may be found in the latter portions of the Burglar Baffler discussion in Chapter 2. This tried and proven circuit worked so well with the Burglar Baffler that it has been used elsewhere on numerous occasions, including here.

The parts list for this circuit is given in Table 6-1.

PRECISION SENTINEL

As mentioned, the Precision Sentinel uses an external crystal for its exceptional accuracy. The 7250 programmable timer is used in this variation of the Sentinel with a few differences. The schematic in Fig. 6-4 shows that the internal time base of the Intersil timer IC has been disabled by pin 13 of IC3 being grounded. This enables pin 14 to be the input. The crystal, XT1, is a 32.768 kHz frequency source. The two resistors and capacitors next to it, R1, R2, C1, and C2, constitute a trimmable network ensuring stable oscillation.

The CD4060, IC1, is a divider that divides by 4,096 to provide a 4 Hz squarewave out on pin 3 that is applied to pin 1 of IC2. The CD4060 is an integrated circuit with all of the active components built right on the chip for an RC or crystal oscillator. Other CMOS counter ICs lack this type of input circuitry. They are merely designed to accept valid digital

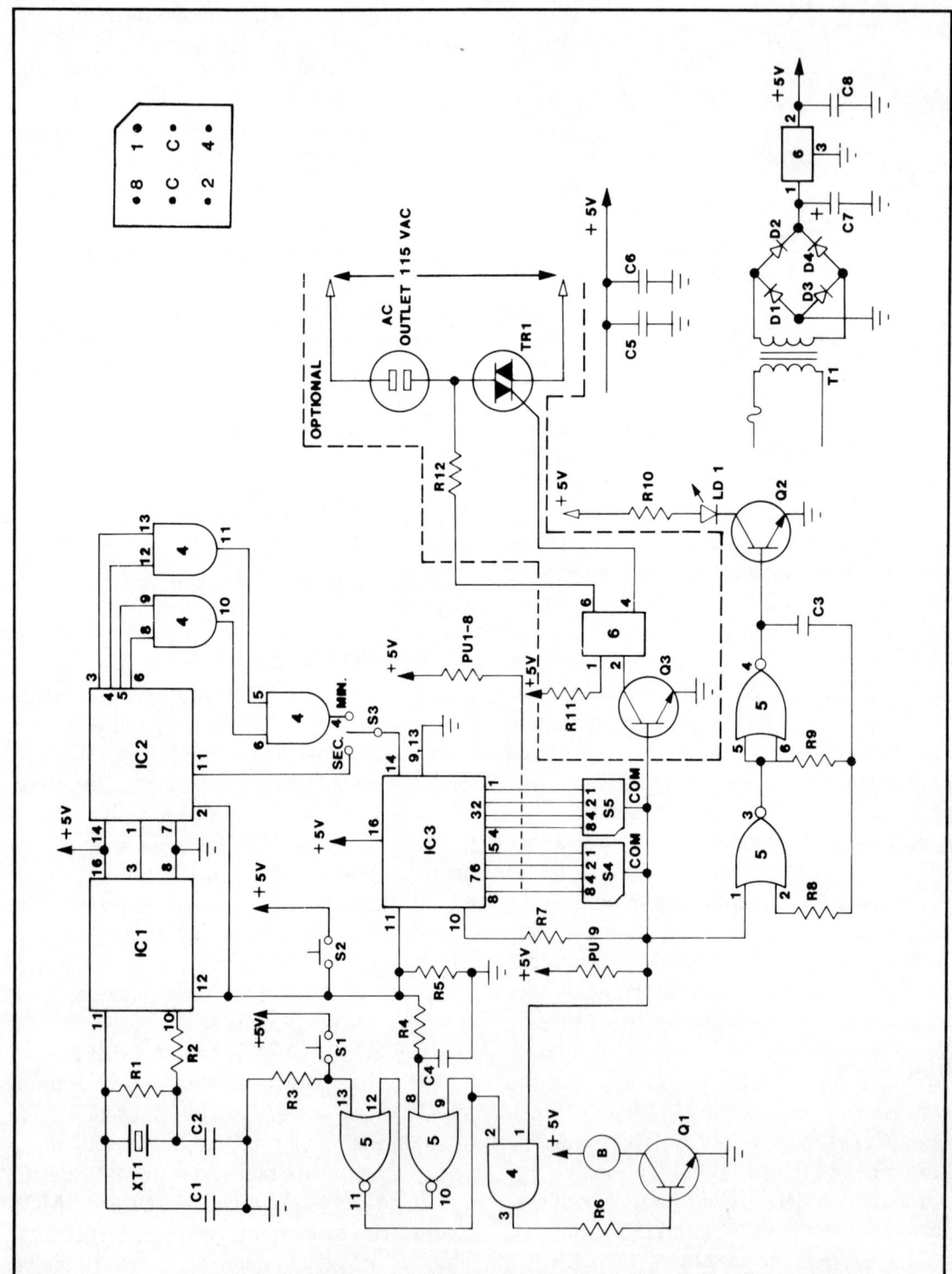

Fig. 6-4. Schematic diagram of the Precision Sentinel.

inputs, not crystal low-amplitude sinewave outputs. This second counter, the CD4024 7-stage ripple counter, is another divider with its first tapped output, pin 11, being a further division by 4 to yield a 1 Hz squarewave.

Note that if switch 3 is in the SEC (seconds) position, the timer, IC3, sees a pulse once per second. IC2 further divides the 1 Hz squarewave and this frequency is decoded to detect a pulse every 60 seconds by the three AND gates within IC4. When the MIN/SEC selector switch is in the MIN (minutes) position, the timer IC experiences one pulse each 60 seconds.

Thumbwheel switches S4 and S5 are the same rotary switches that were shown in Fig. 6-3. Their output is true, not complementary BCD. Look on the schematic and note the notch on the bottom view of the switch. This is for properly orienting the switch.

The 8, 4, 2, 1 designators are the binary weighted outputs. These outputs are pulled up by a single-inline 10-pin resistor network with 9 resistors in it tied to a common pin. Refer to Fig. 6-5. The schematic refers to this as PU1-9 meaning pullup resistors one through nine in the pack. This BCD code forms two digits with S4 controlling the ten's digit and S5 controlling the unit's digit. More specifically, if S4 is set to "3" and S5 is set to "5" and the MIN/SEC switch is set to the MIN position, the timer will buzz after 35 minutes.

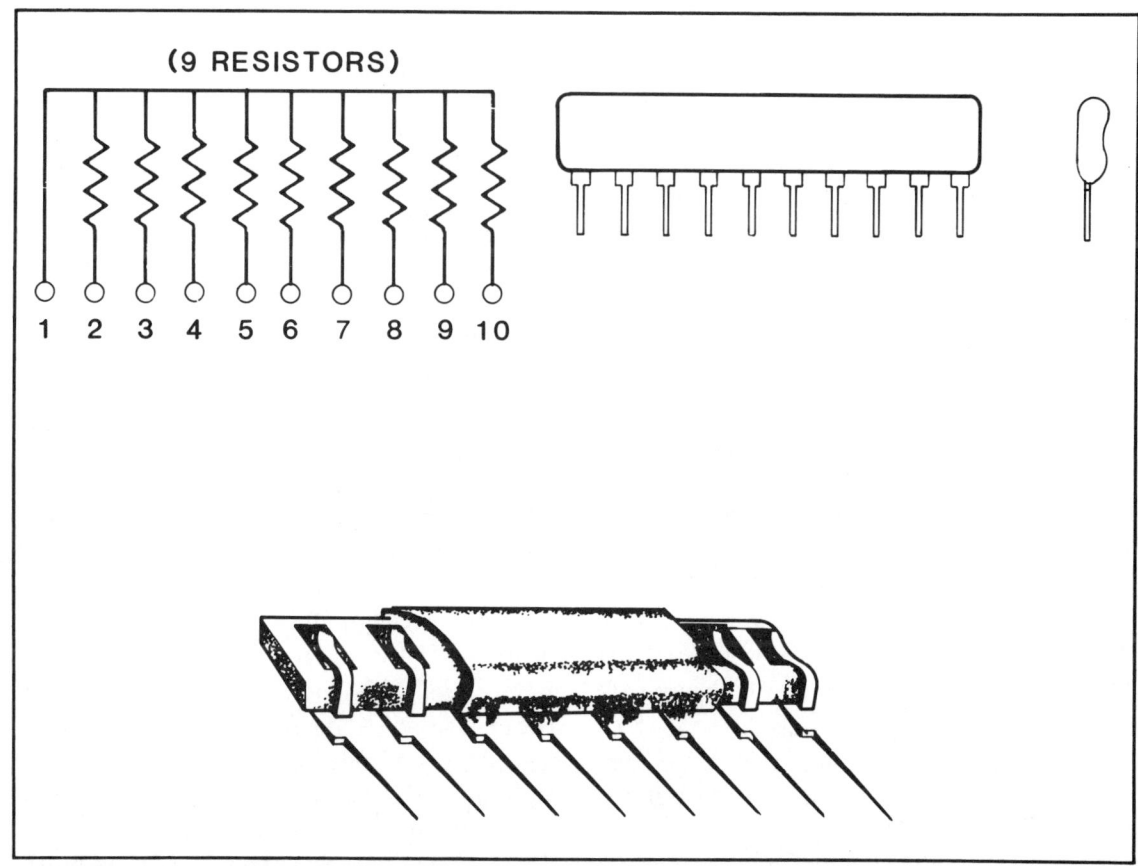

Fig. 6-5. A 10-pin SIP resistor network.

If this buzzer feature is annoying, you may delete it by eliminating R6, Q1, and the buzzer, denoted by an encircled B on the PC board, from the design.

Do not change the MIN/SEC switch during the period the timer is counting down! Switch S2 is depressed to start the countdown and enables the timer IC with pin 10 going low during the countdown. This low also enables the 4 Hz oscillator made from the NOR gates within IC5 and resets the two counters, ICs 1 and 2.

In case you want to substitute component values to accommodate parts on hand or if you want to alter the frequency of this oscillator, its period, T, equals 1.4 × R9C3 with R expressed in ohms and C expressed in farads. The resistor, R8, should be twice as large as R9. It is there to preserve stability when a poorly regulated power supply is used. If you wish, you may want to short this connection and omit this resistor if it would be more convenient.

Incidentally, this oscillator can also be built with NAND gates in place of the NOR gates. If this is done, the formula for the frequency is identical. The only difference is that the logic states for enable and disable are reversed from that of the NOR gate oscillator, but this is really only academic since in both possible configurations the gates are really only used as inverters.

As the timer is counting, the 4 Hz oscillator comprised of R9 and C3 drives the base of transistor Q2 which turns on and off at a 4 Hz rate providing the flashing rate to the LED indicating that the circuit is counting down. When the preprogrammed value is reached, the counter detects this and pin 10, the timer's RESET pin, goes high. This disables the NOR gate oscillator and the buzzer is turned on. Pressing S1, the buzzer reset, will turn it off. Counting begins again when S2 is closed by the microwave motion detector's relay contacts.

The buzzer may be a Sonalert or any 5 V buzzer that works on dc.

The power supply section of this programmable timer is quite simple. It requires a 12 V secondary voltage single-winding transformer or some output voltage close to that value. This is rectified by a full-wave bridge made up of diodes, D1-D4, and filtered by capacitor C7. Capacitor C8 is for noise filtering and ripple. Capacitors C5 and C6 are for decoupling of the ICs and are strategically placed on the board next to the ICs. The regulator, IC6, is a small TO-92 case plastic 3-pin device capable of 100 mA. This will be more than an adequate amount of current for powering this CMOS project. The only concern is to avoid using a buzzer that draws over 40 mA.

The portion of this project's circuitry shown in the dashed box in Fig. 6-2 does not exist on the PC board. It may either be added "as is" on a perf board using Molex pins, as shown in Fig. 2-27, or the ac activation circuitry from the less precise RC time constant version of the Sentinel may be used.

Construction

The Precision Sentinel is easily built with the components listed in Table 6-1 going on the PC boards. Figure 6-6 contains the PC foil pattern. The switches go on the noncomponent sides of the PC board and the buzzer is front panel mountable with their leads going to +5 V and +24 V in the single and quad timers respectively. Figure 6-7 shows the component locations. If you photographically lift the foil pattern from this book, you will end up with a double-sided PC board that naturally will not have any plated-through holes. This is quite acceptable in that some solder connections will have to be made on both sides of the board. This will be obvious as you mount the parts.

Table 6-1. Parts List for the Simple Sentinel.

IC1	CD4060B CMOS divider/oscillator
IC2	CD4024B CMOS divider
IC3	ICM7250 PIE low power programmable interval timer
IC4	CD4082B dual 4-input CMOS AND gate
IC5	CD4001B quad 2-input NOR CMOS gate
Q1	2N2222 general purpose transistor
R3,R5,R7	47 K 1/4 W 5% (50 K equiv.)
R4	39 K 1/4 W 5%
R6	15 K 1/4 W 5%
C3,C4	.01 µF 50 V ceramic 50 V
S2,S3	pushbutton N.O. momentary switches
S1	SPDT switch
S4, S5	ten-position rotary true BCD out screwdriver slot adjustable switches
B	5 V buzzer
Parts from Fig. 6-1B	RC Oscillator from Fig. 6-1B

There is one precaution to note. The screwdriver-slot micro-rotary switches will have to be slightly stood off from the PC board because you will have to solder underneath their bodies to gain soldering access to their two middle pins. A small soldering iron is recommended for this operation. Once soldered, the other side of the micro rotary switch is very accessible and no further physical or mechanical problems exist.

Modifications

Merely counting down a preprogrammed interval of time and then visually or audibly detecting its expiration may not be enough for your application. You may want to control the application of ac power to a device. If this is your requirement, refer to the dotted in section in Fig. 6-4. The npn transistor, Q3, is there to act like an inverting switch. That is, when the timer IC is counting down, pin 10 is low and this turns the transistor off. When the transistor is turned off the collector is high. The transistor's collector is applied to pin 2 of IC6, an optically isolated triac driver. This IC has a gallium arsenide infrared emitting diode (pins 1 and 2) optically coupled to a silicon bilateral switch that is optimally suited for isolated triac driving. The low current required, 10 mA, makes it ideal for this case. The transistor then controls the application of ac to the load via the optoisolator. When the transistor's base is high the transistor conducts with its collector going low. This low on pin 2 of IC6 causes a difference in voltage potentials to be present on the infrared LED within IC6. This condition causes the optotransistor within IC6 to conduct and turns on the gate to the triac, TR1.

This triac should be a "sensitive gate" type since we are attempting to turn on its gate from IC6 with just 10 mA in an effort to conserve power. Motorola 2N6068B to 2N6075B semiconductor devices are sensitive gate triacs that trigger with 3 mA. An "A" suffix replacing the B suffix indicates triggering with 5 mA while no suffix requires 30 mA which IC6 cannot furnish. The various numbers correspond to the repetitive peak off-state voltages. Refer to Table 6-3 for a comparison.

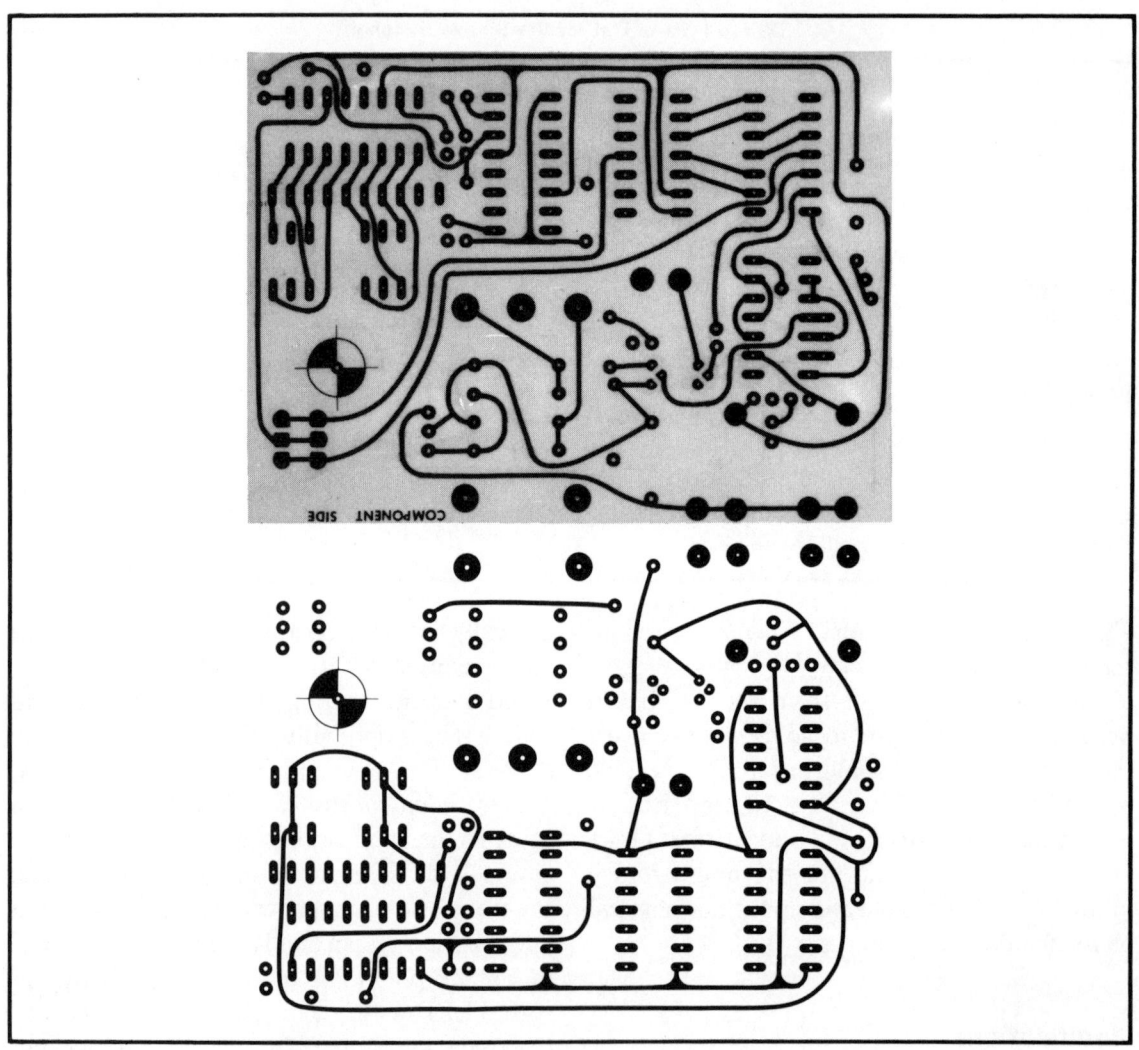

Fig. 6-6. PC foil pattern for the Precision Sentinel.

If you wanted an ac powered device to be on while another was off, you could use paralleled buffers (inverting) from the transistor's collector to the cathode of the second optically coupled triac driver. This way the two would act like the Q and $\overline{Q}$ outputs of a flip-flop in that when one was on the other was off etc. There are applications in the darkroom when this is handy.

The timer does not provide the dotted in circuitry on the PC board. You can tap off pin 10 of IC3 and run this over to a separate perf board.

QUAD PRECISION TIMER

Should you ever have an occasion to require up to four Sentinels at your place of residence or business as an after hours indication that someone has approached, then the circuit in Figs. 6-8 through 6-12 will prove useful. With this circuit, up to four doors or locations can

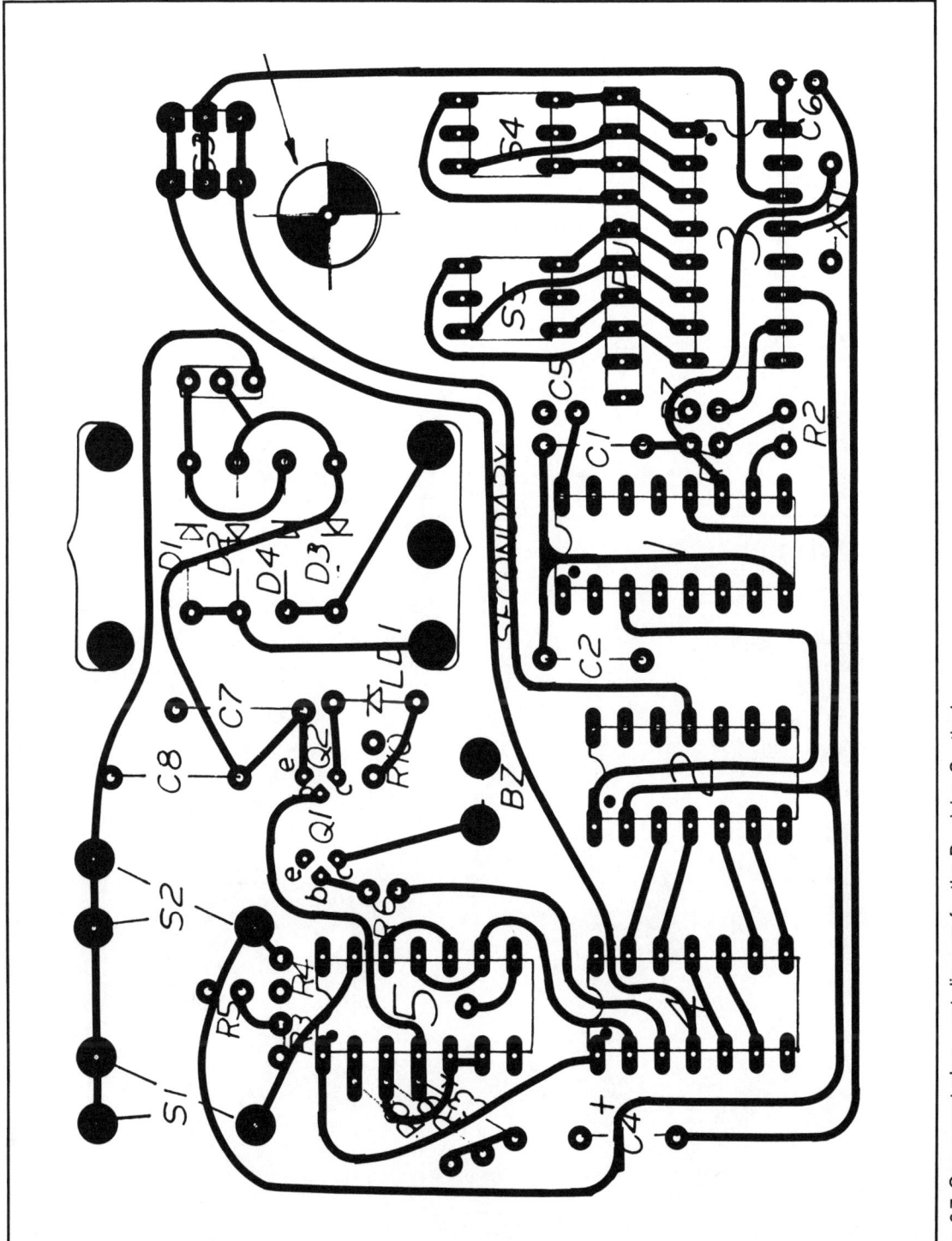

Fig. 6-7. Component placement diagram for the Precision Sentinel.

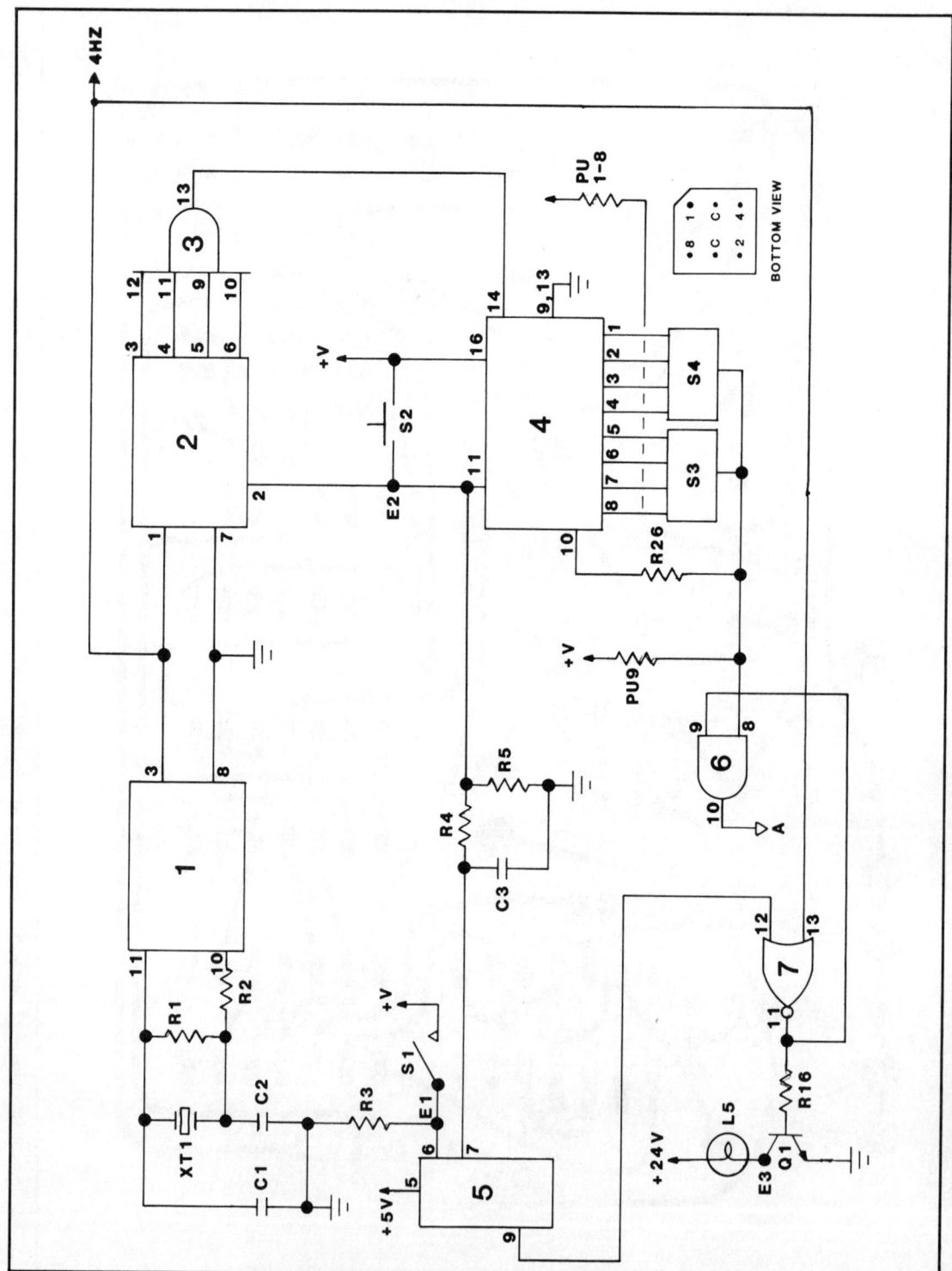

Fig. 6-8. Schematic for the first timer of the Quad Precision Timer.

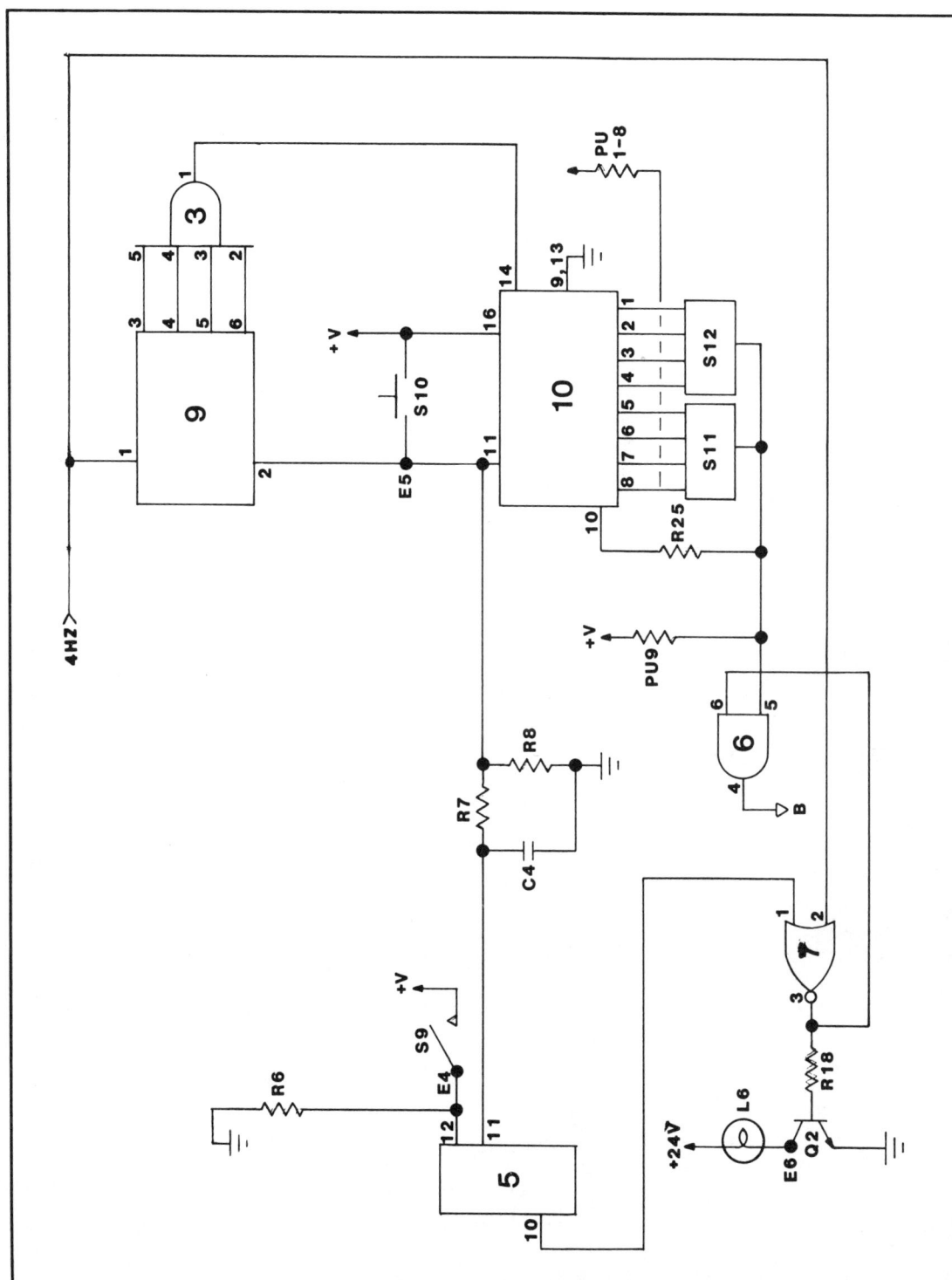

Fig. 6-9. Schematic for the second timer of the Quad Precision Timer.

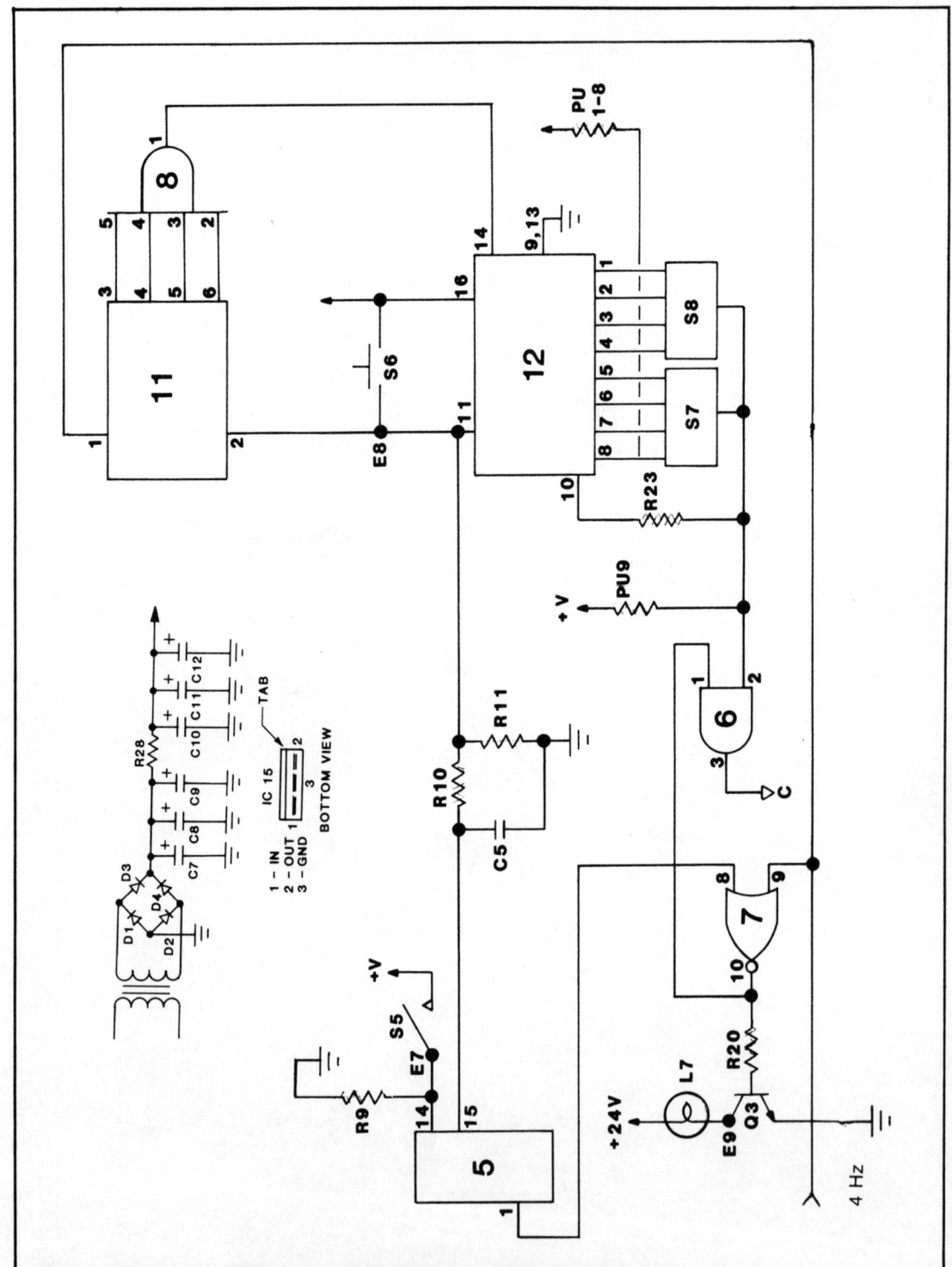

Fig. 6-10. Schematic for the third timer of the Quad Precision Timer, also shown is the power supply.

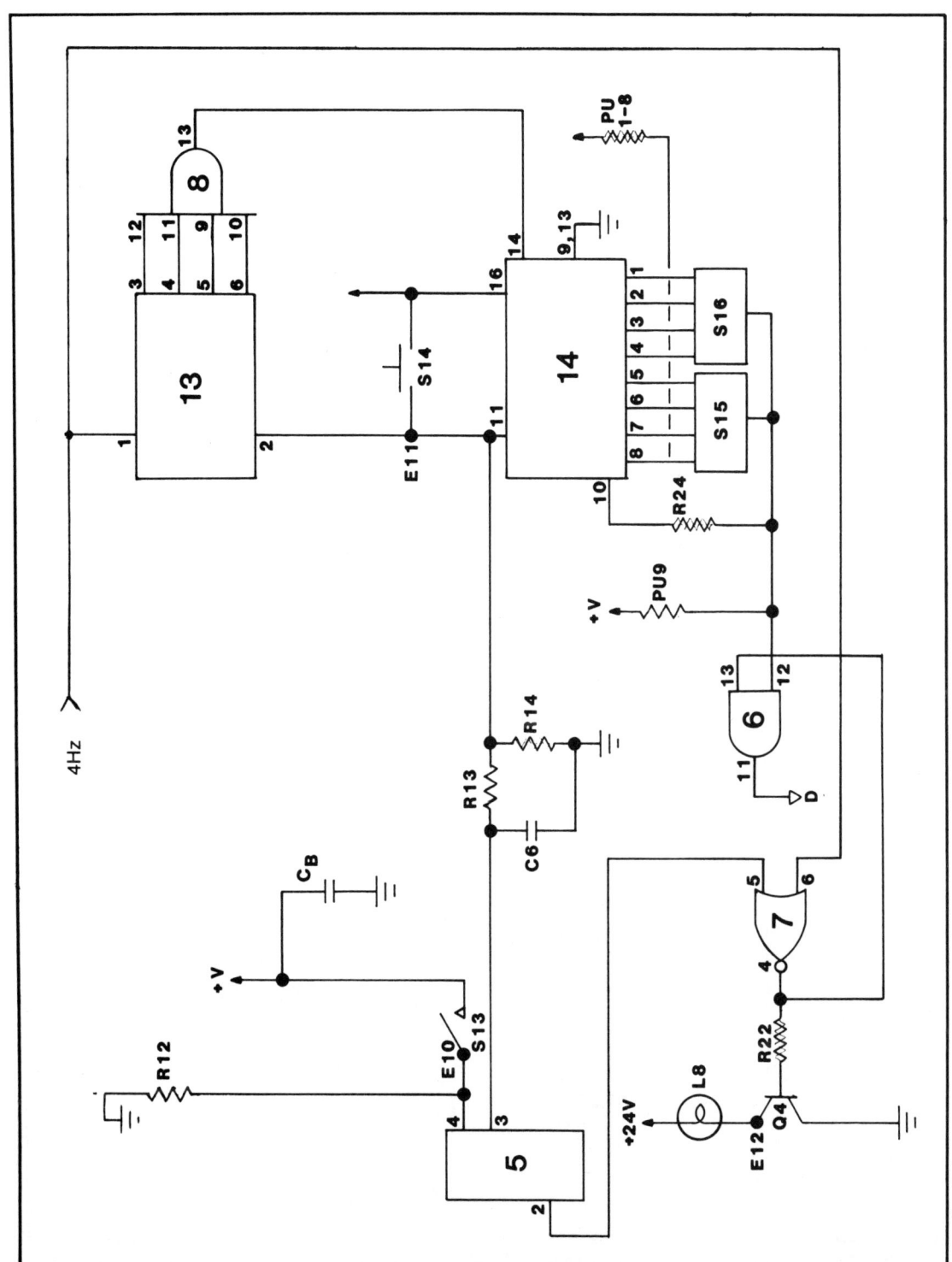

Fig. 6-11. Schematic for the fourth timer of the Quad Precision Timer.

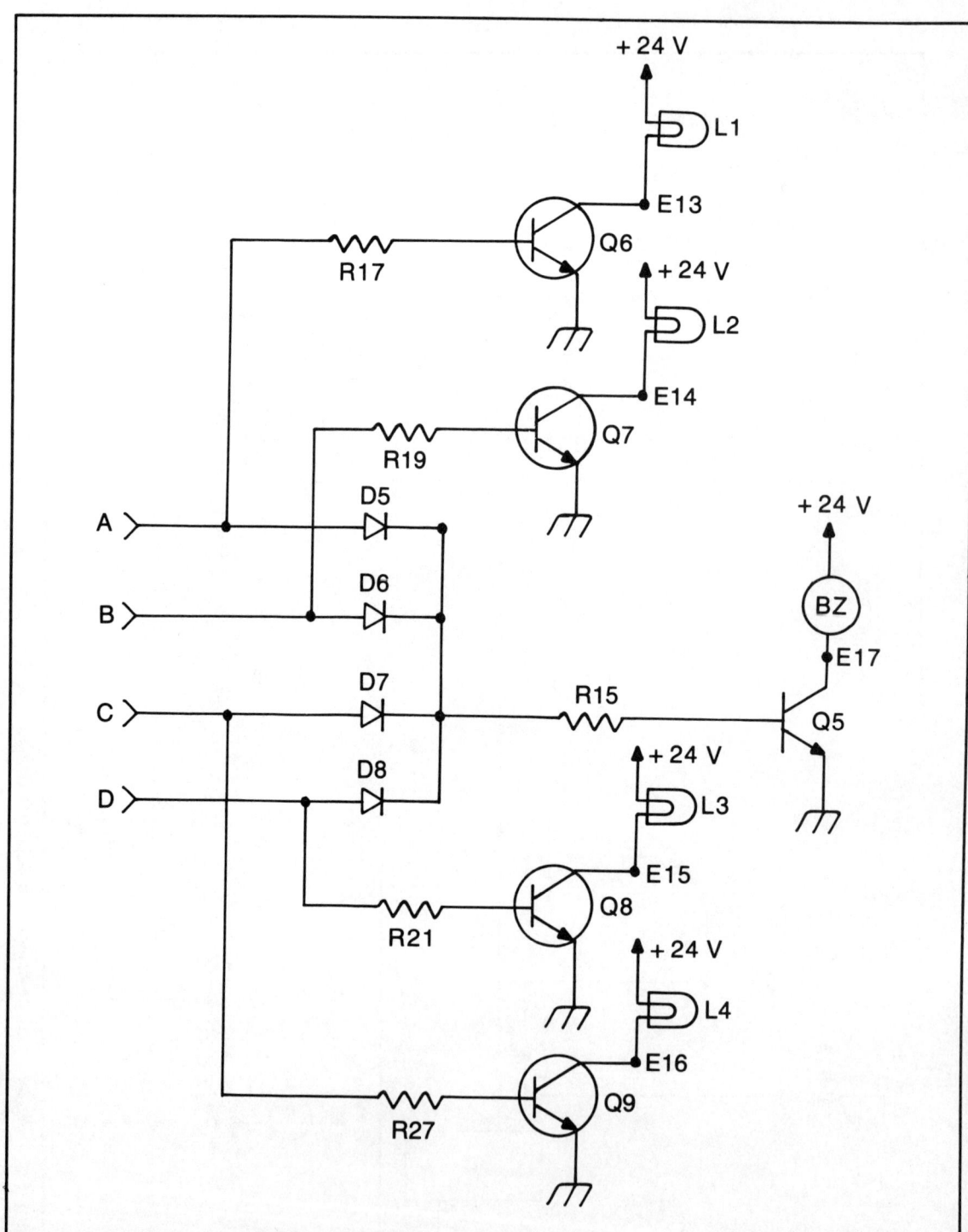

Fig. 6-12. Buzzer and lamp circuit for the Quad Precision Timer.

Table 6-2. Parts List for the Precision Sentinel.

IC1	CD4060B CMOS divider/oscillator
IC2	CD4024B CMOS divider
IC3	ICM7250 PIE low power programmable interval timer
IC4	CD4082B dual 4-input CMOS AND gate
IC5	CD4001B quad 2-input NOR CMOS gate
Q1	2N2222 general purpose transistor
R3,R5,R7	47 K 1/4 W 5% (50 K equiv.)
R1	20 M 1/4 W 5%
R2	330 K 1/4 W 5%
R4	39 K 1/4 W 5%
R6	15 K 1/4 W 5%
C1	27 pF ceramic 50 V
C2	6 to 36 pF ceramic 50 V
C3,C4	.01 μF 50 V ceramic 50 V
S2,S3	pushbutton N.O. momentary switches
S1	SPDT switch
S4, S5	ten-position rotary true BCD out screwdriver slot adjustable switches
B	5 V buzzer
XT1	microminiature 32.768 kHz crystal

be monitored simultaneously. This multiple timer is rather sophisticated and works quite well due to the inherent accuracy of the miniature quartz watch crystal.

In the Sentinel security application, the timer ICs reset switch is replaced by the N.O. (normally open) contacts of the microwave motion detector. The ability to further monitor how long the light is on before it times out by use of red and green lights, just as was done in the keypad based security systems, will prove to be an added feature of interest.

The Quad Precision Timer is very similar to the single timer just described. Compare it to Fig. 6-4. The notable exceptions are that it does not have the switch for selecting minutes or seconds and that it drives eight incandescent lamps at +24 V instead of a single LED, so a heftier voltage regulator is used. It was realized that 4 Hz was already available from the counter so a tap off of that line in this project was used, which saved four 2-input NOR gate oscillators as was used in the single timer project.

Let's explain the operation of one single section in this timer and then examine how all four sections interact with one another. Starting with IC1, this divides the crystal's frequency down to 4 Hz. It is further divided again by IC2 to detect a pulse once per 60 seconds. The same scenario of events transpires as with the single timer except that the cross-coupled NOR latch has been replaced by IC5, a quad cross-coupled NOR gate IC. When the latch is set by switch S1 and IC5 pin 9 is low, this enables NOR IC7 and permits the 4 Hz squarewave to drive the base of transistor Q1 which switches lamp L5 on and off. Lamps L5 through L8 are green to indicate countdown and lamps L1 through L4 are red to indicate ready.

After the timer times out, pin 10 of IC4 goes high. This enables the AND gates within IC6. When the AND gate is enabled and the outputs of the NOR gates within IC7 are high, a high output results. This high output goes to point A. These four outputs (points A through D) cause a high if any of them are high at the transistor's base. This also drives the buzzer, making it sound. Diodes D1 through D4 and resistor R15 actually make up a 4-input OR gate. Those of you familiar with DTL logic will probably recognize this gate. It provides a needed function as a "power" gate to drive the buzzer. Also, as each timer times out you may have a situation in which more than one timer has timed out. How do you know which ones have and which ones haven't since an OR gate (the diode OR gate) detects one or more time expirations? Here is where the other four lamps are useful. As each of the four timers has its respective programmed-in time expire, it creates a high on the inputs to those four diodes. These signals all drive transistors Q6 through Q9 which turn on red lamps L1 through L4.

The thumbwheel switches for these timers are the same as used before. The switches on the right (S3, S11, S7 and S15) correspond to the tens of minutes place. Switches S1, S9, S5, and S13 are for resetting the timers. They all may naturally be reset on an individual basis.

Construction

The Quad Precision Timer could be built on four identical boards or a single board could be made to accommodate all four sections. The part's list for this project is given in Table 6-4. Figures 6-8 through 6-12 contain the schematic. Figure 6-8 shows the derivation of the 4 Hz signal and Fig. 6-10 includes the power supply. Figure 6-8 produces signal A for Fig. 6-12; Fig. 6-9 produces signal B; Fig. 6-10 derives signal C; and Fig. 6-11 produces signal D.

Modifications

If you desire a minutes/seconds switching provision, you could add an SPDT switch with its pole at pin 14 of the timer IC and its two switch contacts switching from pin 11 of the

Table 6-3. Triac Ratings.

Device No.	Repetitive Peak Off-State Voltage
2N6068, A,B	25 V
2N6069, A,B	50 V
2N6070, A,B	100 V
2N6071, A,B	200 V
2N6072, A,B	300 V
2N6073, A,B	400 V
2N6074, A,B	500 V
2N6075, A,B	600 V
All Devices	On State Current 4.0 A
All Devices	Peak Surge Current 30 A
A suffix - A 5 mA gate triggering current. B suffix - A 3 mA gate triggering current.	
An alternate triac, an SK66127, is available from Speciality Electronic Services, Inc. for $2 postpaid. Texas residents add 5% sales tax. Check the list of suppliers at the end of the book.	

Table 6-4. Parts List for the Quad Timer.

C1	27 pF		
C2	20 pF		
C3-C6	.01 µF 50 V ceramic		
C7-C12	100 µF aluminum electrolytic capacitors (radial leads)		
R1	22M	5%	1/4 W
R2	330 K	5%	1/4 W
R3,R6,R9,R12	47 K	5%	1/4 W
R4,R7,R10,R13	47 K	5%	1/4 W
R5,R8,R11,R14	47 K	5%	1/4 W
R15-R22,R27	3.3 K	5%	1/4 W
R23-R26	47 K	5%	1/4 W
R28	47	5%	10 W
PU (4 QTY)	4.7 K	9 resistors/pack, Panasonic Q9472	
Q1-Q9	2N2222 npn silicon transistor		
S1,S5,S9,S13	Momentary contact pushbutton switches (normally open)		
S2,S6,S10,S14	SPSP spring loaded toggle switch		
S3,S4,S7,S8,S11, S12,S15,S16	EECO switches, BCD output, screwdriver slot adjustable (10 positions)		
D1 - D4	Bridge rectifier module, VARO VH248		
D5 - D8	1N4001 silicon diode		
Bz	Buzzer, Mallory SC628 6-28ADC, 2900 Hz		
L1 - L8	Lamp bulbs (8), Chicago Miniature Lamp CM327 Lamp holders with red dome (4), Dialight 162-8430-0931-502 Lamp holders with green dome (4), Dialight 162-8430-0932-502		
IC1	CD4060, Binary Counter & Oscillator		
IC2,IC9,IC11,IC13	Binary Ripple Counter CMOS CD4024		
IC3,IC12,IC10,IC14	ICL 8250C (Intersil) Timer IC		
IC5	CD4043, Quad NOR latch - CMOS		
IC6	CD4081, Quad 1-in-AND gate - CMOS		
IC7	CD4001, Quad 2-in NOR - CMOS IC		
IC15	Voltage regulator (5 V), LM340T-5.0		

XT1 - 32.768 kHz watch crystal, Seiko or Satronics

seconds timer (ICs 2, 9, 11, and 13) and from the output of the quad AND gates on IC3 and IC8. This is the same approach used on the single timer.

7
Automatic Telephone Dialer

THIS CHAPTER ADDRESSES THE USE OF THE ordinary telephone, either rotary dial or tone dial, as a silent alarm project. The chapter begins with an overview of telephones. Then detailed coverage of the Mostek MK5375 Tone/Pulse Dialer IC is provided, followed by a complete description of the actual security project. It automatically dials two operator-entered telephone numbers and transmits a two-tone sound which is heard when the phone receiver is picked up. This two-tone sound is the numeral 1 followed by the numeral 2 keypad frequency, or 697 Hz and 770 Hz respectively. This causes a sound very characteristic of the French or European police cars, which is very attention getting.

TELEPHONE BASICS

The telephone is over 100 years old, yet it is just now undergoing modernization through vast technical changes. This brief overview concentrates on the conventional telephone set as an individual instrument unto itself and does not attempt to examine how the phone is involved in networks, etc.

We will make mention of all telephone set components later as well as use the following terms of which you should be made keenly aware: on-hook, off-hook, pulse dialing, DTMF, switchhook, make and break durations, interdigit interval, pulse period, tone dialing, tone generation and detection, and electrodynamic and electret microphones.

On-Hook

Figure 7-1 is a diagram of a typical telephone set with major functions shown. The ringer circuit is always connected across the line so that it can signal, through an audible device, when there is an incoming call. The remaining portions of the telephone set are electrically isolated from the line by the open contacts of

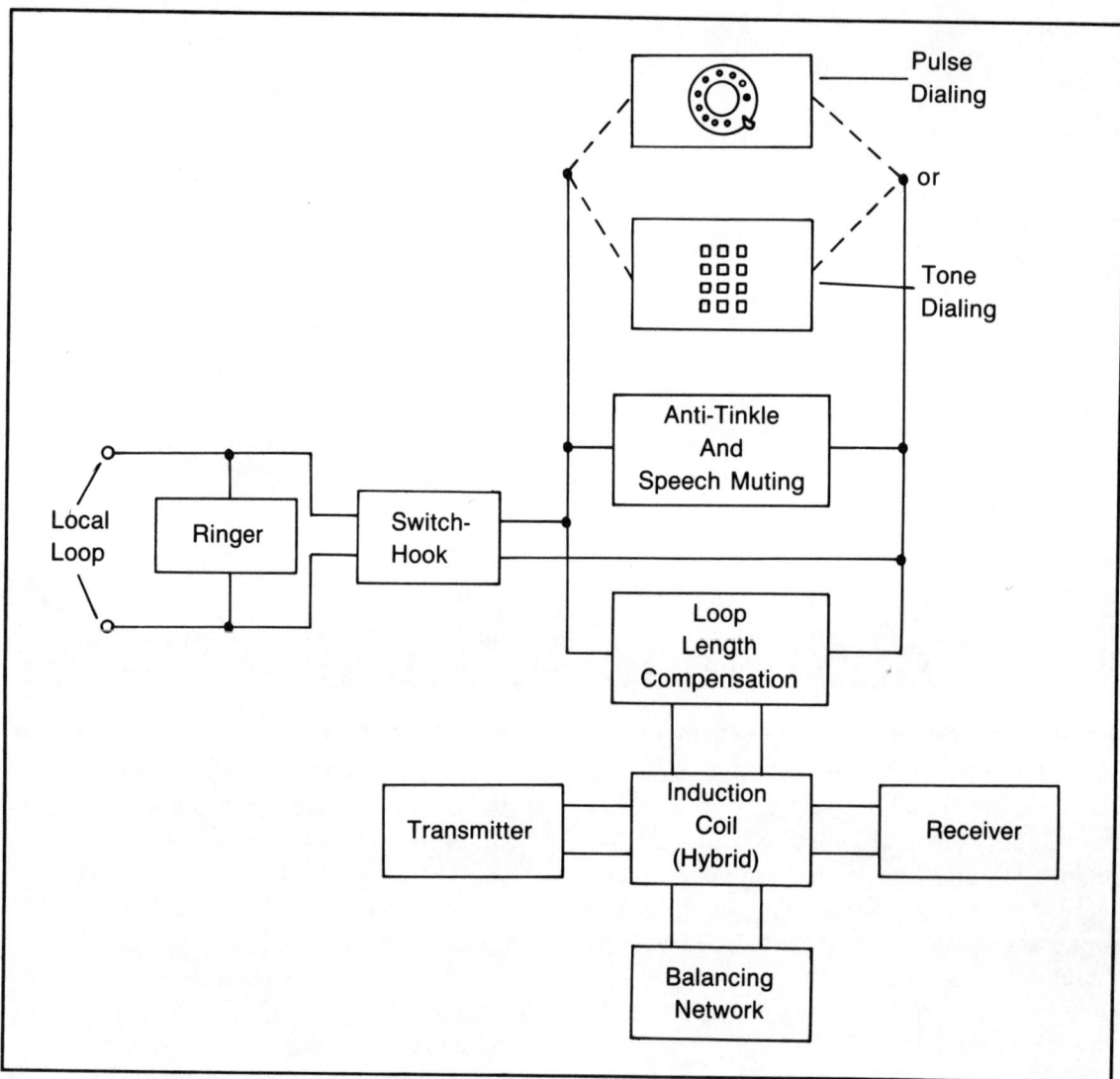

Fig. 7-1. A block diagram for a typical telephone set.

the switchhook when the handset is on-hook. When on-hook, dc current does not flow because of a capacitor that blocks dc from flowing through it.

Off-Hook

When a phone call is to be placed, the handset is naturally lifted off-hook. When this occurs, loop current begins to flow from the central office through a relay in the telephone, and once energized, the closed contacts signal the central office that a subscriber telephone is off-hook. This sequence is shown in Fig. 7-2A. The line finder searches until it finds the line with the off-hook signal and sets up a connection for the switching equipment enabling it to receive the telephone number. Then a tone generator comes on line to direct or signal the caller to begin dialing.

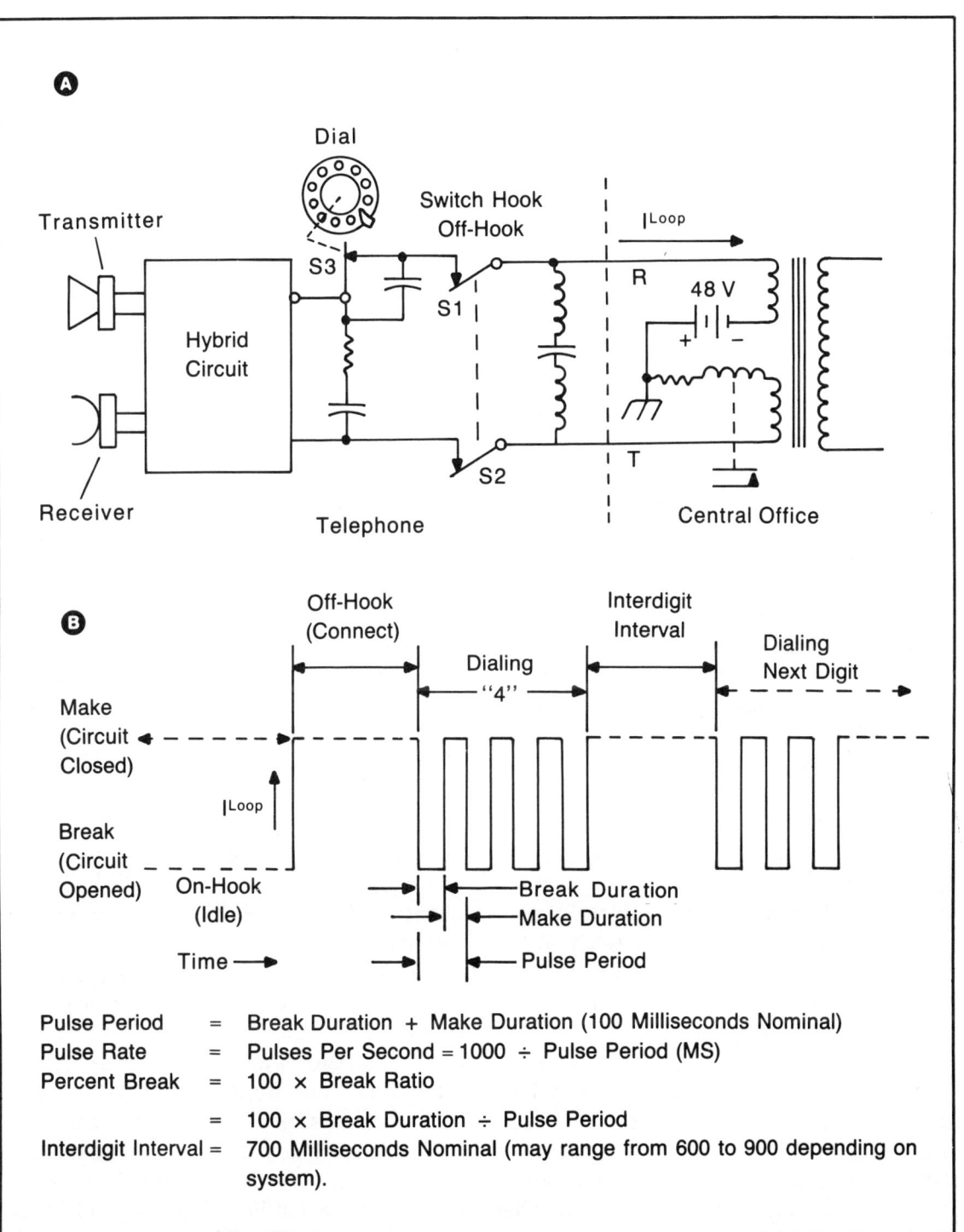

Fig. 7-2. A pulse-dial telephone set with its associated pulses.

Pulse Dialing

Dialing may be accomplished by one of two methods: pulse dialing or tone dialing. Incidentally, this chapter's telephone dialer security project uses a most unique and versatile IC that allows the use of either type of dialing. The pulse dialing convention is with the traditional rotary dial having ten equally spaced fingerholes. The number of pulses resulting from one clockwise dialing motion is dependent upon how far the dial is rotated before being released. There is also a spring, typically residing within the dial, that returns the dial to its initial resting position after having generated a number of pulses. This number is equal to the number of holes rotated. The dial returns at a well-regulated, nearly constant rate because of a governor inside the dial.

The loop is broken during the forward rotation of the dial (the dialing action). Then, as it rotates back, a contact makes and breaks for each number that the dial was moved. Each open and close action of the contact (S3 in Fig. 7-2A) generates a pulse. Note the pulse diagram in Fig. 7-2B. This, along with a predefined timing convention allows telephone numbers to be directed.

The dialing rate is approximately ten pulses per second which limits the dialing speed. One dial pulse consists of both open and closed circuit conditions, as previously mentioned, which correspond respectively to the make and break interval. In the United States, the break interval is 60 milliseconds for a break/make ratio of 60 percent.

Now that the dialing pulses have been generated, how are they detected? This is done at the central office, and it is a problem compounded because the dial pulses are not perfect rectangularly-shaped pulses due to the approximately 0.07 microfarads/mile of parallel capacitance along with a series resistance of 42 ohms per mile and a series inductance of 1.0 millihenries per linear mile of wire.

Tone Dialing

Tone dialing is the more modern and commonly used method today. This system is most predominantly characterized by a telephone set with DTMF (dual tone multiple frequency) capabilities of sending a telephone number. More specifically, the pushbutton keypad, as shown in Fig. 7-3, is used, and this keypad generates two tones when a key is pressed. As an example, if the "4" key were to be pressed, a 770 Hz tone and 1209 Hz tone would be generated.

A typical DTMF circuit is shown in Fig. 7-4. Note that the three switches S1 through S3 are shown in the inactive position and that there are column and row rods that actuate when a key is pressed. This further causes the appropriate S1 and S2 contacts to connect C1 to a tap on L1A and C2 on a tap onto L2A. This results in two resonant circuits composed of an LC network with a keypad selectable "L" or inductance. In other words, the different taps vary the inductance, which in turn varies the resonant frequencies. Twelve different tones are generated from just seven tones; these seven tones are the four column and three row frequencies. Refer to Fig. 7-3 to refresh your memory.

The twelve tones have been carefully selected so that the processing circuits in the central office (called the digit receiver) will not confuse these tones and will be able to distinctly differentiate one from another. This is done with bandpass filters that only pass these DTMF frequencies. Also, the timing relationship previously mentioned ensures that a tone has to be there for 50 milliseconds before it is deemed a valid signal. This helps minimize the

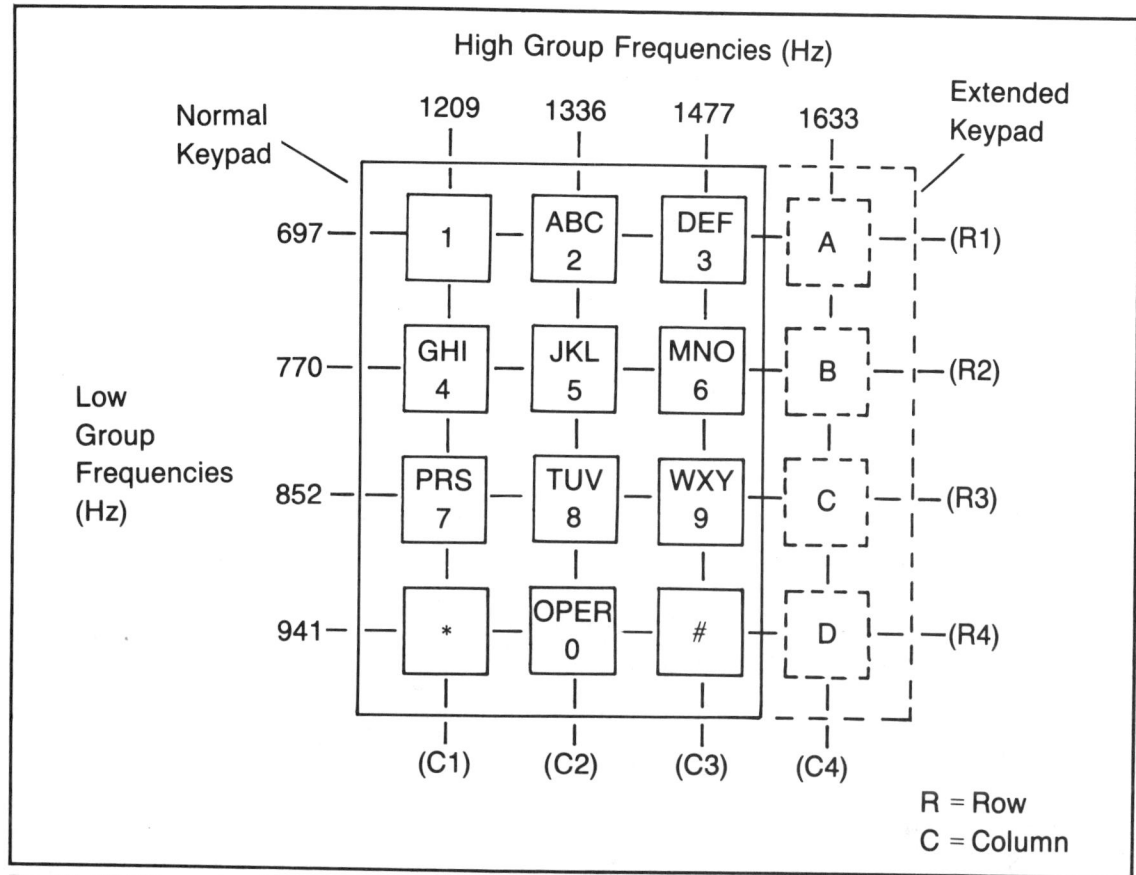

Fig. 7-3. DTMF keypad and frequencies.

possibility of a narrow glitch that is only there for a few microseconds causing havoc with the integrity of the system. Naturally, after the connection has been made and the phone answered, the digit receiver is taken out of the circuit.

DTMF dialing is much faster than pulse dialing because the time to recognize a digit is 50 milliseconds with an equal amount of time for an interdigit interval so that digits are not inadvertently run together. In contrast, pulse dialing uses a 60 millisecond break and 40 millisecond make period plus a large 700 millisecond interdigit interval. A ten digit number (a phone number with area code included) takes about eleven times longer to dial. In addition to this being a time saver to the telephone user, it also helps the telephone company. The company has its digit receiver less busy if the time these numbers are held is less. This translates into savings to the consumer because less capital equipment is required for a given number of lines.

Advantages of DTMF

Let's summarize the preceding discussion that compared the two dialing methods by saying that the DTMF method is superior for the following reasons:

- ☐ Faster dialing.
- ☐ Extensive use of solid state circuits.

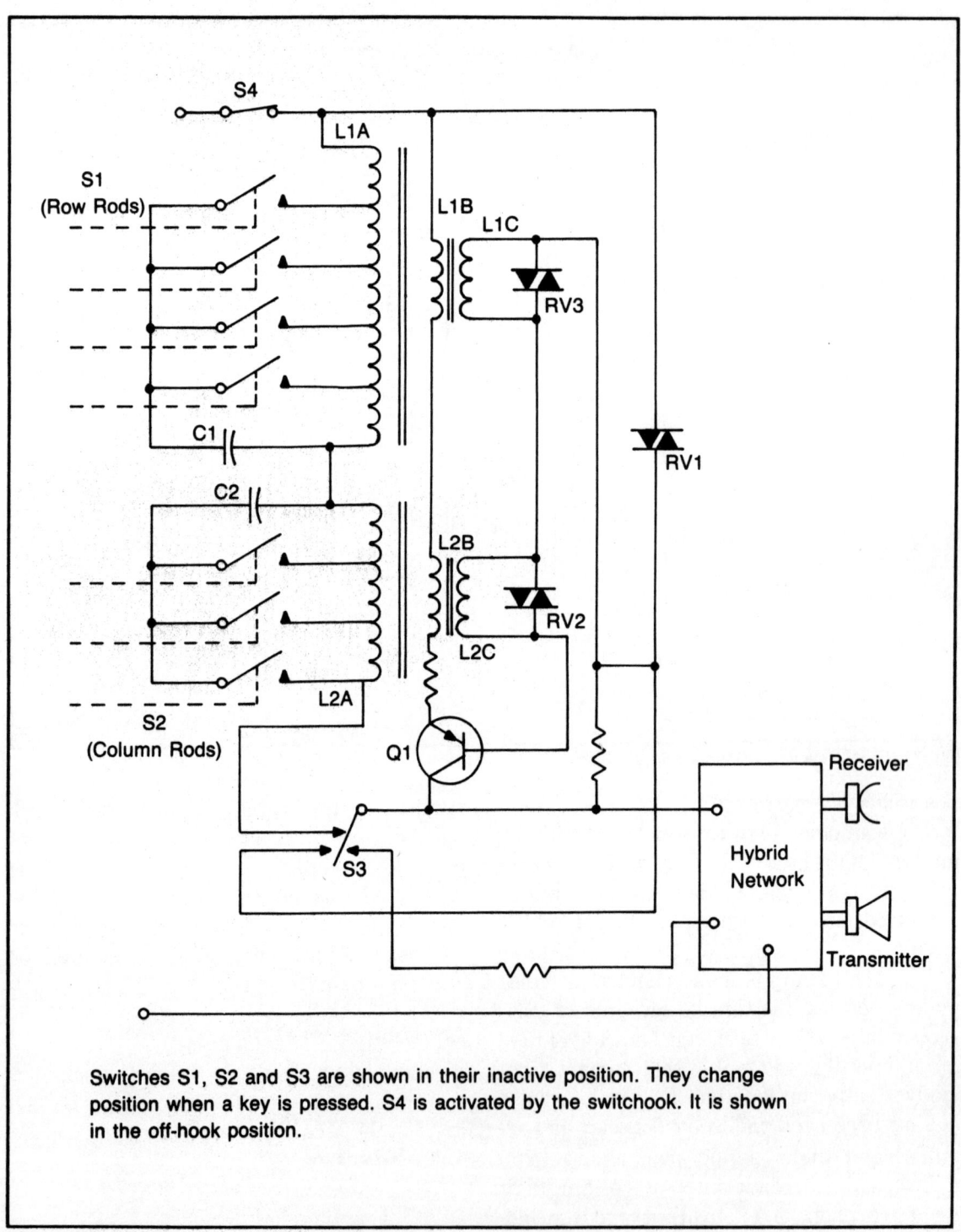

Fig. 7-4. A typical DTMF circuit.

☐ Reduces local exchange equipment requirements.
☐ Easily interfaced with stored program or microcomputer type electronic exchanges.
☐ Easily used for end-to-end signaling after the call has been made.

Transmitter

The part of the telephone handset into which you speak is naturally called the transmitter. It takes acoustic energy transmitted by your voice and converts it to electric energy. In principle, it is very similar to the one invented by Thomas A. Edison some 100 years ago. The output of the transmitter is relatively constant so that by the time it gets to the receiver it suffers from the cause and effect relationship of loop current decreasing as loop length increases. Some means had to be devised by which automatic compensation for variances in for variances in line length would be developed.

The panacea to this problem proved to be a varistor or current sensitive resistor whose resistance changed with respect to current, or actually minute heat production. In the telephone set, the varistor's resistance decreases as the loop current increases, and in effect, this varistor then bypasses some of the current around the transmitter so that the transmitter current is about the same as it is on a long loop.

All microphones, regardless of their type, are electroacoustical transducers. A transducer is a device that changes energy from one type to another. As an example, a phonograph stylus riding along on the grooves of a record's surface experiences varying mechanical pressures because of the depth and angle of cut of the record and these varying minute pressures are sensed and translated, through this transducer action, into to very small electrical currents.

There are many types of microphones, but with the exception of the carbon microphone, there are only two which meet the telephone's requirements of being both rugged and low cost: the electromagnetic or electrodynamic and the electret.

The *electrodynamic* microphone is characterized by a diaphragm attached to either a coil, wire, or ribbon in a permanent magnetic field. The telephone user's voice actuates this diaphragm causing the coil to move which in turn induces a current in the coil proportional to the movement. This current is amplified and eventually transmitted.

The *electret* microphone is a technology that has been around for quite some time but its insertion into the telephone set was only made possible by the recent advent of better dielectric materials and low-cost amplifiers such as FET's (Field Effect Transistors).

The relationship between charge, capacitance, and voltage is given by the following formula:

$$V = \frac{Q}{C}$$

Keeping this relationship in mind, let's realize that an electret is a dielectric (insulator) between two plates (conductors) which constitute a special type of capacitor. It is special because it permanently holds the charge (Q) in the electret material. Interestingly, this electret material is composed of a fluorocarbon material with metallized foil on one side. The material is actually charged by being placed in a corona discharge which forces electrons into the foil with an external electric field. One of the two plates in this unique "capacitor" is the diaphragm of the microphone and the voltage at the terminals varies according to the diaphragm movement. These movements are quite small and must be amplified.

The electret microphone has a high internal impedance and is matched to a low impedance circuit by a source follower FET which is mounted right inside the telephone's microphone capsule. The THD (Total Harmonic Distortion) is excellent, less than 1 percent compared to a THD of 8-10 percent for a carbon granule microphone.

Receiver

The receiver converts electric currents into air pressure detectable by the human ear. A typical electromagnetic receiver is composed of coils of many turns of fine wire mounted or wound on permanently magnetized soft iron cores which drive an armature. One of the salient characteristics of this arrangement, though, is that the electromagnetic receiver be a permanent magnet to provide a constant field bias; otherwise, both the positive and negative currents would push the armature in the same direction. Human speech, with its inherent variances, alternately aids and opposes the permanent magnet and in so doing increases and decreases the movement of the diaphragm. The diaphragm vibrates in accordance with the fluctuating currents and moves the air about it to reproduce the original speech, working on the same principle used by loudspeakers in audio applications.

Ringer

When the central telephone office serving the called subscriber's local loop sends a signal to the called party indicating that a call is waiting, a ringing function occurs. It is imperative that the ring be loud enough to be heard at a distance because the ringing (signaling) function ties up expensive common control equipment in the exchange and this is even more crucial in toll calls.

The way the electromechanical ringer operates is that there is an armature drive mechanism driving a hammer to alternately strike two bells or gongs. The coils within this permanent magnet experience an alternating current which causes an attraction and then an alternate repelling force in turn causing the hammer to strike the bells on alternate half-cycles, producing the ringing sound. The ringing voltage in the United States is approximately 90 volts at 16 to 60 Hz.

Ringing Generator

Historically, the ringing generator was first patented by Mr. Watson. It was a hand cranked magneto producing 75 volts at 17 Hz. In most modern central offices today, the ac ringing generator assumes the form of either a dc motor driving and ac generator or a special solid-state power supply called an inverter which takes dc and converts it into ac without the use of any electromechanical movements. Both approaches to this problem are called ringing generators and are powered by −42 volts. The actual ringing interval in the United States and Europe is 1 second followed by a 3 second pause then a 1 second ringing followed by a 3 second pause, etc.; however, there are some private PABX's that have their own customized or unique ringing conventions.

MK5375 DIALER IC

Let's begin this discussion by listing the IC's nine characteristics which give it its power and versatility.

☐ CMOS Technology provides low-voltage operation.

☐ Converts push-button inputs to both DTMF and loop-disconnect signals.

☐ Stores ten 16-digit telephone numbers, including last number dialed.

☐ Pacifier tone and PBX pause.

☐ Last-number-dialed (LND) privacy.

☐ Manual and auto-dialed digits may be cascaded.

☐ Ability to store and dial both "*" and "#" DTMF signals.

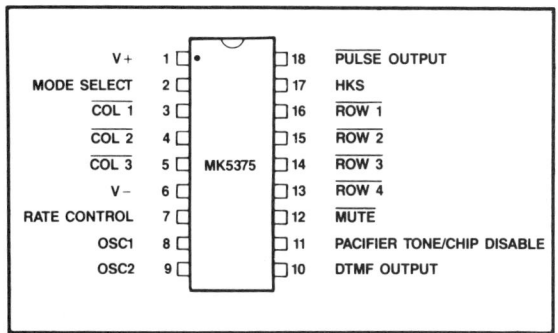

Fig. 7-5. MK5375 pin connection diagram. Courtesy of Mostek.

- [ ] Variable dialing rate.
- [ ] On-chip power-up-clear guarantees data integrity.

Pin Definitions

Probably the best way to really get to "know" this IC is to go through a description of the functions of each one of the IC's 18 pins. We will begin with pin 1 and go right around to pin 18. The pinout is shown in Fig. 7-5.

V+. Pin 1 is the positive supply to the IC. It must be a voltage between 2.5 and 6.0 Vdc.

Mode Select. In normal operations, pin 2 determines the signaling mode used; a logic level 1 (V+) selects tone mode operation. A logic level 0 (V−) selects pulse mode operation. This input must be tied to one of the supplies to guarantee proper dialing. This pin can also be used to force the device into a test mode; this mode of operation is not suitable for normal dialing.

$\overline{COL1}$, $\overline{COL2}$, $\overline{COL3}$, $\overline{ROW4}$, $\overline{ROW3}$, $\overline{ROW2}$, $\overline{ROW1}$. Pins 3, 4, 5, 13, 14, 15, 16 are the keyboard inputs. The MK5375 keypad interface allows either the standard 2-of-7 keyboard with negative common or the inexpensive single-contact (FORM-A) keyboard to be used (Fig. 7-6). A valid key entry is defined by either a single row being connected to a single column or by V− being presented

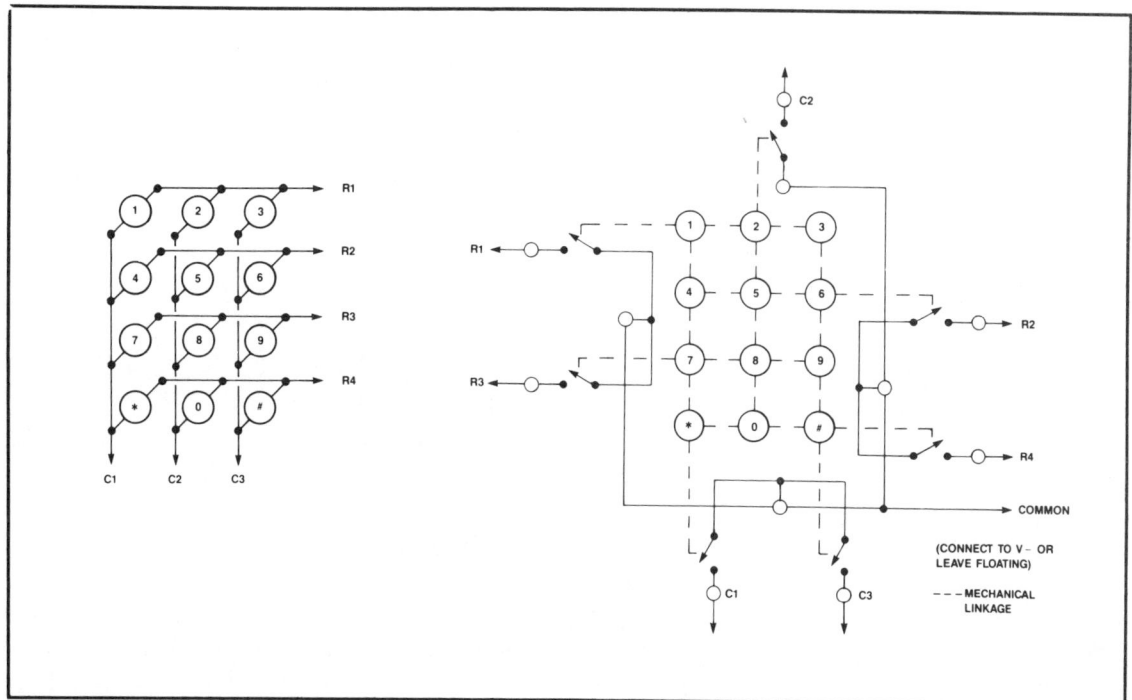

Fig. 7-6. Keypad schematics. Courtesy of Mostek.

145

to both a single row and column. In standby mode, either all the rows will be a logic 1 (V+) and all the columns will be a logic 0 (V−), or vice versa. The keyboard interface logic detects when an input is pulled low and enables the RC (Rate Control) oscillator and keypad scan. Scanning consists of alternately strobing the rows and columns high through on-chip pullups. After both valid row and column key closures have been detected, the debounce counter is enabled. Breaks in contact continuity (bounding contacts, etc.) are ignored for a debounce period (T_{db}) of 32 ms. At this time, the keypad is samples, and if both row and column information is valid, this information is buffered into the LND location.

Rate Control. The Rate Control input (pin 7) is a single-pin RC oscillator. An external resistor and capacitor determine the rate at which signaling occurs in both tone and pulse modes. An 8 kHz oscillator provides the nominal signaling rates of 10 PPS (pulses per second) in pulse mode and 5 TPS (tones per second) in tone mode; the tone duty cycle is 98 ms on and 102 ms off. The RC values on this input can be adjusted to a maximum oscillation frequency of 16 kHz resulting in an effective pulse rate of 20 PPS and a tone rate of 10 TPS. The frequency of oscillation is approximated by the following equation:

$$F^{osc} = 1/(1.49RC).$$

The value suggested for the capacitor (C) should be a maximum of 410 pF to guarantee the accuracy of the oscillator. The resistor is then selected for the desired signaling rate. Nominal frequency (8 kHz) is achieved with component values of 390 pF and 220 kohms. Parasitic oscillations must be taken into account. In our project R14 and C13 are 220 Kohms and 390 pF respectively. C13 is specified as a silver mica type dielectric capacitor.

OSC1, OSC2. Pins 8 and 9 are the input and output, respectively, of an onchip inverter with sufficient loop gain to oscillate when used in conjunction with a low-cost television colorburst crystal. The nominal crystal frequency is 3.579545 MHz and any deviation from this standard is directly reflected in the tone output frequencies. This oscillator is under direct control of the repertory dialer and is enabled only when a tone signal is to be transmitted. During all other times it remains off, and the input has high impedance. The input OSC1 may be driven by an external source.

DTMF OUTPUT. The DTMF Output, pin 10, is connected internally to the emitter of and npn transistor. The collection is tied to V+, as shown on the functional block diagram in Fig. 7-7. The base of this transistor is the output of an onchip operational amplifier that mixes the row and column tones together. The level of the DTMF Output is the sum of a single row frequency and a single column frequency. A typical single-tone sine wave is shown in Fig. 7-8A. This waveform is synthesized using a resistor tree with sinusoidally weighted taps. Fig. 7-8B shows a typical dual-tone waveform. The tone level of the MK5375 is a function of the supply voltage. The voltage to the device may be regulated to achieve the desired tone level, which is related to the supply by either of the following equations:

$T(0) = 20 \text{ LOG } [(0.078V +)/0.775]$ dBm

$T(0) = 0.085(V +)$ Vrms

PACIFIER TONE/CHIP DISABLE. Pin 11 normally has high impedance. Upon acceptance of a valid key input, and after the 21 ms debounce time, a 500 Hz square wave will be output on this pin. The square wave terminates after a maximum of 30 ms or when the valid key is no longer present. The purpose of this pacifier tone is to provide to the user audible feedback that a valid key has been entered.

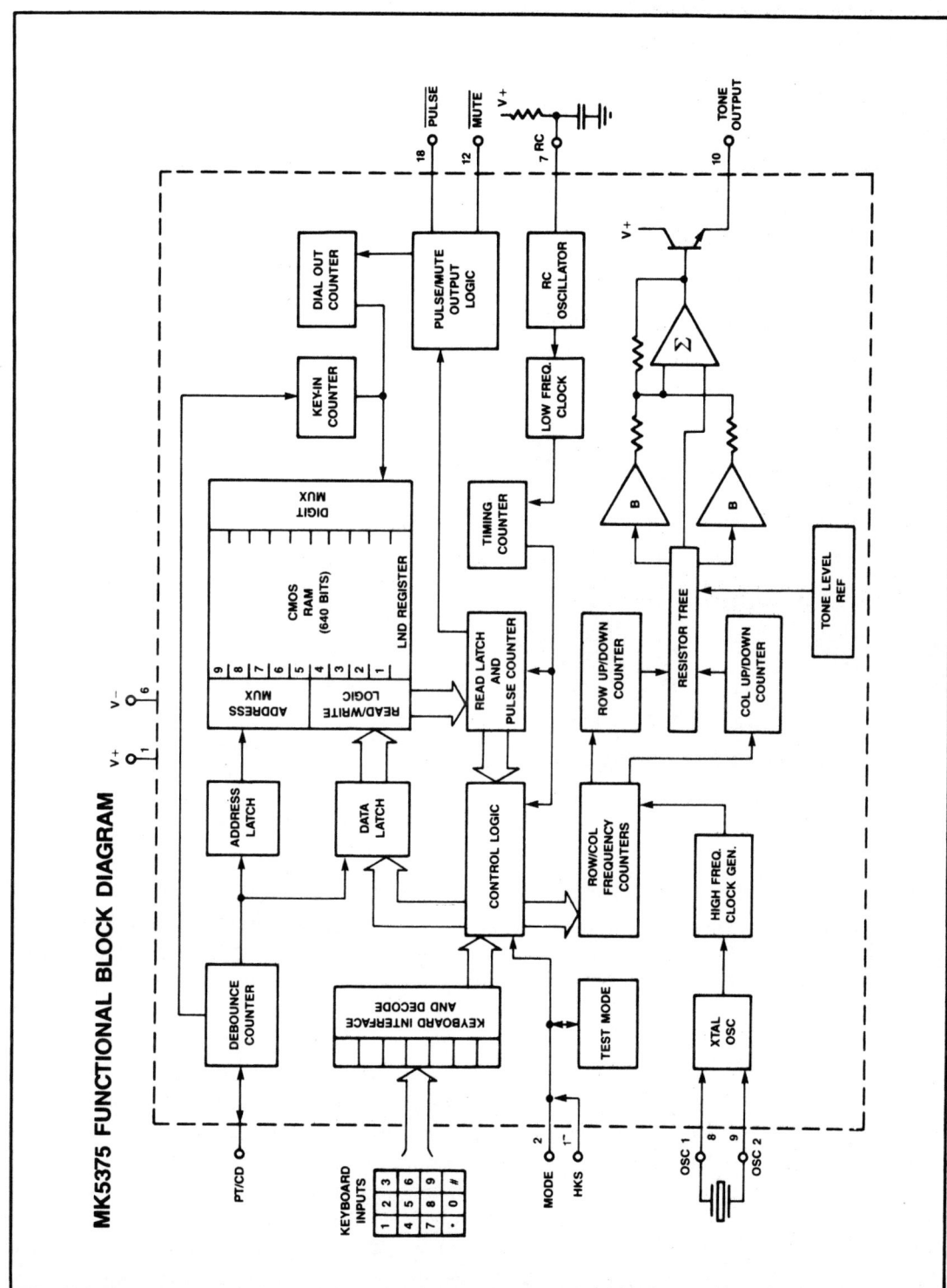

Fig. 7-7. Functional block diagram of the MK5375. Courtesy of Mostek.

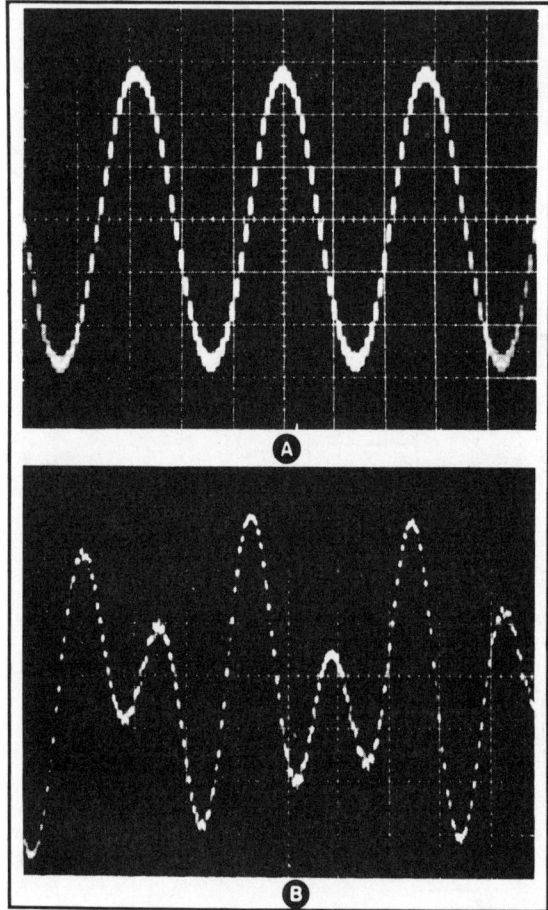

Fig. 7-8. Typical single-tone (A) and dual-tone (B) sinewaves.

This feature is useful particularly for on-hook storage and pulse-mode signaling.

The pacifier tone is not enabled when manually dialing in tone mode. This eliminates any confusion between the audible DTMF feedback and the pacifier tone, and prevents distortion of the DTMF signal by any of the pacifier tone frequency components. In both cases, the tone confirms that the key has been properly entered and accepted; whereas, without the tone, the user will not know if the keys have been properly entered.

Important: This pin also serves as a *chip-disable pin*. Pulling this input high through a resistor will disable the keypad (high impedance) and initialize all counters and flip-flops (memory remains undisturbed). Pulling the input low through the same resistor enables the circuit. For the device to function properly, the resistor to V− (pin 6) is required. This feature is useful in several of the applications described in the Applications section of this chapter.

MUTE OUTPUT. Pin 12 is the mute output for both tone and pulse modes of operation. The timing is dependent upon which mode is being used. The output consists of an open-drain, n-channel device. During standby, the output has high impedance and generally requires an external pullup resistor to the positive supply.

In tone mode, the mute output is used to remove the transmitter and the receiver from the network during DTMF signaling. The output will mute continuously while auto-dialing and during manual DTMF signaling until each digit entered has been signaled. In pulse mode of operation, the mute output is used to remove the receiver or even the entire network from the line. These timing relationships are shown in Fig. 7-9.

HKS INPUT. Pin 17 is a high-impedance input and must be switched high for on-hook operation or low for off-hook operation. A transition on this input will cause the on-chip logic to initialize, terminating any operation in progress at the time. Signaling is inhibited while on-hook, but key inputs will be accepted and stored in the LND register. The information stored in the LND register may be copied into an alternate location only while on-hook. A logic level may be presented to this input, independent of the position of the hook-switch, allowing on-hook operations, such as storage, to be performed off-hook.

PULSE. Pin 18 is an output driven by an open-drain, n-channel device. In pulse mode

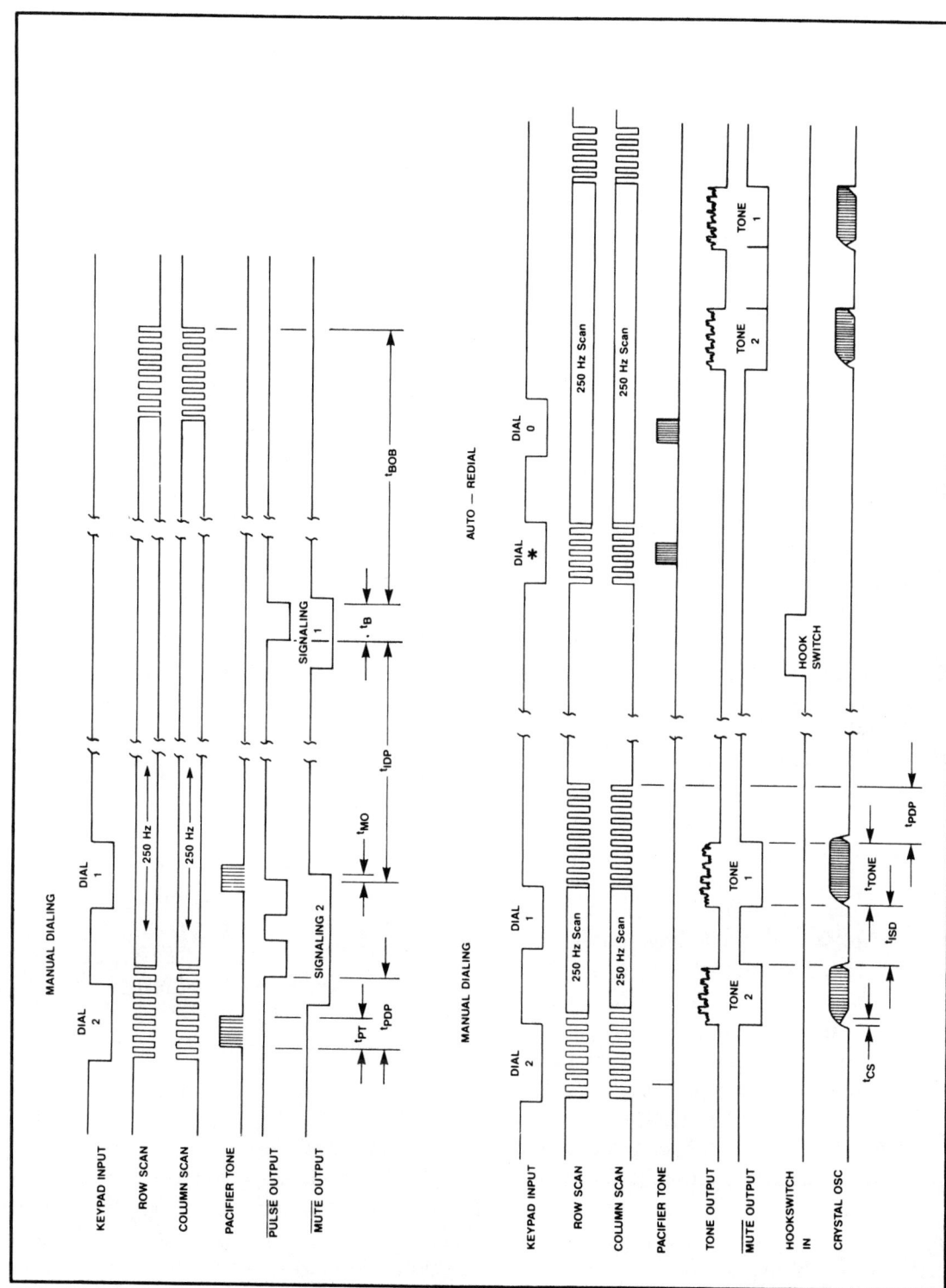

Fig. 7-9. Timing diagrams for both pulse and tone modes. Courtesy of Mostek.

operation, the timing at this output meets Bell Telephone and EIA specifications for loop-disconnect signaling. The Make/Break ratio is set to 40/60 on the standard MK5375. The pulse rate is determined by the RC values selected for the Rate Control, pin 7. **Note:** The standard make/break ratio may not be suitable if the pulse dialing rate is accelerated.

Operation

The MK5375 can be used in low-priced phones with basic 3 × 4 matrix keypads. The block diagram in Fig. 7-7 shows the data and control signal flow between the various functional blocks. The keypad entries are decoded, debounced, and if valid, they are stored into the LND (Last-Number-Dialed) buffer, which acts much like a FIFO (First-In-First-Out) register. Each subsequent entry is stacked in the buffer. Typically, the dialing sequence begins 172 ms after the first digit is accepted in pulse mode operation and 132 ms in tone mode operation. Each digit buffered into the RAM is dialed out with a 98 ms burst of DTMF and an inter-signal time of 102 ms.

Buffering the data into the RAM prior to signaling is an important feature of the repertory dialer. It allows for the use of less expensive keypads, since the user cannot enter the digits too quickly for the system, and the pacifier tone can be used to provide audible feedback following each key entry not generating a DTMF signal. It also guarantees that the data stored in the RAM exactly matches the digits that are dialed.

Manual dialing and auto-dialing can be executed in any order, consecutively or cascaded. The dialer must complete auto-dialing the previous entry before another key is entered. Digits should not be entered while the device is auto-dialing. Most digits would be ignored unless preceded by a control key; in which case, an error in dialing may occur.

The following dial sequences illustrate the functions of the MK 5375. These sequences are for pulse dialing.

Normal Dialing. The "*" (STAR) key is used as the modifier to control repertory functions. All numeric keys will signal normally unless preceded by a modifier. To signal either a "*" or "#", these keys must be entered twice in succession. The first entry is not signaled or stored. (The D in the key sequences is any data.)

| D | * | * | D | D |

LND Privacy. A single "*" input prior to going on-hook or prior to completing off-hook will erase the information stored in the LND buffer.

| D | D | ... | D | * | On-Hook

Auto Dialing (Off-Hook). The key sequence "*", followed by any digit, will auto-dial the number sequence stored in the designated address location while off-hook.

| D | D | ... | D | * | N |
 opt opt   opt

Storage. D is any data (telephone numbers) being entered or dialed. N is the address (memory location) in which numbers are stored. The number sequence stored in the LND buffer can be transferred to one of the other nine permanent locations with the simple sequence "*" followed by the address. New digits may be written into the LND buffer while on-hook. To enter either a "*" or "#" signal, the digit must be entered twice in succession.

| D | D | D | * | N |
 opt opt opt

PABX Pause (Off-Hook and On-Hook). An indefinite pause is stored in a number sequence by entering the "*" key modifier, followed by a "#" key input. When the number sequence is redialed, the dialer will pause when it encounters the "#" entry. A key input will cause it to continue.

Pulse Dialing. Most of the pulse key operations are the same as they were in tone mode; PABX Pause is the only exception. In pulse mode, the pause may be stored as in tone mode, "*#", or with a single "#" input. Two "#" inputs will store two pauses. The "*" key exercises the control function; two "*" inputs will be the same as a single input (multiple inputs are not accepted).

Applications

The MK5375 integrated circuit provides the ability to convert keypad inputs into either DTMF or loop-disconnect signals compatible with most telephone systems. Both modes of signaling utilize loop currents to transmit the desired signaling information to the central office. The schematic in Fig. 7-10 illustrates a typical implementation of the MK5375 dialer IC along with the necessary components required to interface with the telephone line in a tone/pulse application.

In loop-disconnect signaling, each digit dialed consists of a series of momentary interruptions of loop current called "breaks" (i.e., a digit "1" consists of a single break, a digit "2" consists of two breaks, and so on). The pulse output is dedicated to loop-disconnect signaling and controls the flow of loop current through the speech network switching transistors, Q4 and Q5. The mute output, through transistors Q2 and Q3, removes the receiver and transmitter to eliminate loud pops in the receiver caused by switching current through the network. The pulse and mute output signals, as shown in Fig. 7-11 consist of make, break, and interdigital time intervals.

DTMF signaling requires that the loop current be modulated, producing an analog signal on the telephone line. Transistor Q1 modulates the loop current by amplifying the DTMF signal coupled to its base from the tone output. The mute output removes the receiver and transmitter by switching transistors Q2 and Q3. This eliminates any interference with the DTMF signal from the transmitter and cuts down on the amplitude of the DTMF tone heard at the receiver. The timing diagram in Fig. 7-9 illustrates the time relationship between key entries, tone output, and mute output.

The voltage regulator circuit comprising resistor R2, zener diode Z2, and transistor Q6 serves several purposes. In tone mode operation, it provides the regulated supply voltage to the MK5375 which determines the DTMF signal amplitude at the tone output. Varying the supply voltage will vary the DTMF output signal. In pulse mode, it helps provide some isolation from the transients caused by switching the speech network in and out.

During normal off-hook dialing, the MK5375 operates using current from the telephone line. On-hook number storage and memory retention current are supplied by the battery shown in Fig. 7-11. Transistor Q6 prevents the flow of battery current to the speech network.

The rate at which dialing occurs is determined by the values chosen for resistor R1 and capacitor C1. These values can be determined using the equation $F_{osc} = 1/(1.49RC)$. The 3.5795 MHz crystal is used as a reference for synthesizing the DTMF signals and is activated only for the short periods during which these tones are being generated.

The application circuit schematic in Fig. 7-12 gives an example of the various features which can be utilized with the addition of several switches. The example also shows that multiple devices may be used to increase the effective storage capability of the telephone

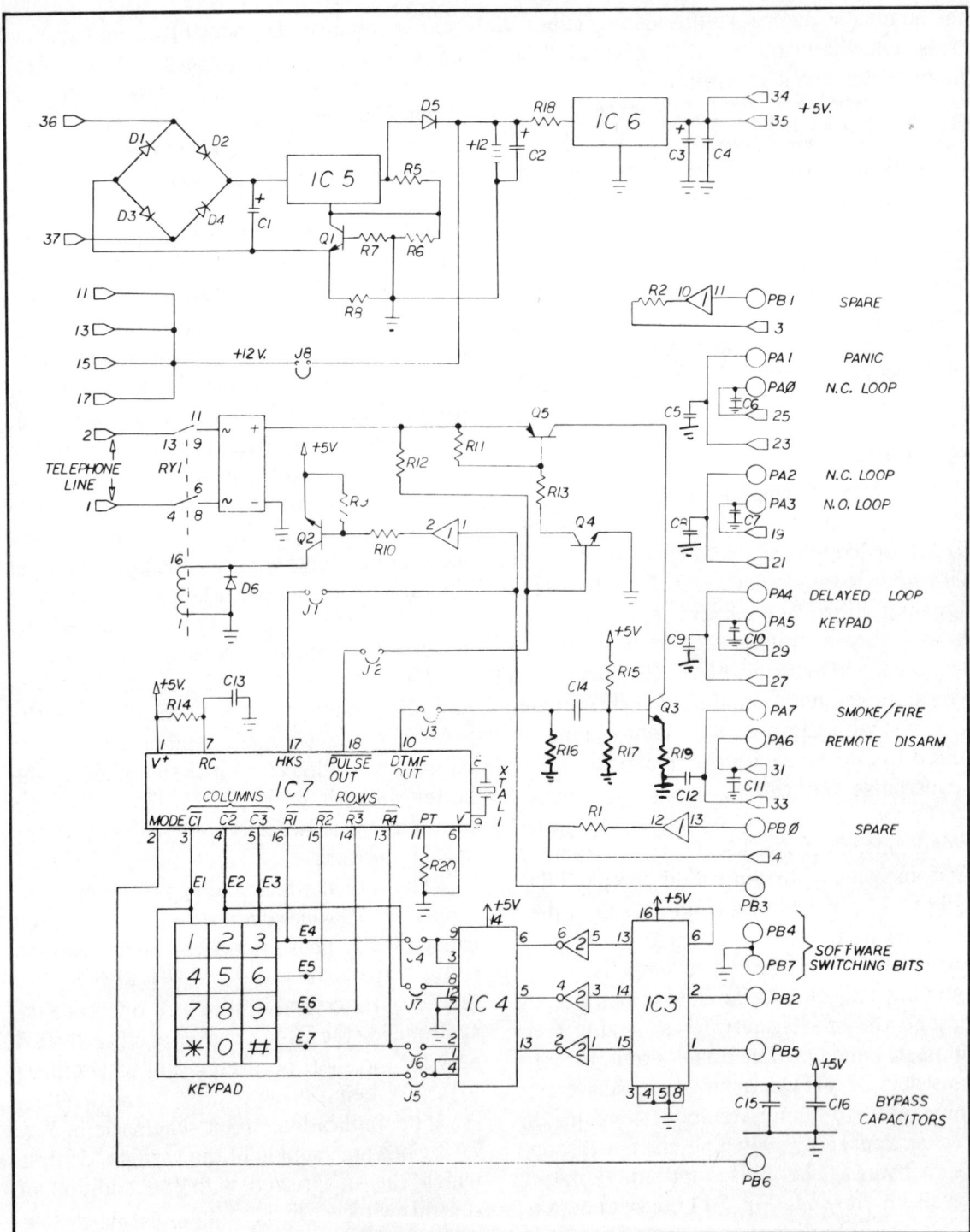

Fig. 7-10. Schematic for the Automatic Telephone Dialer.

Part's List for the Automatic Telephone Dialer.

R1-R2 = 680 1/2 W
R5, R7, R19 = 100 1/4 W
R6, R9, R10 = 1 K 1/4 W
R8 = .33 3 W
R11, R12 = 150 K 1/4 W
R13 = 1.5 K 1/4 W
R14, R20 = 220 K 1/4 W
R15 = 110 K 1/4 W
R16 = 10 K 1/4 W
R17 = 560 K 1/4 W
R18 = 18 3 W

C1 = 1000 µF 25 V
C2 = 470 µF 25 V
C3 = 100 µF 25 V
C4-C12 = .1 µF CERAMIC
C13 = 390 pF SILVER MICA
C14 = 1 µF CERAMIC

D1-D5 = 1N4001
D6 = 1N4148

Q1 = 2N2222
Q2 = T1P127, RCA8203B or equivalent pnp Darlington in a TO-220 Case
Q3, Q4 = 2N5550
Q5 = 2N5401 or equivalent transistor with maximum V_{cb} and V_{ce} ratings of 160 and 150 volts respectively

U1 = 7407 TTL IC
U2 = 7406 TTL IC
U3 = 74LS138 TTL IC
U4 = CD4066 RCA CMOS IC
U5 = LM 350 K STEEL Adjustable Voltage Regulator
U6 = LM 340T-5 5 V. Fixed Voltage Regulator
U7 = MK5375 Mostek IC

Bridge Rectifier = Radio Shack #276-1173 400 V A Bridge
XTAL1 = 3.5795 MHz Radio Shack #272-1310 Color Burst Crystal
RY1 = Radio Shack #275-215 5 V DPDT Relay
Keypad-Wild Rover model KB-001, available from:

    Sintec Company
    P.O. Box 410, 28th street
    Frenchtown, N.J. 08825
    201-996-4093
    Part Number 11291
    $4.50 plus postage

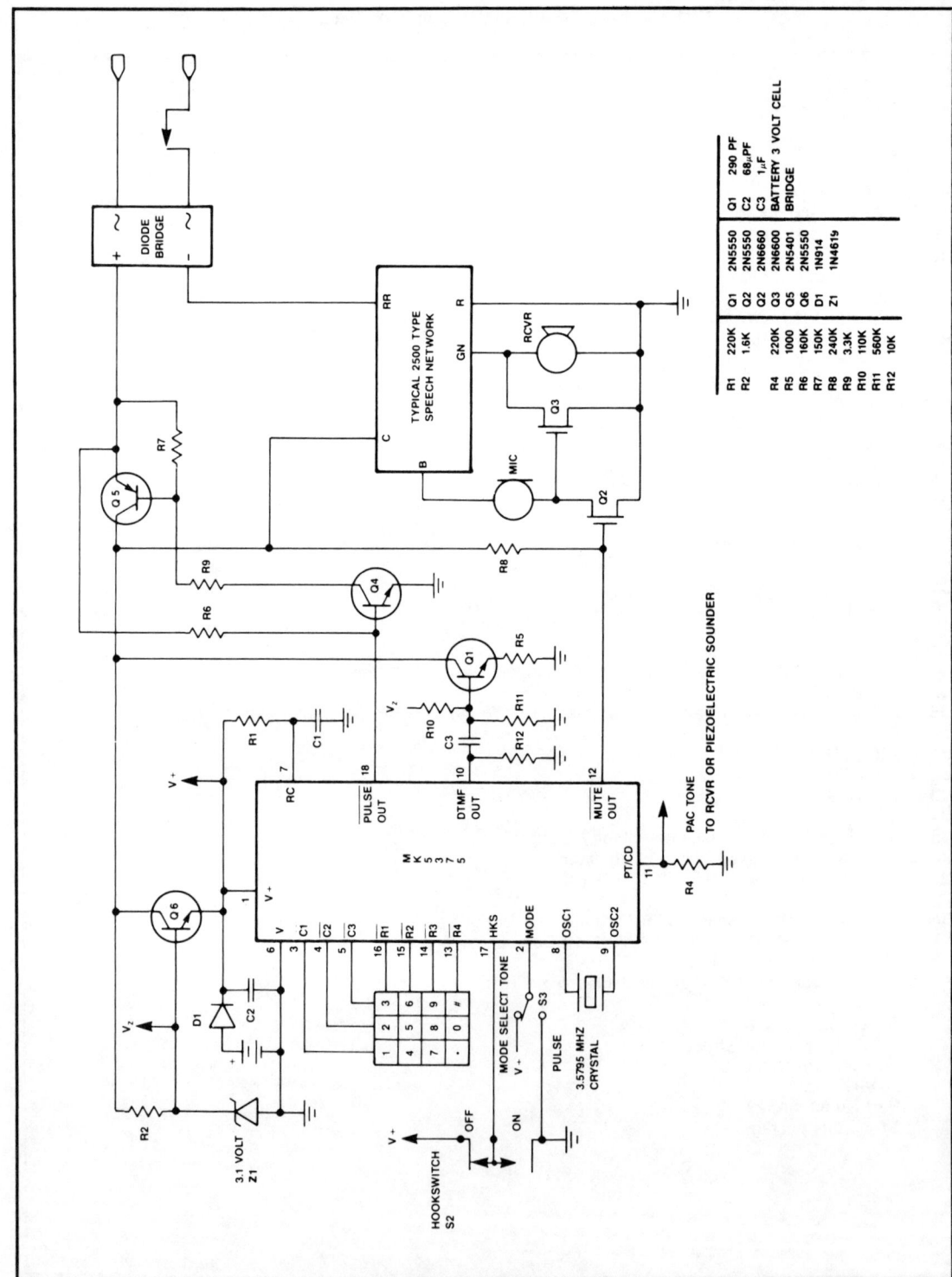

Fig. 7-11. A typical circuit using the MK5375.

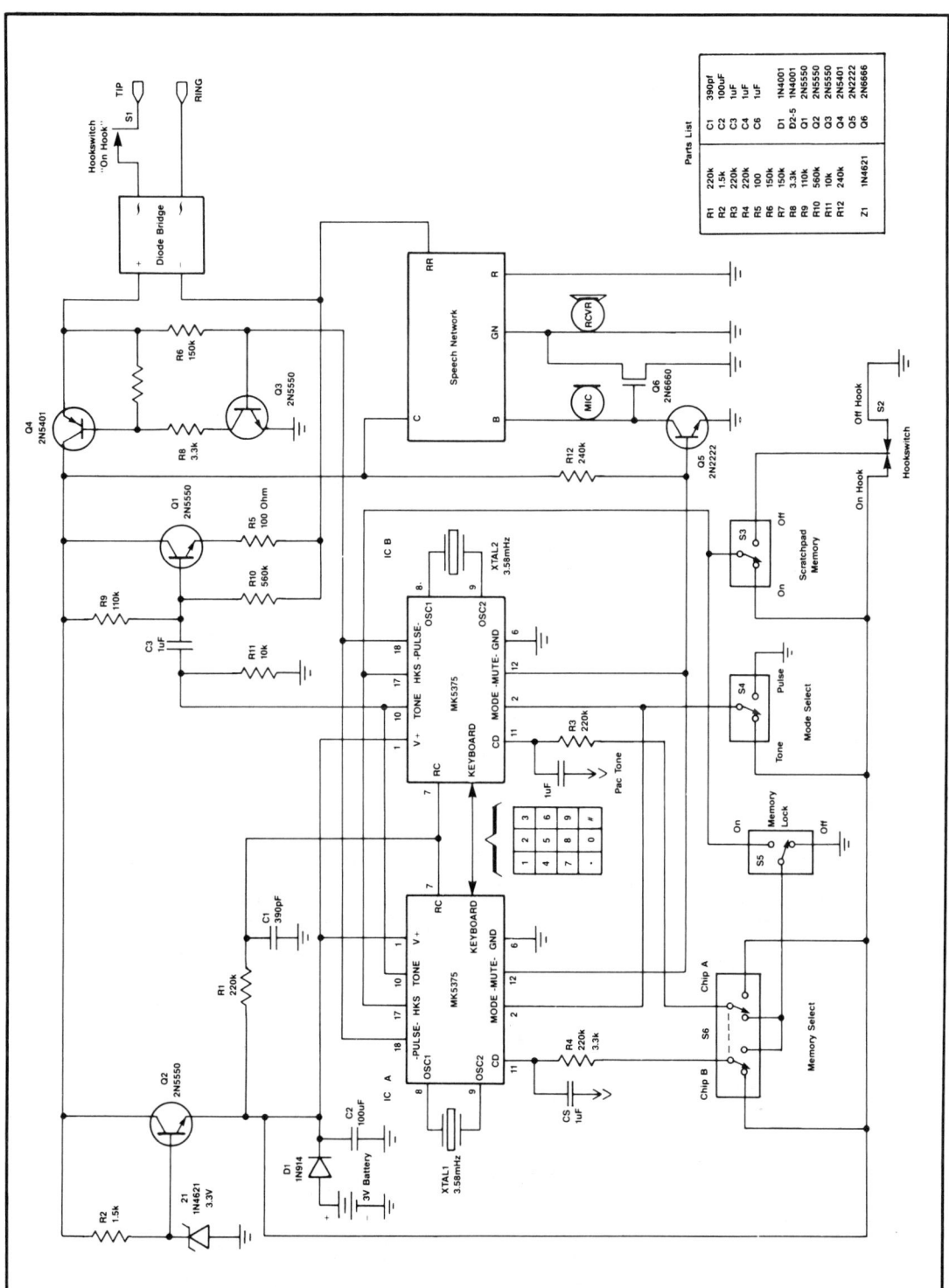

Fig. 7-12. MK5375 application using switches to take advantage of built-in features.

design. Much of the circuitry used to modulate and pulse the line, mute the speech network, and regulate the supply voltage is unchanged from the basic tone/pulse switchable telephone described in Fig. 7-11.

The two devices in Fig. 7-12 are hooked up in parallel with one another except for their oscillator pins and the Chip Disable inputs. A DPDT switch is used to select between the two dialers through the Chip Disable pin; one device is activated while the other is put on standby.

Some applications may include a memory lock switch to prevent any of the data stored to be changed inadvertently. This memory lock switch can take the form of a locking key switch, which would allow only the person with the key to alter data stored in memory.

A scratchpad feature may be implemented to allow off-hook programming of the memory while inhibiting dialing. A switch is added in series with the telephone hook-switch to allow the dialer to be forced into its on-hook key entry mode while the telephone set is off-hook.

TELEPHONE DIALER PROJECT

The basis of this automatic telephone dialer is the delayed entry Perimiguard system as discussed in Chapter 5. The major differences in hardware are the deletion of both the buzzer feature on the keypad entry device and the associated Darlington transistor pair siren drivers. This system is a silent-alarm intrusion-detection system. Therefore, no audible means were required for indicating the detection or discovery of an entry.

The basic design differs from other telephone dialers in that no means are provided for a tape recorder with a prerecorded message to state "an entry has occurred at XXX Main Street etc." This system automatically dials two predetermined numbers in succession which have been entered by the operator or homeowner. Once an intrusion has occurred, the two telephone numbers dialed in are rung and when the receiver is picked up a 30 second succession of two tone pulses occur. These pulses are the very familiar "European police car siren" sound. You may recall from movies shot abroad in which a police chase scene appears that the car's siren makes a warbler of two alternate tone sound. These two tones correspond to the two keypad tones associated with the numbers 1 and 2. Refer to Table 7-3. This two tone convention in lieu of

Table 7-1. Column/Row Key Assignment and Edge Connector Number.

Keypad Numeral	Column Number	Row Number	Edge Connector Number
1	1	1	3 & 4
2	2	1	3 & 2
3	3	1	3 & 6
4	1	2	8 & 4
5	2	2	8 & 2
6	3	2	8 & 6
7	1	3	7 & 4
8	2	3	7 & 2
9	3	3	7 & 6
0	2	4	5 & 4
*	1	4	5 & 2
#	3	4	5 & 6

Note: Pin 1 on the 8-pin keypad's edge connector is grounded and is the pin to the far left viewing the keypad specified in this project from the numeral side up.

the ordinary prerecorded tape message is a more modern approach to security detection because many police departments throughout America now no longer allow these types of calls to be made.

Operation

The ability to enter two phone numbers exists during any time except during the alarm mode, which naturally occurs after an unauthorized entry, or secondly while the system is actually in the process of dialing these two predetermined phone numbers. Entry of these predetermined phone numbers is quite simple. You merely enter the first phone number, press the "*" keypad followed by the number "1". This action enters the phone number into register #1. Likewise, the same procedure is followed for entry of the second number. The only difference is that after the actual phone number and "*" entry you press "2" which enters this second telephone number into the second memory register.

When an unauthorized home entry is detected, the system is set off. The 4 1/2 IC computer will activate all of the functions to dial the phone numbers. The 6502 microprocessor uses the 6532 RIOT's (RAM I/O Timer), B ports, PB2, PB3, PB5, and PB6. In sequence, the MK5375 IC is put into the pulse dialing mode with PB6, and after a short delay, the telephone IC is switched on line through PB3, Q2, U1, and relay RY1. Refer to the schematic in Fig. 7-10 and note that when PB3 goes low the relay (RY1) pulls in and effectively connects to the telephone line. After a short delay, the microprocessor sets PB2 and PB5 low. This selects Y_o out of IC3, a 74LS138 1-of-8 decoder/multiplexer whose output is buffered, inverted, and applied to pin 13 of the CD4066 quad bilateral analog switch. Refer to Fig. 7-13 for an illustration of the four analog switches within this IC. Note on the schematic (Fig. 7-10) that only 3 of the 4 analog switches are used. Pin 13 of this IC controls analog switch A, and the flow of the signal on

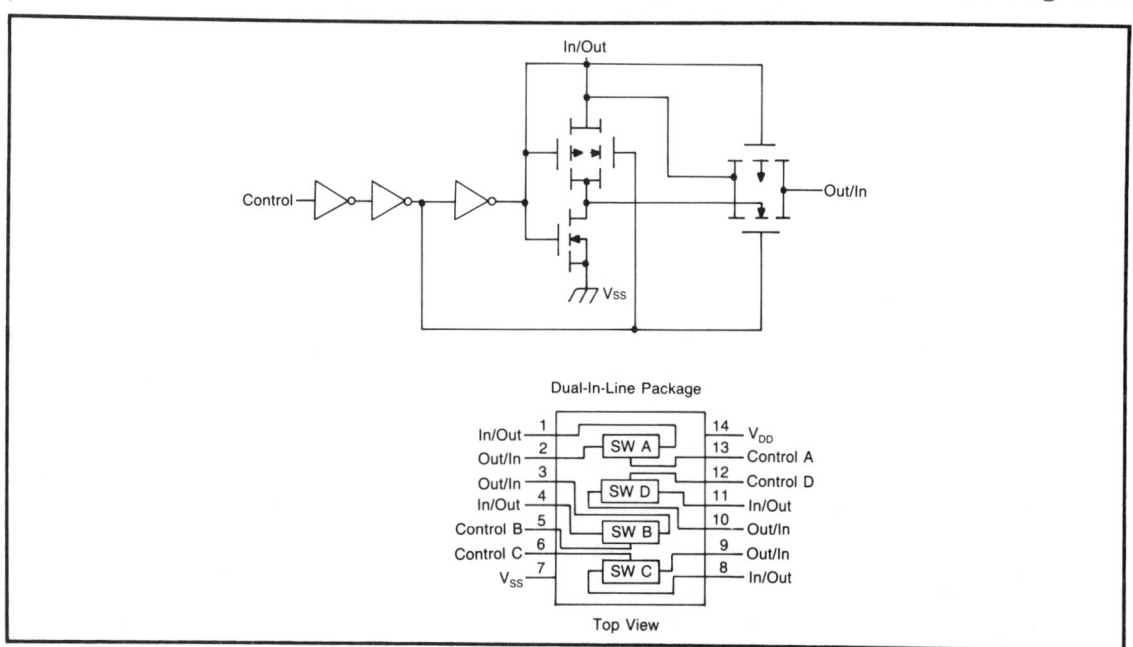

Fig. 7-13. A block diagram of the CD4066 CMOS bilateral analog switch.

pins 1 and 2 connects rows and columns. (Refer to Fig. 7-7 for an illustration of the electrical connections on the keypad.)

Note specifically that when PB2 and PB5 are low this activates the "*" which is the number entry key or the device that prompts the memory or phone number registers that they are about to receive a number. After the "*" is activated, PB2 and PB5 go high and no digits are selected at all. Next, PB2 goes low while PB5 goes high. This selects Y1 which is likewise buffered, inverted by inverting buffer U2, and applied to pin 5 of the quad bilateral switch, analog switch B of U4. This controls the pins 3 and 4 or digit 1 of the keypad. This takes the number entered and stored in memory register 1 and pulse dials it out the MK5375 IC, pin 18, and along with Q4 and Q5, it outputs a string of pulses which go through the bridge rectifier module to the telephone line. After a 15 second delay, the MK5375 is switched to the tone dialing mode by alternately going high then low on PB2 and PB5 of the RIOT. This action selects 1 or 2 in succession and dials out alternate 1 and 2 frequency tones for 30 seconds. In the actual circuit, this physically occurs at pin 10 of the MK5375 on the DTMF pin and goes through an RC network to the base of the transistor Q3 and back out transistor Q5 to the line.

After this 30 second series of alternating tones, PB3 goes high and Q2 and relay RY1 drops out, which effectively disconnects the circuit from the phone line. A 15 second delay allows the system to reset itself before RY1 connects again and the system begins anew with the sequence of PB2 and PB5 from the RIOT pulling in the pulse mode and a "*"; then the second number stored in memory register 2 is dialed while in the pulse mode. After a switch to the tone mode, the two tone sequence is again sent over the phone lines. After this 30 second sequence of pulses, the relay drops out and there is a 5 minute delay. This time out feature is identical to the same feature on the delayed entry perimeter detection project. After the delay, it enters the alarm sequence again and checks to see if the alarm condition has or has not been met. If it has not been met, it goes through a complete sequence of dialing the two numbers again.

If you ever have an occasion to desire to change either one or both of the telephone numbers to be automatically dialed when the alarm condition occurs, this is very easily done. You merely enter the number, press the "*" key on they keypad and then the number 1 is pressed if you wish this to be the new number in memory location 1. Likewise, if you follow the same procedure and press the number 2 key on the keypad after hitting the "*" key, this will enter the new number in memory location 2.

These two memory registers are really volatile RAMs so they not only can be written to but their contents goes away after the removal or a temporary interruption of power to the IC. This should never occur though with the circuit in Fig. 7-10 because of the battery backup feature provided by the LM350 voltage regulator, its associated circuitry, and the 12 volt rechargeable battery.

Components

A PC (printed circuit) board has been laid out for this project. Refer to Fig. 7-14 for a 1:1 scale foil pattern and to Fig. 7-15 for a component placement drawing. Note specifically that the dimensions of this board are identical to the boards used on the two previous Perimiguard detection systems. This approach fortunately enables you to follow all of the same mechanical drawings within Chapter 5 with respect to the hinge, angle bracket, case, etc. Also, the same

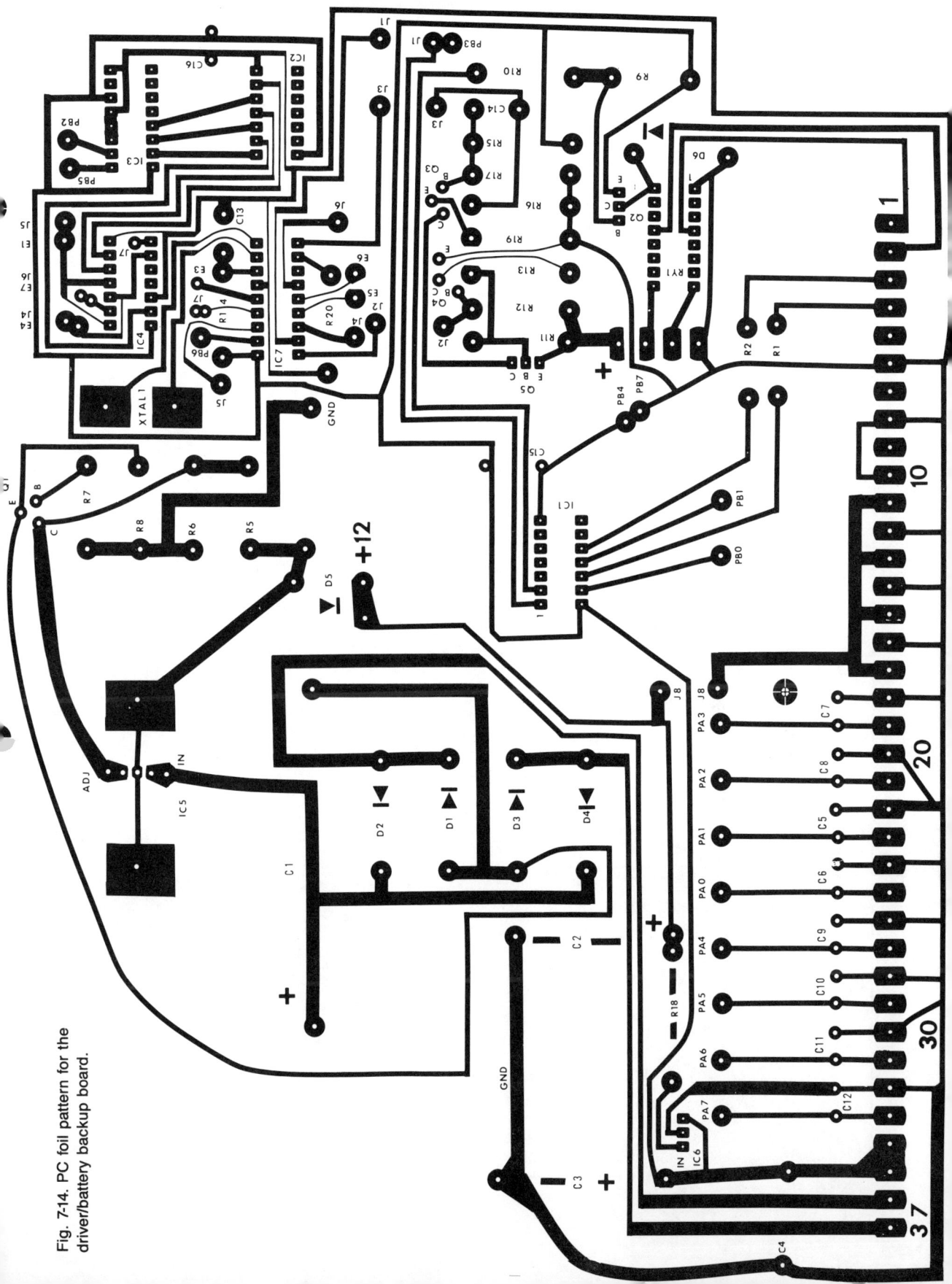

Fig. 7-14. PC foil pattern for the driver/battery backup board.

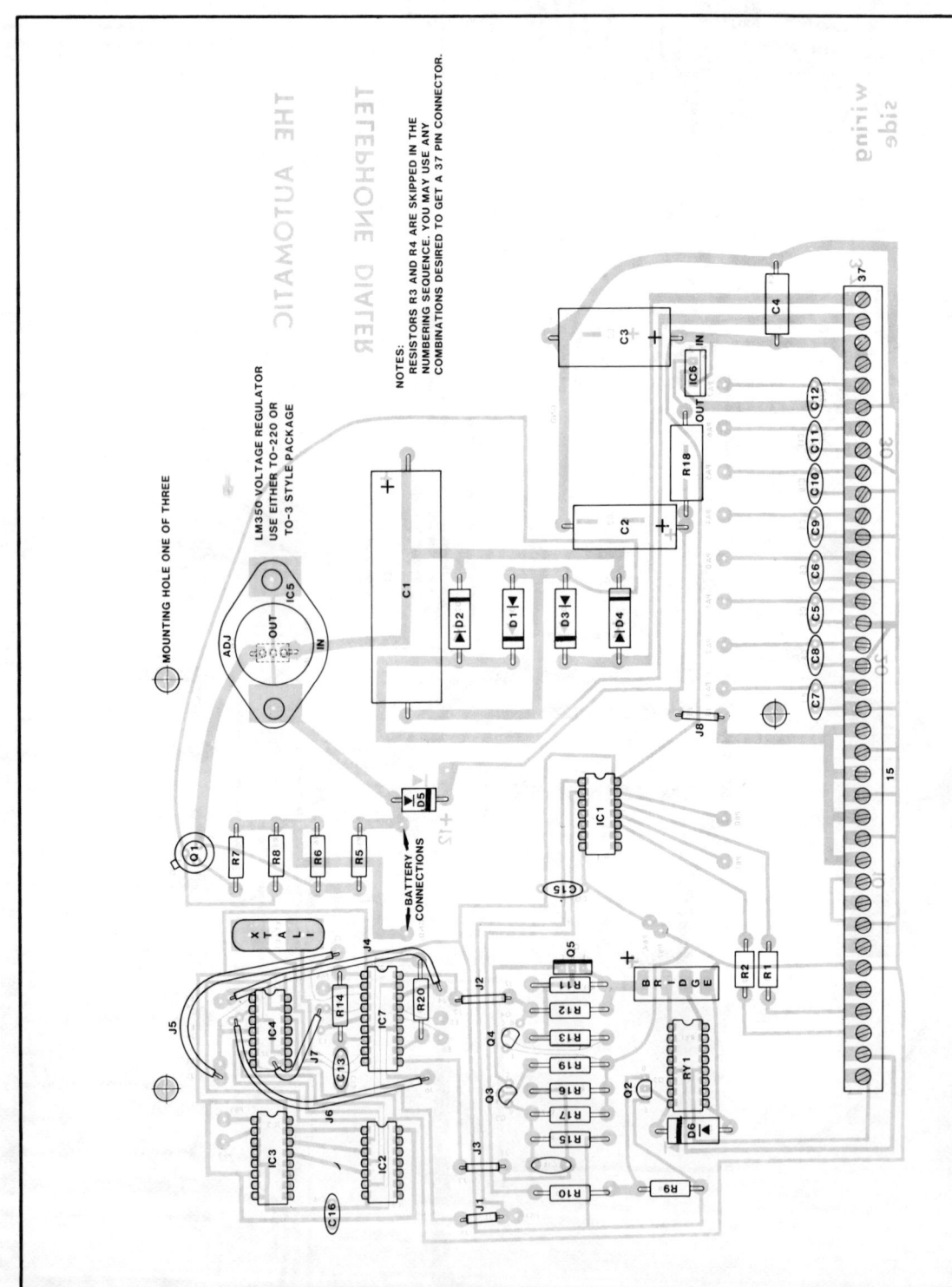

Fig. 7-15. Component placement diagram.

kinds of edge connectors and the same "piggyback" arrangement for the microcomputer/controller board to reside on top of the dialer board can be used.

You will probably recognize much of the circuitry as also being identical. This helped us by not having to reinvent the wheel and helps you by having a standardization of parts. Note the upper half of the circuitry in Fig. 7-10 and also realize that even the same pinout convention was carried over on this PC layout/design. The only hardware considerations to specifically be aware of are that the PC pattern accommodates either a TO-3 cased LM350K STEEL IC voltage regulator or a TO-220 LM350 voltage regulator IC with three inline pins separated by 0.1 inches. This is the same approach that we used in Chapter 5.

The 5 Vdc DPDT (double-pole double-throw) relay was selected for convenience, availability, and electrical performance parameters. The Radio Shack part number is 275-215. It has high reliability silver contacts rated at 1 A at 125 Vac. The relay fits into a standard 16-pin DIP IC socket or PC pattern; however, it only has eight pins brought out by necessity. Alternate pins have judiciously been deleted so that a separation of 0.2 inches or

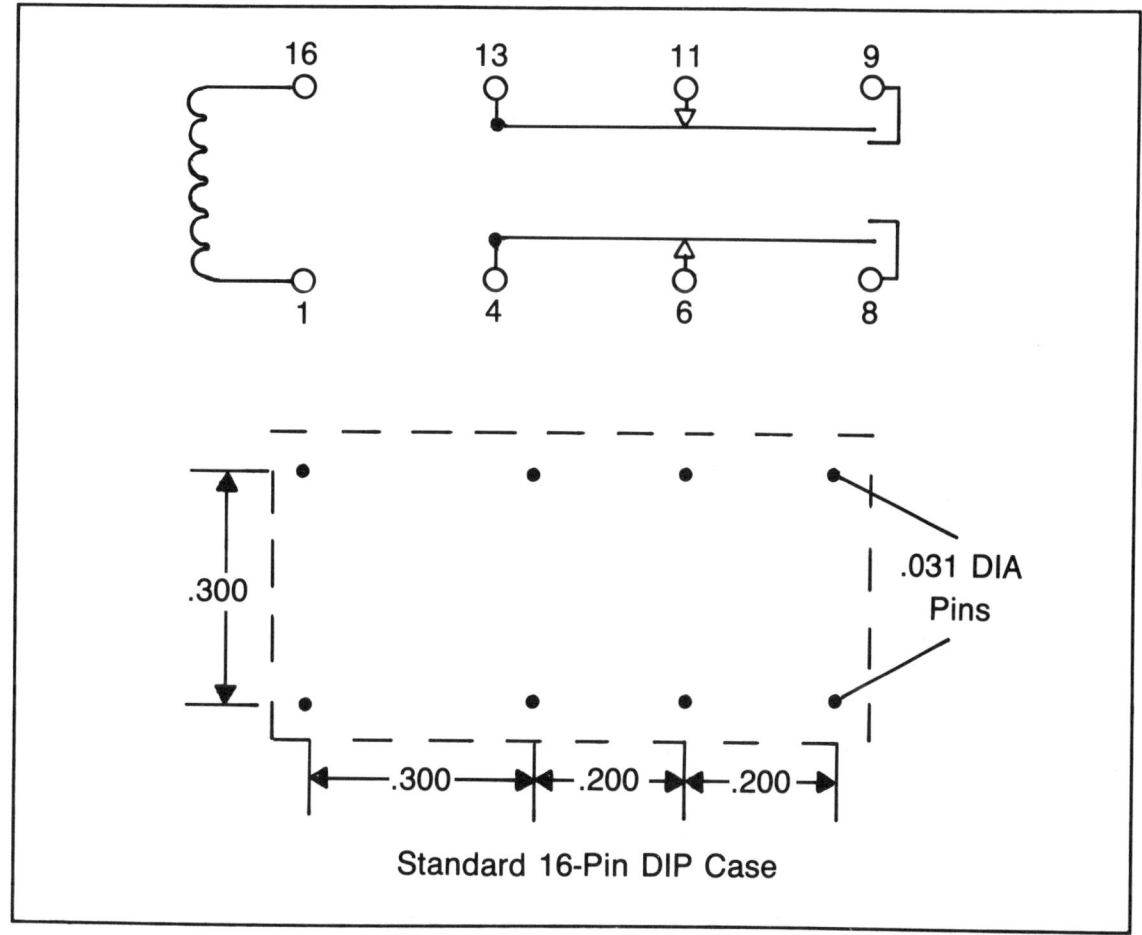

Fig. 7-16. Pin assignment and coil-contact arrangement for the 5 Vdc DPDT relay.

greater always exists between adjacent pins. This is especially prudent when switching larger sums of power. Figure 7-16 shows the pin numbers and coil-contact pin assignments. Incidentally, note that because of the less than equally spaced nonsymetrical staggered pinouts on each side this relay can not ever be incorrectly inserted into the PC board.

The full-wave bridge rectifier specified is Radio Shack part number #276-1173. It is a 400 V, 4 A module with four inline pins. The PC board is laid out to accommodate this one or a similar four pin inline pack with similar pin spacings as long as the electrical parameters are at least 200 V at 2 A.

Board Construction

The PC (printed circuit) board, as shown in Figs. 7-14 and 7-15, illustrates the copper foil pattern and the component placements respectively. This board, as previously stated, is the exact size of the two battery backup/driver boards associated with the Perimiguard projects with and without the delayed entry feature. Therefore, this will allow you to use the same housing cabinet and bracket as previously specified on the two Perimiguard projects. The connectors at the bottom of the board again number 37 in quantity and are the same type.

This PC board is probably slightly more difficult to build owing to the number and position of the jumper wires. These jumper wires were necessary to accommodate a rather complex wiring pattern on a single-sided board. The eight jumpers are labeled J1 through J8 inclusively, and you merely match numbers, that is, wire J1 to J1, J2 to J2 . . . etc. The schematic in Fig. 7-10 clearly labels these jumpers as J1 through J8.

There are also eight additional wires which must be soldered onto the PC board as well.

These eight connectors are from the three columns and four rows, and the last connection is the electrostatic shield on the keypad that requires grounding. These eight wires go to spots on the PC board denoted as E1 through E8 inclusively. Refer to the calculator-type keypad or the so-called matrix switch keypad, the upper illustration in Fig. 7-7. Refer also to Table 7-1 which identifies each key by column and row interaction so that you can perform a continuity check on each of the twelve keys on the keypad to ensure that you have a properly manufactured keypad.

Due to the extremely dense wiring on the PC board around IC4 (the CMOS bilateral quad analog switch), there is a pad under the IC called J7. Solder a wire to this point approximately two inches long and connect it to the other J7 on the PC board between the PB6 and E3 pads. Incidentally, these "E" numbered pads are a convention showing that a wire either enters or leaves the PC board at that spot. Also, there are several other "E" reference designators on the board. These are not to be confused with the E numbered pads with a number following them. These stand alone E designators typically occur in three pad transistor clusters and are placed there to signify an emitter.

Next to the J7 between the PB6 and E3 pads is an adjoining pad. This pad is really the "E2" pad. It was not labelled as such because of insufficient space on an already dense PC board. Look on the schematic and note how E2 and J7 are electrically common to one another. Jumpers J1, J2, J3, and J8 are only one inch jumpers that are directly across from one another. The other four jumpers require a little searching and eventual "matching up" as well as sizing of their conductor lengths for an exact neat fit.

The keypad specified for this project is the

Table 7-3. E Number and Corresponding Keypad Connector Pin Chart.

E Number on the PC Board	Connector Pin on the Keypad
1	4
2	2
3	6
4	3
5	8
6	7
7	5
8	1

Wire the connector pin to the "E" number straight across from it in this table. Pin 1 on the keypad edge connector is the pin to the far left, viewed face up, and is the electrostatic shield which gets grounded. The keypad is a Wild Rover model KB-001.

Wild Rover elastomeric keyboard in the firm's KB series. These 3 × 4 keypads consist of a glass-filled epoxy PC board, high quality elastomeric pad with conductive rubber contacts and high impact ABS plastic keyboard bodies with double-shot molded keys. This keypad offers a matrix schematic in lieu of the common ground. Refer to Fig. 7-7. This means that as a key is pressed a path is completed and two pins on the edge connector will have a very low resistance between them. These two edge connector pins correspond to the row/column entry. More specifically, if you were to press the numeral 6, then you would have very low resistance between pins 6 and 8. Refer to Table 7-1 and Fig. 7-7. You are encouraged to go through and press all twelve keys and run a continuity check on the edge connector pin pairs corresponding to these twelve key closures. This will ensure a properly manufactured keypad.

When you have used Table 7-1 to properly satisfy your keypad testing you will want to install it by wiring it into the PC board. This should come before you mount the microcomputer board. As you may recall from previous projects, the microcomputer board has three holes and is mounted onto the larger PC battery backup/buffer boards by aligning the two sets of three holes with one another and mounting the two boards on top of one another with threaded standoffs for proper and uniform separation. The three pads on the larger telephone dialer PC board are bulleye's or crosshair appearing pads. Wire the keypad, per the instructions in Table 7-2, to the proper "E" numbers.

The maximum electrical stress parameters on these keypads is 12 Vdc @ 20 mA, a contact resistance of less than 500 ohms, and a contact bounce of less than 10 ms. But the contact bounce is no problem since the telephone dialer IC is designed to tolerate such a contact bounce duration. It is interesting to note that the contact resistance is guaranteed to be less than 500 ohms. Since most metallic contact switches, some of which are even coated with precious metals, have resistances in the millohm regions. But remember, these contacts are conductive rubber. They work very well with a predicted life of one million activations specified at 12 Vdc @ 5 mA.

Software

At the beginning of the listing in Appendix B, the program initializes and goes to the start sequence. This entails the checking of the status of RIOT bits PB4 and PB7. These are the software switching bits which enable the microprocessor to distinguish the projects from one another and to vector to the appropriate address in the EPROM corresponding to that particular security project's software. As you will recall, this was done to allow one single EPROM, rather than four separate EPROMs, to collectively contain the programs (four in all) for all of the microprocessor-based security projects in this book.

Keeping this convention well in mind, the telephone dialer software checks these same two bits, PB4 and PB7, and if both are low, this indicates that the telephone dialer program is in effect. This further causes a branching to the delayed-burglar alarm software. This is the same as that previously covered in Chapter 5 with one exception. If PB4 and PB7 are low, the microprocessor directs the program to the dialer routine in order to set the alarm instead of to the alarm system. More specifically, if the microprocessor detects any non "00" two bit code when the PB4 and PB7 RIOT bits are checked, it then goes to the set alarm (SETALR) routine and sets the alarm system to drive both inside and outside alarms in the form of sirens/horns, etc. If, however, the microprocessor reads a "00" two bit code on the RIOT's PB4 and PB7 bits, the phone dialer software is then put into effect. You will recall from observing the schematic in Fig. 7-11 that the Darlington drivers are missing in this circuit. This is merely because this circuit is a silent alarm. Its main function is to dial two telephone numbers, not to drive a loud siren/horn.

This routine resides at FBCC near the end of the EPROM listing. It is called the "telephone dialer routine". This portion of the software generates the appropriate bit to place the telephone dialer IC, the MK5375, in the pulse dialer mode. The next software action is to set the appropriate bits to cause the relay to pull in and connect the telephone line. Refer to the schematic in Fig. 7-10. A 2 second delay is inserted to allow the phone company's equipment to come on line. This is followed by PB2 and PB5 going low which activates the "*" button. After a 1/4 second delay, the buttons on the phone keypad are deselected so that the "*" is not active. This allows the numeral "1" on the keypad to be software selected. Incidentally, you may want to turn back to the hardware description and note that essentially what happened in hardware is being implemented here in the form of driver routines causing certain codes or bits to be manipulated on PB2 and PB5. After the numeral 1 is deselected, the dialing is initialized. Most dialing can be accomplished in 15 seconds in the pulse mode. This is followed by generating a bit to place the telephone dialer IC into the tone dialing mode which means it goes to the SIGNAL subroutine. This software alternately selects the "1" tone for 1 second and then the "2" tone for 1 second. This continues for a total of 30 seconds. After this the signalling stops, the program hangs up the telephone and deselects all of the telephone keypad numerals. A 1 second delay follows allowing the telephone line to clear and to again get a dial tone back on the phone lines.

After this sequence, the program selects pulse dial mode again, connects back up to the telephone line, waits 2 seconds because of a software delay for a dial tone, activates the "*" pushbutton in the same manner as previously described, deselects it after 1 second, activates the "2" pushbutton for 1 second, deselects the "2" pushbutton, waits 15 seconds for the dialer to finish dialing the second number, and then it sets up for tone dialing and alternates the two tones for 30 seconds as before. The telephone is then hung up, goes into a five minute delay loop, and returns back to the burglar alarm subroutine to check all over again if an unauthorized entry has occurred. If it encounters a no entry or set position then nothing else happens; however, if an entry is detected then it dials both numbers again.

Appendices

Appendix A
EMI Supression

A RECENT TELEVISION PROGRAM AIRED HERE in San Antonio concerning security emphasized one point that boggles the mind. That is, of the more than 10,000 alarms activated and answered by either a private security protection agency or by the local police during a recent accounting period, over 95 percent were false alarms. But these had to be answered anyway. The police departments in some parts of the country find this to be such a nuisance and a distraction from their routine police activities that they are seriously contemplating enacting legislation to charge a flat rate for each false alarm. The majority of private security companies already do this to remain solvent. In an effort to remain good citizens and not to perpetuate the "Little Boy who Cried Wolf" syndrome, let's resolve ourselves to squelch as much electromagnetic interference (EMI) as possible and in so doing we'll all have better TV and radio reception as well as more reliable security systems.

This problem is a sensitive one, so let us skirt the actual issue of politics and concentrate on the causes of these alarms. A lot of these false alarms are the result of EMI/rfi interference. Electromagnetic and radio frequency interference actually cause spurious signals to be present with sufficient magnitude to cause false triggering of sensitive security system circuits.

Ten years ago there was only a small fraction of the number of electronic devices now available to consumers: electronic watches, calculators, home computers, video tape recorders, electronic games, electronic toys, CB radios, microwave ovens, thermostats, home security devices, and a variety of controls on new cars. All of these devices emit electromagnetic radiation. In addition, the emphasis on portability in many of these items means that prolonged battery life through power reduction techniques—such as using switching voltage regulated rather than linear voltage regulated power supplies—has assumed far greater importance. Granted, the switchers are about twice as efficient as the linears, but because of their inherent mode of operation, i.e., switching current into an inductor, they are veritable EMI generators. Consequently, shielding becomes essential.

According to FCC chairman Mark Fowler, the number of electronic interference complaints now exceeds 80,000 per year. For example, communications at an East Coast airport were hampered by interference from a "noisy" cash register in a drug store a mile away. In a western state, police communications at 42 MHz were disrupted by interference from coin-operated video arcade games. A home computer was found to affect its owner's TV as well as sets throughout the neighborhood. A fleet of new passenger buses designed for urban use were delivered, but during a test drive, a driver tried to brake as he went downhill and was astonished to discover he had no brakes until he reached bottom. Why? Because the microprocessor-controlled anti-skid devices controlling the brakes had been rendered useless by a commercial TV station's signal lobed in the direction of that particular hill. Once the electronic housings in the buses were shielded, their brakes worked. Background on FCC Rule-Making.

On April 23, 1976, the FCC began a rulemaking proceeding (referred to a Docket 20780, Part 15, Subpart J) for setting realistic limits on VHF and UHF frequency emissions. The law included six categories: class, definitions, emission limits, verification, certification, labeling, and dates of compliance in dealing with radiated EMI/rfi in electronic and electrical industrial devices. In January, 1979, a major computer manufacturer petitioned the FCC to relax some of these proposed standards. In response, the FCC relented on a few minor

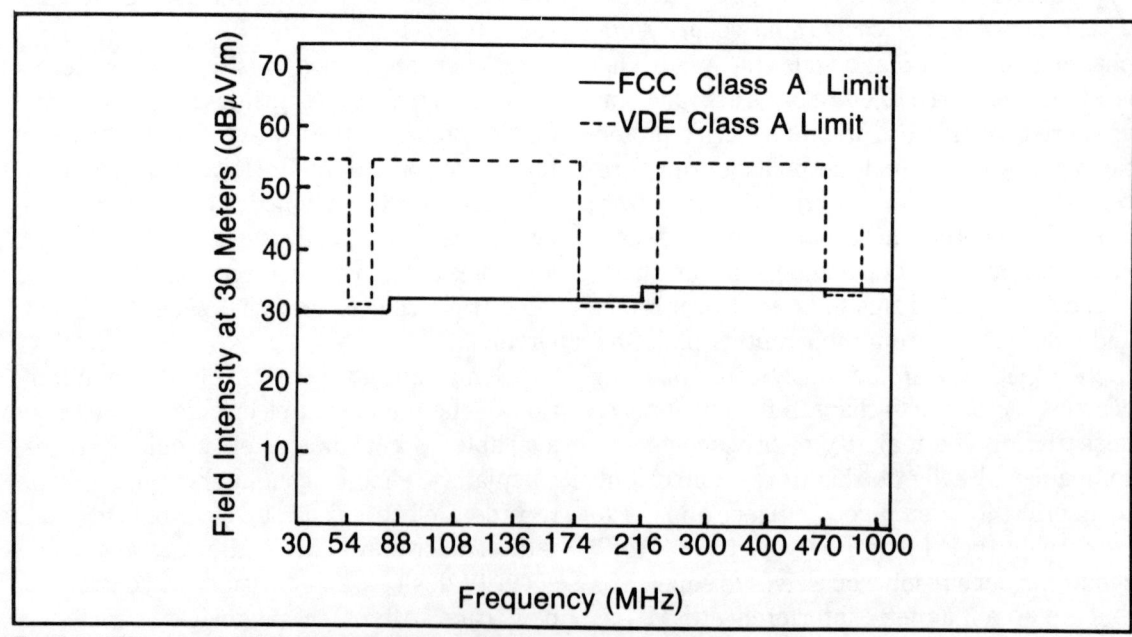

Fig. A-1. VDE versus FCC Standards on EMI emissions for Class A Industrial products.

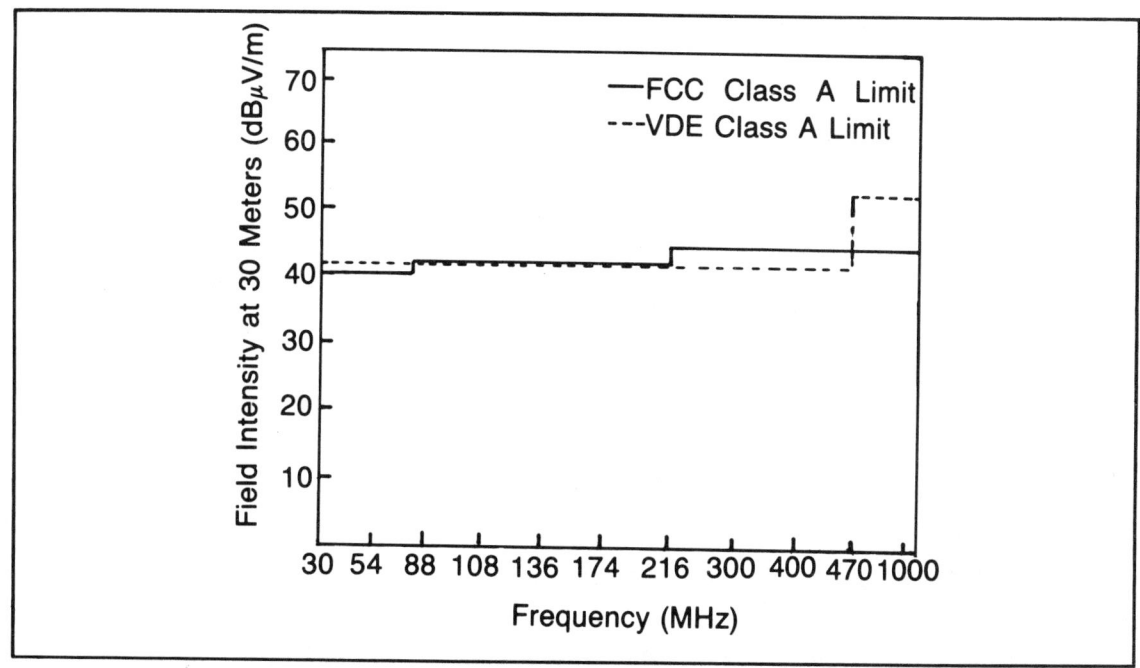

Fig. A-2. VDE versus FCC Standards on EMI emissions for Class B consumer products.

changes and rescheduled the July 1, 1980 compliance date. Other proposals presented are under consideration as well. While Class A products (industrial electronic devices) are of interest, most concern seems to be focused on Class B products—personal computers, electronic games and similar consumer items. (Certain inexpensive electronic games operating at frequencies less than 495 kHz are exempt from the new FCC ruling.)

Emission limits on Class B devices are about three times as stringent as those placed on Class A industrial products. Note in Fig. A-1 and Fig. A-2 how Class A and B limits compare with the West German or generally accepted European standard, the VDE. The German post office has placed half-page ads in newspapers pointing out that items not meeting the specifications contained in the VDE regulation will not have a government proof number. Purchasers of devices without such numbers are liable to prosecution for electronic pollution, therefore, if an American product is to be marketed in West Germany it must be very EMI-proof. But the FCC is tightening up on emissions. For example, as of October 1, 1983, all manufacturers of Class A and B products became subject to the FCC's request for random sampling of products to check compliance with established standards. Any questions should be addressed to your local FCC office or to Art Wall, Office of Science and Technology, FCC, Washington, D.C. 20554.

From the preceding discussion, it should be obvious that the effects of EMI/rfi can be nearly catastrophic to aircraft, mobile communications, electronic braking systems, and a whole host of other forms of electronic-based products. Therefore, with the new October, 1983 FCC rulings, electronic products should be appearing on the market that have been designed with considerably more concern directed toward the suppression and containment of EMI. This is both from a standpoint

Fig. A-3. Metallic adhesive tape to contain EMI emmanations.

of minimizing EMI emissions as well as neutralizing its effects by providing greater shielding effectiveness.

The following 26 figures give a pictorial overview of EMI containment and show representative methods or design approaches for solving these problems. Starting with Fig. A-3 and progressing through to Fig. A-7, we see a bevy of products to contain EMI. Figure A-8 shows a method of spraying plastic enclosures with molten zinc to allow them to be as EMI-proof as metal containers. The methods as shown in Figs. A-3 through A-8 are basically for the containment of EMI so that it cannot radiate through an insulator or a plastic case. Figures A-9 through A-15 all show metallic enclosures. All of them are inherently EMI-proof by virtue of the total metallic sides and ends. Figures A-16 through A-19 show how relatively soft pliable materials can conform to various objects and shapes and remain "soft" while still being impregnated with metallic particles. This method is nearly as effective as a metallic enclosure.

Figure A-20 shows how a CRT or large opening in an instrument can be made less of a radiator of EMI by having the viewing glass fused or impregnated with metallic bifilar (spiral) wound strands, so small that they are nearly invisible while only providing a miniminal amount of visual attenuation as a byproduct, less than that afforded by looking through the visible side of a screen door.

Figures A-21 through A-28 all show how a number of clever devices have been conceived to suppress EMI from radiating to the environment. The devices which would need these types of solutions would be electronic products manufactured previous to October 1983. The FCC finally got tough in 1983.

Fig. A-4. A $99.50 kit containing foil forms, sheets, a magnetic pickup probe and design data to build and test magnetic field shields of various types.

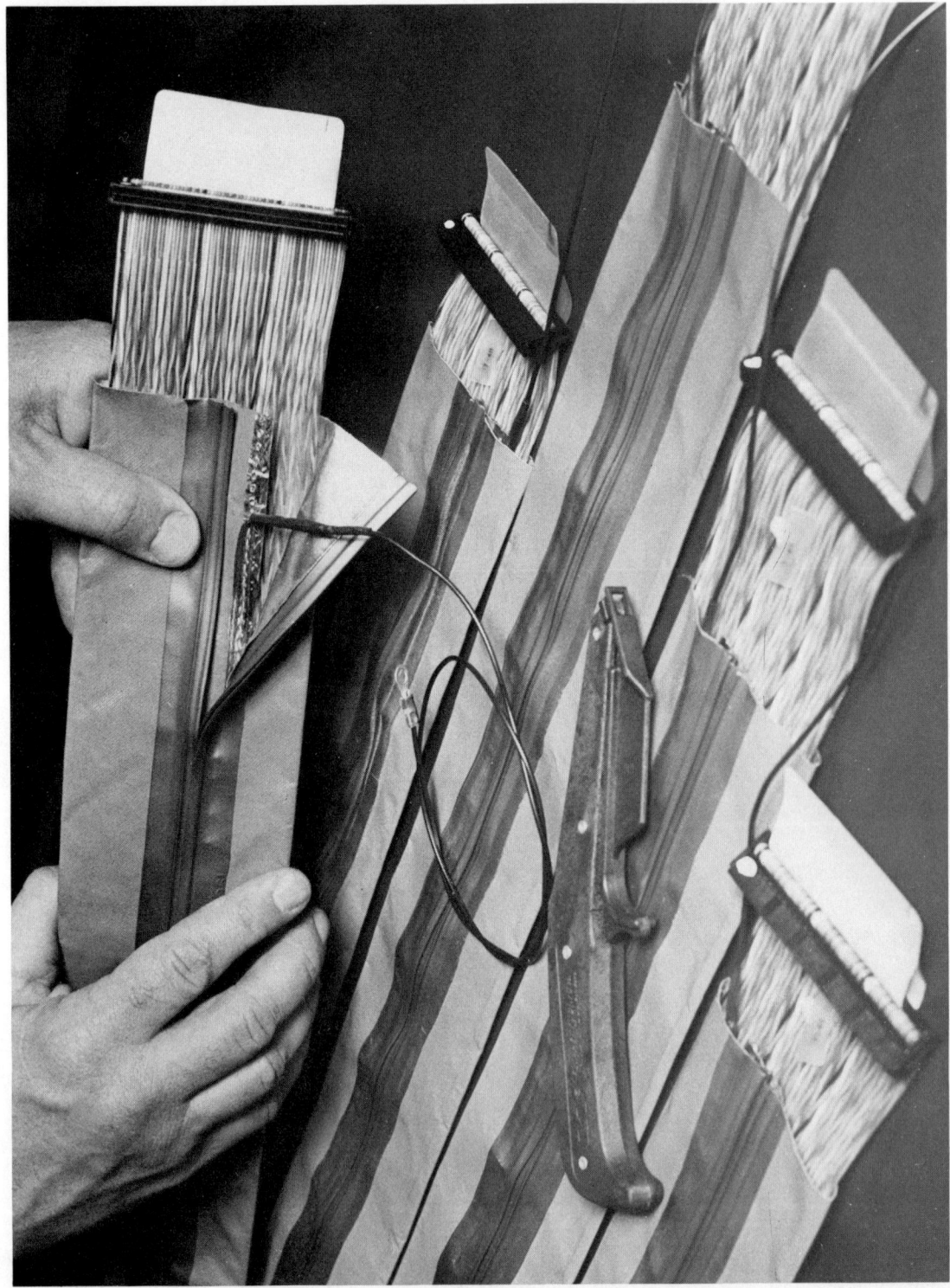

Fig. A-5. Zippertubing "Zip Top" encasement shielding for cable bundles to contain radiated EMI.

Fig. A-6. Ferrite beads to suppress EMI emissions. These are slipped over a wire that is a potential emitter of EMI.

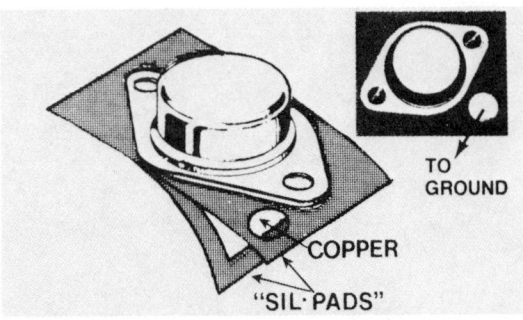

Fig. A-7. A thermal heatsink pad that fits beneath a TO-3 or TO-66 power transistor and does double duty as a heatsink and an EMI/conducted radiation suppressor.

Fig. A-10. Gaskets impregnated with small metallic particles for EMI shielding within these Compac cases.

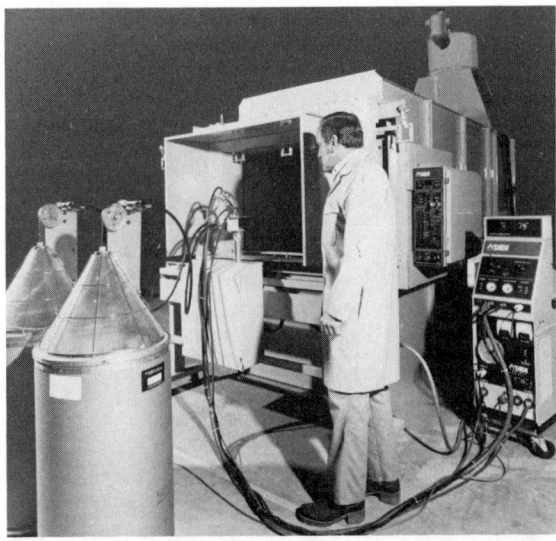

Fig. A-8. A Programmable X-Y Axis sprayer for molten zinc. Used to coat electronic enclosures for enhanced shielding effectiveness for EMI.

Fig. A-11. Nickel plated cases for especially effective rfi shielding.

Fig. A-9. The RFT series of highly shielded cases by compac.

Fig. A-12. A line of rfi shielded cases with interchangeable rf connectors.

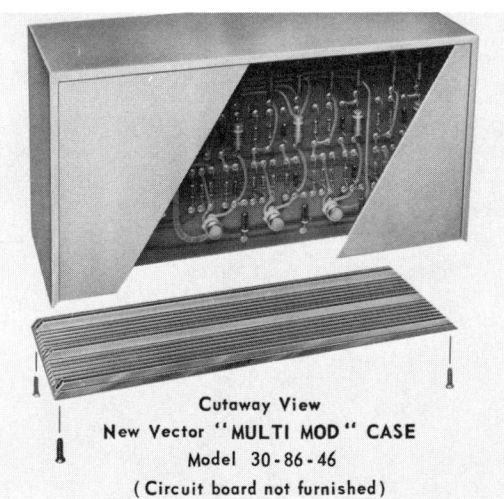

Fig. A-13. A cutaway view of a case manufactured by Vector Electronic Co., Inc. showing how slots are molded into the ends which overlap very tightly for enhanced rfi shielding.

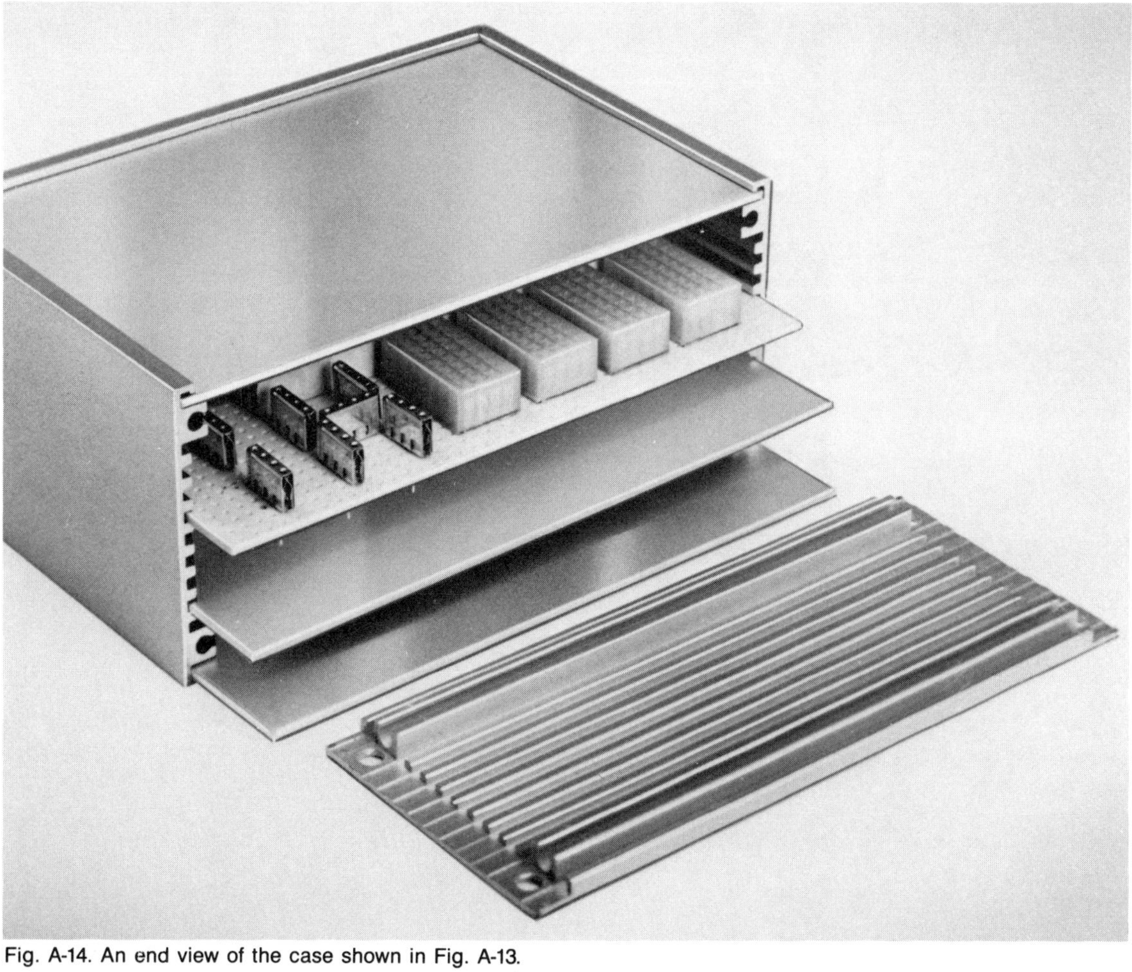

Fig. A-14. An end view of the case shown in Fig. A-13.

Fig. A-15. A more decorative but still rfi tight enclosure.

Fig. A-16. Prestamped gaskets impregnated with metallic particles for EMI containment.

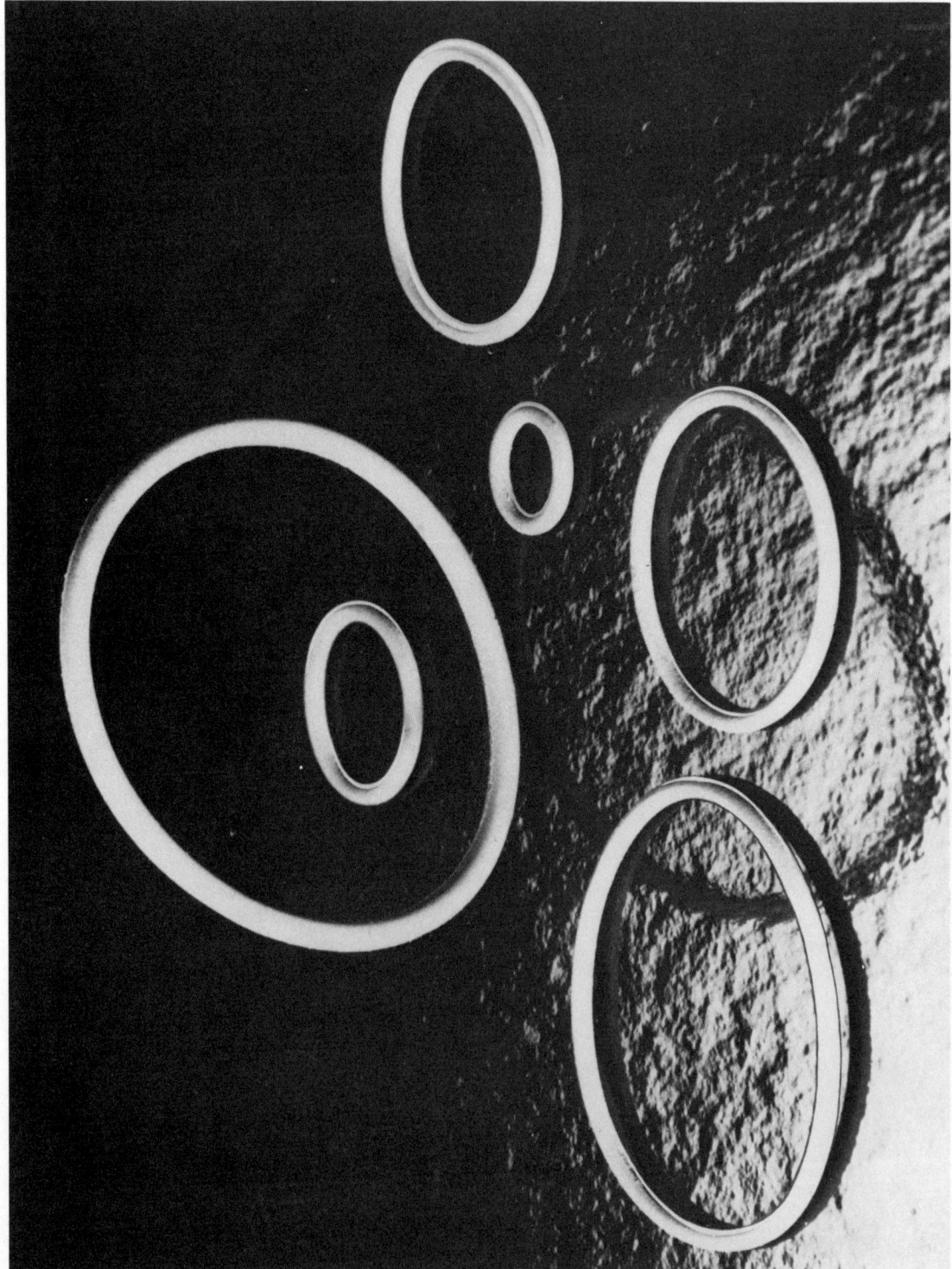

Fig. A-17. Circular grommets or rings used around holes in enclosures, ensuring a tight enclosure and suppressing EMI emission.

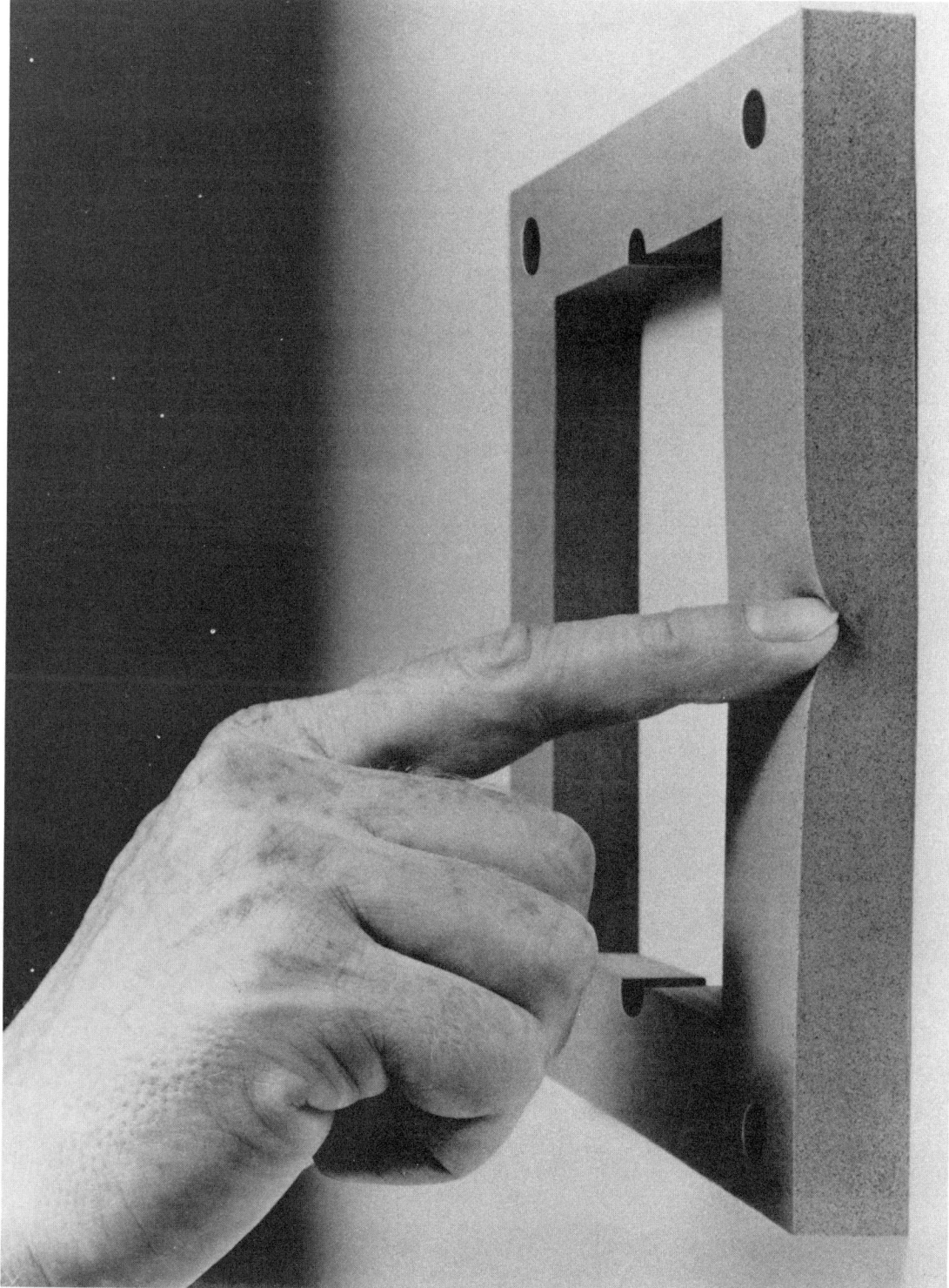

Fig. A-18. A soft metallic particle impregnated elastomer bezel in which an electronic assembly fits. Especially designed for rf/EMI suppression.

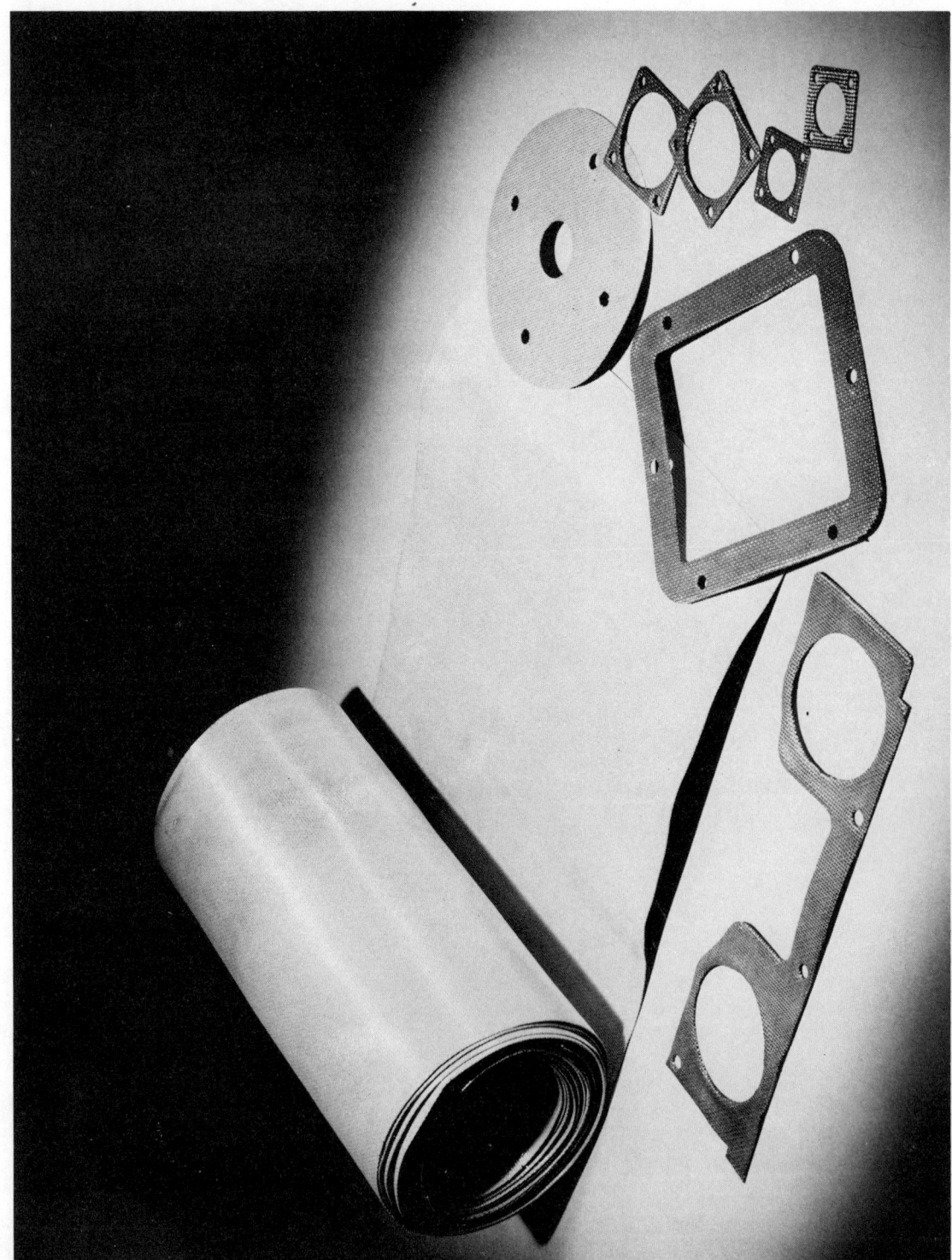

Fig. A-19. Rolls of vinyl sheet material treated for EMI containment.

Fig. A-20. A piece of glass impregnated with fine mesh wires for EMI containment. This glass would typically go over the screen of a CRT to contain radiation.

Fig. A-21. A plug acting as a filter and a suppressor that fits directly into the ac wall outlet. Courtesy of Electronic Specialists, Inc.

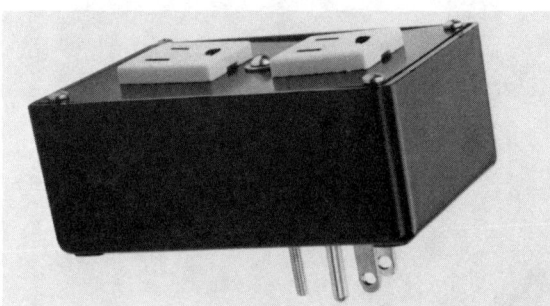

Fig. A-22. A two-stage ultra-fast security circuit that stands guard against damages to phone line or data equipment from spikes or surges common to ac power lines during lightning storms or from switch-gear high voltage, spikes on the line. Courtesy of Electronic Specialists, Inc.

Fig. A-23. Another version of the circuit in the preceding figure, only equipped with a standard telephone connector (RJ-11 type) 4-pin, 6-position standard 2-wire phone line. Courtesy of Electronic Specialists, Inc.

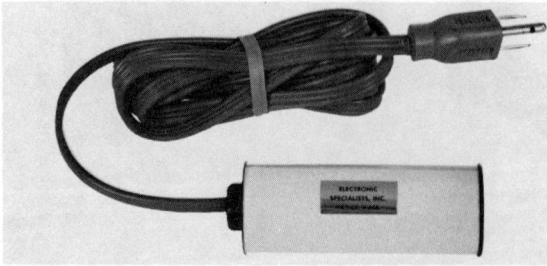

Fig. A-24. A spike suppressor and line hash filter which provides limited lightning protection for direct hits but does ensure against long term line overvoltage. Courtesy of Electronic Specialists, Inc.

Fig. A-25. An audio interference filter for: CB pickup by a phono cartridge, broadcast station pickup by tape decks, police radio pickup by audio mixers/equalizers, airport radar pickup by audio mixers/equalizers, CB radio pickup by cables between the preamplifier and the power amplifier. Courtesy of Electronic Specialists, Inc.

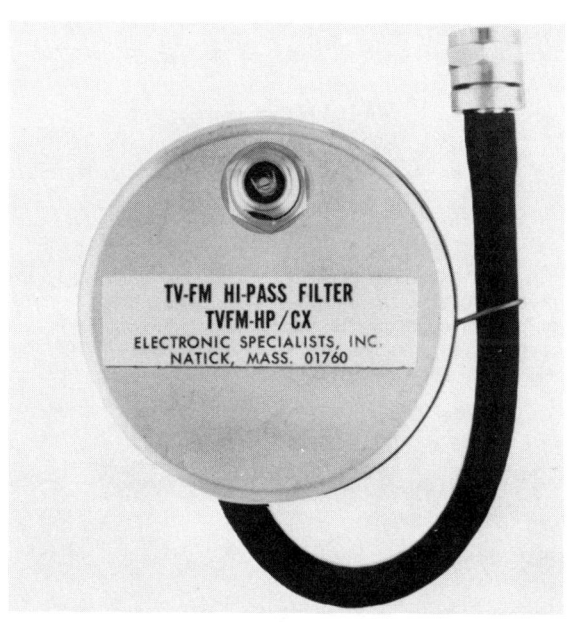

Fig. A-26. A flat twin lead (300 ohm) high-pass filter designed for lightning protection.

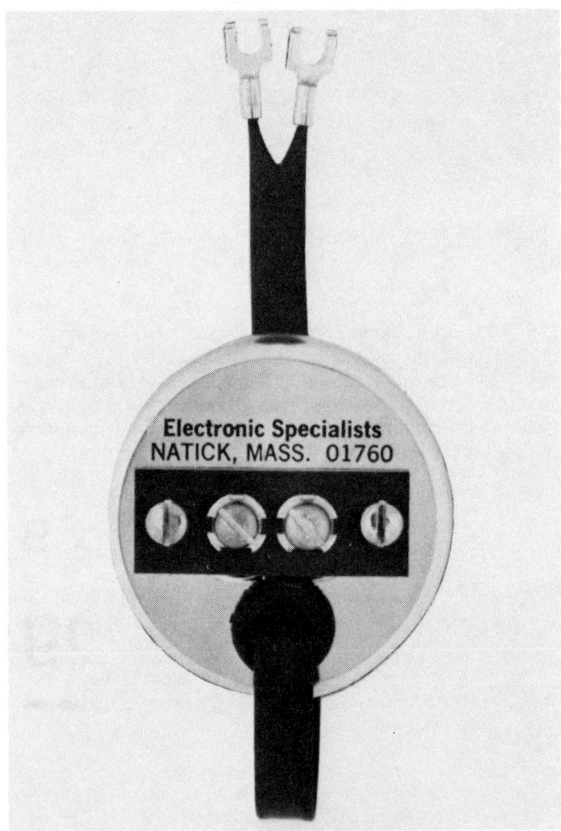

Fig. A-27. A round coaxial cable (75 ohms) for blocking interference from TV, cable TV, CB, police or taxi radios. Courtesy of Electronic Specialists, Inc.

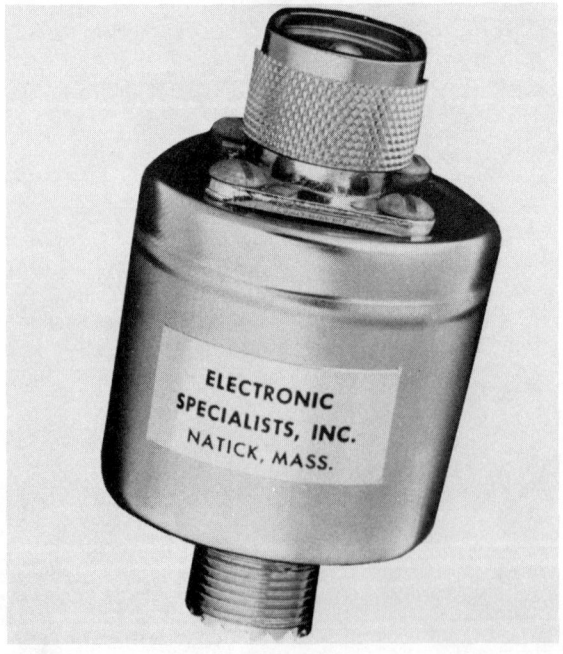

Fig. A-28. A filter designed for lightning protection and suppression of spurious unwanted CB radio signals. Courtesy of Electronic Specialists, Inc.

Appendix B
Program Listing

DEFINITIONS

```
LINE#    ADDR  OBJECT     LABEL  SOURCE           PAGE 0002

01-0020  2000             ;PROGRAM TO RUN SINGLE BOARD 6502 COMPUTER
01-0025  2000             ;AS A BURGLAR ALARM SYSTEM
01-0030  2000             ;
01-0035  2000             ;
01-0040  2000                    .OPT ERR,LIS,SOR
01-0045  2000             ;
01-0050  2000             ;
01-0055  2000             ;
01-0060  2000             ;
01-0065  2000             ;DEFINITIONS
01-0070  2000             ;
01-0075  2000             ;*********************************************
01-0080  2000             ;
01-0085  2000             PORTA  =$00
01-0090  2000             PORTB  =$02
01-0095  2000             DDRA   =$01
01-0100  2000             DDRB   =$03
01-0105  2000             NCLOOP =PORTA           ;PA0  (XXXX XXX1) NORMALLY CLOSED LOOP BIT
01-0110  2000             PRLOOP =PORTA           ;PA1  (XXXX XX1X) PANIC LOOP
01-0115  2000             INLOOP =PORTA           ;PA2  (XXXX X1XX) INSIDE LOOP BIT
01-0120  2000             NOLOOP =PORTA           ;PA3  (XXXX 1XXX) NORMALLY OPEN LOOP BIT
01-0125  2000             DELOOP =PORTA           ;PA4  (XXX1 XXXX) DELAYED ENTRY LOOP BIT
01-0130  2000             KEYPAD =PORTA           ;PA5  (XX1X XXXX) KEYPAD CONTACTS BIT
01-0135  2000             ;                       ;FOR DELAYED ENTRY BURGLAR ALARM
01-0140  2000             KEYSWT =PORTA           ;PA5  (XX1X XXXX) KEY SWITCH BIT FOR
01-0145  2000             ;                       ;KEY CONTROLLED BURGLAR ALARM
01-0150  2000             REMDIS =PORTA           ;PA6  (X1XX XXXX) REMOTE DISABLE LOOP BIT
01-0155  2000             SMODET =PORTA           ;PA7  (1XXX XXXX) SMOKE/FIRE LOOP BIT
01-0160  2000
01-0165  2000             SWB1   =PORTB           ;PB4  (XXX1 XXXX) PROGRAM SWITCH BIT 1
01-0170  2000             SWB2   =PORTB           ;PB7  (1XXX XXXX) PROGRAM SWITCH BIT 2
01-0175  2000             ;
01-0180  2000             ;OUTPUTS
01-0185  2000             ARMLED =PORTB           ;PB0  (XXXX XXX1) RED LED BIT
01-0190  2000             LOKLED =PORTB           ;PB1  (XXXX XX1X) GREEN LED BIT
01-0195  2000             OPTLED =PORTB           ;PB2  (XXXX X1XX) OPTIONAL LED BIT
01-0200  2000             OUTALR =PORTB           ;PB3  (XXXX 1XXX) ALARM SIREN BIT
01-0205  2000             FIRALR =PORTB           ;PB5  (XX1X XXXX) FIRE ALARM BIT
01-0210  2000             WARBUZ =PORTB           ;PB6  (X1XX XXXX) WARNING BUZZER BIT
01-0215  2000             ;
01-0220  2000             ;TIMERS
01-0225  2000             ;
01-0230  2000             STATUS =$05             ;COUNTER STATUS REGISTER
01-0235  2000             ;
01-0240  2000             DIV1DI =$14             ;COUNTER DIVIDE BY 1 ;INTERRUPT DISABLED
01-0245  2000             DIV8DI =$15             ;COUNTER DIVIDE BY 8 ;INTERRUPT DISABLED
01-0250  2000             DI64DI =$16             ;COUNTER DIVIDE BY 64;INTERRUPT DISABLED
01-0255  2000             D1024D =$17             ;COUNTER DIVIDE BY 1024 ;INTERRUPT DISABLED
01-0260  2000             ;
01-0265  2000             DIV1EI =$1C             ;COUNTER DIVIDE BY 1 ;INTERRUPT ENABLED
01-0270  2000             DIV8EI =$1D             ;COUNTER DIVIDE BY 8 ;INTERRUPT ENABLED
01-0275  2000             DI64EI =$1E             ;COUNTER DIVIDE BY 64 ;INTERRUPT ENABLED
01-0280  2000             D1024E =$1F             ;COUNTER DIVIDE BY 1024 ;INTERRUPT ENABLED
01-0285  2000             ;
01-0290  2000             ;
```

DEFINITIONS

```
LINE#    ADDR   OBJECT     LABEL   SOURCE            PAGE 0003

01-0295  2000              ;MEMORY
01-0300  2000              ;
01-0305  2000                      *=$0080
01-0310  0080              ;
01-0315  0080              ;
01-0320  0080              FLAGS   *=*+1             ;LOOP STATUS FLAGS
01-0325  0081              DELYFF  *=*+1             ;DELAYED ENTRY CONTACTS FLIP-FLOP
01-0330  0082              ALARFF  *=*+1             ;ALARM SET FILP-FLOP
01-0335  0083              SETRES  *=*+1             ;SET-RESET FLIP-FLOP
01-0340  0084              TEMPT1  *=*+1             ;TEMPORARY COUNTER FOR 1 SECOND TIMEOUT
01-0345  0085              TEMPT2  *=*+1             ;TEMPORARY COUNTER FOR OTHER TIMEOUTS
01-0350  0086              TEMPT3  *=*+1             ;TEMPORARY COUNTER
01-0355  0087              TEMPT4  *=*+1             ;TEMPORARY COUNTER
01-0360  0088              TEMPT5  *=*+1             ;TEMPORARY COUNTER
01-0365  0089              TEMPT6  *=*+1             ;TEMPORARY COUNTER
01-0370  008A              TEMPT7  *=*+1             ;TEMPORARY RANDOM 3 BIT NUMBER
01-0375  008B              TEMPT8  *=*+1             ;LIGHT DIMMER ATTACK RAMP COUNTER
01-0380  008C              TEMPT9  *=*+1             ;LIGHT DIMMER DECAY RAMP COUNTER
01-0385  008D              TEMPTA  *=*+1             ;NUMBER OF 30 SECOND INTERVALS
01-0390  008E              TEMPTB  *=*+1             ;TEMPORARY COUNTER
01-0395  008F              ;
01-0400  008F              ;
01-0405  008F              ;
01-0410  008F              ;
01-0415  008F              ;*********************************************
01-0420  008F              ;
01-0425  008F              ;
01-0430  008F                      *=$F800           ;PROGRAM STARTS AT HEX ADDRESS F800
01-0435  F800              ;
01-0440  F800                      .OFFSET 8800
01-0445  F800              ;
```

PROGRAM SELECTION AND INITIALIZATION

```
LINE#    ADDR    OBJECT      LABEL    SOURCE          PAGE 0004

01-0455  F800                         ;
01-0460  F800    78          START    SEI             ;DISABLE INTERRUPTS
01-0465  F801    D8                   CLD             ;CLEAR DECIMAL MODE
01-0470  F802    A0 0C                LDY #12         ;IDLE UNTIL ALL IS RESET
01-0475  F804    A2 FF       DELY1    LDX #$FF
01-0480  F806    CA          DELY2    DEX
01-0485  F807    D0 FD                BNE DELY2
01-0490  F809    88                   DEY
01-0495  F80A    D0 F8                BNE DELY1
01-0500  F80C    A2 FF                LDX #$FF        ;INITIALIZE STACK POINTER
01-0505  F80E    9A                   TXS
01-0510  F80F    A5 02                LDA PORTB       ;READ B PORT
01-0515  F811    29 90                AND #$90        ;ONLY LOOK AT PROGRAM SWITCH BITS
01-0520  F813    C9 90                CMP #$90        ;ARE BOTH HIGH?
01-0525  F815    F0 15                BEQ DLYALR      ;THEN GOTO DELAYED ALARM PROGRAM
01-0530  F817    C9 10                CMP #$10        ;IS PB4 HIGH?
01-0535  F819    F0 08                BEQ REGALR      ;THEN GOTO SIMPLE ALARM
01-0540  F81B    C9 80                CMP #$80        ;IS PB7 HIGH?
01-0545  F81D    F0 07                BEQ DIMLIG
01-0550  F81F    C9 00                CMP #$00        ;ARE BOTH LOW?
01-0555  F821    F0 06                BEQ OTHER
01-0560  F823    4C 2F F8    REGALR   JMP ALARM1      ;SIMPLE ALARM
01-0565  F826    4C 20 FB    DIMLIG   JMP LIGDIM      ;JUMP TO RANDOM LIGHT DIMMER
01-0570  F829    4C CC FB    OTHER    JMP DEDIAL      ;JUMP TO DELAYED ALARM WITH
01-0575  F82C                         ;               ;TELEPHONE DIALER
01-0580  F82C    4C B4 F8    DLYALR   JMP DELARM      ;JUMP TO DELAYED ENTRY ALARM
01-0585  F82F                         ;
01-0590  F82F                         ;
```

KEY CONTROLLED BURGLAR ALARM

```
LINE#    ADDR    OBJECT     LABEL   SOURCE              PAGE 0005

01-0600  F82F
01-0605  F82F               ;
01-0610  F82F               ;KEY SWITCH CONTROLLED BURGLAR ALARM
01-0615  F82F               ;
01-0620  F82F   A2 6F       ALARM1  LDX #$6F            ;GET READY TO INITIALIZE PORTS
01-0625  F831   86 02               STX PORTB           ;SET ALL OUTPUTS OF PORTB HIGH
01-0630  F833                       ;                   ;EXCEPT PB4 AND PB7
01-0635  F833   86 03               STX DDRB            ;MAKE ALL B PORTS OUTPUTS
01-0640  F835   A2 00               LDX #$00
01-0645  F837   86 82               STX ALARFF          ;SET ALARM FLIP-FLOP TO NO ALARM STATUS
01-0650  F839   20 98 F9    CHKLOP  JSR CHKNCL          ;CHECK THE STATUS OF THE NORMALLY
01-0655  F83C                       ;                   ;CLOSED LOOP
01-0660  F83C   20 AE F9            JSR CHKNOL          ;CHECK THE STATUS OF THE NORMALLY
01-0665  F83F                       ;                   ;OPEN LOOP
01-0670  F83F                       ;
01-0675  F83F   20 62 F8            JSR CHKSWT          ;CHECK THE STATUS OF THE ARM/DISARM SWITCH
01-0680  F842                       ;
01-0685  F842   B0 09               BCS SETIT           ;IF THE CARRY BIT IS SET, THEN THE SWITCH IS
01-0690  F844                       ;                   ;CLOSED
01-0695  F844   20 9E F8            JSR NOALRM          ;IF NOT SET, THEN DISARM SYSTEM
01-0700  F847                       ;
01-0705  F847   20 78 F8            JSR STLEDS          ;TURN ON THE PROPER LED
01-0710  F84A   4C 39 F8            JMP CHKLOP          ;JUMP BACK TO CHECKING LOOPS AND SWITCHES
01-0715  F84D                       ;
01-0720  F84D                       ;
01-0725  F84D
01-0730  F84D               ;THIS ROUTINE ARMS THE ALARM SYSTEM
01-0735  F84D
01-0740  F84D   A9 FF       SETIT   LDA #$FF            ;ALARM MODE
01-0745  F84F   85 82               STA ALARFF          ;SET ALARM FLIP-FLOP FOR ALARM CONDITION
01-0750  F851   20 A6 F8            JSR CHKFLS          ;CHECK THE STATUS OF THE LOOP FLAGS
01-0755  F854   90 06               BCC OKFLG           ;IF CARRY IS SET, THEN FLAGS ARE OK
01-0760  F856                       ;
01-0765  F856               ;IF THE LOOPS ARE NOT OK, THEN THIS ROUTINE
01-0770  F856               ;TURNS THE SIREN ON
01-0775  F856
01-0780  F856   20 8A FA            JSR SIREON          ;IF NOT OK, THEN TURN THE SIREN ON (ALARM)
01-0785  F859   4C 39 F8            JMP CHKLOP          ;AND CONTINUE CHECKING THE LOOPS
01-0790  F85C                       ;
01-0795  F85C
01-0800  F85C
01-0805  F85C   20 78 F8    OKFLG   JSR STLEDS          ;SET PROPER LED
01-0810  F85F   4C 39 F8            JMP CHKLOP          ;AND CONTINUE CHECKING THE LOOPS
01-0815  F862                       ;
01-0820  F862               ;THIS ROUTINE CHECKS THE KEY SWITCH FOR
01-0825  F862               ;OPEN OR CLOSED CONDITION
01-0830  F862
01-0835  F862   A5 00       CHKSWT  LDA KEYSWT          ;GET STATUS OF KEY SWITCH
01-0840  F864   29 20               AND #$20            ;MASK OFF ALL EXCEPT KEY SWITCH BIT
01-0845  F866   D0 08               BNE OPENS           ;IF NOT ZERO, THEN SWITCH IS OPEN
01-0850  F868                       ;
01-0855  F868   A5 80               LDA FLAGS           ;GET STATUS OF LOOP FLAGS
01-0860  F86A   09 20               ORA #$20            ;SET KEY SWITCH FLAG BIT
01-0865  F86C   85 80               STA FLAGS           ;DO IT
01-0870  F86E   38                  SEC                 ;SET CARRY BIT TO INDICATE SWITCH CLOSED
```

KEY CONTROLLED BURGLAR ALARM

```
   LINE#   ADDR   OBJECT     LABEL  SOURCE           PAGE 0006

01-0875    F86F   60                RTS
01-0880    F870                     ;
01-0885    F870
01-0890    F870   A5 80      OPENS  LDA FLAGS        ;GET FLAG STATUS
01-0895    F872   29 DF             AND #$DF         ;CLEAR SWITCH FLAG BIT
01-0900    F874   85 80             STA FLAGS        ;DO IT
01-0905    F876   18                CLC              ;CLEAR CARRY BIT TO INDICATE SWITCH OPEN
01-0910    F877   60                RTS
01-0915    F878                     ;
01-0920    F878                     ;THIS ROUTINE TURNS ON THE PROPER LED
01-0925    F878                     ;FOR THE STATE OF THE ALARM SYSTEM
01-0930    F878
01-0935    F878   18         STLEDS CLC
01-0940    F879   A5 80             LDA FLAGS        ;GET LOOP STATUS BITS
01-0945    F87B   4A                LSR A            ;SHIFT NORMALLY CLOSED LOOP FLAG BIT
01-0950    F87C   B0 19             BCS OPENL        ;IF CARRY IS SET, THEN LOOP IS OPEN
01-0955    F87E                     ;
01-0960    F87E   4A                LSR A            ;SHIFT NORMALLY OPEN LOOP FLAG BIT
01-0965    F87F   4A                LSR A
01-0970    F880   4A                LSR A
01-0975    F881   B0 14             BCS OPENL        ;IF CARRY IS SET, THEN LOOP STATUS IS WRONG
01-0980    F883                     ;
01-0985    F883
01-0990    F883   A5 82             LDA ALARFF       ;GET STATUS OF ALARM FLIP-FLOP
01-0995    F885   30 09             BMI REDLED       ;IF NEGATIVE, THEN ALARM IS SET SO
01-1000    F887                     ;                ;TURN ON RED LED
01-1005    F887                     ;
01-1010    F887
01-1015    F887   A5 02             LDA LOKLED       ;GET STSTUS OF LOOP OK (GREEN) LED
01-1020    F889   29 FD             AND #$FD         ;TURN IT ON
01-1025    F88B   09 41             ORA #$41         ;TURN RED LED OFF
01-1030    F88D   85 02             STA LOKLED       ;DO IT
01-1035    F88F   60                RTS
01-1040    F890                     ;
01-1045    F890                     ;THIS ROUTINE TURNS THE RED LED ON
01-1050    F890
01-1055    F890   A5 02      REDLED LDA ARMLED       ;GET STATUS OF ARMED (RED) LED
01-1060    F892   29 FE             AND #$FE         ;TURN IT ON
01-1065    F894   09 02             ORA #$02         ;TURN GREEN LED OFF
01-1070    F896   60                RTS
01-1075    F897                     ;
01-1080    F897                     ;THIS ROUTINE TURNS BOTH LEDS OFF
01-1085    F897
01-1090    F897   A5 02      OPENL  LDA LOKLED       ;GET STATUS OF LED
01-1095    F899   09 43             ORA #$43         ;TURN OFF BOTH RED AND GREEN LED
01-1100    F89B   85 02             STA LOKLED
01-1105    F89D   60                RTS
01-1110    F89E                     ;
01-1115    F89E                     ;THIS ROUTINE DISARMS THE ALARM SYSTEM
01-1120    F89E
01-1125    F89E   A9 00      NOALRM LDA #$00
01-1130    F8A0   85 82             STA ALARFF       ;CLEAR ALARM FLIP-FLOP TO NO ALARM STATUS
01-1135    F8A2   20 91 FA          JSR SIROFF
01-1140    F8A5   60                RTS
01-1145    F8A6                     ;
```

KEY CONTROLLED BURGLAR ALARM

```
LINE#    ADDR    OBJECT    LABEL    SOURCE              PAGE 0007

01-1150  F8A6
01-1155  F8A6                       ;THIS ROUTINE CHECKS THE STATUS OF THE FLAGS
01-1160  F8A6                       ;
01-1165  F8A6
01-1170  F8A6    A5 80     CHKFLS   LDA FLAGS           ;GET FLAG STATUS
01-1175  F8A8    6A                 ROR A               ;SHIFT NORMALLY CLOSED LOOP BIT
01-1180  F8A9                       ;TO CARRY BIT
01-1185  F8A9    B0 07              BCS BADF            ;IF CARRY IS SET, THEN LOOP STATUS IS WRONG
01-1190  F8AB    6A                 ROR A               ;SHIFT NORMALLY OPEN BIT TO CARRY BIT
01-1195  F8AC    6A                 ROR A
01-1200  F8AD    6A                 ROR A
01-1205  F8AE    B0 02              BCS BADF            ;IF CARRY IS SET, THEN LOOP STATUS IS WRONG
01-1210  F8B0    18                 CLC                 ;CLEAR CARRY BIT IF FLAGS ARE OK
01-1215  F8B1    60                 RTS
01-1220  F8B2                       ;
01-1225  F8B2
01-1230  F8B2    38        BADF     SEC                 ;SET CARRY BIT IF A FLAG IS BAD
01-1235  F8B3    60                 RTS
01-1240  F8B4                       ;
01-1245  F8B4
01-1250  F8B4                       ;
```

BURGLAR ALARM WITH DELAYED ENTRY

```
LINE#    ADDR    OBJECT     LABEL   SOURCE          PAGE 0008

01-1260  F8B4
01-1265  F8B4    A2 6F      DELARM  LDX #$6F        ;GET READY TO INITIALIZE PORTS
01-1270  F8B6    86 02              STX PORTB       ;SET ALL OUTPUTS OF PORTB HIGH
01-1275  F8B8               ;                       ;EXCEPT PB4 AND PB7
01-1280  F8B8    86 03              STX DDRB        ;MAKE ALL B PORTS OUTPUTS
01-1285  F8BA    A2 00              LDX #$00        ;GET READY TO SET UP PORTA
01-1290  F8BC    86 01              STX DDRA        ;SET ALL A PORTS FOR INPUTS
01-1295  F8BE    86 80              STX FLAGS       ;CLEAR ALL FLAGS
01-1300  F8C0    20 0A FA   LOPOP   JSR CHKKEY      ;CHECK TO SEE IF THE KEYPAD CONTACTS
01-1305  F8C3               ;                       ;ARE CLOSED OR OPEN ON POWER UP
01-1310  F8C3    B0 FB              BCS LOPOP       ;IF CLOSED, LOOP UNTIL OPEN
01-1315  F8C5    A2 00              LDX #$00        ;CLEAR
01-1320  F8C7    86 82              STX ALARFF      ;ALARM FLAG TO NO ALARM STATUS AFTER
01-1325  F8C9               ;                       ;KEYPAD CONTACTS OPEN
01-1330  F8C9               ;                       ;ALARM FLIP-FLOP OFF=$00, ON=$FF
01-1335  F8C9    86 83              STX SETRES      ;INITIALIZE SET-RESET TO RESET VALUE
01-1340  F8CB               ;
01-1345  F8CB               ;
01-1350  F8CB               ;SET-RESET FLIP-FLOP
01-1355  F8CB               ;NOT SET BEFORE = $00
01-1360  F8CB               ;PREVIOUSLY SET = $FF
01-1365  F8CB               ;
01-1370  F8CB               ;
01-1375  F8CB               ;
01-1380  F8CB               ;CHECK LOOP
01-1385  F8CB               ;
01-1390  F8CB    20 98 F9   CHECK   JSR CHKNCL      ;CHECK NORMALLY CLOSED LOOP
01-1395  F8CE    20 AE F9           JSR CHKNOL      ;CHECK NORMALLY OPEN LOOP
01-1400  F8D1    20 C4 F9           JSR CHKPL       ;CHECK PANIC LOOP
01-1405  F8D4    20 DE F9           JSR CHKIL       ;CHECK INSIDE LOOP
01-1410  F8D7    20 F4 F9           JSR CHKDE       ;CHECK DELAYED ENTRY LOOP
01-1415  F8DA    20 0A FA           JSR CHKKEY      ;CHECK KEYPAD CONTACTS
01-1420  F8DD    20 74 FA           JSR CHKREM      ;CHECK REMOTE DISARMING STATIONS
01-1425  F8E0    B0 5B              BCS REDIS       ;IF CARRY SET, THEN
01-1430  F8E2               ;                       ;A REMOTE IS DISABLED
01-1435  F8E2               ;
01-1440  F8E2    20 5E FA           JSR CHKSMO      ;CHECK SMOKE/FIRE DETECTOR LOOP
01-1445  F8E5    B0 4A              BCS SMOKEA      ;IF CARRY IS SET, THEN
01-1450  F8E7               ;                       ;SMOKE/FIRE IS DETECTED
01-1455  F8E7               ;
01-1460  F8E7    A5 82              LDA ALARFF      ;IS ALARM SET?
01-1465  F8E9    C9 FF              CMP #$FF        ;SET
01-1470  F8EB    D0 0E              BNE NOWAY       ;NOT SET
01-1475  F8ED    A5 83              LDA SETRES      ;SEE IF IT HAS ALREADY BEEN SET
01-1480  F8EF    C9 FF              CMP #$FF        ;HAS IT BEEN SET YET?
01-1485  F8F1    D0 1B              BNE ALSET       ;IF NOT, THEN SET IT
01-1490  F8F3    20 83 F9           JSR CHKFLG      ;IF SO, THEN CHECK FLAGS
01-1495  F8F6    90 03              BCC NOWAY       ;IF ALL O.K. THEN CHECK LOOPS
01-1500  F8F8    4C 3D F9           JMP REDIS       ;IF NOT, THEN FIND OUT WHY
01-1505  F8FB    20 2F FA   NOWAY   JSR SETLED      ;TURN ON PROPER LED INDICATORS
01-1510  F8FE    A5 82              LDA ALARFF      ;SEE IF ALARM IS SET
01-1515  F900    C9 FF              CMP #$FF        ;IS IT SET?
01-1520  F902    F0 07              BEQ EXEND       ;IF SO, SKIP RESET
01-1525  F904    A9 00              LDA #$00        ;RESET SET-RESET FILP-FLOP
01-1530  F906    85 83              STA SETRES      ;DOIT
```

BURGLAR ALARM WITH DELAYED ENTRY

```
LINE#    ADDR   OBJECT     LABEL   SOURCE          PAGE 0009

01-1535  F908   20 70 F9           JSR DISARM      ;IF ALARM FLIP-FLOP NOT SET, DISARM
01-1540  F90B   4C CB F8   EXEND   JMP CHECK
01-1545  F90E                      ;
01-1550  F90E   A5 80      ALSET   LDA FLAGS       ;GET LOOP STATUS
01-1555  F910   29 FE              AND #$FE        ;CLEAR (IGNORE) DELAYED ENTRY FLAG
01-1560  F912   85 80              STA FLAGS       ;CLEAR IT
01-1565  F914   20 83 F9           JSR CHKFLG      ;CHECK ALL LOOP FLAGS
01-1570  F917   90 03              BCC GOODFL      ;IF O.K. THEN SETLED
01-1575  F919   4C 3D F9           JMP REDIS       ;IF NOT, CHECK BAD FLAG
01-1580  F91C   20 2F FA   GOODFL  JSR SETLED      ;SET LED FOR PROPER INDICATION
01-1585  F91F   20 C9 FA           JSR DLY20S      ;DELAY FOR 20 SECONDS
01-1590  F922   A5 02              LDA ARMLED      ;GET STATUS OF RED LED & BUZZER
01-1595  F924   09 40              ORA #$40        ;TURN BUZZER OFF (X1XX XXXX)
01-1600  F926   29 FE              AND #$FE        ;TURN RED LED ON (XXXX XXX0)
01-1605  F928   85 02              STA ARMLED      ;DO IT
01-1610  F92A   A9 FF              LDA #$FF        ;SET SET-RES TO SET VALUE
01-1615  F92C   85 83              STA SETRES      ;DO IT
01-1620  F92E   4C CB F8           JMP CHECK       ;GO BACK TO CHECKING LOOPS
01-1625  F931                      ;
01-1630  F931                      ;THIS CODE TURNS ON SMOKE/FIRE WARNING HORN
01-1635  F931                      ;
01-1640  F931   20 98 FA   SMOKEA  JSR SMOKON      ;TURN ON THE WARNING HORN
01-1645  F934   20 A6 FA           JSR TIMOU5      ;TIME FOR 5 MINUTES
01-1650  F937   20 9F FA           JSR SMOKOF      ;AFTER 5 MINUTES TURN HORN OFF AND
01-1655  F93A   4C CB F8           JMP CHECK       ;SEE IF SMOKE/FIRE LOOP IS CLEARED
01-1660  F93D                      ;
01-1665  F93D                      ;
01-1670  F93D   20 74 FA   REDIS   JSR CHKREM      ;CHECK REMOTE DISARM LOOP
01-1675  F940   90 0E              BCC NOTREM      ;IF NOT REMOTE, THEN CHECK DELAYED
01-1680  F942                      ;               ;ENTRY LOOP
01-1685  F942   20 70 F9           JSR DISARM      ;IF REMOTE, THEN DISARM SYSTEM
01-1690  F945   20 74 FA   OPENC   JSR CHKREM      ;AND CHECK UNTIL REMOTE CONTACTS
01-1695  F948   90 FB              BCC OPENC       ;CLOSE AGAIN
01-1700  F94A   20 2F FA           JSR SETLED      ;SET LED FOR PROPER INDICATION
01-1705  F94D   4C CB F8           JMP CHECK       ;AND GO BACK TO CHECKING LOOPS
01-1710  F950                      ;
01-1715  F950   20 F4 F9   NOTREM  JSR CHKDE       ;CHECK FOR DELAYED ENTRY
01-1720  F953   B0 28              BCS DELENT      ;IF DELAYED ENTRY, THEN SET UP DELAY
01-1725  F955                      ;               ;IF NOT THEN ALARM IMMEDIATELY
01-1730  F955                      ;
01-1735  F955                      ;THIS CODE TURNS ALARM SYSTEM TO ALARM FOR 5 MINUTES
01-1740  F955                      ;
01-1745  F955   A5 02      SETALR  LDA PORTB       ;GET STATUS OF SOFT SWITCHES
01-1750  F957   29 90              AND #$90        ;(1XX1 XXXX) MASK ALL BUT SWITCH BITS
01-1755  F959   F0 12              BEQ ISDIAL      ;IF 00, THEN IT IS DIALER
01-1760  F95B   20 8A FA           JSR SIREON      ;TURN THE SIREN(S) ON
01-1765  F95E   20 98 FA           JSR SMOKON      ;TURN SMOKE ALARM ON
01-1770  F961   20 A6 FA           JSR TIMOU5      ;TIME FOR 5 MINUTES
01-1775  F964   20 91 FA           JSR SIROFF      ;TURN THE SIREN(S) OFF
01-1780  F967   20 9F FA           JSR SMOKOF      ;TURN OFF SMOKE ALARM
01-1785  F96A   4C CB F8           JMP CHECK       ;SEE IF SYSTEM IS RESET. IF NOT IT
01-1790  F96D                      ;               ;WILL CONTINUE TO ALARM
01-1795  F96D                      ;
01-1800  F96D   4C CF FB   ISDIAL  JMP DIALER      ;JUMP TO AUTO DIALER ROUTINE
01-1805  F970                      ;
```

195

BURGLAR ALARM WITH DELAYED ENTRY

```
LINE#    ADDR   OBJECT     LABEL  SOURCE           PAGE 0010

01-1810  F970                     ;THIS ROUTINE DISARMS THE SYSTEM
01-1815  F970                     ;
01-1820  F970   A9 00      DISARM LDA #$00         ;SET ALARM FLAG TO OFF
01-1825  F972   85 82             STA ALARFF       ;STORE AT ALARM FLAG
01-1830  F974   85 83             STA SETRES       ;CLEAR SET RESET FLIP-FLOP
01-1835  F976   20 9F FA          JSR SMOKOF       ;TURN OFF SMOKE/FIRE ALARM
01-1840  F979   20 91 FA          JSR SIROFF       ;TURN SIREN OFF
01-1845  F97C   60                RTS
01-1850  F97D                     ;
01-1855  F97D                     ;
01-1860  F97D                     ;
01-1865  F97D   20 C9 FA   DELENT JSR DLY20S       ;IF DELAYED ENTRY, THEN SET UP FOR
01-1870  F980                     ;                ;20 SECOND DELAY
01-1875  F980   4C 55 F9          JMP SETALR       ;SET ALARM AFTER 20 SECOND DELAY
01-1880  F983                     ;                ;AND NO KEYPAD OR REMOTE DISABLE
01-1885  F983                     ;
01-1890  F983                     ;
01-1895  F983   A5 80      CHKFLG LDA FLAGS        ;GET FLAG STATUS
01-1900  F985   6A                ROR A            ;SHIFT N.C. LOOP TO CARRY
01-1905  F986   B0 0E             BCS BAD2         ;BAD LOOP
01-1910  F988   6A                ROR A            ;SHIFT PANIC LOOP TO CARRY
01-1915  F989   B0 0B             BCS BAD2         ;BAD LOOP
01-1920  F98B   6A                ROR A            ;SHIFT INSIDE LOOP TO CARRY
01-1925  F98C   B0 08             BCS BAD2         ;BAD LOOP
01-1930  F98E   6A                ROR A            ;SHIFT N.O. LOOP TO CARRY
01-1935  F98F   B0 05             BCS BAD2         ;BAD LOOP
01-1940  F991   6A                ROR A            ;SHIFT DELAYED ENTRY LOOP TO CARRY
01-1945  F992   B0 02             BCS BAD2         ;BAD LOOP
01-1950  F994   18                CLC              ;ALL LOOPS OK
01-1955  F995   60                RTS
01-1960  F996                     ;
01-1965  F996   38         BAD2   SEC              ;SET ERROR BIT
01-1970  F997   60                RTS
01-1975  F998                     ;
01-1980  F998                     ;
01-1985  F998                     ;SUBROUTINE TO CHECK THE NORMALLY CLOSED LOOP
01-1990  F998                     ;
01-1995  F998   A5 00      CHKNCL LDA NCLOOP       ;GET LOOP STATUS
01-2000  F99A   29 01             AND #$01         ;MASK OFF ALL EXCEPT
01-2005  F99C                     ;                ;NORMALLY CLOSED LOOP
01-2010  F99C                     ;
01-2015  F99C   F0 08             BEQ CLOSE1       ;IF ZERO, THEN LOOP IS CLOSED
01-2020  F99E   A5 80             LDA FLAGS        ;GET FLAG STATUS
01-2025  F9A0   09 01             ORA #$01         ;SET NORMALLY CLOSED LOOP OPEN BIT
01-2030  F9A2   85 80             STA FLAGS        ;RETURN FLAG STATUS
01-2035  F9A4   38                SEC              ;SET CARRY BIT (ERROR)
01-2040  F9A5   60                RTS
01-2045  F9A6                     ;
01-2050  F9A6   A5 80      CLOSE1 LDA FLAGS        ;GET FLAG STATUS
01-2055  F9A8   29 FE             AND #$FE         ;CLEAR NORMALLY OPEN FLAG
01-2060  F9AA   85 80             STA FLAGS        ;RETURN STATUS
01-2065  F9AC   18                CLC              ;CLEAR CARRY BIT (NO ERROR)
01-2070  F9AD   60                RTS
01-2075  F9AE                     ;
01-2080  F9AE                     ;
```

BURGLAR ALARM WITH DELAYED ENTRY

```
LINE#     ADDR    OBJECT      LABEL    SOURCE              PAGE 0011

01-2085   F9AE                         ;SUBROUTINE TO CHECK THE NORMALLY OPEN LOOP
01-2090   F9AE                         ;
01-2095   F9AE    A5 00       CHKNOL   LDA NOLOOP          ;GET STATUS OF LOOPS
01-2100   F9B0    29 08                AND #$08            ;MASK ALL EXCEPT THE
01-2105   F9B2                ;                            ;NORMALLY OPEN LOOP
01-2110   F9B2    D0 08                BNE OK1             ;IF NOT ZERO, THEN LOOP IS OK
01-2115   F9B4    A5 80                LDA FLAGS           ;GET FLAG STATUS
01-2120   F9B6    09 08                ORA #$08            ;SET NORMALLY CLOSED LOOP ERROR BIT
01-2125   F9B8    85 80                STA FLAGS           ;RETURN STATUS
01-2130   F9BA    38                   SEC                 ;SET CARRY BIT (ERROR)
01-2135   F9BB    60                   RTS
01-2140   F9BC                ;
01-2145   F9BC    A5 80       OK1      LDA FLAGS           ;GET FLAG STATUS
01-2150   F9BE    29 F7                AND #$F7            ;CLEAR NORMALLY OPEN LOOP ERROR BIT
01-2155   F9C0    85 80                STA FLAGS           ;RETURN FLAG STATUS
01-2160   F9C2    18                   CLC                 ;CLEAR CARRY BIT (NO ERROR)
01-2165   F9C3    60                   RTS
01-2170   F9C4                ;
01-2175   F9C4                ;
01-2180   F9C4                         ;SUBROUTINE TO CHECK THE PANIC LOOP
01-2185   F9C4                ;
01-2190   F9C4    A5 00       CHKPL    LDA PRLOOP          ;GET LOOP STATUS
01-2195   F9C6    29 02                AND #$02            ;MASK OFF ALL BUT PANIC LOOP
01-2200   F9C8    D0 0C                BNE OK2             ;IF NOT ZERO, THEN LOOP IS OK
01-2205   F9CA    A5 80                LDA FLAGS           ;GET FLAG STATUS
01-2210   F9CC    09 02                ORA #$02            ;SET PANIC LOOP ERROR BIT
01-2215   F9CE    85 80                STA FLAGS           ;RETURN STATUS
01-2220   F9D0    A2 FF                LDX #$FF            ;RESET STACK POINTER
01-2225   F9D2    9A                   TXS                 ;DO IT
01-2230   F9D3    4C 55 F9             JMP SETALR          ;SET OFF ALARM
01-2235   F9D6                ;
01-2240   F9D6    A5 80       OK2      LDA FLAGS           ;GET FLAG STATUS
01-2245   F9D8    29 FD                AND #$FD            ;CLEAR PANIC LOOP ERROR BIT
01-2250   F9DA    85 80                STA FLAGS           ;RETURN FLAG STATUS
01-2255   F9DC    18                   CLC                 ;CLEAR CARRY BIT (NO ERROR)
01-2260   F9DD    60                   RTS
01-2265   F9DE                ;
01-2270   F9DE                ;
01-2275   F9DE                         ;SUBROUTINE TO CHECK INSIDE LOOP (N.C.)
01-2280   F9DE                ;
01-2285   F9DE    A5 00       CHKIL    LDA INLOOP          ;GET LOOP STATUS
01-2290   F9E0    29 04                AND #$04            ;MASK ALL EXCEPT INSIDE LOOP
01-2295   F9E2    F0 08                BEQ CLOSE2          ;IF ZERO, THEN LOOP IS CLOSED
01-2300   F9E4    A5 80                LDA FLAGS           ;GET FLAG STATUS
01-2305   F9E6    09 04                ORA #$04            ;SET INSIDE LOOP ERROR BIT
01-2310   F9E8    85 80                STA FLAGS           ;RETURN STATUS
01-2315   F9EA    38                   SEC                 ;SET CARRY BIT (ERROR)
01-2320   F9EB    60                   RTS
01-2325   F9EC                ;
01-2330   F9EC    A5 80       CLOSE2   LDA FLAGS           ;GET FLAG STATUS
01-2335   F9EE    29 FB                AND #$FB            ;CLEAR INSIDE LOOP ERROR BIT
01-2340   F9F0    85 80                STA FLAGS           ;RETURN STATUS
01-2345   F9F2    18                   CLC                 ;CLEAR CARRY BIT (NO ERROR)
01-2350   F9F3    60                   RTS
01-2355   F9F4                ;
```

BURGLAR ALARM WITH DELAYED ENTRY

```
LINE#    ADDR    OBJECT      LABEL    SOURCE           PAGE 0012

01-2360  F9F4                         ;
01-2365  F9F4                         ;SUBROUTINE TO CHECK DELAYED ENTRY LOOP
01-2370  F9F4                         ;
01-2375  F9F4    A5 00       CHKDE    LDA DELOOP       ;GET LOOP STATUS
01-2380  F9F6    29 10                AND #$10         ;MASK ALL EXCEPT DELAYED ENTRY LOOP
01-2385  F9F8    F0 08                BEQ CLOSE3       ;IF ZERO, THEN LOOP IS CLOSED
01-2390  F9FA    A5 80                LDA FLAGS        ;GET FLAG STATUS
01-2395  F9FC    09 10                ORA #$10         ;SET DELAYED ENTRY FLAG BIT
01-2400  F9FE    85 80                STA FLAGS        ;RETURN STATUS
01-2405  FA00    38                   SEC              ;SET CARRY BIT (ERROR)
01-2410  FA01    60                   RTS
01-2415  FA02                         ;
01-2420  FA02    A5 80       CLOSE3   LDA FLAGS        ;GET FLAG STATUS
01-2425  FA04    29 EF                AND #$EF         ;CLEAR DELAYED ENTRY FLAG BIT
01-2430  FA06    85 80                STA FLAGS        ;RETURN STATUS
01-2435  FA08    18                   CLC              ;CLEAR CARRY FLAG (NO ERROR)
01-2440  FA09    60                   RTS
01-2445  FA0A                         ;
01-2450  FA0A                         ;
01-2455  FA0A                         ;SUBROUTINE TO CHECK KEYBOARD CONTACTS
01-2460  FA0A                         ;
01-2465  FA0A    A5 00       CHKKEY   LDA KEYPAD       ;GET STATUS
01-2470  FA0C    29 20                AND #$20         ;MASK ALL EXCEPT KEYBOARD BIT
01-2475  FA0E    D0 17                BNE OK4          ;IF NOT ZERO, THEN CONTACTS ARE OPEN
01-2480  FA10    A5 80                LDA FLAGS        ;GET FLAG STATUS
01-2485  FA12    09 20                ORA #$20         ;SET KEYPAD ERROR FLAG
01-2490  FA14    85 80                STA FLAGS        ;RETURN STATUS
01-2495  FA16    20 0C FB    AOPEN    JSR DLYVSC       ;DELAY FOR A WHILE
01-2500  FA19    A5 00                LDA KEYPAD       ;GET STATUS
01-2505  FA1B    29 20                AND #$20         ;MASK ALL EXCEPT KEYPAD BIT
01-2510  FA1D    F0 F7                BEQ AOPEN        ;CHECK UNTIL CONTACTS OPEN AGAIN
01-2515  FA1F    A5 82                LDA ALARFF       ;GET ALARM FLIP-FLOP
01-2520  FA21    49 FF                EOR #$FF         ;FLIP IT TO OTHER STATE
01-2525  FA23    85 82                STA ALARFF       ;PUT IN NEW STATUS
01-2530  FA25    38                   SEC              ;SET CARRY BIT (ERROR)
01-2535  FA26    60                   RTS
01-2540  FA27                         ;
01-2545  FA27    A5 80       OK4      LDA FLAGS        ;GET FLAG STATUS
01-2550  FA29    29 DF                AND #$DF         ;CLEAR KEYPAD ERROR FLAG
01-2555  FA2B    85 80                STA FLAGS        ;RETURN STATUS
01-2560  FA2D    18                   CLC              ;CLEAR CARRY BIT (NO ERROR)
01-2565  FA2E    60                   RTS
01-2570  FA2F                         ;
01-2575  FA2F                         ;
01-2580  FA2F                         ;SUBROUTINE TO TURN ON PROPER LED
01-2585  FA2F                         ;
01-2590  FA2F    18          SETLED   CLC
01-2595  FA30    A5 80                LDA FLAGS        ;GET LOOP STATUS FLAGS
01-2600  FA32    4A                   LSR A            ;SHIFT NORMALLY CLOSED LOOP
01-2605  FA33                         ;                ;STATUS TO CARRY
01-2610  FA33    B0 22                BCS LOPEN        ;IF CARRY IS SET THEN LOOP IS OPEN
01-2615  FA35    4A                   LSR A            ;SHIFT PANIC BIT TO CARRY
01-2620  FA36    B0 1F                BCS LOPEN        ;IF CARRY IS SET THEN
01-2625  FA38                         ;                ;LOOP STATUS WRONG
01-2630  FA38    4A                   LSR A            ;SHIFT INSIDE LOOP BIT TO CARRY
```

BURGLAR ALARM WITH DELAYED ENTRY

LINE#	ADDR	OBJECT	LABEL	SOURCE	PAGE 0013
01-2635	FA39	B0 1C		BCS LOPEN	;IF CARRY IS SET, THEN LOOP IS OPEN
01-2640	FA3B	4A		LSR A	;SHIFT NORMALLY OPEN LOOP
01-2645	FA3C		;		;BIT TO CARRY
01-2650	FA3C	B0 19		BCS LOPEN	;IF CARRY IS SET THEN LOOP
01-2655	FA3E		;		;STATUS WRONG
01-2660	FA3E	4A		LSR A	;CHECK DELAYED ENTRY LOOP
01-2665	FA3F	B0 16		BCS LOPEN	;IF CARRY IS SET, THEN LOOP IS OPEN
01-2670	FA41	A5 82		LDA ALARFF	;GET STATUS OF ALARM FILP-FLOP
01-2675	FA43	30 09		BMI REDON	;IF NEGATIVE, THEN TURN ON
01-2680	FA45		;		;RED LED FOR ALARM
01-2685	FA45		;		
01-2690	FA45	A5 02		LDA LOKLED	;GET STATUS OF LOOP OK LED
01-2695	FA47	29 FD		AND #$FD	;TURN ON GREEN LED
01-2700	FA49	09 41		ORA #$41	;TURN OFF RED LED & WARNING BUZZER
01-2705	FA4B	85 02		STA LOKLED	;STORE AT LED COMMAND PORT
01-2710	FA4D	60		RTS	
01-2715	FA4E		;		
01-2720	FA4E	A5 02	REDON	LDA ARMLED	;GET STATUS OF ARMED SYSTEM LED
01-2725	FA50	29 FE		AND #$FE	;TURN RED LED ON
01-2730	FA52	09 02		ORA #$02	;TURN GREEN LED OFF
01-2735	FA54	85 02		STA ARMLED	;STORE AT LED COMMAND PORT
01-2740	FA56	60		RTS	
01-2745	FA57		;		
01-2750	FA57	A5 02	LOPEN	LDA LOKLED	;GET LED STATUS
01-2755	FA59	09 43		ORA #$43	;TURN OFF BOTH RED AND GREEN LED
01-2760	FA5B		;		;AND WARNING BUZZER
01-2765	FA5B	85 02		STA LOKLED	;STORE AT LED COMMAND PORT
01-2770	FA5D	60		RTS	
01-2775	FA5E		;		
01-2780	FA5E		;		
01-2785	FA5E		;		
01-2790	FA5E		;CHECK SMOKE/FIRE LOOP		
01-2795	FA5E		;		
01-2800	FA5E	A5 00	CHKSMO	LDA SMODET	;GET SMOKE LOOP STATUS
01-2805	FA60	29 80		AND #$80	;MASK ALL EXCEPT SMOKE/FIRE BIT
01-2810	FA62	F0 08		BEQ CLOSE4	;IF ZERO, THEN LOOP IS O.K.
01-2815	FA64	A5 80		LDA FLAGS	;GET FLAG STATUS
01-2820	FA66	09 80		ORA #$80	;SET SMOKE/FIRE BIT
01-2825	FA68	85 80		STA FLAGS	
01-2830	FA6A	38		SEC	;SET CARRY BIT (ERROR)
01-2835	FA6B	60		RTS	
01-2840	FA6C		;		
01-2845	FA6C	A5 80	CLOSE4	LDA FLAGS	;GET FLAG STATUS
01-2850	FA6E	29 7F		AND #$7F	;CLEAR SMOKE/FIRE BIT
01-2855	FA70	85 80		STA FLAGS	
01-2860	FA72	18		CLC	;CLEAR CARRY (NO ERROR)
01-2865	FA73	60		RTS	
01-2870	FA74		;		
01-2875	FA74		;		
01-2880	FA74		;CHECK REMOTE DISARM LOOP		
01-2885	FA74		;		
01-2890	FA74	A5 00	CHKREM	LDA REMDIS	;GET LOOP STATUS
01-2895	FA76	29 40		AND #$40	;MASK ALL EXCEPT REMOTE LOOP BIT
01-2900	FA78	F0 08		BEQ CLOSE5	;IF ZERO, THEN LOOP IS O.K.
01-2905	FA7A	A5 80		LDA FLAGS	;GET FLAG STATUS

BURGLAR ALARM WITH DELAYED ENTRY

```
LINE#     ADDR    OBJECT     LABEL    SOURCE              PAGE 0014

01-2910   FA7C    09 40               ORA #$40            ;SET REMOTE STATUS FLAG
01-2915   FA7E    85 80               STA FLAGS
01-2920   FA80    38                  SEC                 ;SET CARRY BIT (ERROR)
01-2925   FA81    60                  RTS
01-2930   FA82                      ;
01-2935   FA82    A5 80      CLOSE5   LDA FLAGS           ;GET FLAG STATUS
01-2940   FA84    29 BF               AND #$BF            ;CLEAR REMOTE FLAG
01-2945   FA86    85 80               STA FLAGS
01-2950   FA88    18                  CLC                 ;CLEAR CARRY (NO ERROR)
01-2955   FA89    60                  RTS
01-2960   FA8A                      ;
01-2965   FA8A                      ;ROUTINE TO TURN OUTSIDE SIREN ON
01-2970   FA8A                      ;
01-2975   FA8A    A5 02      SIREON   LDA OUTALR          ;GET STATUS OF OUTSIDE ALARM
01-2980   FA8C    29 F7               AND #$F7            ;SET OUTSIDE ALARM BIT LOW (ALARM)
01-2985   FA8E    85 02               STA OUTALR          ;SET IT LOW
01-2990   FA90    60                  RTS
01-2995   FA91                      ;
01-3000   FA91                      ;ROUTINE TO TURN OUTSIDE SIREN OFF
01-3005   FA91                      ;
01-3010   FA91    A5 02      SIROFF   LDA OUTALR          ;GET STATUS OF OUTSIDE SIREN
01-3015   FA93    09 08               ORA #$08            ;SET SIREN BIT HIGH (OFF)
01-3020   FA95    85 02               STA OUTALR          ;SET IT
01-3025   FA97    60                  RTS
01-3030   FA98                      ;
01-3035   FA98                      ;ROUTINE TO TURN INSIDE SMOKE/FIRE HORN ON
01-3040   FA98                      ;
01-3045   FA98    A5 02      SMOKON   LDA FIRALR          ;GET STATUS OF FIRE HORN
01-3050   FA9A    29 DF               AND #$DF            ;SET FIRE HORN BIT LOW (ON)
01-3055   FA9C    85 02               STA FIRALR          ;SET IT
01-3060   FA9E    60                  RTS
01-3065   FA9F                      ;
01-3070   FA9F                      ;ROUTINE TO TURN SMOKE/FIRE HORN OFF
01-3075   FA9F                      ;
01-3080   FA9F    A5 02      SMOKOF   LDA FIRALR          ;GET STATUS OF FIRE HORN
01-3085   FAA1    09 20               ORA #$20            ;SET BIT HIGH (OFF)
01-3090   FAA3    85 02               STA FIRALR          ;SET IT
01-3095   FAA5    60                  RTS
01-3100   FAA6                      ;
01-3105   FAA6                      ;
01-3110   FAA6                      ;
01-3115   FAA6                      ;SUBROUTINE TO CHECK FOR 5 MINUTE TIMEOUT ON ALARM
01-3120   FAA6                      ;
01-3125   FAA6    A0 02      TIMOU5   LDY #2              ;SET FOR 2 X 150 SEC. = 300 SEC.
01-3130   FAA8                      ;                    ;OR 5 MINUTES
01-3135   FAA8    84 88               STY TEMPT5          ;SET COUNTER
01-3140   FAAA    A2 96      SETNEX   LDX #150            ;SET FOR 150 X 1 SEC. = 150 SEC.
01-3145   FAAC    86 89               STX TEMPT6          ;SET COUNTER
01-3150   FAAE    20 DC FA   SETIME   JSR DLY1SC          ;DELAY FOR 1 SECOND
01-3155   FAB1    A5 02               LDA WARBUZ          ;GET STATUS OF WARNING BUZZER AND
01-3160   FAB3                      ;                    ;ARM LED
01-3165   FAB3    49 41               EOR #$41            ;ALTERNATE RED LED ON AND WARNING
01-3170   FAB5                      ;                    ;BUZZER OFF OR RED LED OFF AND
01-3175   FAB5                      ;                    ;WARNING BUZZER ON
01-3180   FAB5    85 02               STA WARBUZ
```

BURGLAR ALARM WITH DELAYED ENTRY

```
LINE#     ADDR   OBJECT      LABEL    SOURCE            PAGE 0015

01-3185   FAB7   C6 89                DEC TEMPT6
01-3190   FAB9   D0 F3                BNE SETIME        ;IF NOT ZERO, THEN LOOP SOME MORE
01-3195   FABB   C6 88                DEC TEMPT5
01-3200   FABD   D0 EB                BNE SETNEX        ;IF NOT ZERO, THEN LOOP SOME MORE
01-3205   FABF   60          TIMOUT   RTS               ;RETURN WHEN TIMED OUT
01-3210   FAC0                        ;
01-3215   FAC0                        ;
01-3220   FAC0                        ;SUBROUTINE TO DELAY APPROXIMATELY 1 MILLISECOND
01-3225   FAC0                        ;
01-3230   FAC0   A9 50       DLY1MS   LDA #80           ;SET COUNT FOR 80
01-3235   FAC2   85 15                STA DIV8DI        ;SET DIVIDE RATE FOR 8 CLOCK CYCLES
01-3240   FAC4   A5 14       CKTIME   LDA DIV1DI        ;GET TIMER STATUS
01-3245   FAC6   10 FC                BPL CKTIME        ;IF NOT NEGATIVE, THEN TIMER
01-3250   FAC8                        ;                 ;NOT TIMED OUT
01-3255   FAC8   60                   RTS
01-3260   FAC9                        ;
01-3265   FAC9                        ;
01-3270   FAC9                        ;SUBROUTINE TO DELAY FOR 20 SECONDS
01-3275   FAC9                        ;
01-3280   FAC9                        ;
01-3285   FAC9   A5 02       DLY20S   LDA ARMLED
01-3290   FACB   49 01                EOR #$01          ;TURN RED LED OFF
01-3295   FACD   29 BF                AND #$BF          ;TURN BUZZER ON
01-3300   FACF   85 02                STA ARMLED
01-3305   FAD1   A2 14                LDX #20           ;FOR 20 X 1 SECOND = 20 SECONDS
01-3310   FAD3   A0 01                LDY #1
01-3315   FAD5   86 89                STX TEMPT6        ;SET COUNTER
01-3320   FAD7   84 88                STY TEMPT5        ;SET COUNTER
01-3325   FAD9   4C AE FA             JMP SETIME
01-3330   FADC                        ;
01-3335   FADC                        ;
01-3340   FADC   A9 04       DLY1SC   LDA #$04          ;FOR 4 X 1/4 SECOND = 1 SECOND
01-3345   FADE   85 84                STA TEMPT1        ;STORE TEMPORARY COUNTER
01-3350   FAE0   A9 FA       DLY1S4   LDA #250          ;SET FOR 250 X 1 MS.=1/4 SEC.
01-3355   FAE2   85 86                STA TEMPT3        ;STORE AT COUNTER 3
01-3360   FAE4   20 C0 FA    CKOUT    JSR DLY1MS        ;DELAY FOR 1 MILLISECOND
01-3365   FAE7   20 0A FA             JSR CHKKEY        ;CHECK FOR KEYPAD
01-3370   FAEA   B0 0E                BCS CHANGE        ;IF CHANGED, THEN CHANGE ALARM STATUS
01-3375   FAEC   20 74 FA             JSR CHKREM        ;CHECK FOR REMOTE DISARM SWITCH
01-3380   FAEF   B0 09                BCS CHANGE
01-3385   FAF1   C6 86                DEC TEMPT3        ;DECREMENT COUNTER 3
01-3390   FAF3   D0 EF                BNE CKOUT         ;IF NOT TIMED OUT, THEN CHECK
01-3395   FAF5                        ;SOME MORE
01-3400   FAF5   C6 84                DEC TEMPT1
01-3405   FAF7   D0 E7                BNE DLY1S4
01-3410   FAF9   60                   RTS
01-3415   FAFA                        ;
01-3420   FAFA   A2 FF       CHANGE   LDX #$FF          ;FIX STACK POINTER
01-3425   FAFC   9A                   TXS
01-3430   FAFD   20 9F FA             JSR SMOKOF        ;TURN OFF SMOKE/FIRE WARNING HORN
01-3435   FB00                        ;                 ;IF IT IS ON
01-3440   FB00   A5 82                LDA ALARFF        ;CHECK ALARM STATUS
01-3445   FB02   C9 FF                CMP #$FF          ;IS IT SET?
01-3450   FB04   F0 03                BEQ PART          ;ONLY DO DISARM PART (FIRE/SMOKE)
01-3455   FB06   20 70 F9             JSR DISARM        ;DISARM ALL
01-3460   FB09   4C CB F8    PART     JMP CHECK
```

BURGLAR ALARM WITH DELAYED ENTRY

```
LINE#     ADDR    OBJECT     LABEL   SOURCE          PAGE 0016

01-3465   FB0C                       ;
01-3470   FB0C    A9 04      DLYVSC  LDA #$04        ;SET FOR 4 X 1/4 SECONDS = 1 SECOND
01-3475   FB0E    85 85              STA TEMPT2      ;SET COUNTER FOR 4 COUNTS
01-3480   FB10    A9 FA      OVER1   LDA #250        ;SET FOR 250 COUNTS X 1 MS.=1/4 SEC.
01-3485   FB12    85 87              STA TEMPT4
01-3490   FB14    20 C0 FA   OVER2   JSR DLY1MS      ;DELAY 1 MILLISECOND
01-3495   FB17    C6 87              DEC TEMPT4      ;DECREMENT COUNTER FOR MILLISECONDS
01-3500   FB19    D0 F9              BNE OVER2       ;COUNT SOME MORE IF NOT FINISHED
01-3505   FB1B    C6 85              DEC TEMPT2      ;DECREMENT 1/4 SEC. COUNTER
01-3510   FB1D    D0 F1              BNE OVER1       ;COUNT SOME MORE IF NOT FINISHED
01-3515   FB1F    60                 RTS
01-3520   FB20                       ;
```

RANDOM LIGHT DIMMER

```
LINE#     ADDR   OBJECT     LABEL   SOURCE          PAGE 0017

01-3530   FB20                      ;
01-3535   FB20                      ;
01-3540   FB20   A9 FF      LIGDIM  LDA #$FF        ;MAKE ALL A PORTS OUTPUTS
01-3545   FB22   85 01              STA DDRA        ;DO IT
01-3550   FB24                      ;
01-3555   FB24                      ;MAKE A RANDOM ATTACK RAMP FROM 1/4 SECOND TO 1 3/4 SEC.
01-3560   FB24                      ;
01-3565   FB24   20 B0 FB           JSR RAND7       ;MAKE A RANDOM 3 BIT NUMBER (0-7)
01-3570   FB27   A5 8A              LDA TEMPT7      ;GET NUMBER
01-3575   FB29   D0 07              BNE ZRONOT      ;CANNOT BE ZERO
01-3580   FB2B   85 8B              STA TEMPT8      ;IF ZERO, THEN STORE IT
01-3585   FB2D   E6 8B              INC TEMPT8      ;AND MAKE IT A 1
01-3590   FB2F   4C 34 FB           JMP OKNUM       ;AND CONTINUE
01-3595   FB32   85 8B      ZRONOT  STA TEMPT8      ;STORE NUMBER AT ATTACK RAMP VALUE
01-3600   FB34                      ;               ;IS NUMBER OF 1/4 SECOND INTERVALS
01-3605   FB34                      ;
01-3610   FB34                      ;MAKE A DECAY RAMP BY SUBTRACTING ATTACK RAMP FROM 2 SEC.
01-3615   FB34                      ;
01-3620   FB34   A9 08      OKNUM   LDA #8          ;PUT 8 X 1/4 SECONDS, OR 2 SECONDS
01-3625   FB36   85 8C              STA TEMPT9      ;IN DECAY RAMP VALUE
01-3630   FB38   38                 SEC             ;GET READY TO SUBTRACT
01-3635   FB39   E5 8B              SBC TEMPT8      ;SUBTRACT ATTACK RAMP VALUE FROM
01-3640   FB3B                      ;               ;DECAY RAMP VALUE
01-3645   FB3B   85 8C              STA TEMPT9      ;PUT RESULT IN DECAY RAMP VALUE
01-3650   FB3D   20 B0 FB           JSR RAND7       ;GET 3 BIT RANDOM NUMBER
01-3655   FB40                      ;
01-3660   FB40                      ;MAKE A RANDOM TIME INTERVAL BETWEEN RAMP CYCLES
01-3665   FB40                      ;BY COUNTING FROM 1-7 TIMES 30 SECOND INTERVALS
01-3670   FB40                      ;
01-3675   FB40   A5 8A              LDA TEMPT7      ;GET NUMBER
01-3680   FB42   D0 07              BNE NOTZ1       ;CANNOT BE ZERO
01-3685   FB44   85 8D              STA TEMPTA      ;STORE IT IF ZERO
01-3690   FB46   E6 8D              INC TEMPTA      ;AND MAKE IT A 1
01-3695   FB48   4C 4D FB           JMP OKNUM1      ;AND CONTINUE
01-3700   FB4B                      ;
01-3705   FB4B   85 8D      NOTZ1   STA TEMPTA      ;STORE NUMBER
01-3710   FB4D
01-3715   FB4D
01-3720   FB4D                      ;
01-3725   FB4D                      ; VARIABLE DELAY
01-3730   FB4D                      ;
01-3735   FB4D   A4 8D      OKNUM1  LDY TEMPTA      ;NUMBER OF 30 SECOND INTERVALS
01-3740   FB4F   84 88              STY TEMPT5      ;FROM 1 TO 7 INTERVALS FOR 30 SECONDS
01-3745   FB51                      ;               ;FOR 30 TO 210 SECOND DELAY
01-3750   FB51   A2 1E      SETNE1  LDX #30         ;30 SECOND COUNT
01-3755   FB53   86 89              STX TEMPT6      ;STORE IT
01-3760   FB55                      ;
01-3765   FB55   20 0C FB   SET1    JSR DLYVSC      ;DELAY 1 SECOND
01-3770   FB58   C6 89              DEC TEMPT6      ;DECREMENT SECONDS COUNTER
01-3775   FB5A   D0 F9              BNE SET1        ;IF NOT ZERO, DO SOME MORE
01-3780   FB5C                      ;
01-3785   FB5C   C6 88              DEC TEMPT5      ;DECREMENT NUMBER OF COUNTS
01-3790   FB5E   D0 F1              BNE SETNE1      ;IF NOT ZERO, DO SOME MORE
01-3795   FB60                      ;
01-3800   FB60                      ;
```

RANDOM LIGHT DIMMER

```
LINE#    ADDR    OBJECT      LABEL   SOURCE          PAGE 0018

01-3805  FB60                      ; DO ATTACK RAMP
01-3810  FB60                      ;
01-3815  FB60   20 9E FB     SETIT2 JSR SET250       ;SET 1/4 SECOND DELAY
01-3820  FB63   20 B0 FB     REPEAT JSR RAND7        ;MAKE A 3 BIT RANDOM NUMBER
01-3825  FB66   A5 8A               LDA TEMPT7       ;GET RANDOM NUMBER
01-3830  FB68   18                  CLC              ;GET READY TO ADD
01-3835  FB69   65 00                ADC PORTA       ;ADD RANDOM NUMBER TO PORT A VALUE
01-3840  FB6B   85 00                STA PORTA       ;SET PORTA TO NEW VALUE
01-3845  FB6D   C9 C1                CMP #193        ;IS NEW VALUE 193 OR MORE?
01-3850  FB6F   B0 0C                BCS STOPRA      ;IF SO, THEN STOP RAMP
01-3855  FB71   20 A5 FB             JSR TES250      ;IS 1/4 SECOND UP YET?
01-3860  FB74   B0 03                BCS TOVER       ;IF OVER, THEN GO ON
01-3865  FB76   4C 63 FB             JMP REPEAT      ;IF NOT, THEN ADD SOME MORE NUMBERS
01-3870  FB79                      ;
01-3875  FB79   C6 8C        TOVER  DEC TEMPT9       ;DECREMENT RAMP 1/4 SECOND COUNTER
01-3880  FB7B   D0 E3                BNE SETIT2      ;DO MORE UNTIL RAMP COUNTER=ZERO
01-3885  FB7D   EA           STOPRA NOP              ;STOP ADDING RAMP VALUES
01-3890  FB7E
01-3895  FB7E
01-3900  FB7E                      ;
01-3905  FB7E                      ;DO DECAY RAMP
01-3910  FB7E                      ;
01-3915  FB7E   20 9E FB     SETIT1 JSR SET250       ;SET 1/4 SECOND DELAY
01-3920  FB81   20 B0 FB     REPET1 JSR RAND7        ;MAKE 3 BIT RANDOM NUMBER
01-3925  FB84   A5 8A               LDA TEMPT7       ;GET NUMBER
01-3930  FB86   38                  SEC              ;GET READY TO SUBTRACT
01-3935  FB87   E5 00                SBC PORTA       ;SUBTRACT NUMBER FROM PORTA
01-3940  FB89   B0 02                BCS POSNUM      ;IF NEGATIVE NUMBER, THEN MAKE ZERO
01-3945  FB8B                      ;
01-3950  FB8B   A9 00                LDA #0          ;MAKE ZERO
01-3955  FB8D   85 00        POSNUM STA PORTA        ;STORE NEW VALUE AT PORTA
01-3960  FB8F   20 A5 FB             JSR TES250      ;SEE IF 1/4 SECOND IS UP YET
01-3965  FB92   B0 03                BCS TOVER1      ;IF TIME UP, THEN BRANCH
01-3970  FB94                      ;
01-3975  FB94   4C 81 FB             JMP REPET1      ;IF NOT, THEN DO SOME MORE
01-3980  FB97                      ;
01-3985  FB97   C6 8D        TOVER1 DEC TEMPTA       ;DECREMENT DECAY RAMP VALUE
01-3990  FB99   D0 E3                BNE SETIT1      ;IF NOT ZERO, THEN DO SOME MORE
01-3995  FB9B                      ;
01-4000  FB9B   4C 20 FB             JMP LIGDIM      ;IF ALL, THEN START ALL OVER AGAIN
01-4005  FB9E                      ;
01-4010  FB9E                      ;SET 1/4 SECOND TIMER
01-4015  FB9E                      ;
01-4020  FB9E   48           SET250 PHA              ;STORE ACCUMULATOR
01-4025  FB9F   A9 F4                LDA #244        ;SET TO 244 COUNTS
01-4030  FBA1   85 17                STA D1024D      ;SET TO DIVIDE BY 1024 CLOCK CYCLES
01-4035  FBA3                      ;                ;FOR 244X1024=249.8 MILLISECONDS
01-4040  FBA3   68                  PLA              ;RESTORE ACCUMULATOR
01-4045  FBA4   60                  RTS
01-4050  FBA5                      ;
01-4055  FBA5                      ;TEST 1/4 SECOND TIMER FOR TIMEOUT
01-4060  FBA5                      ;
01-4065  FBA5   48           TES250 PHA              ;STORE ACCUMULATOR
01-4070  FBA6   A5 14               LDA DIV1DI       ;GET TIMER STATUS
01-4075  FBA8   10 03               BPL NOTIME       ;BRANCH IF NOT TIMED OUT
```

RANDOM LIGHT DIMMER

```
LINE#     ADDR   OBJECT      LABEL   SOURCE          PAGE 0019
01-4080   FBAA               ;
01-4085   FBAA   68                  PLA             ;RESTORE ACCUMULATOR
01-4090   FBAB   38                  SEC             ;SET CARRY BIT IF TIMED OUT
01-4095   FBAC   60                  RTS
01-4100   FBAD                       ;
01-4105   FBAD   68          NOTIME  PLA             ;RESTORE ACCUMULATOR
01-4110   FBAE   18                  CLC             ;CLEAR CARRY IF NOT TIMED OUT
01-4115   FBAF   60                  RTS
01-4120   FBB0
01-4125   FBB0               ;
01-4130   FBB0               ; MAKE A 3 BIT RANDOM NUMBER (0-7)
01-4135   FBB0               ;
01-4140   FBB0   A0 02       RAND7   LDY #2          ;DO IT FOR 3 BITS ONLY
01-4145   FBB2   A9 00               LDA #0          ;ZERO TEMP LOCATION
01-4150   FBB4   85 8A               STA TEMPT7      ;DO IT
01-4155   FBB6               ;
01-4160   FBB6   A5 02       NEXBIT  LDA PORTB       ;RANDOM NUMBER PORT
01-4165   FBB8   29 01               AND #$01        ;(0000 0001) MASK OFF ALL EXCEPT LOW BIT
01-4170   FBBA               ;
01-4175   FBBA   F0 09               BEQ NOTONE      ;IF ZERO THEN BRANCH TO NOT ONE
01-4180   FBBC               ;
01-4185   FBBC   38                  SEC             ;IF A '1' SET CARRY BIT
01-4190   FBBD   26 8A               ROL TEMPT7      ;AND ROTATE CARRY BIT TO LS BIT
01-4195   FBBF   88                  DEY             ;DECREMENT BIT COUNTER
01-4200   FBC0   10 F4               BPL NEXBIT      ;IF NOT FINISHED, DO SOME MORE BITS
01-4205   FBC2   4C CB FB            JMP ALLBIT      ;IF FINISHED, THEN GO ON
01-4210   FBC5               ;
01-4215   FBC5   18          NOTONE  CLC             ;IF ZERO, THEN CLEAR CARRY BIT
01-4220   FBC6   26 8A               ROL TEMPT7      ;AND ROTATE CARRY BIT TO LS BIT
01-4225   FBC8   88                  DEY             ;DECREMENT BIT COUNTER
01-4230   FBC9   10 EB               BPL NEXBIT      ;IF NOT FINISHED, THEN DO SOME MORE BITS
01-4235   FBCB               ;
01-4240   FBCB   60          ALLBIT  RTS             ;RETURN WHEN FINISHED
01-4245   FBCC
01-4250   FBCC
```

TELEPHONE DIALER ROUTINES

LINE#	ADDR	OBJECT	LABEL	SOURCE	PAGE 0020
01-4260	FBCC				
01-4265	FBCC			;AUTOMATIC TELEPHONE DIALER ROUTINES	
01-4270	FBCC			;	
01-4275	FBCC			;	
01-4280	FBCC	4C B4 F8	DEDIAL	JMP DELARM	;USES SOME OF THE DELAYED ENTRY
01-4285	FBCF			;	;ALARM ROUTINES
01-4290	FBCF			;	
01-4295	FBCF			;	
01-4300	FBCF	A5 02	DIALER	LDA PORTB	;GET PORT STATUS
01-4305	FBD1	29 BF		AND #$BF	;(XOXX XXXX) SET TO PULSE DIAL MODE
01-4310	FBD3	85 02		STA PORTB	;DO IT
01-4315	FBD5	29 F7		AND #$F7	;(XXXX OXXX) CONNECT DIALER TO
01-4320	FBD7			;	;TELEPHONE LINE
01-4325	FBD7	85 02		STA PORTB	;DO IT
01-4330	FBD9	20 0C FB		JSR DLYVSC	;DELAY 1 SECOND
01-4335	FBDC	20 0C FB		JSR DLYVSC	;DELAY ANOTHER SECOND FOR DIAL TONE
01-4340	FBDF	A5 02		LDA PORTB	;GET STATUS
01-4345	FBE1	29 DB		AND #$DB	;(XXOX XOXX) SET PB2 & PB5 LOW
01-4350	FBE3			;	;TO ACTIVATE "*" PUSHBUTTON
01-4355	FBE3	85 02		STA PORTB	;DO IT
01-4360	FBE5	20 10 FB		JSR OVER1	;DELAY 1/4 SECOND
01-4365	FBE8	A5 02		LDA PORTB	;GET STATUS
01-4370	FBEA	09 24		ORA #$24	;(XX1X X1XX) UN-SELECT PUSHBUTTONS
01-4375	FBEC	85 02		STA PORTB	;DO IT
01-4380	FBEE	20 0C FB		JSR DLYVSC	;DELAY 1 SECOND
01-4385	FBF1	A5 02		LDA PORTB	;GET STATUS
01-4390	FBF3	29 DF		AND #$DF	;(XXOX XXXX)
01-4395	FBF5	09 20		ORA #$20	;(XX1X XXXX) SELECT "1" PUSHBUTTON
01-4400	FBF7	85 02		STA PORTB	
01-4405	FBF9	20 10 FB		JSR OVER1	;DELAY 1/4 SECOND
01-4410	FBFC	A5 02		LDA PORTB	;GET STATUS
01-4415	FBFE	09 24		ORA #$24	;(XX1X X1XX) UN-SELECT PUSHBUTTONS
01-4420	FC00	85 02		STA PORTB	;DO IT
01-4425	FC02	20 66 FC		JSR DLY10S	;DELAY FOR 10 SECONDS FOR
01-4430	FC05			;	;DIALER TO FINISH DIALING
01-4435	FC05			;	
01-4440	FC05	A5 02		LDA PORTB	;GET STATUS
01-4445	FC07	09 40		ORA #$40	;(X1XX XXXX) SELECT TONE DIALING MODE
01-4450	FC09	85 02		STA PORTB	;DO IT
01-4455	FC0B	A2 0F		LDX #15	;DO IT FOR 15 TIMES
01-4460	FC0D	20 6F FC		JSR SIGNAL	;SEND ALTERNATING TONES
01-4465	FC10			;	;FOR 30 SECONDS
01-4470	FC10			;	
01-4475	FC10	A5 02		LDA PORTB	;GET STATUS
01-4480	FC12	09 6C		ORA #$6C	;UN-SELECT BUTTONS & HANG UP
01-4485	FC14	85 02		STA PORTB	;TELEPHONE
01-4490	FC16	20 66 FC		JSR DLY10S	;WAIT 10 SECONDS FOR LINE TO CLEAR
01-4495	FC19	A5 02		LDA PORTB	;GET STATUS
01-4500	FC1B	29 BF		AND #$BF	;(XOXX XXXX) SET DIALER TO PULSE MODE
01-4505	FC1D	85 02		STA PORTB	;DO IT
01-4510	FC1F	29 F7		AND #$F7	;(XXXX OXXX) CONNECT TO TELEPHONE LINE
01-4515	FC21	85 02		STA PORTB	;DO IT
01-4520	FC23	20 0C FB		JSR DLYVSC	;DELAY 1 SECOND
01-4525	FC26	20 0C FB		JSR DLYVSC	;DELAY ANOTHER SEC. FOR DIAL TONE
01-4530	FC29	A5 02		LDA PORTB	

TELEPHONE DIALER ROUTINES

```
LINE#    ADDR   OBJECT      LABEL   SOURCE          PAGE 0021
01-4535  FC2B   29 DB               AND #$DB        ;ACTIVATE "*" PUSHBUTTON
01-4540  FC2D   85 02               STA PORTB       ;DO IT
01-4545  FC2F   20 10 FB            JSR OVER1       ;DELAY 1/4 SECOND
01-4550  FC32   A5 02               LDA PORTB       ;GET STATUS
01-4555  FC34   09 24               ORA #$24        ;(XX1X X1XX) UN-SELECT PUSHBUTTONS
01-4560  FC36   85 02               STA PORTB       ;DO IT
01-4565  FC38   20 0C FB            JSR DLYVSC      ;DELAY 1 SECOND
01-4570  FC3B   A5 02               LDA PORTB       ;GET STATUS
01-4575  FC3D   29 DF               AND #$DF        ;(XX0X XXXX) SET UP TO
01-4580  FC3F   09 04               ORA #$04        ;(XXXX X1XX) ACTIVATE "2" PUSHBUTTON
01-4585  FC41   85 02               STA PORTB       ;DO IT
01-4590  FC43   20 10 FB            JSR OVER1       ;DELAY 1/4 SECOND
01-4595  FC46   A5 02               LDA PORTB       ;GET STATUS
01-4600  FC48   09 24               ORA #$24        ;UN-SELECT PUSHBUTTONS
01-4605  FC4A   85 02               STA PORTB       ;DO IT
01-4610  FC4C   20 66 FC            JSR DLY10S      ;DELAY 10 SECONDS FOR
01-4615  FC4F               ;                       ;DIALER TO FINISH DIALING
01-4620  FC4F   A5 02               LDA PORTB       ;GET STATUS
01-4625  FC51   09 40               ORA #$40        ;(X1XX XXXX) SET FOR TONE DIALING
01-4630  FC53   85 02               STA PORTB       ;DO IT
01-4635  FC55   A2 0F               LDX #15         ;DO IT FOR 15 TIMES
01-4640  FC57   20 6F FC            JSR SIGNAL      ;ALTERNATE TONES FOR 30 SECONDS
01-4645  FC5A   A5 02               LDA PORTB       ;GET STATUS
01-4650  FC5C   09 6C               ORA #$6C        ;(X11X 11XX) UN-SELECT PUSHBUTTONS
01-4655  FC5E   85 02               STA PORTB       ;AND HANG UP TELEPHONE
01-4660  FC60   20 A6 FA            JSR TIMOU5      ;TIME FOR 5 MINUTES
01-4665  FC63   4C CB F8            JMP CHECK       ;AND THEN CHECK AGAIN
01-4670  FC66               ;
01-4675  FC66               ;
01-4680  FC66               ;ROUTINE TO DELAY FOR 10 SECONDS
01-4685  FC66               ;
01-4690  FC66   A2 0A       DLY10S  LDX #10         ;DO IT 10 TIMES
01-4695  FC68   20 0C FB    LESDLY  JSR DLYVSC      ;DELAY FOR 1 SECOND
01-4700  FC6B   CA                  DEX             ;DECREMENT COUNTER
01-4705  FC6C   D0 FA               BNE LESDLY      ;IF NOT ZERO, THEN DO SOME MORE
01-4710  FC6E   60                  RTS
01-4715  FC6F               ;
01-4720  FC6F               ;
01-4725  FC6F               ;ROUTINE TO SEND ALTERNATING TONES OVER THE TELEPHONE
01-4730  FC6F               ;LINES
01-4735  FC6F               ;
01-4740  FC6F               ;
01-4745  FC6F   A5 02       SIGNAL  LDA PORTB       ;GET STATUS
01-4750  FC71   29 DB       MORSIG  AND #$DB        ;(XX0X X0XX) SELECT "1" PUSHBUTTON
01-4755  FC73   85 02               STA PORTB       ;FOR FIRST TONE
01-4760  FC75   20 0C FB            JSR DLYVSC      ;LEAVE TONE FOR 1 SECOND
01-4765  FC78   A5 02               LDA PORTB       ;GET STATUS
01-4770  FC7A   29 DB               AND #$DB        ;(XX0X X0XX) SELECT
01-4775  FC7C   09 04               ORA #$04        ;(XXXX X1XX) "2" PUSHBUTTON FOR
01-4780  FC7E   85 02               STA PORTB       ;SECOND TONE
01-4785  FC80   20 0C FB            JSR DLYVSC      ;LEAVE FOR 1 SECOND
01-4790  FC83   CA                  DEX             ;DECREMENT COUNTER
01-4795  FC84   D0 EB               BNE MORSIG      ;IF NOT ZERO, DO SOME MORE
01-4800  FC86   A5 02               LDA PORTB       ;GET STATUS
01-4805  FC88   09 24               ORA #$24        ;(XX1X X1XX) UN-SELECT PUSH BUTTONS
```

TELEPHONE DIALER ROUTINES

```
  LINE#   ADDR   OBJECT    LABEL  SOURCE            PAGE 0022
01-4810   FC8A   85 02            STA PORTB
01-4815   FC8C   60               RTS
01-4820   FC8D                  ;
01-4825   FC8D                  ;
01-4830   FC8D                    *=$FFF8
01-4835   FFF8                    .OFFSET 8FF8
01-4840   FFF8                  ;
01-4845   FFF8                  ;
01-4850   FFF8                  ;RESET VECTORS
01-4855   FFF8                  ;
01-4860   FFF8                  ;
01-4865   FFF8
01-4870   FFF8   00 F8            .WORD START
01-4875   FFFA   00 F8            .WORD START
01-4880   FFFC   00 F8            .WORD START
01-4885   FFFE   00 F8            .WORD START
01-4890   0000                  ;
01-4895   0000
01-4900   0000                    .END


ERRORS = 0000
```

SYMBOL TABLE 0023

ALARFF	0082	ALARM1	F82F	ALLBIT	FBCB	ALSET	F90E
AOPEN	FA16	ARMLED	0002	BAD2	F996	BADF	F8B2
CHANGE	FAFA	CHECK	F8CB	CHKDE	F9F4	CHKFLG	F983
CHKFLS	F8A6	CHKIL	F9DE	CHKKEY	FA0A	CHKLOP	F839
CHKNCL	F998	CHKNOL	F9AE	CHKPL	F9C4	CHKREM	FA74
CHKSMO	FA5E	CHKSWT	F862	CKOUT	FAE4	CKTIME	FAC4
CLOSE1	F9A6	CLOSE2	F9EC	CLOSE3	FA02	CLOSE4	FA6C
CLOSE5	FA82	D1024D	0017	D1024E	001F	DDRA	0001
DDRB	0003	DEDIAL	FBCC	DELARM	F8B4	DELENT	F97D
DELOOP	0000	DELY1	F804	DELY2	F806	DELYFF	0081
DI64DI	0016	DI64EI	001E	DIALER	FBCF	DIMLIG	F826
DISARM	F970	DIV1DI	0014	DIV1EI	001C	DIV8DI	0015
DIV8EI	001D	DLY10S	FC66	DLY1MS	FAC0	DLY1S4	FAE0
DLY1SC	FADC	DLY20S	FAC9	DLYALR	F82C	DLYVSC	FB0C
EXEND	F90B	FIRALR	0002	FLAGS	0080	GOODFL	F91C
INLOOP	0000	ISDIAL	F96D	KEYPAD	0000	KEYSWT	0000
LESDLY	FC68	LIGDIM	FB20	LOKLED	0002	LOPEN	FA57
LOPOP	F8C0	MORSIG	FC71	NCLOOP	0000	NEXBIT	FBB6
NOALRM	F89E	NOLOOP	0000	NOTIME	FBAD	NOTONE	FBC5
NOTREM	F950	NOTZ1	FB4B	NOWAY	F8FB	OK1	F9BC
OK2	F9D6	OK4	FA27	OKFLG	F85C	OKNUM	FB34
OKNUM1	FB4D	OPENC	F945	OPENL	F897	OPENS	F870
OPTLED	0002	OTHER	F829	OUTALR	0002	OVER1	FB10
OVER2	FB14	PART	FB09	PORTA	0000	PORTB	0002
POSNUM	FB8D	PRLOOP	0000	RAND7	FBB0	REDIS	F93D
REDLED	F890	REDON	FA4E	REGALR	F823	REMDIS	0000
REPEAT	FB63	REPET1	FB81	SET1	FB55	SET250	FB9E
SETALR	F955	SETIME	FAAE	SETIT	F84D	SETIT1	FB7E
SETIT2	FB60	SETLED	FA2F	SETNE1	FB51	SETNEX	FAAA
SETRES	0083	SIGNAL	FC6F	SIREON	FA8A	SIROFF	FA91
SMODET	0000	SMOKEA	F931	SMOKOF	FA9F	SMOKON	FA98
START	F800	STATUS	0005	STLEDS	F878	STOPRA	FB7D
SWB1	0002	SWB2	0002	TEMPT1	0084	TEMPT2	0085
TEMPT3	0086	TEMPT4	0087	TEMPT5	0088	TEMPT6	0089
TEMPT7	008A	TEMPT8	008B	TEMPT9	008C	TEMPTA	008D
TEMPTB	008E	TES250	FBA5	TIMOU5	FAA6	TIMOUT	FABF
TOVER	FB79	TOVER1	FB97	WARBUZ	0002	ZRONOT	FB32

END OF ASSEMBLY = FFFF

Appendix C
Suppliers

SECTION I LISTS DIFFERENT CATAGORIES OF security equipment along with a short definition of each and suggested suppliers. Section II lists the suppliers in alphabetical order.

SECTION I

Alarms, Auto
Devices used to protect autos from theft.
Alertronics, Inc.
Aqualarm, Inc.
Auto-Matic Products Co.
Electronic Locator Co.
Mallory Distributor Products, Inc.
Mountain West Alarm
Radio Shack
Universal Security Instruments, Inc.

Auto-Matic Products Co.
Electronic Instruments Co., Inc.
Electronic Locator Co.
GC Electronics
Mallory Distributor Products, Inc.
Mountain West Alarm
MRL Inc.
NAPCO Security Systems, Inc.
Radio Shack
Universal Security Instruments, Inc.

Alarms, Bells, Sirens, Horns
Audible devices used for sounding an alarm.
Alarm Devices Manufacturing Co.

Alarms, Capacitance
Alarm systems which are activated by a change in capacity.
Systron-Donner

211

Alarms, Remote (Self-Contained)

Self-contained door alarms which sound an alarm when the door is opened.
Continental Instruments Corp.
Mallory Distributor Products, Inc.
NAPCO Security Systems Inc.
Radio Shack

Alarm Systems, Complete

Complete Alarm systems for home use consisting of various types of sensors, hoop-up wire, control circuitry, and an alarm.
Aqualarm Inc. (Belgard Alarm Systems)
Continental Instruments Corp. (Apartment Alarm Systems)
Crismar Corp. (Challenge Alarm System)
Electronic Instruments Co., Inc.
Electronic Locator
Mallory Distributor Products, Inc.
Mountain West Alarm
MRL Inc.
Systron-Donner
Transcience
Universal Security Instruments, Inc.

Electronic Components and Construction Aids

Discrete components, ICs, perf boards, switches, wire, PC board kits, connectors, keypads and other electronics aids.
Datak Corp.
Digi-Key Corp.
Fire Burglary Instruments, Inc.
GC Electronics
Radio Shack
Specialty Electronics

This company can supply all of the following items for the projects in this book.
   1. Microcomputer/controller PC board - $14.00
   2. Buffer Board/Power Supply (Delayed Entry) $24.00
   3. Buffer Board/Power Supply (Without Delayed Entry) $21.00
   4. EPROM already programmed (2716) $10.00
   5. 37-pin edge connector $8.50
   6. 22-pin edge connector $5.00
   7. 18-pin edge connector for microcomputer PC Board $4.00
   8. Triac - used in numerous projects within the book - $2.00 postpaid

Electronic Eye (Photoelectric Detector)

Alarm system which triggers if a light beam emitted from a transmitter to a receiver is interrupted. Devices are available with visible light, infrared light, and pulsed light sources.
Alarm Device Manufacturing Co.
Alerta-Mat Manufacturing Co.
Continental Instruments Corp. (microminiature systems)
Design Controls, Inc. (pulsed-infrared systems)
Mountain West Alarm
Radio Shack
Systron-Donner

Fire Sensors

Devices for detecting fires within a home. Consists of heat detectors, smoke detectors and wireless systems.
Alarm Device Manufacturing Co.
Auto-Matic Products Co.
Electronic Instruments Co., Inc.
GC Electronics
Mallory Distributor Products, Inc.
Mountain West Alarm
NAPCO Security Systems, Inc.
Statitrol
Transcience
Universal Security Instruments, Inc.

Infrared Detectors

Devices for activating an alarm when movement within a fixed area is sensed. Senses changes in infrared body heat to determine movement.
Advanced Devices Laboratory
Mountain West Alarm

Light Switches, Automatic

Automatically turns lights on and off. Activated by photoelectric cells or timers to turn lights on at dusk and off at dawn.
Electronic Instruments Company, Inc.
GC Electronics
LeVan Electronics, Inc.
Mountain West Alarm

Locks, Door

Includes locking mechanisms, night latches, and locks for special-purpose doors.
Adams Rite Manufacturing Co. (special-purpose locks)
Ajax Hardware Corp. (patio locks, night latches)
Belwith International. Ltd. (special-purpose locks)
Illinois Lock Co. (lock mechanisms)
Kwikset Sales & Service Co. (lock mechanisms)
Loxem Manufacturing Co. (night latches)
National Lock Hardware (night latches, door locks)
Proof-Lock International, Ltd. (special-purpose locks)
P.T.I. Dolco (sliding-door locks, jimmy plates, night latches)
Schlage Lock Co. (lock mechanisms)

Master Control Panel

Electronic controls for burglar-alarm systems. Some control panels also contain the actual alarm.
Alarm Device Manufacturing Co.
Adcor Electronics
Aqualarm Inc.
Electronic Instruments Co., Inc.
OMWEI Corp.
Thomas Industries
Universal Security Instruments, Inc.

Microswitch, Leaf

Small switch activated by a metal leaf.
Aqualarm Inc.
Auto-Matic Products Co.
Electronic Instruments Co., Inc.
Mountain West Alarm
Universal Security Instruments, Inc.

Microwave Detector

A device which detects any movement within a given area by changes in transmitted wave patterns. Detector penetrates most walls much like a radar system.
Advanced Devices Laboratory
Mountain West Alarm

Panic Button

A button switch which, when depressed manually, activates an alarm; some are wireless.
Alarm Device Manufacturing Co.
Aqualarm Inc.
Auto-Matic Products Co.
Electronic Instruments Company, Inc.
GC Electronics
Mallory Distributor Products, Inc.
Mountain West Alarm
Radio Shack
Universal Security Instruments, Inc.

Relays

Electrical devices used for activating alarms.

Alarm Device Manufacturing Co.
Electronic Locator Co.
Mountain West Alarm
Radio Shack

Smoke Detectors

Detectors designed to sense smoke and activate fire alarms when smoke reaches a predetermined level.
Alarm Device Manufacturing Co.
Electronic Instruments Co., Inc.
Electronic Locator Co.
Mallory Distributor Products, Inc.
Mountain West Alarm
MRL Inc.
Thomas Industries

Switches, Lock

Switches which turn on and off by means of a key.
Adcor Electronics
Alarm Device Manufacturing Co.
Aqualarm Inc.
Auto-Matic Products Co.
Chicago Lock
Electronic Instruments Co., Inc.
Electronic Locator Co.
Illinois Lock Co.
Mallory Distributor Products, Inc.
Medeco Security Locks, Inc.
Mountain West Alarm
NAPCO Security Systems, Inc.
Radio Shack
Universal Security Instruments, Inc.

Switches, Magnetic

Switches which are activated when small magnets are passed alongside of them.
Alarm Device Manufacturing Co.
Alerta-Mat Manufacturing Co.
Aqualarm Inc.
Auto-Matic Products Co.
Continental Instruments Corp.
Design Controls, Inc.
Electronic Instruments Co., Inc.
Electronic Locator Co.
GC Electronics
Mallory Distributor Products, Inc.
Mountain West Alarm
MRL Inc.
Radio Shack
Sentrol Inc.
Systron Donner
Universal Security Instruments, Inc.

Switches, Mat

Switching devices enclosed in mats. Pressure applied to the mat activates the switch.
Alarm Device Manufacturing Co.
Alerta-Mat Manufacturing Co.
Auto-Matic Products Co.
Electronic Instruments Co., Inc.
Electronic Locator
GC Electronics
Mountain West Alarm
Recora Co., Inc.
Universal Security Instruments, Inc.

Switches, Mercury

When tilted, a mercury switch is activated by a small bubble of mercury which closes the electrical contacts.
Alarm Device Manufacturing Co.
Universal Security Instruments, Inc.

Switches, Pressure

Switch which is activated when either depressed or when pressure on it is relieved; often used to protect doors and windows.
Auto-Matic Products Co.
Electronic Instruments Co., Inc.

Electronic Locator Co.
MRL Inc.
Thomas Industries
Universal Security Instruments, Inc.

Telephone Dialers, Automatic

A device for automatically dialing one or more prescribed numbers and playing a prerecorded message into the phone.
Acron Corp.
Adcor Electronics
Alarm Device Manufacturing Co.
Electronic Instruments Co., Inc.
Electronic Locator Co.
Mountain West Alarm
NAPCO Security Systems, Inc.
OMWEI Corp.
Westinghouse Security System, Inc.

Timer, On/Off

An electric timer which turns any appliance connected to it on and off at prescribed times.

Mallory Distributor Products, Inc.
Mountain West Alarm

Vibration Detector

A device for sensing vibration and activating an alarm whenever a predetermined amount of vibration is sensed.
Alarm Device Manufacturing Co.
Electronic Locator Co.
Mountain West Alarm
Systron-Donner
Universal Security Instruments, Inc.

Window-Foil Sensor

Conductive foil glued to windows and attached to an alarm system. A break in the foil activates an alarm.
Alarm Device Manufacturing Co.
Electronic Instruments Co., Inc.
Electronic Locator Co.
GC Electronics
Mountain West Alarm
Universal Security Instruments, Inc.

SECTION II

Acron Corp.
1095 Towbin Ave.
Lakewood, NJ 08701

Adam Rite Manufacturing Co.
1425 Grand Central Ave.
Glendale, CA 91201

Adcor Electronics
349 Peach Tree Hills Ave., N.E.
Atlanta, GA 30305

Advanced Devices Laboratory
316 Mathew St.
Santa Clara, CA 95050

Alarm Device Manufacturing Co.
(ADEMCO)
165 Eileen Way
Syosset, Long Island, NY 11791

Alcotronics Corp.
Church Road & Roland Ave.
Mt. Laurel, NJ 08057

Alerta-Mat Manufacturing Co.
PO Box 133
San Mateo, CA 94401

Alertronics Inc.
20 Boright Ave.
Kenilworth, NJ 07033

Aqualarm Inc.
4911 W. Rosecrans Ave.
Hawthorne, CA 90250

Auto-Matic Products Co.
1918 S. Michigan Ave.
Chicago, IL 60616

Belwith International Ltd.
1119 E. 63rd St.
Los Angeles, CA 90001

John D. Brush & Co.
900 Linden Ave.
Rochester, NY 14625

Chicago Lock Co.
Chicago, IL

Concord Communications Systems
40 Smith St.
Farmington, NY 11735

Continental Instruments Corp.
3327 Royal Ave.
Oceanside, NY 11572

Crismar Corp.
1275 Post Rd.
Fairfield, CO 06430

Datak Corporation
Guttenberg, NJ

Design Controls, Inc.
111 Cantiaque Rock Rd.
Westbury, NY 11590

Digi-Key Corp.
Highway 32 South Box 677
Thief River Falls, MN 56701
1-800-346-5144

Electronic Instruments Company,
   Inc. (EICO)
283 Malta St.
Brooklyn, NY 11207

Electronic Locator Co.
350 Gotham Parkway
Carlstadt, NJ 07072

Fire Burglary Instruments, Inc.
Houppauga, NY

GC Electronics
400 S. Wyman St.
Rockford, IL 61101

Hillcor Plastics
2661 S. Yates Ave.
Los Angeles, CA 90040

Honeywell Commercial Division
2727 S. Fourth Ave.
Minneapolis, MI 55408

E.F. Johnson Co.
299 Tenth Ave.
Waseca, MI 56093

Kwikset Sales & Service Co.
516 E. Santa Ana St.
Anaheim, CA 92803

LeVan Electronics, Inc.
132 Signal Hill Rd.
Wilton, CO 06897

Loxem Manufacturing Co.
5110 Mercantile Row
Dallas, TX 75247

Mallory Distributor Products, Inc.
PO Box 1284
Indianapolis, IN 46206

Master Lock Co.
2600 N. 32nd St.
Milwaukee, WI 53245

Medeco Security Locks, Inc.
P.O. Box 1075
Salem, VA 24153

Mini-Com Inc.
15500 Lee Highway
Centreville, VA 22020

Mountain West Alarm
4215 N. 16th St.
P.O. Box 10780
Phoenix, Az. 85016
1-800-528-6169

MRL Inc.
5404B Port Royal Rd.
Springfield, VA 22151

NAPCO Security Systems, Inc.
6 Ditomas Court
Copiague, NY 11726

National Lock Hardware
Rockford, IL 11726

OMWEI Corp.
4141 NE 6th Ave.
Fort LAuderdale, FL 33308

On Guard Corp.
350 Gotham Parkway
Carlstadt, NJ 07072

Presto-Matic Lock Co., Inc.
8228 W. 47th St.
Lyons, IL 60534

Proof Lock International, Inc.
750 Third Ave.
New York, NY 10017

P.T.I. Dolco
2350 Curry St.
Long Beach, CA 90805

Radio Shack
2617 W. 7th St.
Fort Worth, TX 76107

Recora Co., Inc.
Powis Road
St. Charles, IL 60174

Robyn International Co.
PO Box 478, Northland Drive
Rockford, MI 49341

Sargent and Greenleaf, Inc.
24 Seneca Ave.
Rochester, NY 14621

Schlage Lock Co.
PO Box 3324
San Francisco, CA 94119

Schwab Safe Co., Inc.
3000 Main St.
Lafayette, IN 47902

Sentrol Inc.
10950 S. W. 5th St., Bldg 250
Beaverton, OR 97005

Simplex Security Systems, Inc.
10 Front St.
Collinsville, CN 06022

(The) Slip Seal Co.
1325 Redondo Ave.
Long Beach, CA 90804

Specialty Electronic Services, Inc.
P.O. Box 3320
San Antonio, TX 78211

Statitrol
Division of Emerson Electric Co.
140 South Union Boulevard
Lakewood, CO 80228

Systron Donner
6767 Dublin Blvd.
Dublin, CA 94566

Teledyne Geotech
3401 Shiloh Rd.
Garland, TX 75040

Thomas Industries
207 E. Broadway
Louisville, KY 40201

Transcience
17 Irving Avenue
Stamford, CN 06902

Universal Security Instruments, Inc.
2829 Potee St.
Baltimore, MD 21225

Victor Peterzell Co.
410 N. Goodman St.
Rochester, NY 14609

Westinghouse Security Systems, Inc.
200 Beta Drive
Pittsburgh, PA 15238

Bibliography

Home Security

Gifford, J. Daniel, *The Automotive Security System Design Handbook,* TAB BOOKS Inc., 1985, Book No. 1734.

Hall, Gerald, *How to Completely Secure Your Home,* TAB BOOKS Inc., 1978, Book No. 758.

Kelly, Clarence M. and Roper, C.A., *Security for You and Your Home . . . A Complete Handbook,* TAB BOOKS Inc., 1984, Book No. 1680.

Roper, C.A., *The Complete Security Handbook,* TAB BOOKS Inc., 1981, Book No. 1320.

Electronic Lock/Switch Entry Enhancement Circuits

Alfke, Peter. "Ten-Digit Keyboard and CMOS Circuit Gives Low-Cost Electronic Lock 151,000 Codes, " *Electronic Design,* September 1, 1978, p. 140.

Dahl, Jerry. "Linear Sense Amplifier Raises Sensitivity of Touch Keyboard," *Electronics,* March 27, 1980, P. 139.

Fahnstock, David E. "SCR Combination Lock," *Popular Electronics,* November, 1971, p. 53.

Fortuna, J. "Foil Car Thieves With 'Digistart' The Electronic Security Lock," *Popular Electronics,* April, 1977, p. 48.

Fox, R. W. "Chapter 17 - 'Optoelectronic Key Lock,'" *Optoelectronics Guidebook* - with tested projects TAB Book #836, copyright 1977 TAB BOOKS, Inc., p. 182.

Freischlag, Eric. "Monitor Circuit Discourages Switch Tampering," *Electronic Design,* December 24, 1981, p. 140.

Gregory, Vern. "CMOS Touch Switches— Convenient, Less $ and Sexy," *EDN,* May 5, 1976, p. 112.

Hung, L. Y. "Sequential Lock Circuit Provides Programmable Key Word Length," *Digital Design,* March, 1981, p. 78.

Merrell, Richard. "A Programmable Combination Logic Circuit," *EDN,* December 5, 1973, p. 84.

Peltzman, Edward S. "Circuit Eliminates Rotary—Switch Bounce Problems," *EDN,* April 20, 1978, p. 132.

Sokol, B. J. "Electronic Lock Boasts Low Cost and Low Power," *Electronics,* July 14, 1981, p. 127.

Solov, Ed. "Electronic Warfare for the Amateur—A Low Cost Alarm System," *CQ,* January, 1984, p. 20.

Stehney, Tom. "Alarm Circuit Avoids False Triggers," *EDN,* August 5, 1979, p. 126.

Wood, Robert D. "Replace Bulky Mechanical Switches with Touch Controls," *EDN,* April 20, 1978, p. 132.

Battery Charger Circuits

Ballinger, Richard. "Circuit Uses Rectifier Forward Drop To Monitor Battery Charger," *Electronic Design,* October 25, 1980, p. 176.

Boasson, Hanan. "Transistors Fix Charging Path for 'No Polarity' NiCd Charger," *Electronic Design,* September 17, 1981, p. 188.

Dobkin, Robert C. "Break Loose From Fixed IC Regulators," *Electronic Design,* April 12, 1977, p. 122.

Frisch, Arnold. "Float Charger Independently Recharges Two Lead-Acid Cells Connected in Series," *Electronic Design,* August 16, 1977, p. 108.

Herrick, Kennan C. "Battery Charger Snaps from Full to Trickle," *EDN,* February 4, 1981, p. 164.

Hung, Huynh Trung. "Ni-Cd-Battery Charger Has Wide Range of Features," *Electronics,* July 14, 1982, p. 155.

Kranz, Paul. "A Simple Battery Charger for Gel Cells Detects Full Charge and Switches to Float," *Electronic Design,* July 19, 1976, p. 120.

Okolowicz, John. "Timing Circuit Burps Battery to Improve Charging Efficiency," *Electronic Design,* June 7, 1977, p. 116.

Okolowicz, John. "Automotive Charging Regulator Gives Overvoltage and Undervoltage Warnings," *Electronic Design,* March 15, 1976, p. 104.

Olson, Hank. "An Automatic Battery Charger Shuts Itself Down," *EDN,* May 20, 1974, p. 77.

Pal, Ajit. "Comparator Circuit Regulates Battery's Charging Current," *Electronics,* October 6, 1981, p. 142.

Panicali, Nat. "Temperature Compensation Ups Power-Pack Performance," *EDN,* September 5, 1980, p. 205.

Pease, Robert A. "Bar-Graph IC Controls Loading on Sun/Wind-Powered Battery Charger," *Electronic Design,* October 11, 1980, p. 212.

Swift, Steven D. and Gunderson, David. "Protect Your Rechargeable Battery," *Electronic Design,* June 7, 1978, p. 112.

Pseudorandom Number Generator Circuits

Anderson, Leonard H. "Uniting Number Generators for Long Bit Patterns," *Electronics,* November 9, 1978, p. 134.

Banes, Vince. "Simulating a Repeatable Pseudorandom Pulse Train," *Electronics,* September 8, 1982, p. 140.

Bardou, Jean Paul. "RC Network Prevents Power-Up Latching in a Pseudorandom Noise Generator," *Electronic Design,* February 5, 1981, p. 142.

Gard, Michael F. "Pseudorandom Tone Generator Produces 16 Tones Over Its Frequency Range," *Electronic Design,* May 24, 1978, p. 254.

Kreindel, Uri and Meir Guttman. "Control Your Shift Register's Length Externally," *EDN,* February 5, 1977, p. 102.

Lacefield, Michael M. "Reader's Circuits," *Popular Electronics,* April, 1977.

Lancaster, Don. "Understanding Pseudo-Random Circuits," *Radio-Electronics,* April, 1975, p. 42.

Marthy, K. R. Srinivasa. "Calculate Pseudorandom Sequence Length," *Digital Design,* February 1979, p. 61.

Mims, Forrest M. "More on Pseudorandom Number Generators," *Popular Electronics,* p. 94.

Pal, Ajit. "Pseudorandom Generator Has Programmable Sequence Length," *Electronics,* October 11, 1979, p. 129.

Pangratz, Heinrich. "Binary Counter Allows a Pseudorandom Generator to Run without Interruption," *Electronic Design,* May 10, 1978, p. 134.

Sward, Wayne. "Four Chips Generate Pseudorandom Test Data," *Electronics,* March 10, 1981, p. 173.

Tanski, Tomasz R. "11-Byte Program Generates 2 Billion Pseudorandom Bits," *Electronics,* October 12, 1978, p. 148.

Wheless, Tom. "Binary Counter Unlatches Multistage, Pseudorandom Noise Generator," *Electronic Design,* October 11, 1980, p. 210.

Wong, Chung M. "NOR Gate Unlatches Pseudo random Noise Generator," *Electronic Design,* June 7, 1980, p. 200.

Workman, Michael. "Digital Pseudorandom Number Generator Produces Analog Noise for Testing," *Electronic Design,* March 31, 1981, p. 196.

Phase-Locked Loop Articles

Buchanan, James E. "Build a High-Frequency Phase-Locked Loop with Common IC Components," *Electronic Design,* August 2, 1977, p. 108.

*Burton, David A. "Two-IC Module Creates Symmetrical Divide-by-3 Circuit," *Electronic Design,* November 26, 1981, p. 248.

Cohen, Herb. "How Phase-Locked Loops Work," *Popular Electronics,* February 1978, p. 32.

Cohen, Herb. "Experimenting with Phase-Locked Loops," *Popular Electronics,* October 1975, p. 47.

Conner, Finis F. "Varactor-Controlled Hybrid PLL Aids Micro-Winchester Disk Drives," *Digital Design,* January 1981, p. 94.

Delagrange, Arthur D., "Lock onto Frequency with Frequency-Lock Loops," *Electronic Design,* June 21, 1977, p. 84.

Delagrange, Arthur D., "Need a Precise Tone? Synthesize Your Own," *EDN,* October 5, 1980, p. 125.

*Dellmo, Russell. "1 1/4 ICs Divide by Three," *EDN,* June 9, 1982, p. 178.

Fadrhons, Jan. "Blend a Wideband PLL with a Narrowband," *Electronic Design,* July 5, 1976, p. 46.

Ferris, Raymond K. "Constant-Bandwidth PLL Tone Decorder Accepts Wide Range of Input Voltages," *Electronic Design,* November 8, 1977, p. 106.

*Getgen, Lawrence E. "Divide Symmetrical Clock Pulses by Odd Numbers, Get a Symmetrical Output," *Electronic Design,* March 1, 1980, p. 110.

Ghosh, S. "The Bandwidth of Phase-Lock Loops," *Electronic Design,* March 15, 1978 p. 84.

Ghosh, Sid and Christian Foster "Phase/Frequency-Locked Loops Handle Random Inputs," *EDN,* February 20, 1980, p. 141.

*Godbole, V. R. "Simplify Design of Fixed Odd-Modulo Dividers," *EDN,* June 5, 1975, p. 77.

Greer, W. T., Jr. and Kean, Bill. "Digital Phase-Locked Loops Move Into Analog Territory," *Electronic Design,* March 31, 1982, p. 95.

Hahn, Marck C. "PLL's Capture Range Equals its Locking Range," *EDN,* September 20, 1977, p. 117.

Hanisko, John Cyril. "Phase Controller + R&C=Lock Indicator," *EDN,* August 5, 1980, p. 132.

Hanisko, John C. "PLL Lock Indicator Uses a Single IC," *EDN,* October 5, 1976, p. 104.

Hanisko, John. "Timer/Counter Functions as Phase-Locked Loop Component," *EDN,* March 20, 1976, p. 98.

Hatchett, John and William Morgan. "Versatile Synthesizer Controls 140 MHz," *EDN,* November 11, 1981, p. 287.

Hatchett, John. "Adding to PLL Chips' Functions Speed RF Synthesizer Design," *Electronics,* October 9, 1980, p. 148.

Jagtap, Vilas and Vidyut Bapat. "Phase-Locked Loops Replace Precision Component Bridge," *Electronics,* August 11, 1981, p. 136.

Jeutter, Dean C. "Detect Sync Gap for Better Data Recovery in Serial PDM Telemetry Systems," *Electronic Design,* December 10, 1981, p. 175.

Kasevich, Lawrence S. "PLL Converts Square Wave into Sine Wave," *EDN,* June 20, 1978, p. 128.

Kinley, Harold. "Troubleshooting Phase-Locked-Loop Circuits," *Popular Electronics,* July 1980, p. 56.

Kirby, Steve. "PLL's Lock Indicator Detects Latching Simply," *Electronics,* April 10, 1980, p. 127.

Leck, R. P. "Reducing a PLL's Even-Order Harmonics," *Electronics,* April 12, 1979, p. 150.

Miron, N., M. N. Ion, and D. Sporea. "C-MOS IC Achieves Triggered Phase-Locked Oscillations," *Electronics,* January 27, 1982, p. 127.

Mollinga, Thomas. "Solve Phase Stability Problem in AM Receivers with PLL Techniques," *EDN,* February 20, 1975, p. 51.6

Moore, A. W. "Phase-Locked Loops for Motor-Speed Control," *IEEE Spectrum,* April 1973, p. 64.

Murthi, Enjeti. "Monolithic Phase-Locked Loops—Analogs Do all the Work of Digitals, and Much More," *EDN,* September 5, 1977, p. 60.

Myers, Harold E. "Synthesizer Techniques," *R. F. Design,* September/October 1980, p. 43.

Pease, Robert A. "Wide-Band Phase-Locked Loops Take on F/V-Conversion Chores," *EDN,* May 20, 1979, p. 145.

Przedpelski, Andrzej B. "Suppress Phase-Lock-Loop Sidebands without Introducing Instability," *Electronic Design,* September 13, 1979, p. 142.

Przedpelski, Andrzej B. "Optimize Phase-Lock Loops to Meet Your Needs—or Determine Why You Can't," *Electronic Design,* September 13, 1978, p. 134.

Pyle, Ronald E. "Phase-Locked Loop Aids in Measuring Capacitance," *Electronics,* May 24, 1979, p. 168.

*Rao, M. V. Subba. "Programmable Divide-By-N Counter Provides Symmetrical Outputs for All Divisors," *Electronic Design,* January 19, 1976, p. 82.

Rohde, Ulrich. "Low-Noise Frequency Synthesizers Using Fractional N Phase-locked Loops," *R. F. Design,* January/February 1981, p. 20.

Roduit, Christophe. "Frequency Meter Uses PLL," *EDN,* January 20, 1979, p. 111.

Sabah, N. H. "PLL Performs Accurate Phase Measurements," *Electronics,* June 19, 1980, p. 158.

Scott, Robert F. "Using PLL for CB Frequency Synthesizers," *Radio-Electronics,* April 1977, p. 43.

Sharpe, C. A. "Speed Up PLLs in Digital Synthesizers," *Electronic Design,* November 22, 1977, p. 124.

Sharpe, Andrew C. "A 3-State Phase Detector Can Improve Your Next PLL Design," *EDN,* September 20, 1976, p. 55.

Smallwood, R. H. "PLL Handles Small, 0.05-Hz Signals," *Digital Design,* July 1980, p. 80.

Stofka, Marian. "Digital-Only PLL Exhibits No Overshoot," *EDN,* May 26, 1982, p. 206.

Wilbur, Ralph. "Op Amp Provides Phase-Locked Loop," *EDN,* May 5, 1979, p. 131.

Zwicker, Robert M. "Phase-Locked-Loop Circuit Multiples Frequencies by 2 to 256," *Electronic Design,* May 24, 1976, P. 94.

*These articles all address digital division by an odd number with a resultant symmetrical squarewave output.

Index

Index

A
ac activation circuit, 28
alarm devices, 93, 211, 212
Automatic Telephone Dailer project, 156
Automatic Telephone Dialer, 137

    board construction, 162, component placement, 160, components, 158, operation, 157, parts list, 153, PC board, 160, schematic, 152 software, 163

B
bells, 211
Burglar Baffler, 13, 14

    ac activation, 28, applications, 39, block diagram, 15, 22, component placement, 32, construction, 29, input gating, 25, modifications, 40, operation of, 18, parts list, 30, PC board, 26, 27, power capacity, 29, precautions, 29, program verification, 21, programming, 21, schematic, 16,17, timing, 36

C
CD4046 CMOS PLL, 40
closed circuit systems, 4
construction aids, 212
control panels, 213
controller, 71
crime, 1

D
DTMF, 140, 141
DTMF, advantages of, 141
dual tone multiple frequency, 140

E
electronic components, 212
EMI supression, 169
Entry Detection System, 59

    battery backup, 66, circuit description, 62, component placement, 67, construction, 69, front panel controls, 69, schematic, 60

EPROM, 72, 94 exclusive-OR, 23

F
FCC, 170
Fire Burglary Instruments, 90
fire detectors, 8, 94
fire sensors, 212
Fire-Lite heat detector, 8

H
home security measures, 3
home security, 1
horns, 211

I
infrared detectors, 213
inner loop, 4
inside loop, 83

K
key switch, 108
keypad, 91

L
LEDs, 34
light controllers, 13
light timer, limitations of, 14
line frequency accuracy, 50
locks, door, 213
loop, 4, 59, 62, 83

M
microcomputer/controller, 71, 83

    assembly instructions, 76, board components, 71, board construction, 75, placement, 77, memory map, 74, PC board, 79,80, power requirements, 71, system checkout, 81, troubleshooting, 75, 78

microcomputer-based project's program listing, 187 microphone, electret, 143 microphone, electrodynamic, 143 microswitches, 213 MK5375, 137, 144 applications, 151, operation, 150

motion detectors, 5, 213
Mountain West Security, 11, 91

O

open circuit systems, 5
outer loop, 4
outside loop, 83

P

panic button, 213
PC boards, 34, 35
Perimiguard with Delayed Entry, 83

circuit description, 83, component placement, 99, final assembly, 102, fire/smoke alarm, 90, installation/checkout, 101, keypad connections, 92, keypad functions, 88, keypad installation, 91, output devices, 86, panic switch, 90, PC board, 100, power capacity, 88, power supply/buffer board schematic, 85, remote disarm, 90, software, 95, troubleshooting chart, 103,

Perimiguard without Delayed Entry, 104

component placement, 110, installation/checkout, 113, PC board, 111 power supply/buffer board, 109, software, 108, troubleshooting chart, 114

photoelectric eye, 212
phase-locked loop, 40

bandwidth, 44, capture range, 44, lock range, 43, low-pass filter, 44 operation, 46, phase detector, 40, theory, 40, transient response, 44, voltage controlled oscillator, 44

PNG, 13 Precision Sentinel, 121

component placement, 127, construction, 124, modifications, 125 parts list, 125, PC board, 124, schematic, 122

program listing for microcomputer-based projects, 187
Programmable Light Dimmer, 13, 40

component placement, 54, modifications, 47, operation, 46, parts list, 51, PC board, 52, schematic, 45, troubleshooting, 57

Programmable Timer, 13, 51

component placement, 54, construction, 50, parts list, 51, PC board, 52,53, precautions, 57, troubleshooting, 57

pseudorandom number generator, 13

Q

Quad Precision Timer, 126

construction, 134, modificatons, 134, parts list, 135, schematic, 128-132

R

RAM, 71
relays, 213
RIOT, 75

S

security system components, 5
sensor, window foil, 215

sensors, 7, 212
Sentinel, 117
Sentrol, 11
Simple Sentinel, 120

parts list, 125, schematic, 119

sirens, 211
6502, 71
smoke detectors, 8, 94, 214
Software Light Dimmer software, 113
Software Light Dimmer, 113, 115
Statitrol SmokeGard, 8
steering diode, 59
suppliers of security products, 211
suppliers, addresses of, 215-217
switches, 9, 111
switches, automatic light, 213
switches, door, 91
switches, lock, 214
switches, magnetic, 11, 214
switches, mat, 214
switches, mercury, 214
switches, pressure, 214
switches, window, 91

T

telephone basics, 137
telephone dialers, automatic, 215
telephone off-hook, 138
telephone on-hook, 137
telephone pulse dialing, 140
telephone receiver, 144
telephone ringer, 144
telephone ringing generator, 144
telephone tone dialing, 140
telephone transmitter, 143
timers, 215
tone/pulse dialer, 140, 144
triac ratings, 134

V

VCO, 44
VDE, 171
vibration detector, 215
voltage controlled oscillator, 44

OTHER POPULAR TAB BOOKS OF INTEREST

Transducer Fundamentals, with Projects (No. 1693—$14.50 paper; $19.95 hard)

Second Book of Easy-to-Build Electronic Projects (No. 1679—$13.50 paper; $17.95 hard)

Practical Microwave Oven Repair (No. 1667—$13.50 paper; $19.95 hard)

CMOS/TTL—A User's Guide with Projects (No. 1650—$13.50 paper; $19.95 hard)

Satellite Communications (No. 1632—$11.50 paper; $16.95 hard)

Build Your Own Laser, Phaser, Ion Ray Gun and Other Working Space-Age Projects (No. 1604—$15.50 paper; $24.95 hard)

Principles and Practice of Digital ICs and LEDs (No. 1577—$13.50 paper; $19.95 hard)

Understanding Electronics—2nd Edition (No. 1553—$9.95 paper; $15.95 hard)

Electronic Databook—3rd Edition (No. 1538—$17.50 paper; $24.95 hard)

Beginner's Guide to Reading Schematics (No. 1536—$9.25 paper; $14.95 hard)

Concepts of Digital Electronics (No. 1531—$11.50 paper; $17.95 hard)

Beginner's Guide to Electricity and Electrical Phenomena (No. 1507—$10.25 paper; $15.95 hard)

750 Practical Electronic Circuits (No. 1499—$14.95 paper; $21.95 hard)

Exploring Electricity and Electronics with Projects (No. 1497—$9.95 paper; $15.95 hard)

Video Electronics Technology (No. 1474—$11.50 paper; $16.95 hard)

Towers' International Transistor Selector—3rd Edition (No. 1416—$19.95 vinyl)

The Illustrated Dictionary of Electronics—2nd Edition (No. 1366—$18.95 paper; $26.95 hard)

49 Easy-To-Build Electronic Projects (No. 1337—$6.25 paper; $10.95 hard)

The Master Handbook of Telephones (No. 1316—$12.50 paper; $16.95 hard)

Giant Handbook of 222 Weekend Electronics Projects (No. 1265—$14.95 paper)

Introducing Cellular Communications: The New Mobile Telephone System (No. 1682—$9.95 paper; $14.95 hard)

The Fiberoptics and Laser Handbook (No. 1671—$15.50 paper; $21.95 hard)

Power Supplies, Switching Regulators, Inverters and Converters (No. 1665—$15.50 paper; $21.95 hard)

Using Integrated Circuit Logic Devices (No. 1645—$15.50 paper; $21.95 hard)

Basic Transistor Course—2nd Edition (No. 1605—$13.50 paper; $19.95 hard)

The GIANT Book of Easy-to-Build Electronic Projects (No. 1599—$13.95 paper; $21.95 hard)

Music Synthesizers: A Manual of Design and Construction (No. 1565—$12.50 paper; $16.95 hard)

How to Design Circuits Using Semiconductors (No. 1543—$11.50 paper; $17.95 hard)

All About Telephones—2nd Edition (No. 1537—$11.50 paper; $16.95 hard)

The Complete Book of Oscilloscopes (No. 1532—$11.50 paper; $17.95 hard)

All About Home Satellite Television (No. 1519—$13.50 paper; $19.95 hard)

Maintaining and Repairing Videocassette Recorders (No. 1503—$15.50 paper; $21.95 hard)

The Build-It Book of Electronic Projects (No. 1498—$10.25 paper; $18.95 hard)

Video Cassette Recorders: Buying, Using and Maintaining (No. 1490—$8.25 paper; $14.95 hard)

The Beginner's Book of Electronic Music (No. 1438—$12.95 paper; $18.95 hard)

Build a Personal Earth Station for Worldwide Satellite TV Reception (No. 1409—$10.25 paper; $15.95 hard)

Basic Electronics Theory—with projects and experiments (No. 1338—$15.50 paper; $19.95 hard)

Electric Motor Test & Repair—3rd Edition (No. 1321—$7.25 paper; $13.95 hard)

The GIANT Handbook of Electronic Circuits (No. 1300—$19.95 paper)

Digital Electronics Troubleshooting (No. 1250—$12.50 paper)

TAB BOOKS Inc.

Blue Ridge Summit, Pa. 17214

Send for FREE TAB Catalog describing over 750 current titles in print.